HISTORY OF
THE BIG
BONANZA

HISTORY OF
THE BIG
BONANZA

AN AUTHENTIC ACCOUNT
OF THE DISCOVERY, HISTORY, AND WORKING OF THE

WORLD RENOWNED
COMSTOCK SILVER LODE OF NEVADA

Including Descriptions of the Various Mines
Situated Thereon; Sketches of the Most
Prominent Men Interested in Them;
Incidents and Adventures Connected
with Mining, the Indians, and the
Country; Amusing Stories,
Experiences, Anecdotes,
etc., etc., and a
FULL EXPOSITION OF THE PRODUCTION OF PURE SILVER

BY
DAN DE QUILLE

INTRODUCTORY BY
MARK TWAIN

114 HISTORIC PHOTOGRAPHS,
ILLUSTRATIONS AND MAPS

PERUSE PRESS
LOS ANGELES

TITLE:
HISTORY OF THE BIG BONANZA:

SUBTITLE:
*An Authentic Account of the Discovery, History, and Working of the
World Renowned Comstock Silver Lode of Nevada, Including Descriptions of the
Various Mines Situated Thereon; Sketches of the Most Prominent Men Interested
in Them; Incidents and Adventures Connected with Mining, the Indians,
and the Country; Amusing Stories, Experiences, Anecdotes, etc., etc.,
and a Full Exposition of the Production of Pure Silver.*

COMPILED WITH 114 HISTORIC PHOTOGRAPHS, ILLUSTRATIONS, AND MAPS

AUTHOR:
Dan De Quille
(William Wright)

INTRODUCTORY:
Mark Twain
(Samuel L. Clemens)

CONTRIBUTOR:
John Ross Browne

PHOTOGRAPHERS, ILLUSTRATORS, AND CARTOGRAPHERS:
Mathew Brady, Grafton Tyler Brown, Elmer Chickering,
James H. Crockwell, W. H. Davenport, T. L. Dawes,
Mark Diederichsen, Andrew A. Forbes, Charles F. Hoffmann,
Robert Kerrigan, Augustus Koch, Lawrence & Houseworth,
Walter Neale, John S. Noe, Timothy H. O'Sullivan,
Roswell Morse Shurtleff, Louis Thors, Carleton E. Watkins,
Charles L. Weed, and True Williams.

EDITOR:
Mark Diederichsen

PUBLISHER:
Peruse Press
Los Angeles, California

FIRST PERUSE PRESS EDITION

FIRST PRINTING:
2013

FRONT COVER:
Timothy H. O'Sullivan, *Cars Coming Out of a Shaft,* 1867,
collodion/albumen. Library of Congress Prints and Photographs Division.

FRONTISPIECE:
W. H. Davenport, *Song of the Honest Miner,* 1876, lithograph.

BACK COVER:
Augustus Koch, *Bird's Eye View of Virginia City,* 1875, lithograph.
Library of Congress Geography & Map Division.

ISBN-THIRTEEN: 978-0615922447
ISBN-TEN: 0615922449

TO
JOHN MACKAY
PRINCE OF MINERS,
AND
"BOSS" OF THE BIG BONANZA,
IS THIS BOOK
RESPECTFULLY INSCRIBED.

Portrait of John Mackay, 1876, True Williams.

"Oh, it's a lively place, you bet!
an oncommon lively place—
reely hexcitin.' I look out of the
winder every mornin' jist to see
how many dead men are layin'
around. I declare to gracious
the bullets flies around here
sometimes like hailstones!"

—Hotel chambermaid,
Virginia City

From *Washoe Revisited*, by John Ross Browne,
Harper's Monthly Magazine, May, 1865.

CONTENTS

CONTENTS

Contents

CONTENTS

Contents

CONTENTS

Contents

Contents

ILLUSTRATIONS

ILLUSTRATIONS

INTRODUCTORY

One easily gets a surface-knowledge of any remote country, through the writings of travellers. The inner life of such a country is not very often presented to the reader. The outside of a strange house is interesting, but the people, the life, and the furniture inside, are far more so.

Nevada is peculiarly a surface-known country, for no one has written of that land who had lived long there and made himself competent to furnish an inside view to the public. I think the present volume supplies this defect in an eminently satisfactory way. The writer of it has spent sixteen years in the heart of the silver-mining region, as one of the editors of the principal daily newspaper of Nevada; he is thoroughly acquainted with his subject, and wields a practised pen. He is a gentleman of character and reliability. Certain of us who have known him personally during half a generation are well able to testify in this regard.

MARK TWAIN
1876

PREFACE

I have put all I had to say into the body of this book; but, being informed that a preface is a necessary evil, I have written this one.

DAN DE QUILLE
1876

Territorial Enterprise Masthead, July 30, 1859, letterpress, William Jernegan and Alfred James. Oldest known facsimile (original lost) of the *Territorial Enterprise*, reproduced in *History of Nevada*, 1881, by Myron Angel (Thompson & West, Oakland). This edition (vol. 1, no. 20) covered a constitutional convention attempting to establish the Territory of Nevada, and was published while the weekly newspaper was still located in Genoa, Nevada.

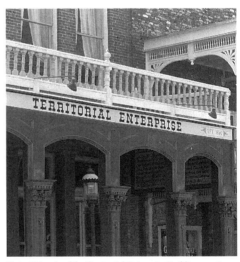

Office of the Territorial Enterprise, (detail from a larger map), 1861, lithograph, Grafton Tyler Brown. Library of Congress Prints and Photographs Division. This illustration shows the first location of the *Daily Territorial Enterprise* in Virginia City at the corner of A Street and Sutton Avenue.

Extant Facade of the Territorial Enterprise Building, 2008, raster, Mark Diederichsen. This is the location on C Street in Virginia City where Dan De Quille and Mark Twain worked together as reporters, though the building was replaced in 1875 after the city-wide Great Fire.

PROLOGUE

Territorial Enterprise, September, 1863:
LITERARY MANIFESTO
By Dan De Quille and Mark Twain

Our duty is to keep the universe thoroughly posted concerning murders and street fighters, and balls, and theaters, and pack-trains, and churches, and lectures, and school-houses, and city military affairs, and highway robberies, and Bible societies, and hay-wagons, and the thousand other things which it is in the province of local reporters to keep track of and magnify into undue importance for the instruction of the readers of a great daily newspaper.

Territorial Enterprise, April 20, 1864:
FRIGHTFUL ACCIDENT TO DAN DE QUILLE
by Mark Twain

Our time-honored confrere, Dan, met with a disastrous accident, yesterday, while returning from American City on a vicious Spanish horse, the result of which accident is that at the present writing he is confined to his bed and suffering great bodily pain. He was coming down the road at the rate of a hundred miles an hour (as stated in his will, which he made shortly after the accident,) and on turning a sharp corner, he suddenly hove in sight of a horse standing square across the channel; he signaled for the starboard, and put his helm down instantly, but too late, after all; he was swinging to port, and before he could straighten down, he swept like an avalanche against the transom of the strange craft; his larboard knee coming in contact with the rudder-post of the adversary, Dan was wrenched from his saddle and thrown some three hundred yards (according to his own statement, made in his will, above mentioned,) alighting upon solid ground, and bursting himself open from the chin to the pit of the stomach. His head was also caved in out of sight, and his hat was afterwards extracted in a bloody and damaged condition from between his lungs; he must have bounced end-for-end after he struck first, because it is evident he received a concussion from the rear that broke his heart; one of his legs was jammed up in his body nearly to his throat, and the other so torn and mutilated that it pulled out when they attempted to lift him into the hearse which we had sent to the scene of the disaster, under the general impression that he might need it; both arms were indiscriminately broken up until they were jointed like a bamboo; the back was considerably fractured and bent into the shape of a rail fence. Aside from these injuries, however, he sustained no other damage. They brought some of him home in the hearse and the balance on a dray. His first remark showed that the powers of his great mind had not been impaired by the accident, nor his profound judgment destroyed—he said he wouldn't have cared a damn if it had been anybody but himself. He then made his will, after which he set to work with that earnestness and singleness of purpose which have always distinguished him, to abuse the assemblage of anxious hash house proprietors who had called on business, and to repudiate their bills with his customary promptness and impartiality. Dan may have exaggerated the above details in some respects, but he charged us to report them thus, and it is a source of genuine pleasure to us to have the opportunity of doing it. Our noble old friend is recovering fast, and what is left of him will be around the Brewery again to-day, just as usual.

Territorial Enterprise, April, 1864:
AN INFAMOUS PROCEEDING
by Dan De Quille

Some three days since, in returning to this city from American Flat, we had the misfortune to be thrown from a fiery untamed steed of Spanish extraction—a very strong extract, too. Our knee was sprained by our fall and we were for a day or two confined to our room—of course knowing little of what was going on in the great world outside. Mark Twain, our confrere and room-mate, a man in whom we trusted, was our only visitor during our seclusion. We saw some actions of his that almost caused us to suspect him of contemplating treachery towards us, but it was not until we regained in some degree the use of our maimed limb that we discovered the full extent—the infamousness of this wretch's treasonable and inhuman plottings. He wrote such an account of our accident as would lead the public to believe that we were injured beyond all hope of recovery. The next day he tied a small piece of second-hand crape about his hat, and putting on a lugubrious look, went to the Probate Court, and getting down on his knees commenced praying—it was the first time he ever prayed for anything or to anybody—for letters of administration on our estate. Before going to the Court to pray he had stuffed the principal part of our estate—consisting of numerous shares in the Pewterinctum—into his vest pocket; also had secured our tooth-brush and had been using it a whole day. He had on our only clean shirt and best socks, also was sporting our cane and smoking our meerschaum. But what most showed his heartlessness and utter depravity was the disposition he made of our boots and coat. When we missed these we applied to Marshall Cooke. The Marshall said he thought he could find them for us. He went on to say that for sometime past he had noticed the existence of a suspicious intimacy between Twain and a nigger saloon keeper, who had a dead-fall on North B street. Proceeding to this palace he found that he was correct in his conjecture. Twain had taken our boots and coat to the darkey, and traded them off for a bottle of vile whiskey, with which he got drunk; and when the police were about to snatch him for drunkenness, he commenced blubbering, saying that he was "overcome for the untimely death of poor Dan." By this dodge he escaped the lock-up, but if he does not shortly give up our Pewtertinctum stock—which is of fabulous vale—shell out our tooth-brush and take off our socks and best shirt, he will not so easily escape the Territorial prison.

P. S.—We have just learned that he stole the crape he tied about his hat from the door knob of Three's engine house, South B street.

Territorial Enterprise, April 1864:
MARK TWAIN TAKES A LESSON IN THE MANLY ART
by Dan De Quille

We may have said some harsh things of Mark Twain, but now we take them all back. We feel like weeping for him—yes, we would fall on his breast and mingle our tears with his'n. But that manly shirt front of his air now a bloody one, and his nose is swollen to such an extent that to fall on his breast would be an utter impossibility.

Yesterday, he brought back all our things and promised us that he intended hereafter to lead a virtuous life. This was in the forenoon; in the afternoon he commenced the career of virtue he had marked out for himself and took a first lesson in boxing. Once he had the big gloves on, he imagined that he weighed a ton and could whip his weight in Greek-fire. He waded into a professor of the "manly art" like one of Howlan's rotary batteries, and the professor, in a playful way he has, when he wants to take the conceit out of forward pupils, let one fly straight out from the shoulder and "busted" Mr. Twain in the "snoot," sending him reeling— not exactly to grass, but across a bench—with two bountiful streams of "claret" spouting from his nostrils. At first his nose was smashed out till it covered nearly the whole of his face and then looked like a large piece of tripe, but it was finally scraped into some resemblance of a nose, when he rushed away for surgical advice. Pools of gore covered the floor of the Club Room where he fought, and he left a bloody trail for half a mile through the city. It is estimated that he lost several hogsheads of blood in all. He procured a lot of sugar of lead and other cooling lotions and spent the balance of the day in applying them with towels and sponges.

After dark, he ventured forth with his nose swollen to the size of several junk bottles—a vast, inflamed and pulpy old snoot—to get advice about having it amputated. None of his friends recognize him now, and he spends his time in solitude, contemplating his ponderous vermillion smeller in a two-bit mirror, which he bought for that purpose. We cannot comfort him, for we know his nose will never be a nose again. It always was somewhat lopsided; now it is a perfect lump of blubber. Since the above was in type, the doctors have decided to amputate poor Mark Twain's smeller. A new one is to be made for him of a quarter of veal.

Territorial Enterprise, April 28 or 30, 1864:
DAN REASSEMBLED
(abridged)
By Mark Twain

The idea of a plebeian like Dan supposing he could ever ride a horse! He! why, even the cats and the chickens laughed when they saw him go by. Of course, he would be thrown off. Of course, any well-bred horse wouldn't let a common, underbred person like Dan stay on his back! When they gathered him up he was just a bag of scraps, but they put him together, and you'll find him at his old place in the *Enterprise* office next week, still laboring under the delusion that he's a newspaper man.

Dissolute Author, 1872, lithograph, Roswell Morse Shurtleff. Illustrated in
Roughing It by Mark Twain, and believed to be modeled after Dan De Quille.

HISTORY OF
THE BIG
BONANZA

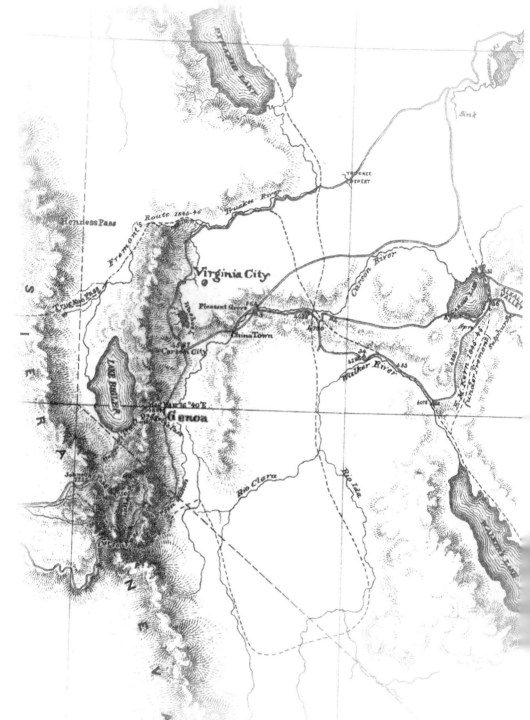

Map of Wagon Routes in Utah Territory (detail), 1859, lithograph, from the *Report of Explorations Across the Great Basin of the Territory of Utah for a Direct Wagon-route from Camp Floyd to Genoa, in Carson Valley,* by Captain James Hervey Simpson. (Note: Lake Bigler on the map is now known as Lake Tahoe.) Library of Congress Geography and Map Division.

CHAPTER I

THE FIRST SETTLERS IN NEVADA

Facts and Fiction—How the Rivers are Lost—
Unwelcome Visitors—The Washoes—Taking in the Pilgrims

The bare mention of a mine of silver calls up in most minds visions of glittering wealth and a world of romantic situations and associations. All no doubt have read the story of the Indian hunter, Diego Hualca, who, in the year 1545, discovered the world-famous silver-mine of Potosi, Peru. How, while climbing up the face of a steep mountain in pursuit of a wild goat, this fortunate hunter laid hold upon a bush, in order to pull himself up over a steep ledge of rocks, and how the bush was torn out by the roots, when lo! wonderful store of wealth was laid bare. In the roots of the upturned bush, and in the soil of the spot whence it was torn, the eyes of the lone Indian hunter beheld masses of glittering silver.

Having all our lives had in mind this romantic story, and having a thousand times pictured to ourselves the great, shining lumps of native silver, as they lay exposed in the black soil "before that Indian, who stood alone in a far-away place on the wild mountain, we are apt to imagine that something of the same kind is to be seen wherever a silver-mine exists. Besides, we have all heard the stories told by the old settlers of the Atlantic States in regard to the wonderful mines of silver known to the Indians in early days.

Hardly a State in the Union but has its legend of a silver-mine known to the red-men when they inhabited the country. This mine was pretty much the same in every State and in every region. Upon the removal of a large flat stone an opening resembling the mouth of a cavern was seen. Entering this, you found yourself in a great crevice in the rocks, and the sides of this crevice were lined with silver, which you forthwith proceeded to hew and chip off with a hatchet kindly furnished you by your Indian guide. You worked rapidly, as, according to contract, you had but a limited time to remain in the mine. When the Indian at your side announced your, time up, the tomahawk was taken from your hand, even though you might have an immense mass detached, save a mere clinging thread.

Only men who had saved the life of some Indian of renown were ever led to these silver caverns and they were invariably obliged to submit to be blindfolded, so that none of them were ever able to find their way back to the mines they had been shown.

These and kindred stories have placed masses of native silver, and deposits of rich ores of silver very near to the surface of the ground, in the popular mind. No doubt there are many places in the world where native silver exists almost upon the present surface, as was the case in the Potosi mine, in Peru, and as was the case with the rich deposit of silver ore first found on the Comstock lode, but those who visit the present mines of the Comstock will find little in them that at all agrees with their preconceived notions of silver-mines. On the surface they will find nothing that is glittering, nothing that is at all romantic. The soil looks much the same as in any other mountainous region, and the rocks seem to have a very ordinary look to the inexperienced eye. The general hue of the hills is a yellowish-brown, and all about through the rents in the ashen-hued sagebrush which clothes the country, peep jagged piles of granite—the bones of the land, showing through its rags.

In sketching the history of the famous Comstock silver lode of Nevada, however, and of the bonanza mines, situated on that lode, it seems proper to begin by giving a brief account of the first settlement of the country, when known as Western Utah, and under Mormon, if under any rule; also, to chronicle what is to be gathered in regard to the finding of gold-diggings in that region, the working of which finally resulted in the discovery of the richest silver-mines in the world.

Nevada, as at present bounded, extends from the 35th to the 42d degree of north latitude, and from the 114th to the 120th degree west longitude from Greenwich.

The area of the State is 112,190 square miles, or 71,801,819 acres. Assuming the water-surface of the several lakes in the State to cover an area of 1,690 square miles, or 1,081,819 acres, there remain 110,500 square miles, or 70,720,000 acres as the land-area of the State.

I do not know that this is correct to the fraction of an acre, but, when the quality of the greater part of the land is considered, I don't think anybody is likely to come along and make trouble about the measurement.

The Sierra Nevada Mountains, with long lines of snowy peaks towering to the clouds, form the western boundary of the State and rise far above any mountain ranges lying to the westward in the Great Basin region, a region largely made up of alkali deserts and rugged, barren hills, yet a country abounding in all manner of minerals.

The rivers of Nevada are none of them of great size. They all pour their waters into lakes that have no outlet, where they sink into the earth or are dissipated by the active evaporation that goes on in all this region during the greater part of the year. Each river empties into its lake, or what in that country is called its "sink." Not a river of them all gets out of the State or through any other river reaches the sea.

This condition of the rivers of Nevada was once thus curiously accounted for by an old mountaineer and prospector. Said he:

"The way it came about was in this wise—The Almighty, at the time he was creatin' and fashionin' of this here yearth, got along to this section late on Saturday evening. He had finished all of the great lakes, like Superior, Michigan, Huron, Erie and them—had made the Ohio, Missouri and Mississippi rivers, and, as a sort of wind-up, was about to make a river that would be far ahead of anything he had yet done in that line. So he started in and traced out Humboldt River, and Truckee River, and Walker River, and Reese River, and all the other rivers, and he was leadin' of them along, calkerlatin' to bring 'em all together into one big boss river and then lead that off and let it empty into the Gulf of Mexico or the Gulf of California, as might be most convenient; but as he was bringin' down and leadin' along the several branches— the Truckee, Humboldt, Carson, Walker, and them—it came on dark and instead of trying to carry out the original plan, he jist tucked the lower ends of the several streams into the ground, whar they have remained from that day to this."

Carson River and Carson Valley were named in honor of Kit Carson, the famous Indian fighter, trapper, and guide, who visited that region as early as 1833. He was accompanied by old Jim Beckworth, once chief of the Crow Indians, three Crow Indians and some white trappers—nine men in all. The party passed over the Sierra Nevada Mountains to California.

Thirteen years later when with Col. J. C. Frémont, Kit Carson followed his old trail in crossing the Sierras, going in the direction of Bear River, and

Christopher (Kit) Carson, c. 1860s, collodion/albumen, Mathew Brady. Library of Congress Prints and Photographs Division.

at last, ascending a high hill in the neighborhood of where Rough-and-Ready, California, now stands, Kit struck a landmark he well remembered. Pointing out the blue peaks of the Marysville Buttes, seen far away in the smoky distance, he said: "Yonder lies the valley of the Sacramento!"

At the time of the discovery of silver, the principal settlement in that part of Utah which afterwards became the Territory and eventually the State of Nevada, was at Genoa, now the county-seat of Douglas county and situated about fourteen miles south of Carson City, the capital of the State. To all who crossed the Plains, on their way to the gold-fields of California, in the early days, Genoa was known as "Mormon Station," a name it continued to bear for some years. Even after the name had been changed to Genoa, many of the old settlers persisted in calling the place Mormon Station.

The first building of a permanent character erected in Genoa was built by Col. John Reese, who came from Salt Lake City early in the spring of 1851 with a stock of dry-goods. This first structure was a large log-house, covering an area of forty-five square yards, was in the form of an L and at one time formed two sides of a pentagon-shaped fort. Colonel Reese bought the land on which the town of Genoa now stands, with a farm adjoining, of Captain Jim, of the Washoe tribe of Indians, for two sacks of flour.

Besides the settlement at Mormon Station, a settlement, also by Mormons, was commenced in the spring of 1853 at Franktown, Washoe Valley. Quite a little hamlet was formed at Franktown; and others of the colony settled at various points along the west side of the valley at the base of the Sierra Nevada Mountains. Several Mormon families still reside in this neighborhood and occasionally the voice of the Mormon preacher is yet to be heard.

Orson Hyde, a man of considerable note at Salt Lake, had in charge the spiritual and temporal welfare of the Mormon settlements in the early days, he being both preacher and Justice of the Peace.

At this time in the history of the country there was no town in Eagle Valley, where Carson City now stands. The first building erected in that neighborhood was at Eagle Ranche, from which ranch the valley took its name. This place was afterwards better known as King's Ranche, a name it still bears. Two or three houses were next built on the present site of Carson City, but the town was not regularly laid out until 1858, when the land was purchased by Major Ormsby, who gave the place the name it now bears.

Although these early settlements were made upon lands belonging to the Washoe Indians, a tribe of considerable strength at the time, yet no very serious battles were ever had with them. The whites, however, who were at first a mere handful, Mormons and "Gentiles," all told, stood in considerable awe of the redskins. They were obliged to quietly endure not a few insults from some of the bullies of the tribe, who had a fashion of walking into houses and making themselves at home in the cupboards. They were often exceedingly insolent, and when only women and children were found at a house, always managed to frighten them into giving up most of the provisions about the place.

In one instance, however, an Indian who went to the house of a Gentile, when the only occupants were a boy about twelve years of age and his sister still younger, met a fate he-little anticipated. The Indian, after regaling himself in the pantry, began threatening the children with a roasting at the stake, for the purpose of enjoying their fright; and, finally, whipping out a big knife, began "making believe" to take the scalp of the little girl. The boy, it would seem, thought they had had about enough of this foolishness, as he went into an adjoining room, took down his father's rifle and returning to where the brave was flourishing his knife and enjoying himself, shot him dead in his tracks.

The Indian killed was one of the worst in the Washoe tribe, and was greatly dreaded in all the settlements. The father of the boy who rid the country of the much-feared Indian bully, was obliged to "pull up stakes" at once and fly to California for safety.

The Washoes inhabited the eastern slope of the Sierras, and made the stealing of the stock of the settlers both their business and their pleasure. Like crows they sat looking down into the valleys from the tops of the rocky buttresses of the mountains, and when they saw the coast clear, down they came and gathered in as many animals as they were able to drive.

Whenever the whites were so incautious as to collect for the purpose of enjoying a ball or any such social festivity, the Washoes were pretty sure to know of the affair, and seldom neglected to swoop from their mountain fastnesses, gathering up and driving away whatever animals they could find. The trail of the Indian depredators,

Washoe Indians—The Chief's Family, 1862, collodion/albumen, attributed to Charles L. Weed (Lawrence & Houseworth). Library of Congress Prints and Photographs Division.

when followed, was generally found marked with the remains of roasted horses—the Washoes having a great fondness for horse-flesh. On the occasion of a ball in Dayton, as late as 1854, the Washoes came down and "gobbled up" all the horses of the revellers. The Indians appeared to think this cunning and a very good joke.

Although Colonel Reese had about his big log-house at Mormon Station, a strong stockade, that defense was never required as a protection against the Washoe Indians. The tribe has dwindled away until at the present day those remaining are few and miserably poor, ragged, filthy, and spiritless. They now cling to the skirts of the white man and stand in awe of all surrounding tribes of Indians, even in time of peace.

The settlements thus far mentioned were all scattered along the eastern base of the Sierra Nevada Mountains, but as early as 1851, there were erected a few temporary structures, principally canvas houses, at various points to the eastward, along the line of the main "Emigrant Road." This, the then grand highway across the continent, after passing through some of the worst and most dreaded deserts between the Rocky Mountains and the Sierras, led to the well-watered and fertile valley of the Carson, a region that doubtless seemed almost a paradise to the weary emigrant, who for months and months had been toiling over rugged mountains and across sterile plains.

Mormon Station being directly on the old Hangtown (afterwards Placerville) Road, then the principal route over the Sierras, drove a thriving trade with the thousands and tens of thousands of adventurers who were then pushing their way toward the gold-fields of California. Seeing that there was money in this trade, not a few adventurers, principally from Salt Lake and California, established posts on the line of the road to the eastward of Mormon Station and Eagle Ranche, a few even pushing out a considerable distance into the deserts. The majority of these traders, however, returned to California each season, following in the wake of the last emigrant-trains that came in over the Plains, and there remained until the tide of emigration began to pour in again the next year.

These traders furnished the "pilgrims" cheap luxuries at outrageously high prices, traded for their disabled cattle and swindled them in every possible manner, as they all considered the emigrant their lawful prey.

CHAPTER II

THE SEARCH FOR GOLD

"Washing"—Celestials at the Diggings—Original Papers—
Primitive Amusements—Jacob Job's little Game—A Delusion and a Snare

Gold was first discovered in Nevada in the spring of 1850, by some Mormon emigrants. They had started for California, but so early in the season that when they arrived at the Carson River they learned that the snow on the summit of the Sierra Nevada Mountains was still too deep to allow of their being crossed. This being the case, the party encamped on the Carson to await the opening of the road.

Having nothing else to do, some of the men of the party began prospecting for gold. Their camp on the river being at no great distance from the mouth of the Gold Cañon, the largest cañon in the neighborhood, they were naturally attracted to it and there began their prospecting operations.

Although they knew but little about mining, and had only pans with which to wash the gravel, they found gold sufficiently plentiful to enable them to make small wages. It does not appear, however, that the discoverers worked them longer than until they were able to continue their journey to California.

Other emigrants coming in and encamping on the river learned of the discovery of gold in the cañon, and, being anxious to begin gold-digging as soon as possible, did some prospecting along the bed of the ravine.

But the gold being fine (*i.e.,* like dust—in fine particles), and the quantity not being up to their expectations, nearly all pushed on to California, where they expected to make fortunes in a few weeks or months; as all believed, that they, through their superior acuteness, would find places in some of the dark and secret gulches of the Sierras where they would be able to gather pounds of golden nuggets.

Finally, Spofford Hall, of Fort Wayne, Indiana, arrived across the Plains and, thinking it a good point at which to establish a permanent station, erected a substantial log-house at a point not far from the mouth of the Gold Cañon. This was for some time known as Hall's Station. Afterwards it was known as McMartin's Station, the property having been purchased by James McMartin, a man who came across the Plains with Mr. Hall. This house stood on ground now covered by the town of Dayton and was still being used as a store at the time of the discovery of silver, it being then owned by Major Ormsby, killed at Pyramid Lake, in 1860, in the first battle with the Paiutes.

This discovery of gold at the mouth of Gold Cañon was undoubtedly that which led to the discovery, some years later, of the Comstock lode—the first step, as it were, to the grand silver discovery of the age. At the head of Gold Cañon are situated a number of the leading mines of the Comstock range.

In the spring of 1852 a considerable number of men began working on the lower part of Gold Cañon, most of them using rockers in their mining operations. As these men did well, making from $5 to $10 per day, the number of miners on the cañon was considerably greater in the winter and spring of 1853, there being as many as two or three hundred men at work. As there was little water in the bed of the cañon except during the winter and spring months, few miners were to be seen at work in summer—seldom more than forty or fifty.

As the miners worked their way up the cañon from bar to bar, a new town was eventually founded at a point a few miles above the first

Gold Cañon Where Gold Was First Discovered in Nevada, c. 1890, dry plate/collotype, James H. Crockwell. Library of Congress Prints and Photographs Division. Old, abandoned placer gold mining equipment, including sluice boxes, still remained at the mouth of Gold Cañon when Crockwell took this photograph.

settlement at its mouth. This was a little hamlet of a dozen houses of all kinds, and was christened Johntown. In this little town or "Camp," as such places are usually styled in mining countries, lived Henry Comstock, who gave his name, some years later to the great silver lode; also, Peter O'Riley and Patrick McLaughlin, the discoverers of the Comstock vein. "Old Virginia" (James Finney, or Fennimore), in whose honor Virginia City, the great mining town of Nevada, was named, was also a resident of Johntown in the early days, as were several other persons who are now classed among the worthies of the Comstock range.

A Miner Using the Rocker, 1862, collodion/albumen, attributed to Charles L. Weed (Lawrence & Houseworth). Library of Congress Prints and Photographs Division. This photo was used as the model for an illustration in the first edition of *The Big Bonanza* purportedly depicting "Old Virginia" at his rocker, however, James Fennimore died the year before.

From about 1856 up to 1858, Johntown was the "big mining town" of Western Utah—at least was the head-quarters of most of the miners at work in the country. All told, the camp contained only about a dozen buildings, some of which were mere shanties, but many of the miners preferred to camp out during the spring and summer months—they had no use for houses.

A large number of Chinamen being at work at the mouth of the cañon, near where the gold was first discovered, that place finally became known as "Chinatown," a name which it long retained, though the whites who settled there did not much fancy the name. They gave the place the name of Mineral Rapids, but this did not take; then there was danger of it being christened Nevada City, but the citizens rose in their might and at a meeting, held November 3rd. 1861, the name of Dayton was unanimously adopted, and Dayton it has ever since remained.

The Chinamen mentioned, forty or fifty in number at first, were brought over from California, in 1856, to work on a big water-ditch, by means of which water was to be brought to the Gold Cañon mines from the Carson River. Finding they would be allowed to mine in certain places, others followed, and at one time not less than one hundred and eighty Mongolians were at work at the lower end of the Cañon.

The Celestials probably found very good pay, even in the places where they were allowed to plant their rockers, as it is said that the bars for some miles up the cañon paid well when first worked, there being places where an ounce per day was taken out.

The cañon continued to pay pretty fair wages for some years, and was still being worked at the time of the discovery of silver and the grand silver excitement which immediately followed.

Literature was not neglected at this early period in the history of Washoe. There were, even in the early days when Johntown was the great mining centre of the country, two spicy weekly papers published in the land. They were written on foolscap, often several sheets, and, by being assiduously passed from hand to hand, were widely circulated in the several settlements. These papers were everywhere eagerly read. One, called the *Scorpion,* was published at Genoa, and was edited by S. A. Kinsey; the other was published at Johntown and was edited by Joe Webb. It was called *The Gold-Cañon Switch.* These papers were both published between the years 1854 and 1858.

The people of Johntown, though not numerous, were jovial. They were fond of amusements of all kinds. Nearly every Saturday night a "grand ball" was given at "Dutch Nick's" saloon. As there were but three white women in the town, it was necessary, in order to "make up the set," to take in Miss Sarah Winnemucca, the "Paiute Princess" (daughter of Winnemucca, chief of all the Paiutes). When the orchestra—a "yallerbacked fiddle"—struck up and the 'French four' was in order, the enthusiastic Johntowners went forth in the dance with ardor and filled the air with splinters from the puncheon floor. When a Johntown "hoss" balanced in front of the "Princess" he made no effort to economise shoe-leather.

Even in those early days and in that primitive community, the "beast of the jungle" was known in the land. The "boys" were not allowed to languish for want of amusement. When their sacks of gold-dust became painfully plethoric, and too heavy to be conveniently packed around, Jacob Job, the leading merchant of the place used to deal faro for them "out of hand;" that is, he took the cards from his hand and laid them out on the table, instead of drawing them from a box such as is used in the game by regular "sports."

Billy Williams, a man who had a ranch up in Carson Valley, occasionally came down to Johntown in seasons of great auriferous affluence, and dealt for the boys a little game called "Twenty-one." Faro, out of hand, and Twenty-one, with Williams at the helm, usually sent all the male Johntowners back to their toms and rockers, each man financially a total wreck.

About 1857—58 the diggings along Gold Cañon showed signs of failing, all the best bars and banks being pretty well worked out. It was only occasionally that a rich spot could be found, and most of the miners were only making small wages. That this was the case is evident from the fact that about this time the Johntowners, the mining men of the land, began to scatter out through the country and make prospecting raids in all directions among the hills.

In 1857, several men from Johntown, struck gold-diggings on Six Mile Cañon. This cañon heads on the north side of Mount Davidson, while Gold Cañon, in which gold was first found, heads on the south side of the same mountain. The heads of the two cañons are about a mile apart, and through the eastern face of Mount Davidson, across a sort of plateau, runs the Comstock Silver lode. The lode (or lead), extends across the heads of both cañons, and the gold that was being mined in both came from the decomposed rock of the croppings of the vein.

Thus, it will be seen, these early miners were approaching the great silver lode from two points—on Gold Cañon towards the south, and on Six Mile Cañon toward the north side of Mount Davidson. But not a man among them knew anything of what was ahead. They were only working for gold and were looking for that nowhere but in the gravel of the ravines; none of them having thought of looking for gold-bearing quartz veins.

The men who were mining on Six Mile Cañon first struck paying ground, at a point nearly a mile below the place where silver ore was afterwards found in the Ophir mine. The gold was in clay, which was so tough that before it could be washed out in rockers it was necessary to "puddle" it—that is, put it into a large square box or a hole in the ground, and dissolve it by adding a proper quantity of water and working it about with hoes or shovels. Even working in this way, the men were able to make from five dollars to an ounce per day. The gold found at this distance down the cañon was worth about $13.50 per ounce.

The miners on Six Mile Cañon sold their dust in Placerville, California. Being acquainted with some California boys who were mining in a place called 'Coon Hollow, our Washoe miners were in the habit of buying a certain quantity of fine dust of them, which they mixed with the gold from Six Mile Cañon, when they were able to sell the whole lot at such a price as was equal to fifteen dollars per ounce for their own dust. As they worked further up the ravine, toward the Comstock lode, the gold deteriorated so rapidly in weight, color and value, that this game could no longer be played. The gold-buyer looked upon the mixture of Six Mile Cañon and 'Coon Hollow products and pronounced it a delusion and a snare.

CHAPTER III

ADVENTURES OF EARLY PROSPECTORS

The Mysterious Brothers—What was Found in a Shaft—
Pike's Great Discovery—"Stuff They Make Compasses of"—
Wonderful Travelling Stones

Two young men who were mining in Gold Cañon, suspected the existence of silver-mines in the country at least five or six years before silver was actually discovered. These men were Hosea B. and Edgar Allen Grosch, sons of A. B. Grosch, a Universalist clergyman of considerable note, and editor of a Universalist paper at Utica, New York. The Grosch brothers were well educated and had considerable knowledge of mineralogy and assaying.

They came to Gold Cañon in 1852, from Volcano, California, and engaged in placer-mining. In 1853 and 1854, they appear to have become convinced that there was silver to be found in the country, and did a good deal of prospecting in various directions among the neighboring mountains, doubtless in search of silver ore.

In their cabin, which stood near the present town of Silver City, about a mile above Johntown, they are said to have had a library consisting of a considerable number of volumes of scientific works; also chemical apparatus and assayer's tools.

They did not associate with the miners working on the cañon, and were very reticent in regard to what they were doing. They, however, informed a few persons that they had discovered a vein of silver-bearing quartz and it was well known among the miners that they had formed a company for the purpose of working their mine. The majority of the members of their company were understood to be in California (about Volcano), and in one of the Atlantic States. Mrs. L. M. Dettenreider, one of the early settlers of the country, and a lady who had befriended the brothers, was given an interest in their mine, and at one time had in her possession a piece, of ore from it. This ore, they assured her, contained gold, silver, lead, and antimony.

Mrs. Dettenreider, who is a resident of Virginia City, says she always understood that the mine discovered by the Grosch brothers was somewhere about Mount Davidson, and thinks they may have obtained their ore somewhere along the Comstock lead.

In 1860, I saw their old furnaces unearthed, they having been covered up to the depth of a foot or more by a deposit of mud and sand from Gold Cañon. They were two in number and but two or three feet in length, a foot in height and a foot and a half in width. One had been used as a smelting and the other as a cupel furnace. The remains of melting-pots and fragments of cupels were found in and about the furnaces, also a large piece of argentiferous galena, which had doubtless been procured a short distance west of Silver City, where there are yet to be seen veins containing ore of that character, some of which yield fair assays in silver.

In the spring of 1857, Hosea Grosch, while engaged in mining, stuck a pick in his foot, inflicting a wound, from the effects of which he died, in a few days. In November of that year, while on his way to Volcano, California, Allen, the surviving brother, was caught in a heavy storm in the Sierra Nevada Mountains, and had his feet frozen so badly that amputation was necessary, from the shock of which operation he died. With the brothers was lost the secret of the whereabouts of their silver-mine; if they ever discovered any silver except that contained in the ore of the veins of argentiferous galena I have mentioned.

After the discovery of the old furnaces of the Grosch brothers in 1860, there was much search by miners in the neighborhood for the mine they had been prospecting, but no mine was ever found.

In a sort of sink on the side of a large mountain, at the foot of which stood the cabin and furnaces of the brothers, was found an old shaft. Here was supposed to be the spot where they had worked, and the place was "located" ("claimed" or "preempted"), and called the "Lost Shaft."

About the first discovery made by the locators, when they began cleaning out the shaft, was the body—a sort of mummy—of a Paiute squaw, who had been murdered some years before by members of her tribe, who had tumbled her remains into the old shaft.

After finding this "dead thing," the owners of the claim let a contract for the further sinking and exploration of the old shaft. The men who took the contract soon gave it up. They said they could not work in the shaft; that stones were falling out of its sides without cause. Others took the contract, and each party of miners that went to work in the shaft gave it up, saying that their lives were endangered by the stones which suddenly and at unexpected times, jumped out of its sides. A tunnel was then started to tap the ledge on which the old shaft was supposed to have been sunk, but it was never completed. It is now well known that the old shaft was sunk by a party of Gold Cañon miners in 1851, they having taken it into their heads that from this curious-looking pit or sink in the side of the mountain came all the gold found below in the cañon.

There was also a story current among the miners, in 1860, that before starting on the trip over the Sierras which resulted in his death, Allen Grosch boxed up the library and all the chemical and assaying apparatus, and *cached* the whole somewhere about Grizzly Hill, the mountain at the base of which stood the cabin occupied by the brothers. There was much search by curious miners in the neighborhood for this supposed deposit of valuables. They crawled under the edge of shelving rocks, peered into crevices among the cliffs, and probed all suspicious-looking stoneheaps, but no bonanza of scientific apparatus was ever discovered. When Allen Grosch left to go over the mountains to California, Comstock was placed in charge of the cabin, and it is very probable that whatever books and apparatus there may have been were carried away by such visitors as took a fancy to them, and thus were scattered and lost.

In the summer of 1860 I was camped on a branch of Gold Cañon, near where the old stone-cabin of the Grosch brothers stood. I had a score or more of neighbors, whose tents were pitched on the banks of the ravine, or who, having no tents, made the willows on the bars their shelter. One hot day in July, one of the men, a big, long-legged Missourian, started up the mountain to see what he could find. One object probably was to look for the Grosch scientific "bonanza," but, being a man who had no more knowledge of ores and minerals than a Paiute, he was quite sure to make some remarkable discovery, no matter in what direction he traveled.

He had been absent some hours when, looking up towards the summit of Grizzly Hill, we saw a cloud of dust moving down the face of the mountain. In the midst of this whirling cloud, we caught occasional glimpses of a man, bounding along like a wild goat. Rocks disturbed by his feet, rolled down the steep slope of the mountain, adding greatly to the dust and commotion. All in camp were soon out gazing at the unusual spectacle, and all wondered what had happened to "Pike," who by this time had been recognized by his long legs and reckless manner of handling them.

Some thought that a bear or some other wild beast was in pursuit of Pike, as he charged down the steep mountain in a manner so reckless that it was very evident he was taking no thought of the risk he ran of breaking his neck.

Over jutting ledges and through huge patches of loose, sliding rock, bounded Pike, and soon he came rushing wild-eyed into camp.

Rivulets of perspiration were coursing down his dust-covered cheeks; dust whitened the ends of his long black locks, and dust seemed to fly from his nostrils as, puffing and blowing, he made his way into our midst.

In both hands he held a quantity of black-looking rock. As soon as he could get his breath he said: "Boys, I've struck it! There's millions of tons of it! Millions on millions—enough to make the whole camp rich!"

"Well, what is it Pike?" asked some one. "Is it silver, gold, or what?"

"It is what none of you fellers would ever have found: it's the stuff they make compasses of!"

"Make compasses of! What do you mean?" asked the men. "Mean! I mean just what I say, that it is the stuff they make compasses of—surveyors' compasses, mariners' compasses, and all them kind of compasses that pint to the North Pole. None of you would ever have found it; you wouldn't have knowed what it was!"

"Well, where is it? Where is this big thing?"

"Way up yander on top of the mountain," said Pike, pointing towards the summit of Grizzly Hill. "There's a whole ledge of it—a ledge fifty foot wide!"

"But how do you know that the stuff is good for anything?" asked the boys. "How do you know that it is what compasses are made of?"

"How do I know? Easy enough. Just look here, will you!"

Pike then took a piece of the rock weighing about five pounds, and placing one end of it in the midst of a handful of smaller pieces, ranging from the size of a pea to that of a hulled walnut, the whole mass of small fragments was lifted up and remained clinging to the larger lump of rock.

"See that!" cried Pike, glancing at one and another of the men about him: "What did I tell you? and there is millions more where I got this!"

All were now really a good deal interested in the rock found by Pike, and in the powerful magnetic qualities it exhibited, as the large lumps would pick up and hold suspended fragments weighing over an ounce.

"The way I come to find it," now explained Pike, "was this: I found the big ledge of black, heavy rock, and taking up a chunk of it began trying to break off a slice from the main ledge. As I hammered away, I noticed that all the little bits of rock pounded loose stuck to the chunk I held in my hand. I thought at first that there was pine-gum on the chunk, but could find none, then it all at once flashed into my mind, and I said—'I've struck it! This is the stuff they make compasses of!' Then you just ought to have seen me make tracks down the mountain."

"We saw you!" said the men.

Pike then went on to say, that his discovery was one of the most important, in many respects, that had been made in modern times. It would be of incalculable advantage to navigation and would increase the navies of the world a thousand-fold. He even went so far the next morning (which showed that his brain had not been idle during the night) as to assert that hereafter there would be no difficulty about reaching the North Pole. All that would be necessary, he said, would be to place a block of about ten tons of his rock on the bow of a ship, when, without the aid of sail or rudder, and in spite of adverse winds and ice floes, the vessel would plough its way up through the oceans of the north and never stop until its nose rested against the side of the Pole.

Pike had several assays of his "find" made, and it was weeks before he could be made to believe that it was not something of more value than magnetic iron ore.

Some years after Pike's great discovery, a prospector who had been roaming through the Pahranagat Mountains, the wildest and most sterile portion of southeastern Nevada, brought back with him a great curiosity in the shape of a number of traveling stones. The stones were almost perfectly round, the majority of them as large as a hulled walnut, and very heavy, being of an irony nature. When scattered about on the floor, on a table, or other level surface, within two or three feet of each other, they immediately began traveling toward a common centre, and then huddled up in a bunch like a lot of eggs in a nest. A single stone removed to a distance of a yard, upon being released, at once started off with wonderful and somewhat comical celerity to rejoin its fellows; but if taken away four or five feet it remained motionless.

The man who was in possession of these traveling stones said that he found them in a region of country that, though comparatively level, is nothing but bare rock. Scattered about in this rocky plain are a great number of little basins, from a few feet to two or three rods in diameter, and it is in the bottom of these basins that the rolling stones are found. In the basins they are seen from the size of a pea to five or six inches in diameter. These curious pebbles appeared to be formed of loadstone or magnetic iron ore.

CHAPTER IV

WHAT THEY DISCOVERED
"That Blasted Blue Stuff"—"Old Pancake"—A Discovery—
John Bishop's Story—Unearthly Treasure

To return to the notions of the early miners and others, in regard to the existence of silver in Nevada. Few, it would seem, besides the Grosch brothers, and one or two of their intimate friends, ever dreamed of there being any silver-mines in the country. Had there been anything said about the existence of silver, those who made predictions that it would be found, would not have been slow to remind their friends of the fact as soon as the first discovery of silver was made. Some of the Johntowners say that, in 1853, a Mexican who was hired by them and who worked a few days in Gold Cañon, tried to tell them that he was of the opinion that there were silver-mines in the mountains above them. The man spoke no English, therefore was unable at that time to make himself understood; now that the silver-mines have been found, all seems plain enough.

Pointing to the large fragments of quartz rock lying along the bed of the cañon, the Mexican said: *"Bueno!"*—good! Then pointing toward the mountain peaks about the head of the cañon, and giving his hand a general wave over them all, he cried emphatically: *"Mucho plata! mucho plata!"* "Much silver! much silver! all above you in those hills," was what the

Mexican said by word and gesture.

The men who were at work with the Mexican remember this, because during the two or three days he was at work with them he several times uttered the same words and went through the same pantomime. All that the miners understood of what the fellow was driving at was, "lots of money, gold," somewhere above them in the mountains.

The fact is, that silver was so little in the minds of the early miners, and they knew so little about any ore of silver, that when they at last found it, they did not know what it was and cursed it as some kind of heavy, worthless sand of iron, or some other base metal, that covered up the quicksilver in the bottom of their rockers and interfered with the amalgamation and saving of the gold they were washing out. They damned this stuff from the rising of the sun till the going down thereof, and worked in it for a considerable length of time before anybody knew what it was. Until after an assay of the "blasted blue stuff" had been made, the miners were all working in blissful ignorance of silver existing anywhere in the country.

In the spring of 1858, which the snow was going off and water was plentiful, the men who had worked in Six Mile Cañon the year before, with a number of other miners from Johntown, returned to their diggings. The newcomers set to work on the cañon above the claims of those who had mined there the previous year, planting their rockers wherever they found a spot of ground that would pay wages.

Among those who came to mine on Six Mile Cañon at this time were Peter O'Riley and Pat McLaughlin, the discoverers of the Comstock silver lode, and "Old Virginia" who gave his name to Virginia City, under the streets of which now lie the bonanza mines.

Nick Ambrose, better known in that country as "Dutch Nick," also moved up to Six Mile Cañon, following his customers in their exodus from Johntown. Nick came not to mine, but to minister to the wants of the miners. He set up a large tent and ran it as a saloon and boarding-house. The boys paid him $14 per week for board and "slept themselves;" that is, they were provided with blankets of their own, and rolling up in these, they just curled down in the sagebrush, wherever and whenever they pleased.

The liquid refreshment furnished these miners by Nick was probably the first of that popular brand of whisky known as "tarantula juice" ever dispensed within the limits of Virginia City. When the boys were well charged with this whisky it made the snakes and tarantulas that bit them very sick.

At this time, H. T. P. Comstock was engaged in mining on American Flat Ravine, a branch of Gold Cañon, a short distance above the point where Silver City now stands. He was working with a "tom" (a contrivance for washing auriferous gravel which combines the principles of the rocker and the sluice-box), and, the water used in the tom being some distance below where his "pay-dirt" was found, he had a number of lusty Paiute Indians employed in packing the dirt to where he was engaged in washing it and supervising things in general, as became the proprietor of the "works."

The ground worked was not so rich as to greatly excite anyone, it being about, as the Chinamen say, "two pan, one color," therefore it is not likely that the Indians received wages that gave them a very exalted opinion of mining as a regular business.

At that time Comstock, whose name is now heard in all parts of the world in connection with the great silver lode bearing his name, was familiarly known to the miners of Johntown and neighboring mining camps as "Old Pancake." This name was given him by his brother miners because he was never known to bake any bread. He always had—or imagined he had—so much business on hand that he could spare no time to fool away in making and baking bread. All of his flour was worked up into pancakes. And even as, with spoon in hand, he stirred up his pancake batter, it is said he kept one eye on the top of some distant peak and was lost in speculations in regard to the wealth in gold and silver that might rest somewhere beneath its rocky crest.

Meantime, while "Old Pancake" was thus toiling in American-Flat Ravine, and utilizing the native muscle of the land in his struggles with the stubborn matrix of auriferous deposits, the miners on Six Mile Cañon were steadily working along the channel of the same, picking out the richer places, and the gold extracted was gradually becoming lighter in color and weight, consequently less valuable; a condition of things that puzzled them all not a little. As, at that time, the presence of silver was not suspected, the miners could not imagine what was the matter with the gold, further than that there seemed to be some kind of bogus stuff mixed with it in the form of an alloy. This light metal, whatever it might be, seemed gradually taking the place of the gold and changing the color of the dust. As a small percentage of silver alters the color of a great quantity of gold, the value per ounce was not so much reduced as one would have supposed from looking at it; but in the value there was a slight but steady decrease.

The miners on Six Mile Cañon worked on in the fall of 1858 with tolerable success—making small wages—until it became so cold that the water they had been using in rocking was frozen up, when all hands broke up camp and returned to Johntown, to go into winter quarters.

In January 1859, there came a spell of fine weather, when some of the Johntowners struck out in various directions, for the purpose of prospecting; water being plentiful in all the ravines, owing to the melting of the snow.

On Saturday, January 28, 1859, "Old Virginia," H. T. P. (Pancake) Comstock, and several others struck the surface diggings at Gold Hill, and located a considerable number of claims. They claimed the ground for placer-mining but had no idea of there being a rich vein of gold and silver-bearing quartz underlying the whole region upon which they were staking off their gravel-mines.

They had struck upon the little knoll to which the name of Gold Hill was soon after given, which knoll stood at the north end of the site of the present town of Gold Hill. Although at first mistaken for placer-diggings, the ground forming this hillock was in reality nothing more than a great mass of the decomposed croppings of the Comstock lode. This discovery was made at a point on the head of Gold Cañon about a mile south of where, a few months later, silver was discovered in the Ophir mine, at the head of Six Mile Cañon. John Bishop, one of the men who made this strike, thus describes the manner of it. I give his own words:

"Where Gold Hill now stands, I had noticed indications of a ledge and had got a little color. I spoke to 'Old Virginia' about it, and he remembered the locality, for he said he had often seen the place when hunting deer and antelope. He also said that he had seen any quantity of quartz there. So he joined our party and Comstock also followed along. When we got to the ground, I took a pan and filled it with dirt, with my foot, for I had no shovel or spade. The others did the same thing, though I believe that some of them had shovels. I noticed some willows growing on the hillside and I started for them with my pan. The place looked like an Indian spring, which it proved to be.

"I began washing my pan. When I had finished, I found that I had in it about fifteen cents. None of the others had less than eight cents, and none more than fifteen. It was very fine gold; just as fine as flour. Old Virginia decided that it was a good place to locate and work.

"The next difficulty was to obtain water. We followed the cañon along for some distance and found what appeared to be the same formation all the way along. Presently Old Virginia and another man who had been rambling away, came back and said they had found any amount of water which could be brought right there to the ground.

"I and my partner had meantime had a talk together and had decided to put the others of the party right in the middle of the good ground.

"After Old Virginia got back we told him this, but were not understood, as he said if we had decided to 'hog' it we could do so and he would look around further; but he remained, and when the ground was measured off, took his share with the rest.

"After we had measured the ground we had a consultation as to what name was to be given the place. It was decidedly not Gold Cañon, for it was a little hill; so we concluded to call it Gold Hill. That is how the place came by its present name."

The new diggings were discovered on Saturday, and the next day (Sunday) nearly all the male inhabitants of Johntown went up to the head of Gold Cañon to take a look at and "pass upon" the new mines. The majority of the sagacious citizens of the then mining metropolis of the country did not think much of the new strike. They had placer-mines near at home, five miles below, that prospected much better. However, "Old Pancake" and some of others interested in the new diggings, blowed about them as being the big thing of the country.

Although the prospects at first may not all have been as large as stated by Bishop, who is quoted above, yet Comstock, Old Virginia, and party soon reached very rich dirt—very much richer than Comstock had ever found in any part of his American Ravine claim, where he worked the braves of the Paiute tribe. Starting in at about $5 per day, they were soon making from $15 to $20, and for a time even more to the man. Believing they were working placer-mines, they were at times moved too far away from the main deposit of decomposed croppings, when they made small wages until they got back and started again on the right track.

It was not long before most of the Johntowners had moved to Gold Hill, camping under the trees at first, then building shanties and eventually putting up substantial log-houses.

Thus was first discovered, located, and worked that portion of the Comstock lode lying under the town of Gold Hill, and containing the Belcher, Crown Point, Yellow Jacket, Imperial, Empire, Kentuck, and other leading mines of the country— mines that have yielded millions upon millions in gold and silver bullion.

It was not, however, until these mines had been worked for two or three years, that they were positively known to be silver-mines and a continuation of the Comstock lead, then being so successfully mined upon a mile north, at Virginia City.

CHAPTER V

DISCOVERY OF THE GREAT COMSTOCK MINE

Discovery of the Great Comstock—What they threw Away—
Old Pancake Arrives—Questionable Rights—
Sold and "Sold"—Locking up "Old Virginia"

In the spring of 1859, a considerable number of miners returned to Six Mile Cañon, to work. They now made their headquarters at Gold Hill, where two or three log-houses including a large log boarding-house, had been erected.

Peter O'Riley and Pat McLaughlin set to work well up at the head of the ravine, where the ground began to rise toward the mountain. They used rockers and found small pay. They continued to work at this point until about the 1st of June, 1859, gradually extending their operations up the slope of the hill, in the hope of finding something better. They had started a little cut or trench up the hill and were washing the dirt taken from this in their rockers. Before they started the cut they were making only from $1.50 to $2 per day; in the cut their pay was even less. They were becoming discouraged, and were thinking of going to Walker River to try their luck, placer-mines having been found in that region the year before, but concluded to work on where they were a few days longer—probably in the hope of being able to raise money with which to go to Walker River.

Having but a small stream of water, it became necessary for them to dig a hole as a sort of reservoir, in which to collect it for use in their rockers.

They set to work a short distance above the little cut in which they were mining, to make the needed reservoir or water-hole, and at a depth of about four feet, struck into a stratum of the rich decomposed ore of the Ophir Mine, and of the now world-famous Comstock silver lode.

The manner in which the grand discovery was made, was much less romantic than in the case of the discovery of the celebrated silver-mine of Potosi, Peru. What our miners found, was not glittering native silver, but a great bed of black sulphuret of silver—a decomposed ore of silver filled with spangles of native gold. This gold, however, was alloyed with silver to such an extent that it was more the color of silver than of gold.

The gold dug in the placer-mines of California, is worth from $16 to $19 per ounce, whereas, the gold taken from the croppings of the Comstock was worth no more than $11 or $12 per ounce.

When the discoverers struck into the odd-looking, black dirt, they only thought that it was a sudden and rather singular change from the yellowish gravel and clay in which they had been digging. As any change was welcome, the luck in which they had been working considered, they at once concluded to try some of the curious-looking stuff in their rockers.

The result astounded them. Before, they had only been taking out a dollar or two per day, but now they found the bottoms of their rockers covered with gold as soon as a few buckets of the new dirt had been washed. They found that they were literally taking out gold by the pound.

However, as the gold they were getting was much lighter in color and weight than any they had found below on the cañon, or even on the surface in their cut, they began to fear that all was not right. They thought that, after all, what they had found might be some sort of "bogus stuff"—base metal of some new and strange kind.

It is not strange that these impecunious miners, tinkering away there on the side of a lone, sage-covered mountain, with their rockers, should have felt a little alarmed on account of the great quantity of gold they were getting, as in a few weeks after the discovery had been made—and the work had been advanced further into the croppings of the lode—they were taking out gold at the rate of $1,000 per day. This they were doing with the rockers. Taking the harder lumps left on the screens of the rockers, one man was able to pound out gold at the rate of $100 per day in a common hand-mortar.

In the evening of the day on which the grand discovery was made by O'Riley and McLaughlin, H. T. P. Comstock made his appearance upon the scene.

"Old Pancake," who was then looking after his Gold Hill mines, which were beginning to yield largely, had strolled northward up the mountain, toward evening, in search of a mustang pony that he had out prospecting for a living among the

Henry Tompkins Paige Comstock, 1876, illustration.

hills. He had found his pony, had mounted him, and with his long legs dragging the tops of the sage-brush, came riding up just as the lucky miners were making the last clean-up of their rockers for the day.

Comstock, who had a keen eye for all that was going on in the way of mining in any place he might visit, saw at a glance the unusual quantity of gold that was in sight.

When the gold caught his eye, he was off the back of his pony in an instant. He was soon down in the thick of it all— "hefting" and running his fingers through the gold, and picking into and probing the mass of strange-looking "stuff" exposed.

Conceiving at once that a wonderful discovery of some kind had been made, Old Pancake straightened himself up, as he arose from a critical examination of the black mass in the cut, wherein he had observed the glittering spangles of gold, and coolly proceeded to inform the astonished miners that they were working on ground that belonged to him.

He asserted that he had some time before taken up 160 acres of land at this point, for a ranch; also, that he owned the water they were using in mining, it being from the Caldwell spring, in what was afterwards known as Spanish Ravine.

Suspecting that they were working in a decomposed quartz vein, McLaughlin and O'Riley had written out and posted up a notice, calling for a claim of 300 feet for each and a third claim for the discovery; which extra claim they were entitled to under the mining laws.

Having soon ascertained all this from the men before him, Comstock would have "none of it." He boisterously declared that they should not work there at all, unless they would agree to locate himself and his friend Manny (Emmanuel) Penrod in the claim. In case he and Penrod were given an interest, there should be no further trouble about the ground.

After consulting together, the discoverers concluded that, rather than have a great row about the matter, they would put the names of Comstock and Penrod in their notice of location.

This being arranged to his satisfaction, Comstock next demanded that 100 feet of ground on the lead should be segregated and given to Penrod and himself for the right to the water they were using—he stoutly asserting that he not only owned the land, but also the water, and, as they had recognized his right to the land, they could not consistently ignore his claim to the water flowing upon it. In short, he talked so loudly and so much about his water-right that he at last got the 100 feet, segregated, as he demanded. This 100 feet afterwards became the Spanish or Mexican mine, and yielded millions of dollars.

Comstock would probably not so easily have obtained what he demanded, had the men who made the discovery been fully aware of its great value. They, however, did not know that the "blue stuff" (sulphuret of silver), which they had dug into, was of any value, and even the gold itself seemed altogether too plentiful as well as a good deal "off color."

Comstock had probably at some time posted up a notice claiming 160 acres of land, somewhere in that neighborhood, as a ranch, but if he did so he never had his notice recorded. Men in those days, while roving about the country, very frequently wrote out and stuck up notices claiming land, springs, the water of streams, quartz veins, gravel deposits, or anything else that they might for the moment think valuable, but unless such claims were properly recorded and worked they could not be held, as all miners and others well knew—a mere notice expiring at the end of ten days, when the property might be taken up, recorded and held by the first man that came along. Comstock had some show of right to the water and to the placer-mines along the upper part of Six Mile Cañon, as the year before, he, Old Virginia and Penrod, had bought of old Joe Caldwell a set of sluice-boxes and the water of a spring. However, the possession of a set of sluices on the cañon and a right to use water from a certain spring in the neighborhood, by no means gave Comstock or his friends the right to lay claim to a vein of quartz found in a hill somewhere in their section of the country. John Bishop, who bought Old Virginia's interest in the sluices, gravel-diggings and water, got no share of the quartz vein discovered by Pete O'Riley and Pat McLaughlin, though he managed to get in on the lead, locating the mine known as the Central No. 1; now a part of the California, one of the bonanza mines with millions of ore in sight.

Bishop put up the first arastra ever built on the lead, starting it up two or three days before that of the Ophir folks began running. He sold his interest in the Central No. 1. for $4,000 and shortly afterwards the purchasers sold the same ground for $1,800 per foot—now (as incorporated in the California mine) the ground is selling at over $50,000 per foot, and John Bishop still works, as a miner, at Gold Hill.

After Comstock had managed to become largely interested in the new discovery, and after the gold taken out by O'Riley and McLaughlin had been carried down to Gold Hill and exhibited and examined, there was at once a great local excitement in regard to the new diggings, and all were anxious to get an interest in the claim, or on the lead as near to the original discovery as possible.

Those who were finally recorded in the Ophir notice as original locators were the following persons: Peter O'Riley, Patrick McLaughlin, H. T. P. Comstock, E. Penrod, and J. A. ("Kentuck") Osborne. The men named had one-sixth each of 1,400 feet of ground on the lead and, in addition, Comstock and Penrod had 100 feet segregated to them, making 1,500 feet taken up by the party.

The 100 feet of Comstock and Penrod, though in the midst of the 1,400 feet of ground, was not reckoned as a part of the Ophir claim and was soon sold and worked as a separate mine, under the name of the Mexican or Spanish mine.

The Ophir claim was the first that was located, as a quartz claim, at any point on the Comstock lode, though as early as February 22nd, 1858,

Old Virginia made a location on a large vein lying to the westward of the Comstock. This vein is known as the Virginia lead or Virginia croppings. It has never yielded much ore, but contains vast quantities of base metal of various kinds.

At one time it was thought by some that this would prove to be the main or "mother" lead of the range, as at the surface, and for a considerable distance below the surface, the Comstock vein dipped west toward it. Parties bought Old Virginia's claim, and began suit against the Ophir Company, asserting that the lead on which they were at work was the same as that located, in 1858, by Old Virginia. It was a sort of speculation on the part of those who brought the suit, and it is understood that they succeeded in obtaining $60,000 from the Ophir Company.

At the beginning of this suit it was necessary, if possible, to produce the original notice placed upon the croppings of the lead by Old Virginia, but the parties to whom he had sold his claim could never get him sufficiently sobered up to show where it could be found. Growing desperate, they at length seized the old fellow one evening, and thrusting him into the mouth of a big tunnel, closed and locked upon him a heavy iron gate. The next morning when they went to the tunnel they found Old Virginia sober, but very savage.

He would say nor do nothing until they had taken him down town and given him half a tumbler of whisky. This swallowed, he was ready for business. He marched directly up the side of the mountain, and going straight to a large tower of croppings, drew out a small block of rock, and lo! behind it was seen snugly stowed the much-desired notice.

It was probably on account of his having made this location that Old Virginia was given the credit of having been the discoverer of the Comstock lode, his interest in which he was said to have sold for an old horse, a pair of blankets, and a bottle of whisky. He sold a third interest in the sluices, water, and diggings in the cañon to John Bishop, for $25.

James Hart, who had an interest in the sluices, and diggings in the cañon, sold his right to be "considered in" on the big discovery to J. D. Winters, of Washoe Valley, for a horse and $20 in coin. In this way Winters got into the Ophir as one of the locators, and from this came the "old horse" story that has always been saddled upon Old Virginia—to fix it still more firmly upon the old fellow, the bottle of whiskey was added.

CHAPTER VI

THE DISCOVERY OF SILVER

"Old Pancake's" Weakness—Naming the town—
An Astounding Disclosure—Going to the Diggings—A Grand Discovery

Once Comstock got into the Ophir claim he elected himself superintendent and was the man who did all of the heavy talking. He made himself so conspicuous on every occasion that he soon came to be considered not only the discoverer but almost the father of the lode. As it was all Comstock for a considerable distance round the Ophir mine, people began to speak of the vein as Comstock's mine, Comstock's lode, and the lead throughout its length and breadth came to be known as the Comstock lode, a name which it bears to this day; while the names of O'Riley and McLaughlin, the real discoverers, are seldom heard, even in the city that stands on the spot where they first opened to the light of the sun the glittering treasures of the vein.

Even after the Ophir claim had been duly recorded and its owners had gone regularly to work upon it, they had no idea that the ore contained anything of value except the gold that was found in it.

For some weeks they dug down the rich decomposed silver ore, washed the gold out of it, and let it go as waste—throwing it anywhere to get it out of the way of the rockers. They not only did not try to save it, but they constantly and conscientiously cursed it.

Being very heavy, it settled to the bottom of their rockers, covered up the quicksilver they contained, and prevented the thorough amalgamation of the gold. The miners all thought well of the diggings, but for this stuff. It was the great drawback. In mining on Gold Cañon, they had been bothered with a superabundance of black sand and heavy pebbles of iron ore, but this new, -bluish sand was a thing which they had never before encountered anywhere in the country.

Notwithstanding their trouble with the sulphuret of silver, they were taking out gold at the rate of a thousand dollars or more per day; their dust selling at about $11 per ounce. In some spots they obtained from $50 to $150 in a single pan of dirt.

About this time some ladies from Genoa visited the mine, attracted by the reports which had reached their town of its great richness. Comstock was delighted, showed them everything and very gallantly offered each lady a pan of dirt, a piece of politeness customary in California in the early days when ladies visited a mine. "Old Pancake" was anxious that each of the ladies should get something worth carrying home, therefore by means of sly nods and winks gave one of the workmen to understand that he was to fill the pans from the richest spot.

One of the ladies was young and very pretty. Although the other ladies had each obtained from $150 to $200 in her pan, Comstock was determined that something still handsomer should be done for this one. Therefore, when her pan of dirt was being handed up out of the cut (*i.e.,* the open drift run into the lead), he stepped forward to receive it, and as he did so, slyly slipped into it a large handful of gold which he had taken out of his private purse. The result was a pan that went over $300, and "Old Pancake" was happy all the rest of the day.

Although Comstock had a passion for possessing rich mines, and appeared to have a great greediness for gold, yet no sooner was it in his possession than he was ready to give it to the first man, woman, or child that asked for it, or to recklessly squander it in all directions. Anything that he saw and took a fancy to he bought, no matter what the price might be, so long as he had the money. The article to which he had taken a momentary fancy, once purchased, he presented it to the first person that appeared to admire it, whether that person was white, red, or black.

As work progressed, and the opening made in the hillside penetrated further into the lead, the silver sulphuret, which had at first been found in a decomposed condition, began to grow more firm. In order to work it in the rockers it was necessary to pulverize much of it by beating it with the poll of a pick or sledge-hammer. Even then there were many lumps which it was necessary to pound in a mortar, and soon much of the ore began to assume the form of a tolerably firm rock, when it became necessary to work it in arastras—an old Mexican contrivance for grinding up gold and silver-bearing quartz.

The Arastra, 1876, illustration.

As soon as the grand strike had been made at the Ophir mine by O'Riley and McLaughlin, there was a great rush to that neighborhood; not only of miners from Johntown, Gold Hill, and Dayton (then known as Chinatown), but also from the agricultural sections of the country—from Washoe Valley, Tracker Meadow and from Carson and Eagle Valleys.

Claims were taken up and staked off for a great distance north and south of the Ophir mine in the direction the lead was shown to run by the huge croppings of quartz that came to the surface, and towered far above the surface, in various places.

It was not long before other companies had found pay, and soon there was in the place quite a lively little camp, the miners living in brush shanties, houses made of canvas, or camping in the open air in the sage-brush flats.

At this time the camp was spoken of, in documents placed upon the records, as "Pleasant Hill" and as "Mount Pleasant Point;" in August, 1859, it was designated as "Ophir" and "the settlement known as Ophir," and in September, as "Ophir Diggings." In October the place is first mentioned as "Virginia Town," but a month later it was proposed to "change the name of the place from Virginia Town to Wun-u-muc-a, in honor of the chief of the Py-utes." Old Winnemucca, chief of all the Paiutes was not so honored, and in November, 1859, the town was first called Virginia City, a name it has ever since retained.

Comstock says the way the place came to take the name of Virginia City was this:

"'Old Virginia' was out one night with a lot of the 'boys' on a drunk, when he fell down and broke his whisky bottle. On rising he said—'I baptize this ground Virginia.'"

For a time the old settlers had the new diggings all to themselves and were hard at work with their rockers, saving only the gold and paying no further attention to the silver than to curse it for interfering with their operations; but in a few weeks after the discovery had been made, there was suddenly stirred up in California a whirlwind of excitement that swept over the Sierras, and not only overwhelmed these first miners on the Comstock, but swept them almost out of sight.

About the 1st of July, 1859, Augustus Harrison, a ranchman living on the Truckee Meadows, visited the new diggings about which so much was then said in the several settlements. He took a piece of the ore and going to California shortly afterwards carried it to Grass Valley, Nevada county. He gave the specimen, as a curiosity, to Judge James Walsh, a resident of Grass Valley, who took it to the office of Melville Atwood, an assayer in the town. The ore was assayed and yielded at the rate of several thousand dollars per ton, in gold and silver.

All were astonished and not a little excited when it was ascertained that the black-looking rock which the miners over in Washoe—as the region about the Comstock lode was called—considered worthless, and were throwing away, was almost a solid mass of silver. The excitement by no means abated when they were informed by Mr. Harrison that there were tons and tons of the same stuff in sight in the opening that the Ophir Company had already made in the lead. It was agreed among the few who knew the result of the assay, that the matter should, for the time being, be kept a profound secret; meantime they would arrange to cross the Sierras and secure as much ground as possible on the line of the newly-discovered silver lode.

But each man had intimate friends in whom he had the utmost confidence in every respect, and these bosom friends soon knew that a silver-mine of wonderful richness had been discovered over in the Washoe country. These again had their friends, and, although the result of the assay made by Mr. Atwood was not ascertained until late at night, by 9 o'clock the next morning half the town of Grass Valley knew the wonderful news.

Judge Walsh and Joe Woodworth packed a mule with provisions, and mounting horses, were off for the eastern slope of the Sierras at a very early hour in the morning. This was soon known, and the news of the discovery and their departure ran like wildfire through Nevada county. In a few days hundreds of miners had left their diggings in California and were flocking over the mountains on horseback, on foot, with teams, and in any way that offered. Many men packed donkeys with tools and provisions, and, going on foot themselves, trudged over the Sierras at the best speed they were able to make.

CHAPTER VII

REMINISCENCES OF EARLY MINING DAYS
The Old Record Book—Strange Notices—Curious Houses—
A Modern Robinson Crusoe—Before the World—Mills and Arastras

When news began to be received in various parts of California from the first parties of these adventurers, upon their arrival in Washoe, their reports were confirmatory of all that had before been said and imagined of the new mines, and an almost unparalleled excitement followed. Miners, business men, and capitalists flocked to the wonderful land of silver that had been found in the wilderness of Washoe, beyond the snowy peaks of the Sierras.

The few hardy first prospectors soon counted their neighbors by thousands, and found eager and excited newcomers jostling them on every hand, planting stakes under their very noses and running lines round or through their brush-shanties, as regardless of their presence as though they were Paiutes. The handful of old settlers found themselves strangers, almost in a single day, in their own land and their own dwellings.

There were numerous sales of mining claims almost daily, at what then was thought high prices, and the hundreds who were unprovided with money with which to purchase mining ground swarmed the hills in search of ledges that were still undiscovered and unclaimed. The whole country was supposed to be full of silver lodes as rich as the Comstock, and the man who was so fortunate as to find a large unoccupied vein, containing rock of a color similar to that of the Ophir, considered his fortune made.

The Mining Recorder of the district now drove a thriving trade; he could hardly record the locations of mining claims as fast as they were made.

Some of these notices were literary curiosities, particularly those to be found in the old Gold Hill book of records.

V. A. Houseworth, the "village blacksmith," was the first Recorder at Gold Hill, and the book of records was kept at a saloon, where it lay upon a shelf behind the bar. The "boys" were in the habit of taking it from behind the bar whenever they desired to consult it, and if they thought a location made by them was not advantageously bounded they altered the course of their lines and fixed the whole thing up in good shape, in accordance with the latest developments.

When the book was not wanted for this use, those lounging about the saloon were in the habit of snatching it up and "batting" each other over the head with it.

The old book is now in the office of the County Recorder, at Virginia City, and is beginning to be regarded as quite as curiosity. It shows altered dates, places where leaves have been torn out, and much other rough usage.

The majority of the notices of location recorded by the early miners are very vague. The first notice recorded in the book is one of the location of a spring of water by Petcr O'Riley and Patrick McLaughlin. It reads:

"We the undersigned claim this spring and stream, for mining purposes."

Nothing is said about where the spring is located. For aught the person reading the record can discover, it may be in California or Oregon.

In the book are scores of locations made and recorded in the same loose manner. Many of the recorded notices read:

"We the undersigned claim 2,000 feet on this quartz lead, ledge, lode, or vein, beginning at this stake and running north."

Not a word is said about where the stake is to be found. No wonder that the lawyers drove a thriving trade in the early days of Washoe!

During the progress of a mining suit in the early days the lawyers quarrelled for nearly two days about a certain stump from which one of the parties to the suit desired to begin the measurement of their claim. They produced witnesses who said they could identify the stump, and the next morning the court adjourned, and jury and all concerned went out to take a look at the landmark in question. No stump could be found. The parties of the opposite side had dug it up the night before and packed it away. Not even the spot where it was supposed to have stood could be found, so completely had the ground been levelled in all directions.

I give the following verbatim copy of the original location notice of the Yellow-Jacket mine—a mine that has yielded many millions of dollars—as it stands on the old Gold Hill records:

NOTICE:
That we the undersigned claim Twelve hundred (1200) feet of this Quartz Vain including of its depths & Spurs commencing at Houseworth claim & running north including twenty-five feet of surface on each Side of the Vain. This Vain is known as the Yellow Jacket Vain. Taken up on May 1st. 1850,—recorded June 27th, '59.

H. B. Camp.
John Bishop.
J. F. Rogers.

The claim was called the Yellow Jacket because of the fact of the locators finding a nest of yellow-jackets in the surface rock while they were digging about for the purpose of prospecting the vein. Future developments proved this claim to be on the Comstock lode.

What the locators meant by "depths," in their notice, was dips—no matter in what direction the "vain" might dip, they desired to put on record their right to follow it.

Many notices read—"This vein with all of its dips, spurs, angles, and variations." The word "variations" was presumed to capture everything in the vicinity.

A practice prevailed among the early miners of locating quartz ledges as "twins." This was when they found two parallel veins so near together that they feared, in case of their locating but one, that parties would take up the other and give them trouble in some way. None of the twins ever became famous.

The owners of the Ophir, and some of the adjoining claims on the Comstock lead, continued to use rockers and arastras for some time after it was ascertained that what was at first supposed to be worthless, was silver ore of the richest description, but they no longer threw the "blue stuff" away. It was all saved and sacked up for shipment to San Francisco, thence to England for reduction. Many arastras were running, and the camp soon presented quite a bustling appearance. The first house erected in Virginia City, was built by Lyman Jones, who is still a resident of Nevada. It was a canvas structure, 18 x 40 feet in size, and stood near the present corner of B Street and Sutton Avenue, at no great distance from the Ophir Mine.

It was kept as a boarding-house and saloon. Mr. Jones opened his house with two barrels of "straight" whisky, but being of an accommo-dating disposition and wishing to suit all tastes, he dignified the contents of one of these barrels with the name of brandy. As alcohol was the foun-dation of nearly all the liquors seen in the country at that time, it made little difference by what name they were announced to the consumer, Mr. Jones had an old sluice-box for a bar, and the bar fixtures were by no means numerous or costly.

At this time the Ophir Company were in the habit of bringing their gold-dust to Mr. Jones's house, and leaving it for safe-keeping, and fre-quently he had in his place as high as twenty and thirty thousand dollars.

As the walls of his "hotel" were constructed of nothing more substantial than a single thickness of cotton cloth, safer places might have been con-ceived of, in which to deposit such an amount of gold. At length, when the grand rush from California came, and adventurers of all kinds swarmed along the lode, Mr. Jones refused to any longer act in the capacity of banker to the Ophir folks, as he did not care to run the risk of having his throat cut for gold not his own,—in fact did not want his throat cut at all.

At first it was almost impossible to procure lumber of any kind for build-ing purposes, and the houses erected were principally of canvas; though a few rough stone-houses were soon built and the miners constructed cabins of the rough rocks lying about on the sides of the hills. Many dug holes a few feet square in the sides of steep banks, and covering these with a roof of sage-bush and dirt announced themselves "at home" to their friends.

As winter came on, not a few who had been living in tents or the open air, betook themselves for shelter to the tunnels they had begun to run into the hills; widening out a place at some distance back from the mouth for bedroom and parlor.

Some of those who thus made habitations of tunnels did their cooking in the open air, under a brush-shed placed in front; others, displaying more industry and ingenuity, made a kitchen some distance back in their under-ground quarters, working a hole up to the surface of the earth, through which the' smoke of their fire found egress, presenting the curious appearance of a small semi-active volcano, when seen at a distance by one who knew nothing of the subterranean lodging-house whence the smoke proceeded.

A Scotchman tunnelled into a hill of dry and soft rock near Silver City and excavated a habitation in which he dwelt for years, and in which he finally died. He worked out several chambers of considerable size in the rock, one of which was his library and contained three or four hundred volumes of books, principally of a religious character.

His place was on a secluded ravine, a mile from the town, and he led the life of a hermit; indeed, his home not a little resembled the rock-dwelling of Robinson Crusoe. He had been educated for the ministry in his youth,

Silver City, from South End of Town, c. 1890, dry plate/collotype, James H. Crockwell. Library of Congress Prints and Photographs Division.

and now in his old age, became again a student and gave nearly his whole time to pious meditations. During pleasant weather, in summer, the ladies of Silver City frequently visited the recluse on the Sabbath, when, sitting on a bench at the mouth of his subterranean habitation, he would talk beautiful sermons to them.

In 1859, when the discovery of silver was made, the only wagon-road in all the country was the old Emigrant Road; coming in across the Plains, passing through Carson Valley and thence ascending and crossing the Sierra Nevada Mountains to California, by the way of Placerville.

Virginia City being situated on a sort of sloping plateau, on the eastern face of Mount Davidson, at the height of over 6,000 feet above the level of the sea, was a place difficult of access. Wagons could be used in the surrounding valleys, but Virginia City could receive no freight except such as could be carried up the mountain on the backs of pack-mules. Soon after the discovery of silver, however, companies located routes for wagon-roads to the place, and began the difficult work of building them, blasting out passage-ways in many places through solid rock along the sides of cañons shut in by almost perpendicular walls. Men swarmed on these roads during their construction, the explosion of heavy blasts was almost constant along the cañons, and

Water Carrier to Shaft, 1862, collodion/albumen, attributed to
Charles L. Weed (Lawrence & Houseworth). Library of Congress Prints and Photographs Division.

it was not many months before they were completed, when lumber, timber, and many other much-needed articles, that could not be packed on the backs of mules, poured into Virginia City whose streets were soon crowded with huge "prairie schooners"—as the great mountain wagons are called—drawn by long lines of mules or horses, all musical with bells.

The completion of a practicable wagon-road to Virginia City was at that time considered a great achievement, but now locomotives rush and shriek round the mountain steeps up which the patient mules tugged and groaned in former days.

While the wagon-roads were being built, the miners were not idle. Supplies for their use could readily be packed up the mountain, and the rich silver ore, securely sewed up in canvas bags, made convenient return loads for the trains of pack-mules. In a month or two the several companies working on the Comstock discontinued the use of rockers and arastras. The richest of their ore was sacked up and sold for shipment to Europe, and that of a lower grade was piled up in dumps and ore-bins to be worked in mills in the country at some future day.

The following extract from the *Territorial Enterprise,* then published as a weekly newspaper at Genoa (it is now published as a daily and weekly at Virginia City, and is the leading paper of the city and state), will give some idea of what was being done three months after the discovery. The item was published on Saturday, October 1, under the title of "The Mines:"

"The mines at Virginia Town and Gold Hill are exceeding the most sanguine expectations of their owners. At Virginia Town, particularly, the claims on the main leads promise to excel in richness the far-famed Allison lead in California in its palmiest days.

"Claims are changing hands at almost fabulous prices. No fictitious sales either, but *bona-fide* business operation. The main lead, on which is the celebrated Comstock and other claims, appears to be composed of ores producing both silver and gold, and the more it is prospected the richer it is proving.

"Donald Davidson & Co., of San Francisco, have purchased 200 tons of the rock, containing gold and silver in conjunction, at $2,000 per ton, and are shipping it to England by way of San Francisco, for assay. (Smelting is meant.) Other pretties are investing heavily. All that are now interested are but making preliminary arrangements for next spring, when we may expect to find an amount of either dust or ore sent from that section that will astonish some of the now incredulous ones in California."

They were not only welling and shipping large quantities of ore at this time, but were also beginning to work ores in mills and water-power arastras on the Carson River, near Dayton. In October, 1859, Logan & Holmes had a four-stamp mill in operation (by horse-power) at Dayton, which crushed four tons of ore per day, and Messrs. Hastings & Woodworth had two water-power arastras running, which reduced three tons each per day. The ore being worked by these mills was from Gold Hill, where the ore of the vein as yet contained only gold, they not yet having penetrated to a sufficient depth to reach the silver.

CHAPTER VIII

THE FATE OF THE DISCOVERERS
Thieves in the Camp—An Unpleasant Joke—
Sales of Mining Property —Smelting on a Small Scale—
What They Got from the Furnaces

Although occupying the western portion of Utah Territory, the laws under which the people of the Comstock range were at this time living were of their own making. At a meeting held by the miners of Gold Hill, June 11, 1859, the following preamble and "rules and regulations" were unanimously adopted:

> *Whereas,* The isolated position we occupy far from all legal tribunals, and cut off from those fountains of justice which every American citizen should enjoy—renders it necessary that we organize in body politic for our mutual protection against the lawless and for meting out justice between man and man, therefore we, citizens of Gold Hill, do hereby agree to adopt the following rules and laws for our government—
> RULES AND REGULATIONS.
> SEC. 1. Any person who shall wilfully and with malice aforethought take the life of any person, shall, upon being duly convicted thereof, suffer the penalty of death by hanging.
> SEC. 2. Any person who shall wilfully wound another, shall upon conviction thereof, suffer such penalty as the jury may determine.
> SEC. 3. Any person found guilty of robbery or theft, shall, upon conviction, be punished with stripes or banishment, as the jury may determine.
> SEC. 4. Any person found guilty of assault and battery, or exhibiting deadly weapons, shall, upon conviction, be fined or banished, as the jury may determine.
> SEC. 5. No banking games, under any consideration, shall be allowed in this district, under the penalty of final banishment from the district.

At the present day all manner of gambling games are allowed by the State laws and are licensed by the towns and cities. In the original documents, preserved in the old Gold Hill book of records, there are given several additional sections, but as they relate to matters not of general interest to the reader I have omitted them. One of these provides that "No Chinaman shall hold a claim in this district."

As may be seen, the laws of the first settlers were few and to the point; they were for use, not for ornament or the puzzling of the common understanding. In each settlement were in force some such "rules and regulations" as these. The man who broke one of the "rules" was sure to suffer a strict enforcement of the "regulations."

In August, 1859, two thieves who gave the names of George Ruspas and David Reise, stole a yoke of cattle at Chinatown (now Dayton), and driving them to Washoe Valley, offered them for sale at a price so low that they were at once suspected of having stolen the animals. They were arrested, and it having been proved that the cattle had been stolen from the ranch of a Mr. Campbell, near Dayton, the sentence of the jury was that they have their left ears cut off, and that they be banished the country.

The trial was held under a big pine-tree, near the western shore of Washoe Lake, at the base of the Sierra Nevada Mountains. Jim Sturtevant, an old resident of Washoe Valley, was appointed executioner. He drew out a big knife, ran his thumb along the blade, and not finding its edge just to his mind, gave it a few rakes across a rock. He then walked up to Reise and taking a firm hold on the upper part of the organ designated by the jury, shaved it off, close up, at a single slash.

As he approached Ruspas, the face of that gentleman was observed to wear a cunning smile. He seemed very much amused about something. The executioner, however, meant business, and tossing Reise's ear over to the jury, who sat at the root of the pine, he went after that of Ruspas, whose eyes were following every motion made and whose face wore the expression of that of a man about to say or do a good thing.

Sturtevant pulled aside the fellow's hair, which he wore hanging down about his shoulders, and lo! there was no left ear, it having been parted with on some previous and similar occasion.

Here was a fix for the executioner! His instructions were to cut off the fellow's left ear, but there was no left ear on which to operate.

The prisoner now looked him in the face and laughed aloud. The joke was so good that he could no longer restrain himself.

Sturtevant appealed to the jury for instructions. The jury were enjoying the scene not a little, and being, in a good humor, said that they would reconsider their sentence; that rather than anyone should be disappointed the executioner might take off the prisoner's right ear, if he had one.

The smile faded out of the countenance of Ruspas as he felt Sturtevant's fingers securing a firm hold on the top of his right ear. An instant after, Sturtevant gave a vigorous slash, and then tossed Ruspas, ear over to the jury, saying as he did so, that they now had a pair of ears that were "rights and lefts" and therefore properly mated.

This little ceremony over, the pair of thieves were directed to take the road leading over the Sierras to the beautiful "Golden State." They went, not as Adam and Eve left paradise, "dropping some natural tears," but as a pair of twin lambs are seen to depart when in the spring-time the farmer has whacked off their too luxuriant tails—went dropping blood.

There have been numerous stories told in regard to the amount of money received by Comstock for his interest in the Ophir mine and other mining property on the Comstock lode at Virginia City, some of which are far from the truth. The sale made by Comstock to Judge Walsh is recorded in the books of Virginia mining district and is dated at the "mining village or settlement known as Ophir," August 12, 1859. I make the following extract in regard to the amount to be paid—and what was eventually paid:

"For and in consideration of $10 to me in hand paid, and for the further consideration of ten thousand nine hundred and ninety dollars to be paid by James Walsh, according to the provisions and terms of an obligation executed by him to me this day, 'I have bargained and sold,'" etc.

The description of the property sold is as follows:

"One undivided one-sixth part of 1400 feet, said 1400 feet being now worked by myself, Penrod, Osborne, McLaughlin, Riley, and other owners, and known as Comstock & Co.'s claims, and owned jointly by myself, James Cary and others our associates; also, one undivided half of 200 feet of mining ground being worked by the California Company at the present time under an agreement made with me; also, all my right, title, and interest in and to certain mining claims at Six Mile Cañon diggings, being the claims known as the Caldwell claims; also, one-half the water-right known as the Caldwell Springs, situated on the hill above the said village of Ophir, and being the springs supplying the workings on the first-mentioned 1,400 feet—the present owners in said 1,400 feet being only entitled to the use of said water so long as they continue to be owners; also my recorded title, to a ranch on which the aforesaid village of Ophir is located, together with the springs on the lower part of said ranch. Also, the surface-diggings on the first-mentioned 1,400 feet and one-sixth of all improvements, animals, arastras, and all other property belonging to the company working the first-mentioned 1,400 feet."

If Comstock had a ranch recorded which covered the site of Virginia City, the page containing such record must have been one in the old book of records of Gold Hill district. At first all claims located in Virginia district were recorded at Gold Hill.

September 23, 1859, Pat McLaughlin, one of the discoverers of the silver, sold his interest, one-sixth, in the Ophir mine for $3,500. Peter O'Riley, the other original discoverer, held on to his interest in the mine longer than any of the original locators, and received for it about $40,000, with back dividends amounting to four or five thousand dollars. Osborne received $7,000 for his ground.

V. A. Houseworth, the recorder at Gold Hill, who had trade for one-fourth of one-sixth interest in the mine, sold that interest to Judge Walsh, in September, 1859, for $3,000. All of these men supposed at the time that they were obtaining a big price for their interests in the mine. They knew nothing about silver-mines and feared that the deposit discovered might suddenly "peter" out.

November 30, 1859, E. Penrod sold to Gabriel Maldarnardo, a Mexican miner, his interest in the 100 feet of ground segregated to himself and Comstock, at the time the Ophir mine was located. The deed given on this occasion is quite a curiosity. It shows that the legal genius who drew it up was determined to corral all that was in sight in the way of "tenements, hereditaments" and "appurtenances." It reads:

> "For and in consideration of $3,000, to him in hand paid, this day, E. Penrod has remised, released, and quit-claimed, and by these presents do remise, release and quitclaim unto said party of the second part and his heirs and assigns forever, all his right, title, and interest in and to the undivided one-half of one hundred feet of a certain Quartz Lead known as the reserved claim of Comstock, Penrod, & Co., on the original location of the said company at Virginia City, near the head of Six Mile Cañon, in Virginia Mining District, said Territory of Utah, said claim known as the Spanish claim, together with all and singular the tenements, hereditaments and appurtenances thereunto belonging, or in anywise appertaining, and the reversion and reversions, remainder and remainders, rents, dues, and profits thereof. And, also, all the estate, right, title, interest, property, possession, claim, and demand whatsoever, as well in law as in equity, of said party of the first part, of, in, or to the above-described premises, and every part and parcel thereof, with the appurtenances, to have and to hold, all and singular the above-mentioned and described premises, together with the appurtenances, unto the said party of the second part, to his heirs and assigns forever."

This tremendous document held the property, and Maldarnardo soon after coming into possession of it, erected two small smelting-furnaces and began working the ore of the mine after the Mexican fashion.

The furnaces would hold but about fifty pounds of ore each yet he managed to melt out a considerable amount of bullion— gold and silver mingled. The bullion, as it came from the furnace, was worth about $2.25 per ounce. The blast for the furnace was furnished by means of a common blacksmith's bellows. It was a slow process, and was soon abandoned, though quite a number of cakes of bullion of considerable value were shipped to San Francisco during the time the furnaces were in operation.

CHAPTER IX

COMSTOCK'S MATRIMONIAL VENTURE
"Old Pancake" Courting—Catching a Runaway Wife—
Women and Mischief—Always the Same—
Winnie and his Wife—Seeking a New Bonanza

A short time before he sold his mining interests in Virginia City, Comstock was smitten by the tender passion and made a venture in the matrimonial time. It appears that a Mormon from Salt Lake, a little sore-eyed fellow named Carter, landed at the diggings one day with his wife and all his worldly effects on board of a dilapidated wagon, drawn by a pair of sorry nags.

The man said he desired to go to work, and if he could find employment would take up his residence in the diggings.

Comstock looked upon the fair features of the wife, and his susceptible heart was touched—his soul went out toward her as she sat there in the end of the little canvas-covered wagon, mournfully gazing out from the depths of her calico sun-bonnet. Having charge of the Ophir mine, as superintendent, Comstock hired the man and set him to work, being determined to keep the woman in the camp.

The Mormon pair made their home in their wagon, and in the course of a week or two it was observed that Comstock spent most of his time in the neighborhood of the vehicle, was all the time hanging about it. Finally he was one day seen seated upon the wagon tongue, smiling upon all nature, with the Mormon wife engaged in combing his hair. The next morning both Comstock and the wife were missing. The hair-combing had meant business—showed the sealing of a compact of some kind. The pair had made a bee-line for Washoe Valley, where a preacher acquaintance of Comstock's—one of the old settlers of the country—married them after the manner of the "Gentiles."

The next day Comstock and bride went to Carson City, and while there receiving the congratulations of friends, the Mormon husband suddenly appeared upon the scene.

There was for a time a considerable amount of blowing on both sides, Comstock producing his certificate of marriage and asserting that it was the right he stood upon. Finally, to settle the difficulty, Comstock agreed to give the ex-husband a horse, a revolver, and $60 in money for the woman, and so have no more bother.

This was agreed to and Carter took the "consideration" and started off. After he had gone a distance of two or three hundred yards, Comstock shouted after him and told him to come back. When he had returned, Comstock demanded of him a bill of sale for his wife, saying that the right way to do business was "up and up;" he wanted no "after-claps"—didn't wish to be obliged to pay for the woman a dozen times over.

Carter then made out and signed a regular bill of sale, which Comstock put in his wallet and then waved the man away.

In a few days Comstock had business at San Francisco. He left his bride at Carson City and started over the mountains. When he had reached Sacramento, word was sent him that his wife had run away with a seductive youth of the town, and that the pair were on their way to California by the Placerville route.

Comstock was all activity as soon as this news reached him. He engaged the services of half a dozen Washoe friends whom he found at Sacramento, and all hands hastened to Placerville, where they waited for the runaways, who were on foot, to come in.

In due season they arrived and were pounced upon. Comstock and his wife had a long talk in private.

At length Comstock made his appearance and told his friends that it was all right, there would be no more trouble, as his wife was sorry for what she had done and would now live with him right along and be a good wife to him. All congratulated "Old Pancake" upon having brought his affairs to a conclusion so satisfactory

Wishing to bring forth his wife and have her tell his friends how good she was going to be in the future, Comstock presently went to the room in which he had left her. No wife was there! While Comstock had been talking with his friends and receiving their congratulations, his wife had climbed out of a back window and was off again with her young lover.

"To horse! to horse!" was then the cry, and soon Comstock's friends had mounted and were away. Not a moment was to be lost if the fugitives were to be captured, and the pursuit began at once. Comstock himself was not idle. He went forth into the town and offered $100 reward for the capture and return of the runaways. He also went to a livery-stable and hired all the teams about the establishment, sending forth upon the search all who could be induced to go.

Most of those who accepted teams went off pleasure-riding, and would not have disturbed the runaways had they found them. One man who went out on the search, however, was a California miner who happened to be in Placerville "dead broke." He wanted the reward, and when he started out he meant business.

The next day this man walked the runaways into Placerville in front of his six-shooter. Comstock was delighted, and at once paid the man the $100 reward. He then took his wife away to a secure place in the upper story of a building, and locked her up in a room in order to have another talk with her.

Meantime, his friends had charge of the young fellow who was making a business of stealing Comstock's wife. They shut him up in a room at the hotel where they were stopping, and placed a man over him as a guard, until they could consult together in regard to what was to be his fate— at least this was what the young fellow was given to understand.

Soon after dark the guard told the young man that it had been decided to take him out and hang him. The guard pretended to regret that they were going to be so rough with the young fellow and finally told him that if he could manage to escape it would be all right. "Now," said he, "I am going out to the bar to take a drink and if I find you here when I come back it will be your own fault."

The young fellow was not found nor was he ever seen in the town again.

By practicing eternal vigilance, Comstock managed to keep his wife that winter, but in the spring, when the snow had gone off and the little wild-flowers were beginning to peep up about the rocks and round the roots of the tall pines, she watched her chance and ran away with a long-legged miner who, with his blankets on his back, came strolling that way.

Mrs. Comstock finally ceased to roam; she came to anchor in a lager-beer cellar in Sacramento.

The fate of Carter, the Mormon who sold his wife to Comstock, was tragic. After making the sale he mounted the horse he had received in part payment for his spouse, and crossing the Sierra Nevada Mountains by way of Hope Valley and the Big Trees, went down into California. There he fell in with an emigrant train and courted and married a young girl, all within a week. The next spring he came to Virginia City with his wife. He had lived there but a short time before his wife learned of his having sold a recent wife to Comstock, when she left Carter's bed and board and sued for and obtained a divorce. She then married a Mr. Winnie, of Gold Hill.

At that time it was the fashion to take up mining ground in the names of women. Carter had caused some claims to be located in his wife's name, and after she was divorced from him and married to Winnie, kept running to see her about these claims, wishing to get some share of them back. The frequent visits of Carter were not relished by Winnie, and he and Carter had several wars of words. At length, one day when Carter came and was bothering Mrs. Winnie about the mining ground, she went out and called in her husband, who was at work near at hand. As Winnie entered the house the battle was opened by Carter drawing his revolver and shooting three fingers off Winnie's left hand. Winnie then turned loose with his six-shooter and killed Carter in his tracks. Some time after this, in a similar argument Winnie had a few fingers—less than half a dozen—shot off his right hand.

Winnie afterwards went to Honey Lake Valley, where his wife was thrown from a horse, dragged over the ground, and killed.

After Comstock's wife ran away with the strolling miner he thought best to let her continue her travels unmolested. He opened a store at Carson City with the money received for his mining interests in Virginia City and also had a branch-store at Silver City, a town on Gold Cañon, about three miles below Gold Hill, which was laid out in the summer of 1859.

He soon broke up in the mercantile line, losing everything. He trusted everybody—all went to his stores and purchased goods without money and without price, and at last his old friends the Paiute Indians came in and carried away the remnants. Comstock made them all happy, male and female, by passing out to them armfuls of red blankets and calico of brilliant hues.

His stock in the Carson store was as good as was seen in most trading establishments of the kind at that day, but his Silver City branch never amounted to much, the stock consisting principally, as the miners said, of blue cotton overalls, pick-handles, rusty bacon, "nigger" shoes, and "dogleg" tobacco.

After losing all of his property, Comstock left Nevada and went to Idaho and Montana, through which countries he wandered and prospected for some years, always hoping that some day he should come upon a second Comstock lode. He was always ready to join every expedition that was fitted out' to explore new regions, as the "big thing" seemed to him to be ever just ahead.

In 1870 he joined the Big Horn expedition in Montana, and this was his last undertaking. When near Bozeman City, on September 27th, 1870, he committed suicide by shooting himself in the head with his revolver. The Montana papers said it was supposed that he committed the act while laboring under temporary aberration of mind, and this was doubtless the case, as his was by no means a sound or well-balanced brain.

CHAPTER X

A LETTER FROM COMSTOCK
*"Old Pancake's" Story—Roughing It—The Fate of Old Virginia—
Ole Comstock Dead—A Man who Drank but Little*

The following letter from H. T. P. Comstock was originally published in the *St. Louis Republican,* some years ago, and gives a good idea of the man and his mental condition during the latter years of his life. He was always very eccentric, and even during the time he was in Washoe, in the early days, was considered by many persons to be "a little cracked" in the "upper story"—was a man flighty in his imaginings. The first part of the letter, with the date, is lacking and was no doubt left off as being merely introductory and unimportant, by the papers which republished it after it reached the Pacific Coast. The letter was written from Butte City, Montana,

Some of Comstock's statements are correct, but the greater part of what he says is a mere jumble and shows a wavering mind. His letter begins:

"These men, there in Washoe, are interested in misrepresenting the facts about the Comstock lode; they fear my claims to the water, the town site of Virginia and other interests they have swindled me out of. It is just what they are afraid of exactly; and that's what everybody in Washoe is afraid of. I shall yet have my say, I am writing a history of my life and all those fellows had better stand from under. Now I want to tell the whole truth about the Comstock lode: I'll try to do it and I want you to publish it. If you are gentlemen you will do it—it is nothing more than right. Here it is:

"I, Henry Thomas Paige Comstock, first went to that country—the Washoe—from Mexico, in 1853; roved all around California, and went back to Mexico that year; went back then to Washoe, in the spring of 1854, and staid there. My home was in Santa Fe, when in Mexico. I, old Joe Caldwell, Elmore & Co., partners of mine for twelve years, were the first men who ever worked in that section.

"Worked there in 1855—56 on surface-diggings, prospecting all the while for silver ore. The Grosch brothers worked at what is now known as Silver City. One of them, Hosea, stuck a pick in his foot and died in my cabin. The other, Allen, died near Sugar-Loaf, California. This was three years before the Comstock lode was discovered.

"The first discovery of the Comstock lode was made in this way: In the middle of January, 1859, I saw some queer-looking stuff in a gopher hole; I ran my hand in and took out a handful of dirt and saw silver and gold in it. At that time, big John Bishop and old Virginia were with me, when I found it; they were sitting upon the side of the hill. Gold Hill, a couple of hundred yards from me. I took up five claims. A couple of weeks from that time, and where the Ophir is now located, I found the same prospects, and told the boys at Gold Hill I was going to work as good a mine as the first discovery; did not know at the time there was a lead of that description there, Riley and McLaughlin were working for me at the time of the Ophir discovery, I caved the cut in and went after my party to take up the lead and form my company. Manny Penrod, Peter Riley, Patrick McLaughlin, 'Kentuck,' or Osborne, and myself formed a company. With my party I opened the lead, and called it Comstock lode; that is the way they came by their interests; I gave it to them.

"We started to rocking with my water; had only a small quantity to rock with. We made from five to ten and twelve pounds a day, and the dust was from $9 to $12 an ounce—went that at Brewster's bank, Placerville, California, where I did my business.

"I continued owning the claim, locating 1,400 feet out for myself, for the use of my water to the company. I also located the Savage claim; showed the ground to old man Savage. I located the Gould & Curry—went into the valley and got old Daddy Curry to come down, and put him in possession of it.

"I also owned the Hale & Norcross, and kept Norcross for a year to work in that ground. I also owned the principal part in Gold Hill and leased it out to Walsh and Woodruff—leased to them 950 or 760—don't now remember which. Now I will tell you how I sold it; it has never been told as it ought to be told throughout the United States for my benefit, and it shall be.

"Sandy Bowers, I gave him his claim of 20 feet in Gold Hill. Bill Knight, I gave him his claim; Joe Plato, I gave him his. Joe is dead now, and his widow is awful rich.

"I was working this claim, the Ophir, and taking out a good deal of ore; I did not know what the ore was worth, being in the wilderness then, with no road to get out or into from California. It was an awful wilderness! I took several tons of the ore and transported it by ox-teams, to best advantage through the mountains of California, and Judge Walsh was my agent and helped me.

"Now during this time I was taking out large gold and silver specimens, and took one specimen, weighing 12 pounds, and boxed it up and ordered it sent to Washington City. I instructed John Musser, a lawyer at Washoe, to send it; I don't know whether it ever reached there or not. I wanted Congress to see it, and the President, for it was the first gold and silver ore mixed ever found in the United States.

"I went on working, and Judge Walsh and Woodruff were there for two months, trying every day to buy me out. My health being bad I sold the claim to them on these terms: I was to get $10,000, and did get it at last; and I was to receive one-eleventh of all that ever came out of the claim during my natural life, and at my death was to will it to whoever I pleased; also, to receive $100 per month.

"That was the contract; and two men, Elder Bennett and Manny Penrod, witnessed it; but my health was bad, and before I had the contract of sale recorded, Woodruff and Walsh sold it out, Having taken no lien on the property, I never got a dollar, from that day to this, except what was at first received.

"I am a regular born mountaineer, and did not know the intrigues of civilized rascality, I am not ashamed to acknowledge that. Well, I had a store in Carson City and was lying in the back room sick and helpless. I told Ed. Belcher to take all my papers, and the contract between Judge Walsh and Woodruff and myself, and put them under my pillow. I could speak, but couldn't help myself a bit. They all said I would die, and said: 'Boys, let's pitch in and help ourselves!' And they did pitch in; and I never saw the papers afterwards. And the Gold Hill I leased to Walsh and Woodruff; and then Frink and Kincaid got it, and I never got anything for it; and the 160 acres of ground on which Virginia City is built is my old recorded ranch. I used to raise all my potatoes and vegetables on it, and had the Indians do the work for me.

"Virginia City was first called Silver City. I named it at the time I gave the Ophir claim its name. Old Virginia and the other boys got on a drunk one night there, and Old Virginia fell down and broke his bottle, and when he got up he said he baptized that ground Virginia—hence Virginia City—and that is the way it got its name. At that time there were a few tents, a few little huts, and a grog-shop; that was all there was. I was camped under a cedar-tree at that time—I and my party.

"I am now living at Butte City, in Montana Territory. The quartz in Montana is very rich quartz, and the Cable claim is next to the Comstock, but gold in place of silver. There is a greater variety of minerals in Montana than in any country I have ever explored. There are tin mines here. I discovered them myself; and there are alabaster mines here. Silver, vastly rich, and gold very rich. The Flint Creek mines—oh, God! how rich! This is bound to be a rich country, but we are a long way from market and have to go slow.

"And the Butte mines, too, they are vastly rich, but very much mixed with other metals—that is, a great many of them—and Highland has a good many rich leads now open and opening.

"This is a country second to none on the globe, in point of mineral wealth and in the precious metals. Now, you newspaper men have got me in your papers, I want to say a word about myself. I am a man that has been through the wars. I was in the Black Hawk war; was with Black Hawk when he died. I was in the Mexican war, and all through in the patriot war in Canada; had three brothers in it—I was the youngest; they are all dead now.

"I am the son of old Noah Comstock, living in Cleveland, Ohio. He has been largely engaged in the lumber and hotel business there. I have been in the wilderness since a child; was bound to the American Fur Company; my boss died and that's the way I got with old Black Hawk. My first recollection was packing traps; trapped all over Canada, Michigan, and Indiana; but the Rocky Mountains have been my home; I have been a guide these years and years. I was born in Canada, and am now near fifty years of age.

— HENRY T. P. COMSTOCK.

James Fennimore, better known as James Finney and familiarly called "Old Virginia," by all the old settlers of Washoe, he being a native of the State of Virginia, came to the mines on Gold Cañon, in 1851. He came from the Kern River country, California, where he had a "difficulty" with a man, and, believing he had killed him, took a little walk across the Sierra Nevada Mountains, dropping the name of Fennimore and calling himself James Finney.

Although fond of the bottle, Old Virginia was by no means a loafer. He had his sprees, but these were generally followed by seasons of great activity.

He was very fond of hunting, and when not engaged in mining or prospecting he was ranging the mountains and valleys in search of deer, antelope, and mountain sheep. He was interested in nearly all the enterprises of the early Johntown and Gold Hill mines but missed being in the Ophir at the time of the discovery of silver, having sold his interest in the Six Mile Cañon diggings the previous season.

He was killed in the town of Dayton, in July, 1861, by being thrown from a "bucking" mustang that he was trying to ride while a good deal under the influence of liquor. He was pitched head first upon the ground, suffered a fracture of the skull, and died in a few hours. At the time of his death he was possessed of about $3,000 in coin and had been talking of returning soon to his native State.

I one day met a Paiute Indian in Virginia City who recollected both Comstock and Old Virginia very well. Fifteen or twenty stalwart Indians, who had been engaged at driving wood and timber on the Carson River, had visited Virginia for the purpose of expending their earnings in the purchase of blankets and other staples. Among the number was an Indian who appeared to be forty-five or fifty years of age. Something that he said about the changed appearance of the place induced me to ask him how long he had known the town.

"Well," said he, speaking pretty fair English, "long time. When me first come here, no house here; all sagebrush. Me work here first time me come for Old Birginey (Old Virginia). Yes; me work for Old Birginey down in Six Mile Canyum."

"At mining?" I asked.

"Yes; minin'. Me heap pull um rocker. Me that time know Comstock— Ole Comstock. You Sabe him?"

"Yes;" said I, "have seen him. He is dead now. Got broke, up in Montana; bad luck all the time; got crazy and shot himself through the head with a pistol.

"Hum! Ole Comstock dead," said the old warrior musingly, "dead! Well, Ole Comstock owe me fifty-five dollar. That money gone now. Well, same way Ole Birginey. He owe me forty-five dollar when he die."

"How did he die?" I asked.

"Well, you see he die down to Dayton long time ago. Ole Birginey he all time drink too much whisky. One day he bully drunk, he get on pony; pony he run, he buck one bully buck and Ole Birginey go over pony head. One foot stay in stirrup and pony drag ole man on ground and kill him. Me help dig one grave, bury Ole Birginey, down Dayton, by Carson River. Well, well," said the old redskin, reflectively, "hoss kill um Ole Birginey, Comstock he kill heself. Comstock owe me fifty-five dollar; Ole Birginey owe me fortyfive dollar! Me think," shaking his head, "maybe both time too much whisky!" The sage old Paiute was mistaken as regarded Comstock; he was a man who drank but little.

CHAPTER XI

OLD VIRGINIA AND HIS STORIES

Prospecting for a Dinner—A Skunk Story—
O'Riley's Mistake—A Duel: Curious Consequences—
Flight of the Victor—O'Riley and His Gun

Old Virginia used to tell of a terrible fight that took place one evening in Gold Hill. The stakes, he said, were two short bits (twenty cents). The fight lasted half an hour and was most stubbornly contested on both sides. The contest was, as he would here explain, between his appetite and his "drinketite." He held stakes, and for a good while was unable to decide which had won. At last, however, drinketite got his opponent down and kept him down so long that he decided in his favor, and all three struck out for the nearest saloon—appetite grumbling at him all the way about his decision.

As has been already mentioned, Old Virginia was a great hunter. When not engaged in mining or prospecting, he was off in the hills with his gun; most generally alone wandering and philosophizing through the wilderness as he viewed the stupendous works of nature. He used to tell a story of a feast he once had in the desert regions of the Humboldt, which was quite amusing. It ran as follows:

Old Virginia's Fisher Story.

"In '53, six or eight of us were out on a huntin' trip and camped on the Humboldt River, down to'ards the sink of the same.

"We'd been havin' miserable luck. Couldn't strike any game and had 'bout devoured what grub we'd carried out with us when we left Johntown. This being the case, we nat'rally had to keep stirrin' about to try to skeer up somethin' that would do to eat. So, one afternoon, when the pot was 'bout empty, all hands struck out to try for something in the way of game; some goin' one way and some another.

"Old Captain Crooks and one or two more, went off down the river, while the rest of our fellers struck back from the stream and kind o' promiscuously diversified themselves out across the sand-hills and sage-brush flats in search of sage-hen and rabbits; you see we couldn't expect to find big game in that section—deer, and antelope, and them sort of fellers.

"I finally went off up the river alone. I jogged along up the stream, 'bout half a mile, and then laid down in a big bunch of weedy-lookin' bushes. As I was reposin' thar in the silence, gazin' up at the deep blue sky, I fell to ruminatin' on the unsartinty of all things here below—on what is above, and why we are here.

"I had jist arrived at the conclusion that man can no more help bein' born than a blade of grass can stay in the ground when spring comes; and, as the blade of grass can't help fadin' and dyin' when winter comes on, so man goes out of the world with about as little say in the matter as when he comes into it.

"All of this I was a-thinkin' about as I lay thar lookin' up' at the sky, half-way noticin' a solitary raven as was a sailin about high above. I'd fixed it up that thar was a great head mind up in them blue heavens somewhar, as was a-seein' to all matters for me and the grass, and that things was liable to work jist about as that mind willed, whether me and the grass made a fuss about it or not, when all at once I heerd a small racket, near me in some dry grass.

"Erectin' myself cautiously, and peepin' over the top of my clump of bushes, I seed a all-fired big skunk, rootin' under the dry, matted grass near the brink of the river. He war lookin' after mice, worms, bugs, grass-nuts, and sich like provender.

"I brought my gun to my shoulder and knocked the unsuspectin' critter over so dead that he never kicked. He was jist as good game as I wanted—I wouldn't have traded him for any number of blue-meated rabbits.

"Bein' shot in jist the right spot, thar wasn't a particle of smell about him. You see I'd knocked over many sich fellers back in Ole Virginney and knowed percisely whar to hold on him to do the work. Many's the fine fat one I'd cooked and devoured! But it's not every place whar they'll eat skunk— it's a thing that runs in streaks and through sartain settlements, as you may say.

"This was a prime feller! I think I never, in all my experience, killed a finer or fatter one. I shouldered my game and trudged back to the camp, which I found vacant. None of the boys had yet returned.

"I sat down and skinned my skunk, then tuck and hid the skin in some low' bushes, a few rods from camp, in order that none of the fellows might know the exact natur of the game I'd brought in.

"If they knowed it war a skunk, not one of 'em would eat a bite of it-some people's so prejudiced, you know 'bout outside appearances and the little nat'ral peculiarities of birds and beast.

"Well, to'ards night, Captain Crooks and all the fellers got into camp, and not one of them had killed a thing. They soon spied the fine plump animal I had hangin' up on a stake, near camp, and wanted to know what for critter it war. I told 'em I didn't know for sartin—the blame thing ruther headed my time, and I war convarsant with most of the four-footed quadrupeds perambulatin' the present hemisphere; yet I reckon the thing might do to eat on a pinch.

"All hands now wanted to see the skin. I pretended to look for it, then told 'em I'd seed the dogs a worryin' with somethin' a bit ago' and ruther guessed they'd drug the skin into the river.

"Captain Crooks seemed to be took with a idea. Says he: 'Was it a kinder brownish-black lookin' thing, with a kinder middlin'-like bushy tail?'

"'What would it be apt to be if it was that way?' says I.

"'A fisher,' says he.

"'Is a fisher good to eat?' says I.

"'Yes, fisher's bully eatin',' says he.

"'That's the way its tail looked,' says I

"'How about the color?' says he.

"'Air fishers as good as rabbit?' says I.

"'Much bulleyer!' says he.

"'Then,' says I, 'you've guessed the color.'

"The old Captain then turned to the boys and said he knowed it was a fisher the moment he sot eyes on it, and he hadn't seen one for goin' on eleven year, now.

"Then he went to braggin' so much about what good eatin' fisher was, that the boys all got awful anxious to be tryin' some of the critter.

"But the Captain said fisher warn't good till it had first been well parboiled; that we must put him in the camp-kettle and bile him that night, then stew him down in a pan for breakfast.

"When we went to bed we left the fisher gently simmerin' over the fire, and by mornin' he was not only biled, but too much so —was biled to rags.

"The Captain looked a litle puzzled at this phernominon, but the boys said it was all the better.

"We fried as much of the animal as we could stack into two pans and had a reg'lar feast of fisher; as the fellers all believed the thing to be.

"Old Captain Crooks was delighted. He had his plate filled about five times, and told the boys, as all were squatted in a circle round about on the ground, how he used to have big times up in Wisconsin a catchin' and a cookin' of fishers.

"I'd finished my breakfast and started to go and ketch up my horse, when I came to the skunk skin, layin' in the bushes whar I'd hid it away. An idea popped into my head. I looked at the great black-and-white, woolly hide, then at the ole Captain, who, with his knife and fork balanced acrost his fingers, was showin' the boys how to set a trap for a fisher. He still had in his lap 'bout half a plate of greasy, steamin' fisher stew, and the fellers was all still a shovelin' in fisher, watchin', between mouthfuls, the trap the Captain was fixen up for 'em.

"'I'll do it!' says I, to myself. Pickin' up the skin by 'bout six of the long white hairs in the end of the tail, I marched up to where all war squatted.

"'Hyar, fellers,' says I, 'blame me if hyar ain't that dam fisher skin now!'"

"Gentlemen, if I war to talk from now till next week I could'nt do full justice to what follered! Old Captain Crooks was just raisin' a forkful of stew to his mouth, when he ketched sight of that air skin. The fork dropped from his hand; his eyes bugged out like, the horns of a snail, and a sort of convulsive shudder shook his whole animal system as he yelled: 'Skunk, by all that's stinkin' and nasty!"

"'Skunk, by thunder!' howled all the rest in chorus.

"Sick! well, I need'nt mention what follered. But, fellers, that like ter cost me my life—that trick did. When them boys finally got convalescent and riz up and come for me, it was close papers for a time.

"Ole Captain Crooks picked one lock o' hair out o' my head before I had time to make the least explanation, It tuck awful hard swearin' to make them fellers believe I had'nt never seed a skunk afore."

Peter O'Riley, in the early days, when mining on Gold Cañon and along Six Mile Cañon, was an honest, hard-working, good-natured, harmless kind of man, yet when aroused displayed a most fierce and ungovernable temper. When he flew into a passion he was ready to do anything or use any kind of weapon that first came to hand. Even then, he showed, in this, signs of that insanity in which he ended his days. Many instances of his exhibitions of blind and furious rage are related by the early miners.

During these early days a sham duel was got up at Johntown between O'Riley and a young man named Smith, a miner working in Gold Cañon. As in most real duels, there was a woman in the case, a girl living up in Carson Valley. Both O'Riley and Smith found pleasure in the smile of the young girl in question, and the light of her eyes was as sunshine to their hearts. O'Riley was so much smitten that he would sometimes go and work all day on the farm of the father without money and without reward of any kind, other than the pleasure of being near the daughter during the time he was taking his meals. Such hard-working love as this must have been strong and honest. As O'Riley could neither read nor write the "boys" fixed up letters purporting to come from the girl, in which she expressed unbounded love for both men, but the trouble was that for the life of her she could not say which she most loved. At last there came a letter in which she said she had thought of a way of deciding the matter. O'Riley and Smith were to fight a duel, and her hand was to be the prize of the victor.

O'Riley was ready for this at once, for, as I have said, he was a man who was quite desperate when the deeper feelings of his nature were aroused, and Smith, though he pretended to dislike the proposition, finally agreed to stand up to the rack; there appearing to be no other way in which the difficulty could be settled.

It was left to the friends of the principals to make the necessary arrangements. These decided that as but one of the men could have the girl, the duel should be to the death. They therefore announced that the fight must be with double-barrelled shotguns, at twenty paces.

The appointed time arrived, and the rival lovers were placed in position, each armed with a shotgun. The guns were heavily charged with powder and paper-wads, but O'Riley, who was in downright earnest and thirsted for blood, supposed that all was on the square and that each barrel of both guns contained not less than nine revolver-balls.

At the word, both men fired; but O'Riley, who was determined to put his rival out of the way, turned loose with both barrels of his gun, firing his second barrel almost before the smoke had drifted away from the muzzle of the first.

Young Smith fell groaning to the ground, where his brother who was standing near with his left hand filled with the blood of a chicken, ran to him, crying: "Oh! my poor brother, my poor brother!" at the same time smearing his brother's breast with the blood he held in his hand.

O'Riley was brought to the spot by his seconds, and while they were asking the seconds of the opposite side if their man had received satisfaction, the brother of the man lying on the ground suddenly drew his six-shooter, and shouting: "You have killed my brother, now I'll have your life!" made at O'Riley, who ran like a deer for the house of a neighbor, where he knew a loaded shotgun was kept.

As he ran, the brother of the man supposed to be killed, occasionally fired his pistol, causing O'Riley to do some lively zigzaging, after the manner practiced by the Paiute Indians under similar circumstances.

The farce of the duel having been carefully studied in all of its details, long before going upon the ground, and knowing that at this stage of its progress O'Riley would go for this shotgun, the boys had rammed tremendous charges into both barrels of the ponderous old family weapon, putting a' number of paper wads down upon the powder.

Leaping into the house and getting possession of the gun, O'Riley rushed out and was about to make his way across Gold Cañon, when his pursuer, now dangerously near, blazed, away at him again with his revolver.

O'Riley, standing on the brink of the cañon, wheeled about and let drive at his relentless pursuer. He had cocked both barrels of the gun and both went off together, the breech striking him full on the nose and mouth, sending him rolling fifteen or twenty feet to the bottom of the cañon. He landed in active retreat, however, and went up through the cañon like an antelope.

O'Riley made directly for the village of Franktown, distant twelve miles, over the mountain, and remained there some two weeks, though the Johntowners several times sent word to him to come back and work his claim—that he had not killed Smith, that all was right and the duel was only a sham affair.

But not a word of all this would O'Riley believe. He had seen his rival stretched upon the ground in his gore, had heard his dying groans, and was not to be fooled back to Johntown to be shot by the incensed Smiths or hanged by the miners of the camp. Taking with them young Smith, the man supposed to have been killed in the duel, a party of Johntowners went over to Franktown to see O'Riley. No sooner did the latter see that Smith was really alive than he flew into a terrible rage and it was all that the friends on both sides could do to prevent shooting that was not sham and bloodshed in earnest. Peace was finally made by young Smith agreeing to renounce all pretensions to the hand of the young lady.

Peter O'Riley, one of the discoverers of the Comstock lode, as has been stated, held his interest in the Ophir mine, longer than any of the original locators, and realized nearly $50,000. He seemed to be "fixed" for the remainder of his days. Being a man used to roughing it all the days of his life, his wants, both real and imaginary, were few. Had he placed his money at interest he could have taken his ease all the rest of his days. But he built a big stone hotel in Virginia City, and then allowed persons to persuade him that he was a great man, a man of financial genius, who should make himself felt in the stock-market. As he could neither read nor write, he was obliged to find persons to do that part of the business for him. He and his assistants then speculated—speculated until one day "poor old Pete" found himself with pick, shovel, and pan, on his back, again going forth to prospect; as we have seen Comstock wandering in unrest through the wilds of Montana.

Being a spiritualist and having always the latest advices from the ghosts of the departed, in regard to mines and all else worth knowing about, O'Riley did not find it necessary to wander as far as to Montana. The spirits pointed out a place in the foothills of the Sierra Nevada Mountains, where they said was stored up far more gold and silver than in the whole Comstock

The place shown O'Riley by the spirits was nothing more than a bed of rotten granite. Here he toiled alone at running a tunnel—worked for two or three years—under all manner of difficulties.

The ground in which he was at work was full of water, and caves frequently occurred in his tunnel. The work of many weeks was often lost in a moment by a cave, which crushed in his timbers and drove him back almost to where he first began; but the spirits said there was a whole mountain of silver and gold ahead, and he believed them and persevered.

He was without money but not without friends. One and another of his friends among the old settlers, purchased for him what he required in the way of provisions and tools. As he worked alone in his dark tunnel, month after month, far under the mountain, the spirits began to grow more and more familiar. They swarmed about him, advising him and directing the work. As he wielded pick and sledge, their voices came to him out of the darkness which walled in the light of his solitary candle, cheering him on; voices from the chinks in the rocks whispered to him stories of great masses of native silver at no great distance ahead, of caverns floored with silver and roofed with great arches hung with stalactites of pure silver and glittering, native gold.

The spirits talked so much with him in his tunnel under the mountain, and had made themselves so familiar then, that at last they boldly conversed with him under the broad light of day, and in the city as well as in the solitude of the mountains. He was heard muttering to them as he walked the streets, and a wild and joyous light gleamed in his eyes as he listened to their promises of mountains of gold and caves of silver.

News at length came that O'Riley had been caved on and badly hurt; then that the physicians had pronounced him insane.

When he recovered from his hurt, he was anxious to return to his tunnel—the spirits under the mountain were calling to him—but he was sent to a private asylum for the insane, at Woodbridge, California, and in a year or two died there; the spirits to the last lingering about him and heaping on him reproaches for having left the golden mountains and silver caverns they had pointed out to him.

CHAPTER XII

MISLED BY THE "SPIRITS"

The Great Oil-tank—An Untapped Reservoir—
Going in and Coming out—Experiences of Those Who Stayed—
Approach of Spring—"Zephyrs" and Avalanches—
A Rather Long Night—Queer Incidents

Comstock was a believer in spirits. Mrs. L. S. Bowers—one of the early settlers at Johntown and at Gold Hill, and now known as the "Washoe Seeress," on account of her many predictions about fires in the mines and rich bodies of ore—is a Spiritualist, and very many of the early settlers and those who were one way and another connected with the discovery of silver in Nevada, were Spiritualists. Old Virginia was also a believer in "spirits." O'Riley was not the only person who did mining in Nevada under the direction of the spirits. Much money has been lost in that country with spirit superintendents in charge of the work.

The most ridiculous work of the kind ever done there however, under the direction of spirits was that by some parties who were led to believe that Mount Davidson—the mountain on the side of which Virginia stands and which towers nearly 2000 feet above the city—was an immense tank of oil.

This was about the time of the excitement in regard to the oil wells of Pennsylvania; while "Coal-oil Tommy" was "swinging round the circle."

The great coal oil revelation was made through an old lady of Virginia City who was a great medium, and the great oil deposit, according to this old lady and her spirits, was near the summit of Mount Davidson.

To Joe Grigg, an engineer at the old Savage mining-works, the medium made known the spot where the great subterranean lake of oil was to be found. Joe got some tools and began a tunnel in the flinty granite, or rather gneiss, which was stratified and stood as would the shingles on a house if turned upside down. For a long time Joe dug away in his tunnel, encouraged by new revelations almost daily.

The medium could see the oil and was carefully observing the progress of the tunnel. Joe was getting closer and closer to the vast reservoir every day. At last it seemed to Joe that he must be almost on the point of breaking through into it. Just ahead of him the medium could see the great lake of oil—an oleaginous ocean. Joe, at work away up there all alone on the steep slope of the mountain began cogitating on the situation and became frightened. It seemed altogether too big a thing—too great an abundance of oil. Then, too, he began to think of the consequences to the town, and the innocent and unsuspecting inhabitants thereof. There he was, blasting and banging away on the mountain-side, with a mere shell of granite—perhaps not ten inches thick—between himself and the great lake. He pondered upon the matter until at last he became afraid to continue, and decided the blast he was then putting in, should be his last. He feared even that might break through the shell of rock and set on fire the great lake of oil. In imagination he already saw this vast tank of oil pouring down the side of the mountain, overwhelming and destroying the city.

In this emergency the spirits were again consulted. They declared that a large iron pipe must be procured and laid from the tunnel down into the town, when the oil might be tapped and its flow controlled. The spirits also asserted that the time for forming a company had now arrived and advised that certain persons be let into the secret. Joe having hitherto been "going it alone."

The persons to whom the secret of the existence of the great subterranean reservoir of oil was made known were nearly all spiritualists. The "Mount Davidson Oil Company" was formed, and all concerned kept very quiet about the matter in hand.

All was now in readiness for tapping the oil so soon as the pipe could be procured and laid. In order that they might not lack the pipe, the medium—who was at the head of the company and was managing the whole business—proceeded to levy an assessment of $5 per share on the capital stock. That assessment exploded the whole arrangement. Every shareholder turned tail and "got out of the wilderness." To this day that lake of oil remains untapped, and—as it is not likely that the spirits would lie about the small matter of a few million hogshead of coal-oil—Mount Davidson stands to-day the greatest natural reservoir of oil in the known world.

Patrick McLaughlin, who, with Peter O'Riley, made the discovery of silver in the Ophir mine, was alive at last accounts (in 1875) and was at work at the Green mine, San Bernardino county, California. He was doing the cooking for some half-dozen men, employed at the mine named. He sold his interest in the Ophir mine for $3,500 and probably received considerable sums for shares owned by him in other mines on the Comstock range, all of which he doubtless lost in speculations of various kinds—speculations undertaken with a view to securing millions. Few of those who were original locators anywhere along the Comstock lode received large prices for their claims, and in a few years all were again as poor as before the silver was found. Those who bought and continued to buy at what seemed like enormous figures were they who have made the most money out of the mines.

The first winter after the discovery of silver: 1859—60, was one of the severest the country has known. As I have already stated, there were very few buildings in Virginia City that were worthy of the name. The majority of the inhabitants lived in mere shanties and in underground caves and dens—a tribe of troglodytes.

Many men who were in the country during the summer and fall, left for California before winter set in, some with the intention of returning and others cursing the country. These last were men who had for years been working in the placer-mines of California and who had rushed over the mountains to Washoe as soon as news reached them of the great wages being taken out with rockers. They supposed there were extensive placer-mines in the new region. When they found none but such as had already been gutted by the Johntowners and the Chinese who had worked about the mouth of Gold Cañon, they wanted nothing more to do with the country. They had no taste for working quartz veins or for deep mining of any kind. They lingered in the country till toward fall, hunting for rich pockets in veins of quartz that appeared to be gold-bearing, then rose up and in a flock crossed the Sierras to the more congenial hills, flats, and gulches of the "Golden State."

Many persons, however, remained at Virginia City, Gold Hill, Silver City, and Dayton, and a rough time they all had of it before spring. The first snow fell on the 22nd of November; it snowed all day, and four days later again set in, when snow fell to the depth of five or six feet, cutting off all communication between Gold Hill and Virginia, though the two towns were but a mile apart. The worst of the winter was between this time and the 1st of February. In December many cattle were dying of cold and hunger about Chinatown (Dayton), where they had been sent to find a living in the valley along the Carson River. Not only cattle, but also horses, donkeys, and animals of all kinds died of cold and hunger. Most of them starved to death. It was impossible to procure food for them.

In March, 1860, hay was selling at 50 cents per pound and barley at 40 cents. Men could not afford to keep horses, and therefore shot them or let them wander away into the valleys and flats and take their own time about dying. Food for man was about as dear as that for beast. Flour sold for $75 per 100 pounds in Virginia City; coffee at 50 cents per pound, and bacon at 40 cents. Lumber was worth $150 per thousand feet, and all else in proportion. None of the settlers starved, but the stomachs of many of them had frequent holidays. Fuel was scarce, it being necessary to pack it through the deep snow from the surrounding hills, where, at that time, was to be found a sparse growth of stunted pines and cedars. The stoves of the saloons and lodging-houses were well patronized. Bean-poker and old sledge were the principal amusements, aside from talking over the great expectations, which all cherished. Every man who had a claim expected to sell it for a fortune when spring came.

Little work could be done in the mines, but that little showed them to be growing richer and richer for every foot of progress made or depth attained. The excitement was at fever heat in California, and a grand rush of capitalists was expected as soon as the mountains could be crossed. This being the case, those who were wintering in Washoe though physically uncomfortable were comfortable in spirit. Gold lent its hue to all of their visions of the future.

Some Indians lingered in the neighborhood, and they were quite as hard up for provisions as the whites. They frequently came to the cabins of the miners to beg food. On such occasions—like some white beggars—they began business by presenting a paper to be read. The paper very often read as follows:

"This Indian is a damned old thief. He will steal anything he can lay his hands on. If he comes about your camp, break his head.

"—A Friend"

In the early part of February it began to grow warm. Many days were almost as warm as summer, but of nights it continued to freeze. Building soon began, and in March many houses were going up in Virginia City, in all directions, and the town was roughly laid out for many a mile along the Comstock lead. People began to flounder through the snow from California, during the latter part of February, and early in March began to cross the Sierras in swarms. Great hardships were endured by some of-the first parties that crossed the mountains, and a few persons lost their lives in storms that suddenly arose.

Although there was much fine weather in February, March, and April, snow-squalls were of frequent occurrence in May and even as late as June; this, however, was not particularly out of place in that country; it still does the same way out there. It is a region that has no climate of its own. What climate it has is blown over the Sierras from California and comes in fragments. But for the towering, snow-clad peaks of the Sierra Nevada Mountains, Nevada would have a climate similar to that of California, but these mountains chill all the "weather" that passes over them.

They may be having a fine, warm rain in California, but any portion of it that reaches Nevada is transformed during its passage over the Sierras and descends in the shape of snow. Owing to the altitude of Virginia City, whenever clouds shut" off the sun for any considerable length of time it becomes cold.

The early settlers at Virginia made the acquaintance of the "Washoe zephyr" during this first winter of their sojourn in the town. This "zephyr," as it is sarcastically termed, is a furious westerly gale which is a frequent visitant during the fall and spring months. It appears to come sweeping from the Pacific Ocean, passing over California, and only plunging down to the earth when it has crossed the Sierras. It made wild work that first winter with the frail tenements of the first settlers. Canvas-houses, tents, and brush-shanties were scattered right and left.

During the prevalence of a zephyr, early in the spring of 1860, some enterprising Washoeite performed the feat of stealing a hot stove. A canvas-house occupied by a lone woman was blown down, and while she was gone to find some men to set it up, her stove disappeared, and never more was seen.

Avalanches also put in an appearance, and in March, a man who was cutting wood on a hill just north of Virginia was buried by one, and his body was not recovered till the snow had melted away. Avalanches are still of occasional occurrence, and several lives have been lost and a number of buildings demolished in the southern part of Virginia City, by heavy slides of snow rushing down the side of Mount Davidson into the western suburbs of the town.

In the spring of 1860, an avalanche which fell near Silver City, covered the mouth of a tunnel in which half a dozen miners were living. It came down in the night when they were all asleep. At the usual hour in the morning some of the men awoke, but finding it still dark, turned over and went to sleep again. Others of the party did the same. After a time all were tired of sleeping and began talking about what a long night it seemed. However, they concluded it was all right, and each again addressed himself to the task of trying to sleep the night through. All would not do, and in an hour or two they were again discussing the apparent great length of the night, wondering, also, whether or not all hands might not be unusually wakeful.

At length, one of the party said he would go out to the mouth of the tunnel and see if he could perceive any sign of the approach of daylight. On reaching the mouth of the tunnel, he ran his nose into a solid bank of snow. The exclamation of surprise he uttered, brought all to their feet. They soon comprehended the situation. Luckily they had several shovels in the tunnel. Lighting a candle, they set to work, and in half an hour had dug their way out, when they found that it was almost sundown.

When warm weather came, and men and money were pouring in from California, those who had wintered in the several new towns of Washoe forgot all the troubles they had had and all the hardships they had passed through. They were on the alert to sell claims, and many did realize handsome little fortunes, as all the new comers were wild with excitement, and all were anxious to get hold of ground near the mines. Newcomers who had no money, prospected for new leads, or "jumped" the claims of parties who had made locations the previous fall. This made times lively, and numerous battles, with guns and pistols were the result.

One day while a battle was raging at a claim on the hillside, near the town, a big long-legged fellow, with a knife and pistol slung to his belt, started up to where the fight was raging, on a dead run. Those who were watching the affair said: "Now, we shall see the fur fly, when that fellow gets on the ground!" When about half way up the hill, a pistol ball came along and took off a portion of his goatee. He never for an instant ceased to run, but as the ball cut through his goatee he spun round on his heel and the running he did after that was all in the other direction. From his start till his return, his gait was unbroken.

An honest Dutchman who, at great pains and expense, had built him a cabin in the northern part of the place, came into town one evening to make some purchases. When he went home he found his cabin jumped. To add insult to injury the jumpers were fiddling and dancing, had a lot of whisky, and were having a regular house-warming. The Dutchman had to go and raise an army of his friends before he could drive the intruders out. It was three or four days before he regained possession of his cabin. Such occurrences were not rare, and persons were often placed in very annoying situations.

CHAPTER XIII

EARLY MINING

"Bring Out Your Injunction"—Testing Ores for Gold—
Testing Ores for Silver—A Fire Assay—
Valuable Donkeys—The Washoe "Canary"

During the spring of '60, two mining companies were at war about their locations, and one company threatened the other with an injunction. There had been considerable talk among members of the threatened company about this injunction being put on their claim. Two green Irishmen of the company, who heard this, and who were at work on the claim, concluded that they would keep a bright lookout for this injunction. They had no idea what it was like, but if anything of the kind was going to be put upon their claim they'd see about it. Every day they kept a bright eye open for the injunction, but saw nothing stuck up anywhere about their claim that looked like one.

About this time, however, it so happened that a party of surveyors were engaged in running out a road in that neighborhood. The surveyors arrived at the disputed claim just at noon, and, leaving their theodolite standing on the line they were running, went into town to get dinner. Pat and Mike were also away at dinner, but got back to their claim before the party of surveyors returned. It so chanced that the theodolite had been left standing on the bank

immediately above the cut in which the two sons of Erin had been at work. The first thing that caught the eye of Pat and Mike, was the large and costly instrument, standing on the bank, as though on guard over the cut in which they had been working.

"By the powers 'o war, Pat!" cries Mike, "what divilish thing is that, standing there on its three legs?"

"It looks like some quare kind of patent invintion," said Pat, "wid all of its brass muzzles and stop-cocks. What would it be, anyhow?"

"Well, now," said Mike, "I wondther if it isn't the thaving injunction thim rascally divils over beyant have been swearin' they'd put upon the claim?"

"By the sivin churches, ye've said it!" yelled Pat. "Let's afther it!"

Initial Point and Instrument, 1862, collodion/albumen, attributed to Charles L. Weed (Lawrence & Houseworth). Library of Congress Prints and Photographs Division. Theodolite used in survey of the Sutro Tunnel.

With this, one seized a pick, the other a crowbar, and rushing upon the theodolite they smashed it into a hundred pieces, crying—"This for all of yer infernal injunctions!" Pat flung one leg of the instrument as far as he could send it, yelling: "To the divil wid all injunctions!" Mike sent another whirling down the hill, shouting: "Bring on yer injunctions, we're the lads that can knock the stuffin' out of the best and the biggest of thim!" Just as the pair had succeeded in "bustin' up the injunction" the party of surveyors returned. The interview between them and the two Irishmen was short, but, as Pat afterwards acknowledged, it was "mighty improvin."

The newcomers who swarmed across the Sierras spread along the Comstock range for miles, pitching their tents and establishing their camps wherever wood and water were to be found. Having thus established their headquarters they scouted out on prospecting expeditions in all directions among the hills. In places on the ravines and in the flats, where good water and some grass were to be found, there were to be seen considerable villages of tents and brush shanties.

Of evenings, when the prospectors returned from the hills, there was a big time among them, as they exhibited specimens of ore from the ledges they had discovered and compared notes. All gathered about and opinions were passed in regard to the value of the ores brought in.

The next business was to test the ores for the precious metals. In gold-bearing quartz, small specks of gold were often to be seen with the naked eye or aided by a small magnifying glass, such as every prospector carried in his vest pocket for use in the examination of ores. If gold could be seen at all, either with the naked eye or the glass, it was considered a good sign. In order to further test the specimen, it was then either beaten to a powder in a mortar or was ground as fine as flour on a large flat stone, using a smaller stone for a muller. This pulverized ore was then placed in a "horn," a little canoe-shaped vessel made of the split horn of an ox, when it was carefully washed out, much as auriferous gravel is washed in a pan. The gold, in case the ore experimented upon contained that metal, was found lying in a yellow streak in the bottom of the horn; generally small particles of gold dust, almost as fine as flour.

This was the test for gold, and any miner was able to judge, from the "prospect" obtained in his horn, whether or not the quartz from which it came was rich enough to pay for working in a mill.

In testing ores for silver, the miners in the early days used acids. If a specimen of ore was supposed to contain silver, it was pulverized in the same way as gold-bearing quartz, then was placed in the horn and the lighter matter it contained washed out. When that which remained in the horn appeared to be principally sulphurets and other metalline matter, the washing ceased. The heavy residuum was then washed from the horn into a matrass (a flask of annealed glass, with a narrow neck and a broad bottom). Nitric acid was then poured into the matrass until the matter to be tested was covered, when the flask was suspended over the flame of a candle or lamp and boiled until the fumes escaping (which are for a time red) came off white the boiling operation was then presumed to be completed.

When the contents of the matrass had been allowed to cool and settle, the liquid portion was poured off into a vial of clear, thin glass, called a test-tube. A few drops of a strong solution of common salt was now poured into the test-tube. If the ore operated upon contained silver, the contents of the test-tube would at once assume a milky hue. This would begin at the top of the liquid in the tube, where the salt solution first touched the solution of silver in the acid and would be seen to gradually descend to the bottom of the vial. If there was much silver in the ore, the milky matter formed was quite thick, and clinging together descends to the bottom of the tube in the form of little ropes.

Muriatic acid poured into the tube produced the same effect as the solution of salt and water. The white matter formed was the chloride of silver.

In case the prospector had any doubt about what he had obtained being genuine chloride of silver, he held the test tube in the strong light of the sun for a few minutes, when the chloride would be seen to assume a rich purple color—a color which no photographer would ever mistake. Those who wish to try this experiment may do so anywhere. If no silver ore is to be had a few filings of a silver coin, or anything containing silver, may be used. The boiling in nitric acid may be performed in a small saucer of ordinary table ware and a common vial may be used in lieu of a test-tube.

The chloride of silver obtained in the bottom of the tube may easily be reduced to the metallic state. To do this it is dried and placed in a small hole scooped out in a piece of charcoal, when the flame of a candle is blown upon it until it is melted, and a bright little button of pure silver is obtained. Lead ore (galena) treated with nitric acid, as in testing silver ore, will produce a chloride somewhat resembling that of silver, but is more granular in appearance, does not turn purple in the light of the sun, and is dissolved in twenty times its bulk of water; whereas washing with water does not dissolve the chloride of silver, no matter how many times the washings are repeated.

If the presence of copper is suspected in the ore tested for silver, a bit of bright iron wire or the blade of a penknife may be dipped into the solution obtained from the specimen, either before or after adding the salt, when, if copper be present, the wire or knife will show a coating of it in the metallic state.

Chloride ores of silver cannot be tested by the acid method—they being chloride of silver in advance of the operation. These ores must be subjected to the test of a fire assay—must be smelted in a crucible. This being the case, our prospectors were not utterly cast down when their pet specimens failed to show silver when tested by the acid process. They at once declared that the silver was in the form of a chloride, and were not satisfied that they were not millionaires, until they had carried their specimens to some assay office and had a regular fire assay made. Then, when the certificate of the assayer came, they were generally obliged to take a back seat, receiving the imprecations of the camp. Occasionally, however, a "big assay" was obtained. Then there was a grand excitement. Every man in the camp wanted the lucky man to put him down in his notice of location for a claim of 200 feet—the amount of ground that could be taken up by one man under the revised laws of the district. In order to get an interest in a claim that promised to turn out a "big thing," there was much pulling and hauling, buzzing and log-rolling, among the miners who knew of the "strike."

The miners all did their own cooking, but this was no great task, as when you had mentioned slapjacks, beans, bacon, and coffee, you were at the bottom of the bill of fare. A few men, however, in every camp, developed a decided genius in the art culinary and concocted some wonderful dishes, the raw material at hand considered.

About three-fourths of the prospecting miners who came over from California, packed their traps on the backs of donkeys, and, driving these before them, boldly, if not swiftly, scaled the Sierras. These donkeys became a great nuisance about the several camps. All became thieves of the most accomplished type. They would steal flour, sugar, bacon, beans, and everything eatable about the camp. They would even devour gunny sacks in which bacon had been packed, old woollen shirts and almost everything else but the picks and shovels. The donkeys would be seen demurely grazing on the flats and on the hillsides when the miners left camp in the morning to go out prospecting, but all the time had one eye upon every movement that was made. Hardly were the miners out of sight ere the donkeys were in the camp, with heads in the tents devouring all within reach. When the miners returned the donkeys were all out picking about on the hillsides, as calmly as though nothing had happened; but the swearing heard in camp, as the work of the cunning beasts came to light, would have furnished any ordinary bull-driver a stock of oaths that he could not exhaust in six months.

One of these donkeys—too confiding—was caught in the act. Many of the miners used a kind of flour, called "self-rising." There was mixed with it when it was ground all of the ingredients used in the manufacture of yeast powders. All the miner had to do in making bread from this flour was to add the proper quantity of water and mix it, when it "came up" beautifully. The donkey in question had struck a sack of this flour and had eaten all he could hold of it. He then went down to a spring, near the camp, and drank a quantity of water. When we came home that evening Mr. Donkey was still at the spring. The self-rising principle in the flour had done its work. The beast was round as an apple and his legs stood out like those of a carpenter's bench. He was very dead. Here was one of the thieves. Cunning as he had been, he was caught at last, and with "wool in his teeth."

A queer genius thus described the donkey, called by everybody in that region, "The Washoe Canary":

"SOME ACCOUNT OF YE WASHOE CANARY.

"Let it be proclaimed at the outset that ye Washoe canary is not at all a bird; and, though hee hath voice in great volume, lyke unto that of a *prima donna,* yet is hee no sweet singer in Israel. Hee is none other than ye ungainly beaste known in other landes as ye jackass. You may many times observe ye Washoe canary strolling at hys leasure high up on the side of ye craggy hill and in ye declivous place, basking in ye picturesque and charging hys soul wyth ye majestic. Hee rolleth abroad hys poetic eye upon ye beauties of nature; yea, expandeth hys nostryls and drinketh in sublimity.

"Hee looketh about hym upon ye rocks and ye sage-bushes; he behold-eth ye lizard basking in ye sun, and observeth ye gambols of ye horned toad. Straightway hys poetic imagination becometh heated, he feeleth ye spirit upon him; hee becometh puffed up with ye ardent intensity of hys elevated sensations; he braceth outwardly hys feet and poureth forth in long-drawn, triumphant gushes hys thunderous notes of rapture, the meanwhile wielding hys tayle up and down in the most wanton manner. Hys musick does not approach unto ye ravishing strains whyche descended through ye charmed mountain of Alfouran, and overflowed with melody the cell of the hermit Sanballad. It hath, in some parts, a quaver more of Chinese harmoniousness.

"A wild, uneducated species of canary was thought worthy of mention in ye booke of Job, among the more note-worthy beasts and birds of ye earth; now, how much more worthy of description must be the cultivated and highly accomplished warbler whyche is ye subject of this briefe hys-tory? We shall presently see that hee will compare favorably with any fowl or beaste of whyche we have mention in ye goode booke. Of ye leviathan we read—'Who can come to him with a double bridle?' But, ah! who dare come to ye Washoe canary wythe a Spanish-bitted double bridle, two rope halters and a lasso? Again, of ye leviathan: 'Lay thine hand upon hym, remember the battle, do no more.' Verily, I say of ye Washoe canary—lay thine hand upon hym, remember hys heeles, do no more.

"Of ye behemoth it is said: 'He moveth hys tayle lyke a cedar,' but when ye Washoe canary giveth vent to hys sudden inspiration in an impromptu vocal effort he moveth hys tayle like unto two cedars and one pump-handle.

"Again, of ye behemoth—'He eateth grass as an ox.' Ye Washoe canary not only eateth grass, but in ye wild luxuriance of hys voluptuous fancy, and hys unbounded confidence in hys digestive capacity, rioteth in ye most reckless manner on sage-brush, prickly-pears, thorns and greasewood.

"Of ye horse: 'He smelleth ye battle afar off and saith, 'ha, ha!'' Now, not any horse can further smell out a thing presumed to be hidden—sugar, bacon, and ye lyke—than ye Washoe canary—then, indeed, hys 'yee-haw' far surpasseth the 'ha, ha!' of a horse-laugh. What are ye wings of ye pea-cock or ye feathers of ye ostriche to ye fierceness of hys foretop and ye widespread awfulness of hys ears?

"Of ye horse: 'He swalloweth ye ground in fierceness and rage.' Now, ye Washoe canary swalloweth woolen shirts, old breeches, gunny sacks and dilapidated hoop-skirts when in a state of pensive good nature—what, then, must we suppose hym capable of swallowing, once hys wrath is enkindled and all ye fearful ferocity of hys nature is aroused; Such is ye Washoe canary. Be in haste at no time to proclaim a victory over him."

CHAPTER XIV

MIGRATION ON A LARGE SCALE

*The Migratory Instinct—The Paiute War—Battle of Pyramid Lake—
Second Expedition—The Survivors of the Slaughter*

On the Pacific Coast there is felt every spring a kind of unrest—men of all classes feel as if they should go somewhere. This feeling is particularly strong among miners, and they look about to see if some region cannot be thought of into which they may make a prospecting raid. Others feel like going up into the mountains, or some wild and far-away region, on general principles—just to be rambling and seeing something new and picturesque. To desire to be on the move when spring opens appears to be natural to all mankind—to be a sort of animal instinct implanted in the human race, and an instinct probably never wholly eradicated by the influences of even the most refined civilization.

With the opening of spring, our Indians and all savage tribes of people are on the move. Even among wild animals the same migratory instinct is to be observed. Bear, deer, elk, and other animals that have wintered in the valleys, move up into the mountains, when the snow has disappeared under the warmth of the returning sun. The spring unrest is doubtless now much less strong within us, than at that remote period when we sported tails, yet we still retain in some degree this instinct of our former savage state; it is still in us, and at each return of the season for breaking up camp and moving out of winter quarters it takes possession of us. In the older settled communities, the people may not think of wandering to any great distance, but even there the farmer feels best when he is rambling in his farthest fields, and his wife prefers working in her garden and roving in the open air, to remaining in her house.

No doubt in the dim and distant ages of the past—when we still retained our caudal appendages—spring was a stirring season with the race. There was then a general awakening of the tribes. Knowing nothing, at that time, of the means by which we might provide artificial warmth, when the rigors of winter began to be felt we all left the mountains. Descending into the deepest and most sheltered valleys, we there hibernated, as best we might, in the mouths of caves and in sunny nooks among the hills, till the spring sun again warmed us into life. When it was judged time to be on the move toward the mountains, the sagacious elders probably took up their position on some prominent ledge of rock above the sheltering ravine in which the winter had been passed, and addressed the assembled tribe. What a glad chorus of yelps applauded the sage chatterings of the orators, and what a wildly exultant waving of tails was there when it was known all were to migrate "to fresh woods and pastures new!"

The discovery of the silver mines in Nevada gave all an excellent opportunity of gratifying their migratory instincts, and miners and men of all classes and all trades and professions flocked over the Sierras, in the spring of 1860.

At first they came on foot, driving donkeys or other pack-animals before them, or on horseback, riding where they could and leading their horses where the snow was soft, but soon sleighs and stages were started, and in some shape floundered through with their passengers. Saddle trains for passengers were started, however, before vehicles of any kind began to run, and the snow passed over was in many places from thirty to sixty feet in depth.

At first there was not sufficient shelter for the newcomers, and they crowded to overflowing every building of whatever kind, in all the towns along the Comstock range. But houses were rapidly being built in all directions, and the weather soon became warm enough to allow of camping out in comfort almost anywhere; men who had rolled up in their blankets and slept on the snow, high up on the frosty Sierras, did not much mind sleeping in the open air on the lower hills.

The newcomers from California not only prospected in the neighborhood of Virginia, Gold Hill, Silver City, and all the hills surrounding these towns and the Comstock, but scouted out in all directions to the distance of from fifty to one hundred miles. They generally went in parties of from five or six to a dozen or more men, and when they traveled any great distance, were mounted, and had pack animals with them, to carry their provisions and tools.

The excitement in regard to the mines discovered and being worked, those newly found and those yet to be found—in regard to town sites, mill sites and all manner of property in the new land—was at its greatest height, when that occurred which for a time paralyzed every industry, and alike brought business and prospecting to a stand. A Pony rider—the mail was then being carried across the Plains and over the Sierras to California by Pony Express—came in and reported that the Paiute Indians, till then friendly toward the whites, had burned Williams' Station, on the Carson River, thirty-one miles below Dayton, and had murdered two or three men whom they found in charge.

The news that the Paiutes were on the war path, and had begun killing and burning, spread like wild-fire through the several towns and settlements of the country. It was determined that the murderous redskins should be punished. There was a call for volunteers in all the towns, and the call was promptly responded to everywhere.

The news of the burning of Williams' Station, and the murders there, reached Virginia City May 8th, 1860, and May 9th a party of 105 men, volunteers from the several towns, under command of Major Ormsby, of Carson City, marched down the Carson River for the purpose of overtaking the Indians, and inflicting upon them a proper chastisement.

As I am not writing a history of Nevada I shall leave a detailed account of the "Indian war" to be given by some future writer. I shall but briefly sketch this first and last Indian trouble in Nevada, not attempting to give the names of more than a few of the men who were prominent participants in the battles at Pyramid Lake.

The men under Major Ormsby were poorly armed, badly mounted, and almost wholly unorganized. The majority of the men thought that there would not be much of a fight. They thought they should probably have a bit of a skirmish with the Indians, kill a few of them, capture a lot of ponies, and on the whole have rather a good time. Major Ormsby and a few of the leading men and old settlers doubtless knew the Indians better, but most of the recent arrivals from California who volunteered on the occasion thought it would turn out a sort of pleasure excursion. They were woefully disappointed. Finding no Indians at Williams' Station on his arrival there, Major Ormsby and command marched toward Pyramid Lake, known to be the headquarters of the Paiute tribe in that region of country, and distant less than two days' march.

The Pyramid and Domes—in Pyramid Lake, 1867, collodion/albumen, Timothy H. O'Sullivan. Library of Congress Prints and Photographs Division.

On the morning of the 12th of May, on the Truckee River, at a point about three miles from Pyramid Lake, they found a party of Indians occupying a strong position on a rocky hill. They attacked these Indians, who retreated after firing a few shots, falling back along the sides of a ravine.

As the Indians fell back they continued a scattering fire. The whites charged into the ravine in pursuit. They had proceeded some distance when a body of two or three hundred Indians suddenly confronted them, pouring into their ranks in quick succession several deadly volleys.

On the side of the whites many men and horses fell at this spot. The volunteers were staggered by this sudden onslaught, and made but a feeble reply to the fire of the enemy. At this critical juncture it was observed that the Indians were gathering in the ravine behind them, when a precipitate retreat was made for a piece of woods on the river. The Indians hotly pursued them, firing as they advanced. At the edge of the wood the whites dismounted and tried to make a stand, but the Indians gathered from all sides, pouring in a rapid and galling fire, killing several men and horses. The men were then ordered to mount for another charge. While this was being done the Indians rushed forward, firing and yelling, throwing the whites into a confusion which ended in a precipitate and disorderly retreat.

Many men had no horses, and these fell an easy prey to the elated and victorious savages who pursued the whites a distance of fifteen or twenty miles, even overtaking and killing men who were tolerably well mounted.

The trail of the retreating volunteers was strewn with dead bodies, saddles, guns, knives, pistols, and blankets, thrown away when the chase became desperate, and every man was trying to save his own life. Of the 105 men who went into the fight 76 were killed and a few wounded, slightly, who managed to escape.

Among the killed was Major Ormsby, the commander of the expedition, an old resident in the country; and Henry Meredith, a young lawyer from Nevada City, California, a man well-known and highly esteemed on the Pacific Coast. At the first volley fired by the Indians, in the cañon into which the command had been entrapped, Meredith was wounded and fell from his horse, but rose on one knee and fired three shots from his revolver as the foe advanced upon him.

When the survivors of this slaughter reached Virginia City and told the news of the defeat, the excitement was intense. In all the towns it began to be feared that the Indians, elated by their victory, would come in and sweep everything before them. It was said that there were 500 warriors in the fight at Pyramid Lake and it was supposed that the Paiutes could muster 5,000 men. Dispatches were sent to California for regular troops, and as the news spread men volunteered and companies were formed in Sacramento, Nevada City and Downieville, California. Men also volunteered again in the several Washoe towns, and soon an army of several hundred men, regulars and volunteers, was in the field for the effectual putting down of the savages.

CHAPTER XV

TROUBLE WITH THE INDIANS

An Unlucky Dutchman—Skirmishing—An Appeal to Indian Justice—
After the Scalps—Old Gus. and his "Injun"

Meantime there was a grand panic in the several towns along the Comstock range. Many men, women, and children at once left for California. The night after the survivors of the fight at Pyramid Lake came in, it was reported in Virginia City and Gold Hill that the Indians were advancing in full force and were but twenty miles away. This news caused a grand stampede, many men suddenly remembering that they had business on the other side of the Sierra Nevada Mountains.

At Virginia City, during this season of alarms, the women and children who remained were corralled for safety in a large stone hotel, that was being built by Peter O'Riley, and the walls of which were up to such a height that it made a pretty fair sort of a fort.

There were frequent night alarms and at times it was reported that the Indians were on their way up Six Mile Cañon to attack the town. There were but two classes of persons in the place, those who were not at all frightened, and those who were frightened almost out of their wits.

One night when there was an alarm at Virginia, a Dutchman got his partner to let him down into a shaft, about fifty feet in depth, thinking that about the safest place that could be found in case of an Indian raid.

After the Dutchman had been deposited at the bottom of the shaft his partner went down into the town. He had been there but a short time before a lot of horses and mules were stampeded somewhere down the cañon and came charging up toward the town with great clatter. All thought the Indians were surely coming this time, and not a few went out of the town by the back trails and struck out for California.

Among these was the Dutchman's partner. In his fright he thought only of himself. The poor Teuton roosted at the bottom of the shaft for three days and nights before he was discovered, and was almost dead when taken out.

The people of Silver City determined to stand their ground. They were on the war-path. Just above their town, on Gold Cañon, rugged rocks rise to the height of two hundred feet or more, leaving a very narrow pass. This place is called the Devil's Gate, and here the Silverites determined to make the Indians smell "villainous saltpeter." They went up on top of the Devil's Gate, and built a stone fort about two rods in diameter. The genius in command of this enterprise then bored out a pine log, hooped it with iron bands, and mounting it in the fort as a cannon, filled it full of pieces of scrap-iron, bits of chain, and the like. The muzzle was so pointed that when fired it would sweep the cañon for a great distance, making it very unpleasant for any Indians who might happen to be jogging up that way.

After the war was over, some parties one day concluded to fire this wooden gun off. They took it from the fort and carried it to a considerable distance back on the hill, rigged a slow match to it, and then got out of the way.

When the explosion finally came, the air was filled in all directions, for many rods, with pieces of scrap-iron, iron bands, and chunks of wood. Had it ever been fired in the fort it would have killed every man near it.

At Virginia City, when the news of the defeat at Pyramid Lake came, among other business transacted was the unanimous adoption of the following resolution:

"*Resolved,* That during the next sixty days, or until the settlement of the present Indian difficulties, no claim or mining ground within the Territory, shall be subject to re-location, or liable to be jumped for non-work."

This gave many persons who had urgent business in California an opportunity of going over and attending to it—doubtless many started soon after voting upon the resolution.

On the 24th of May, the second expedition against the Indians left Virginia City. It consisted of a force of 207 regular soldiers and 549 volunteers, all armed with minie-muskets and well equipped in every respect.

The regulars had with them two twelve-pounder mountain howitzers, and all felt in starting out that they were now prepared to give the Indians a good substantial battle, in case they should be found in fighting humor.

About noon, June 2nd, the Paiutes were found in force near the old battle-ground at Pyramid Lake, and fire was opened on them.

As soon as the firing began, the plain, the ravines, hillsides, sand-drifts, and mountain tops seemed alive with Indians.

The battle was short and decisive. The Indians were severely punished. They lost 160 killed and had a great many wounded, while the whites had but two men killed and only three or four wounded. Captain E. F. Storey, from whom Storey county, Nevada, takes its name, was shot through the lungs, and died in camp in the evening. Captain Storey was taking aim at an Indian who was lying behind a rock at the time he received his death wound. The Indian was too quick for him and got the first shot. Storey's men instantly riddled the fellow.

This expedition brought in the remains of Meredith and Major Ormsby. The bodies of many of the dead were found to have been horribly mutilated. About the place where the bodies of the volunteers were found, the ground, for the space of two hundred yards, was beaten as solid as a brick-yard. Appearances indicated that the Indians had taken these men alive, and had held a big dance about them before killing them.

After this battle no more was seen of the Indians in a long time, and there has been no trouble with them since.

In September of that year, Winnemucca, chief of the tribe, visited Fort Churchill, (a fort that was built on the Carson River, near Williams' Station, after the last battle at Pyramid Lake,) accompanied by several leading men of his tribe. The old fellow said that he not only desired at that time, but at all other times had desired, to live at peace with the whites. The late trouble had been brought about by a few Bannocks, a lot of Shoshones and Pitt River Indians, with some bad Paiutes. The whites had, he said, charged in among his people without seeking an interview with him and he had defended himself to the best of his ability. He hoped that the peace would be permanent, and desired that the whites and Paiutes should now become firm friends and allies.

After the trouble was all over the cause of it was ascertained. It was this: In the absence of Williams, proprietor of the station where the massacre, as it was called, occurred, two or three men left in charge had seized upon two young Paiute women and had treated them in the most outrageous manner, keeping them shut up in an outside cellar or cave for a day or two.

The husband of one of the women coming in search of his wife, heard her voice calling him from the place in which she was hidden. When he attempted to go to his wife's assistance the men at the station beat him and drove him away, threatening to kill him if he did not leave at once.

Pah-Utes of Pyramid Lake, 1868, collodion/albumen, Timothy H. O'Sullivan.
Library of Congress Prints and Photographs Division.

It so happened that the women who had been outraged were of the branch of the Paiute tribe living at Walker Lake who had married men of the Bannock tribe. The Indian who was driven away from the station hastened to Walker Lake and informed the chief man there of the outrage, asking him to send a band of braves to punish the men at the station. But the sub-chief at Walker Lake would send no men.

The wronged Indian then went to Old Winnemucca, who said he would send no men, that he wanted no trouble with the whites. His advice was that the whites be informed of the outrage, and requested to punish the men in their own way, in accordance with their laws.

Not satisfied with this, the Bannock went to young Winnemucca, the war chief. Here he was given the same advice that he had already received from the old chief. Thirsting for vengeance, the man then hastened to his own country and his own chief.

When the chief of the Bannocks had heard the man's story he at once gave him thirty of his best men, and told him to go and avenge the wrong that had been done him. He went and the result is known.

After killing the men and burning the station, the Bannocks marked their return trail with blood. They murdered in cold blood several small parties of unarmed prospectors. The bodies of these were not discovered until after the last fight at Pyramid Lake, when the murders were charged to the account of the Paiutes.

Old Winnemucca was not at the first fight at Pyramid Lake, he being on the Humboldt River at the time, but young Winnemucca, the war-chief, was there, and commanded.

Before the fight began he showed a white flag and wished to explain matters, but a man among the whites, who had a telescope rifle, fired and killed an Indian who showed himself on the rocks, and thus precipitated the battle which ended so disastrously for the whites.

When the volunteers returned victorious from the second battle, they were the heroes of the hour, until some of them began to walk into stores and help themselves to clothing.

They called this mode of obtaining clothing "pressing" it, and declared that it was a military necessity. Some of the merchants thought they were "pressing" it a little too strong when they began to help themselves to fine calf-skin boots and cassimere pantaloons, and in two or three instances fights ensued in which pistols were used, one of the merchants and two or three of the raiders receiving severe wounds. This "pressing" was done by a "hoodlum" class that came over the Sierras among the volunteers. These were the men who took Indian scalps after the battle. In one instance one of them found an Indian lying with his back broken by a minie musket-ball. Drawing his bowie-knife he proceeded to scalp the-poor devil alive. As he was sawing away at the tough scalp, the Indian spat in his face. This had the desired effect—the white butcher drew his revolver and blew out the Indian's brains. The officers allowed no scalping, yet two or three scalps found their way to Virginia City.

"Old Gus," an old Dutchman, marched about the town, from saloon to saloon, with an Indian bow stuck in the muzzle of his musket, at the end of which dangled a scalp. This gave "Old Gus" all the whisky he wanted. Wherever he came it was: "Hurrah for Old Gus, he got his Injun!"

The captain of one of the volunteer companies afterwards told me that in passing over the ground after the fight he chanced to come upon Old Gus, behind a rock, industriously engaged in skinning the head of a dead Indian, meanwhile calmly smoking his pipe.

CHAPTER XVI

STATE OF SOCIETY

Organization Begun—In Search of the Gold—Fighting Sam Brown—
The Knife and the Pistol—Pugnacious Periods

Owing to the breaking out of the war with the Paiutes, and to the fact that the precious metals existed in solid quartz, and, in most instances, far beneath the surface, where it could only be reached by means of deep shafts or long and expensive tunnels, many men who came to the country early in the spring of 1860, left in disgust.

Hundreds of prospectors came in the expectation of being able to find rich placer-mines, or at least large deposits of decomposed quartz, rich in gold, which they might wash out with rockers and sluices, as they were accustomed to wash the auriferous gravel of the California gold-fields. Being unable to find anything of this kind, except the ground already taken up and being worked at Virginia and Gold Hill, these men said that, though rich, the mines were of "no extent," and made haste to return to those they had left on the western slope of the Sierras, in the Golden State.

The Indian troubles greatly assisted many of these men in a speedy arrival at the conclusion that Washoe was no good country in which to abide. Few of those who first rushed to the country possessed sufficient capital to enable them to undertake the expensive works required for the proper opening and development of the claims they had located, and not being able to sell a "pig in a poke," they wanted nothing more to do with silver mining, while many of those who had the means lacked faith in the value of the leads discovered.

The business of working silver mines was then new to our people, and at first they depended much on what was told them by the Mexican silver miners who flocked to the country. Mexicans were in great demand. The man who had the word of a Mexican that his lead or his location was "bueno," felt that his fortune was made. It has since been suspected that many of these Mexicans were but "vaqueros" from the "cow counties" of California, who knew no more of silver and silver mining than a Digger Indian. They were shrewd enough, however, to keep their own counsel, and any man who spoke the Spanish language was supposed to have mined all his days in the richest silver mines of Mexico.

There were, however, undoubtedly in the country many old and skilful Mexican miners—skilful after the fashion of mining in Mexico—and with what our people were able to learn of these men, and what they soon themselves discovered, it was not long before very good work was being done, both in the mines and in the works erected for the reduction of the ores.

In the reduction of ores much that was of great practical value was learned from the scientific Germans who flocked to the mines, men who had had much experience in the silver mines of their own country, both in mining and in the working of ores. Although rapid progress was made in mining and milling, in building roads and making substantial improvements of all kinds, Washoe was a region almost destitute of laws of any kind, and all carried pistols and knives at their belts, each man a "law unto himself."

The people of Western Utah, now Nevada, were supposed to be living under Mormon law, but the laws of the Saints were distasteful to the Gentiles and they would have nothing to do with them. They preferred living under some such "rules and regulations," as we have seen were adopted at Gold Hill, in June, 1859, or to settle their difficulties in a fair fight. Such a dislike had the people to the Mormon laws that they early began to agitate the matter of a separation from Utah and the erection of a new Territory out of its western half. Delegates were sent to Congress to urge this, but nothing was accomplished, and at length the people took the matter into their own hands and determined to secede from Utah.

A convention was called, and met at Genoa, July 18th., 1859, when steps were taken for the formation of a "Provisional Government." A "Declaration" and "Constitution" were drafted, submitted to a vote of the people, and adopted. An election for Governor and members of the Legislature was held, and, December 15th, 1859, this Legislature met at Genoa, the capital, organized, received the "first annual message" of Governor Roop, passed a number of resolutions, appointed a few committees, and then adjourned. This was their first and last adjournment; they never met again. The silver mines were discovered and Governor Roop and all hands had other things to think of. The new population created by the grand rush to the mines so altered the whole face of affairs that it was considered inexpedient and impolitic to proceed further in the Provisional Government at that time. The discovery of silver and the rapid settlement of the country soon brought the people of Western Utah to the notice of Congress: the Territory of Nevada was created, and in July, 1861, Governor Nye and a number of the Federal appointees arrived in the country and set in motion the wheels of a government that was in accord with the feelings and traditions of the people. In 1860, however, the Mormon laws were the only laws left to the people; the Legislature of the provisional government having adjourned before making any new laws. Having an abundance of "rules and regulations," with that ready-reckoner the revolver, laws were not much missed for a time; besides, all were too eagerly engaged in the pursuit of wealth in the shape of mines of silver and gold to give much serious attention to matters political.

Soon after the last battle at Pyramid Lake, prospecting parties again began to scout out into the wild and then unknown and unexplored regions lying to the eastward and southward of the Comstock range. Stories of wonderful discoveries of all kinds in these regions kept the people in the several mining towns and settlements in a constant state of excitement. Reports of these new discoveries, greatly exaggerated in most instances, reaching California, a return tide of miners from that State soon set in. The marvellous richness of the Ophir and other Comstock mines continuing, and constantly increasing, capitalists came flocking back to Virginia and Gold Hill, and it was not long before all enterprises were in a condition as flourishing as before the Indian troubles began. With the miners and capitalists also came gamblers of both high and low degree, roughs, robbers, thieves, and adventurers of all kinds, colors, and nationalities. Not a few noted and well-known desperadoes arrived and walked the streets and presided in the saloons as "chiefs." It was the ambition of men of this class to be considered as being "chief" in whatever town they might conclude to infest. Early in the spring of 1860, Sam Brown, known all over the Pacific Coast as "Fighting Sam Brown," arrived at Virginia. He was a big chief, and when he walked into a saloon, a side at a time, with his big Spanish spurs clanking along the floor, and his six-shooter flapping under his coat-tails, the little "chiefs" hunted their holes and talked small on back seats.

In order to signalize his arrival and let it be known that he was no "King Log," Sam Brown committed a murder soon after reaching Virginia. He picked a quarrel one night in a saloon with a man who was so drunk that he did not know what he was saying, ripped him up with his bowie-knife, killing him instantly; then, wiping his knife on the leg of his pantaloons, walked across the saloon, lay down on a bench and went to sleep. After this, where was the chief who dared say that Sam Brown was not the *big* chief? Sam had then killed about fifteen men, doubtless much in the same way as he killed the last man. Not long was Sam chief in Washoe. He took a ride down into Carson Valley, and stopping at Van Sickle's Station, near Genoa, took a shot or two at the barkeeper, then mounted his horse and rode away. Van Sickles was soon informed of what had occurred, and mounting a fast horse, with a heavily-loaded double-barrelled shotgun in his hand, started in pursuit. He overtook the desperado before he reached Genoa. Sam no doubt felt that his hour had come, for an enraged ranchman on his track meant business, as he well knew—it was very different from having to do with a "chief." Sam turned in his saddle and began firing, as Van Sickles approached; but the ranchman was uninjured, and raising his shotgun riddled the great fighter with buckshot, tumbling him dead from his horse, just in the edge of the town of Genoa. Thus died "Fighting Sam Brown"— died with his "boots on," an end which all "chiefs" dread.

After the death of Sam Brown, numerous chiefs rose up and there were many bloody fights in regard to the succession. Also, there were many bloody fights in which the chieftainship was not the mooted question. Having knives and pistols ever at hand, men of all classes too frequently used them. The reports of pistols were heard almost nightly, and in passing along the streets frequent stampedes from the gambling houses were to be seen. As innocent parties were as likely to be killed as the persons engaged in the shooting, those who were not directly interested in a fight always withdrew when pistols were drawn in a saloon or gambling-house. At such times they came out into the street much as a flock of sheep would go through a gap in a fence with a dog at their heels.

The street gained they turned and stood peeping back. If the war did not presently begin they gradually ventured to return and resume their interrupted occupations and pleasures, not expecting an apology from the gentlemen who had inconvenienced them.

Thus were those not directly engaged in mining, or other productive industry worrying along.

CHAPTER XVII

EARLY COMSTOCK MINING OPERATIONS
In the Heart of the Bonanza—Inside the Mine—
Extraordinary Experiments—"Process Peddlers" and Their Devices—
The Value of Tailings—Neat Way of Making Rings—
Waste of Gold and Silver

In the mines rapid advances were soon made, both in the development of the various claims and in the machinery and appliances used. Whereas, the first shafts sunk were mere round holes, precisely similar in every respect to an ordinary well, now began to be seen well-timbered square shafts of two or more compartments; the old hand-windlasses gave place to horse-whims and to steam hoisting machinery, and large and substantially constructed tunnels took the place of the "coyote holes" which were at first run into the hills.

The first steam hoisting and pumping machinery seen on the Comstock lead was put in at the Ophir mine, in 1860. The machinery was driven by a fifteen-horse-power donkey-engine. The mine was at that time being worked through an incline (an inclined shaft) which followed the dip of the vein. A track was laid down in this incline and a car was lowered and hoisted through it by steam-power. The pump then used had a pipe but four inches in diameter, and it was hard work to keep the mine drained, even at the slight depth then attained. At this time the dip of the vein was to the west, and all supposed that that was the true dip of the Comstock lode: on this account locations lying to the west of the Comstock were considered to be much more valuable, and were much more sought for than those lying to the east. The westward dip of the great lode would carry it directly into and under Mount Davidson, on the eastern slope of which, and 1500 feet below its summit, the croppings of the vein made their appearance; all, therefore, were desirous of obtaining mining ground on the side of Mount Davidson and the mountains flanking it north and south. But when the depth of 300 feet had been attained in the Ophir mine, the lead began to straighten up and soon assumed its true dip to the east, at an angle of about forty-five degrees, a dip it has maintained ever since, and not only at that particular point, but throughout its entire length of nearly three miles.

When the true dip of the vein had been ascertained, it was then seen that its apparent dip to the west was owing to the pressure of the superincumbent rock and earth, on the steep side of the mountain, having pressed down the upper part and bent it over to the east. When those who had located claims on the side of Mount Davidson, and adjacent mountains, saw the Comstock lead thus turning tail and leaving them, they stood aghast. Those who had located to the eastward and had mourned because they could do no better, were now happy men—the Comstock was making toward them.

In December, 1860, the Ophir folks had attained a depth of but 180 feet in their mine. They were working down in the heart of the bonanza, or rich ore-body, and at that depth the breadth of ore was forty-five feet. No such great width of ore had ever before been seen, and the miners were at their wits' end to know how to work it and keep up the superincumbent ground—how to support such a great width of ground with timbers, was the question. The ordinary plan of using posts and caps would not do, as posts of sufficient length could not be obtained, and, even though they could be had, would be inadequate to the support of the great weight and pressure that would be brought to bear upon them. In this emergency the company sent to California for Mr. Philip Deidesheimer, a gentleman who had had much practical experience both in the mines of Germany and those of the Pacific coast.

After Mr. Deidesheimer arrived and was placed in charge of the mine as superintendent, he worked upon the problem before him for three weeks before he arrived at a satisfactory solution. He then hit upon the plan of timbering in "square sets" which is still in use in all the mines on the Comstock, and without which they could not be worked. The plan was to frame timbers and put them together in the shape of cribs, four by five or six feet in size, piling these cribs one upon another—but all neatly framed together—to any desired height. Thus was the ground supported and braced up in all directions. Where the vein was of great width, a certain number of these cribs could be filled in with waste rock, forming pillars of stone reaching up to the wall of rock to be supported—up to the roof of the mine.

Previous to the invention by Mr. Deidesheimer of the system of timbering by means of "square sets," the only supports used in the mines were round logs cut on the surrounding hills. These logs were from sixteen to thirty-five feet in length. When of the latter length they were manufactured, that is, were made of two logs spliced and held together by means of iron bolts and bands. Owing to the stunted character of the pines and cedars found in the neighborhood it was almost impossible to procure a log more than twenty feet in length. After setting up two of these long logs, a log about eighteen feet long was placed upon them as a cap. These posts and caps were placed as close together as they could be made to stand, but then would not hold up the ground when it began to slack and swell from exposure to the air.

Timbering of A Mine. 1876, Illustration showing square-set timbering.

Besides this difficulty there was no safe way of working either above or below these sets, in the vein. To take out ore, either under or over the timbers, loosened them and caused a disastrous cave. Many accidents happened and many men lost their lives while this method of timbering was practiced, but no lives have ever been lost in timbering by the square-set or Deidesheimer plan. In the mines at Gold Hill was where the timbers thirty-five feet in length were used, and there was where the greatest number of accidents happened; but in the Ophir mine, timbers sixteen feet long had been used.

When the miners of Gold Hill heard of the new mode of timbering practiced in the Ophir mine, they went up to Virginia to see it, and found it was just what was required. Mr. Deidesheimer sent some of his carpenters down to Gold Hill to show the workmen there how to frame the new timbers, and how to set them up. In 1861 this style of timbering was adopted along the whole line of the Comstock and has been in use ever since. The Ophir was probably the first mine in any part of the world where such a system of timbering became a necessity, as no orebody of such great width had ever before been found. Nothing seen in the Comstock mines more surprises and pleases the mining men of Europe than this mode of timbering. It is a thing none of them has ever before seen or thought of, and its utility is so strikingly obvious that they can hardly find words in which to adequately express their great admiration of it.

In 1861, Mr. Deidesheimer prevailed upon the Ophir Company to put up a forty-five horse-power engine, an eight-inch pump and improved hoisting machinery for the incline of the mine. The company thought this a fearfully extravagant move, and were almost frightened out of their wits when this "tremendous" machinery was first mentioned. Now there is hardly anything in the shape of a mine anywhere along the Comstock range on which there is not in operation more powerful and costly machinery.

Interior Ophir Hoisting Works, The Cages, c. 1876, collodion/albumen,
Carleton E. Watkins. California State Library.

Workmen in the Mine, 1862, lithograph, plate from a Gould & Curry Silver Mining Company stock prospectus. California State Library.

Engine Room, 1862, lithograph, plate from a Gould & Curry Silver Mining Company stock prospectus. California State Library.

At the depth of 180 feet, at what was called the third gallery, the width of the ore was, as I have said, 45 feet; at the fourth gallery it became 66 feet in width, and the miners were delighted to find that the new timbers supported the ground in the most perfect manner. At this time the ore extracted from this first bonanza was assorted as it was extracted. That which would average $1,000 per ton was sacked up and shipped to England for reduction, while the remainder was piled up as second and third-class ore, to await the erection of proper mills for working it at home. At the Mexican and other mines in the neighborhood, about the same disposition was at this time being made of the ores taken out, while at Gold Hill they had not yet attained a sufficient depth to reach the silver, and were working their ores for gold alone; though much silver was obtained with the gold.

The first mill started up for the reduction of silver ores was that known as the "Pioneer," located at the Devil's Gate, just where the warlike "Silverites" built their fort at the time of the Indian troubles. Other mills started up within a few days after this first one went into operation and soon there were many at work in all directions. The early millmen knew but little about working silver ores, and all manner of experiments were tried with a view to the thorough amalgamation of the silver contained in the rock that was crushed. This, in the opinion of most superintendents of mills, was to be accomplished by the use of chemicals. A more promiscuous collection of strange drugs and vegetable decoctions never before was used for any purpose. The amalgamating pans in the mills surpassed the caldron of Macbeth's witches in the variety and villainousness of their contents. Not content with blue-stone (sulphate of copper), salt, and one or two other simple articles of known efficacy, they poured into their pans all manner of acids; dumped in potash, borax, saltpetre, alum, and all else that could be found at the drug-stores, then went to the hills and started in on the vegetable kingdom. They peeled bark off the cedar-trees, boiled it down till they had obtained a strong tea, and then poured it into the pans where it would have an opportunity of attacking the silver stubbornly remaining in the rocky parts of the ore. The native sage-brush, which everywhere covered the hills, being the bitterest, most unsavory, and nauseating shrub to be found in any part of the world, it was not long before a genius in charge of a mill conceived the idea of making a tea of this and putting it into his pans. Soon, the wonders performed by the "sage-brush process," as it was called, were being heralded through the land. The superintendent of every mill had his secret process of working the silver ore. Often, when it was supposed that one of the superintendents had made a grand discovery, the workmen of the mill were bribed to make known the secret. To guard as much as possible against this, the superintendent generally had a private room in which he made his vile compounds. "Process-peddlers," with little vials of chemicals in their vest pockets, went from mill to mill to show what they could do and would do, provided they received from $5,000 to $20,000 for their secret. The object with many inventors of "processes" appeared to be to physic the silver out of the rock, or at least to

Sacking the Tailings, Gould & Curry Mill, 1862, collodion/albumen, attributed to Charles L. Weed (Lawrence & Houseworth). Library of Congress Prints and Photographs Division.

make it so sick that it would be obliged to loose its hold upon its matrix and come out and be caught by the quicksilver lying in wait for it in the bottom of the pans. Had it been in the dark ages that these experiments were in progress, the efficacy of the blood of human victims would doubtless have been tried; they would occasionally have hoisted an honest miner up from the subterranean depths and cut his throat over a pan. The "process-peddlers" finally became a worse nuisance than even lightning-rod men have been—the limited space of country to which they were confined being considered—and the millmen became disgusted with all the patent processes—their own as well as those of others—and soon little, save salt and blue-stone, was used in the pans. It was found that thorough grinding and careful working of the ore was what was required.

During the first few years that they were experimenting on the Comstock ores, in the many new and inefficient mills, millions of dollars in silver and gold were lost in the tailings; that is, in the pulverized ore that ran away from the mills after it had been operated upon in the pans, settlers, and other apparatus for the saving and amalgamation of silver by the wet-process. These tailings flowed from the mills into the cañons and were swept down into the Carson River, thence down to the "sink" or lake into which the river empties. These millions still lie in the bed of the Carson River and in the bottom of the sink. Had any man thought of saving these tailings in the early days of milling, by putting a flume into Gold Cañon and running them to some flat or valley where they could have been dumped in a great heap, all that is now lost would have been saved, and the originator of the enterprise would have made half a dozen big fortunes. The Mexicans knew the value of these tailings and worked them, but they always do things on such a small scale that what they obtained was a mere trifle, and nobody thought of collecting the whole of the tailings running to waste in the cañons and saving them in bulk; besides, the price of milling at that time was so high—about $50 per ton—that the general impression was that it would not pay to save the whole mass of tailings.

Two Mexicans were at work all one summer in Gold Cañon, at Silver City, at concentrating and working the tailings that were flowing down the stream, a mere rill of muddy water. They caught the tailings in a small reservoir, from which they took them and spread them on a table that stood at an inclination of about thirty degrees. They then threw water over the tailings with a small dipper, beginning at the top of the table and gradually working downward until they reached the bottom, at which point, where the end of the table rested on the ground, would be found some pounds of sulphuret of silver, with some particles of amalgam and quicksilver that had escaped from the mills. This they placed upon a platform of boards, called a "*patio*" and when several hundred pounds had been saved, sulphate of copper, salts, and quicksilver, in proper proportions, were added to the mass of sulphuret and tailings, and the whole was mixed up as builders mix mortar. When thoroughly mixed, the whole mass was drawn together into a round heap, and allowed to stand and sweat and digest in that shape for a certain number of hours. It was then spread out and worked over, giving it the benefit of the air for a time, when it was again heaped up to digest. This being several times repeated, the operation was complete, and the silver, amalgamated with quicksilver, was washed out in a pan or rocker. This is the famous Mexican "*patio*" process on a small scale. At the mines in Mexico they have large, circular *patios,* paved with stone or tamped with tough clay, in which

The Patio Process, Gould & Curry Mill, 1862, collodion/albumen, attributed to Charles L. Weed (Lawrence & Houseworth). Library of Congress Prints and Photographs Division.

horses are driven about to tread and knead the pulverized and moistened ore. It is, however, the same thing in effect as the process described above. The two Mexicans mentioned worked all summer, and the supposition was that they were about "making grub," but after they left, the butcher of whom they obtained their meat stated that they took away with them about $3,000 each; that they were in the habit of bringing their bullion to his shop every Saturday night to weigh it, therefore he knew what they had been doing all the time, but had promised to keep their secret, as they were afraid of being driven away before winter if it were known that they were making money.

After freshets in the cañon the miners used to go out and collect amalgam by digging it out of the crevices in the rocks with knives, or scooping it out with spoons. Having retorted this, they would take it to a blacksmith's forge, and make rings out of it by melting it and pouring it into a mould cut in an adobe or piece of brick. In this way they made rings that would weigh an ounce or more, and of nights, when going into town to have a good time with the "boys," would slip three or four of these rings upon the fingers of their right hands, for use in lieu of brass knuckles.

Notwithstanding all these evidences of the richness of tailings it was long before men began to work them in any regular or scientific manner. At length, however, shallow flumes were put up on the cañons in which the tailings were concentrated and the sulphurets caught on strips of coarse blanketing placed in the bottom of the sluices, and, finally, huge reservoirs were constructed in which the whole of the tailings were caught and saved in bulk, it being found that they could be worked at an expense not exceeding four or five dollars per ton. With the tailings there is always caught more or less amalgam and quicksilver. It appears to be impossible to save all the gold and silver contained in ore by any one process; indeed, after it has been worked over several times, and in several different ways, the tailings that finally escape still contain gold, silver, and quicksilver, but a much larger per cent is at present saved than formerly.

CHAPTER XVIII

Loss of the Precious Metals
Floating Treasure—Where the Quicksilver Goes—
An Unanswered Question—Floating Away

The divisibility of quicksilver, and also of silver and gold, as shown by the milling operations conducted in Nevada, is incomprehensibly great, and would seem to be almost unlimited; particularly in the case of the metal first named. A globule of quicksilver may be divided until no longer visible to the naked eye, and, indeed, until scarcely visible under a microscope, and yet even the most minute subdivision shall be found to contain both gold and silver. How infinitesimally small, then, must be the particles of silver and gold contained in one of these almost invisible and immeasurable globules of mercury!

In regard to the remarkable divisibility of the precious metals, the following instance maybe given in illustration: The superintendent of a water mill on the Carson River, when working for a considerable length of time an ore in which gold largely predominated, used every precaution to guard against loss. In addition to the usual settling-tanks, he caused to be dug in the ground a number of large pits, into which the waste water flowed after leaving the tanks.

After leaving these pits, the water passed off in a small flume, and to the eye appeared as clear as the water of the purest mountain stream. For the sake of experiment, the superintendent coated a copper bowl with quicksilver, and placed it in such a position that the water from the flume should fall into it. He also placed in the flume, below the bowl, some copper riffles, properly coated with quicksilver. Although the water passing through the flume appeared to be perfectly clear, yet at the end of three months the bowl and riffles were cleaned up and over $100 in amalgam was obtained.

Morgan Mill, Carson River, c.1876, collodion/albumen, Carleton E. Watkins. California State Library.

This mill is driven by water taken from the Carson River, and carried for a considerable distance through a large wooden flume. At one time it became necessary to shut off the water, for the purpose of repairing this flume. In making the repairs it was found that in many places that the heads of the nails driven into the bottom of the flume were thickly coated with amalgam. Within a distance of about three rods along the flume, the workmen engaged in making repairs collected over an ounce of amalgam. The water flowing through the flume was taken from the river, below a number of large mills, and, though far from being clear, would never have been suspected to contain floating quicksilver in such quantity as to form collections of amalgam on the heads of iron nails. In order that quicksilver may amalgamate with iron, the iron must be scratched or polished while immersed in the quicksilver; it will therefore be seen that much amalgam must have passed by before the accidental occurrence of the conditions under which the collection of amalgam on the heads of the nails could begin. As a beginning, a passing pebble must have pricked through a globule of quicksilver just at the moment when it was rolling over the head of a nail. By a succession of these accidental collisions the head was finally covered with quicksilver, and the collection of amalgam then went on rapidly.

As further evidence that quicksilver in considerable quantities floats in the water of flumes and streams, below reduction-works, in a state of invisible division, and yet carries with it the precious metals, I may give an additional instance. At a mill on the Carson River one of the workmen required a piece of copper. Remembering to have seen some old sheets of that metal lying near the waste-gate of the flume, through which water was brought to the wheel of the mill, he went to the spot and hauled them out of a puddle in which they were lying. Much to his surprise he found the sheets heavily coated with amalgam and so eaten up by quicksilver that they were as thin as writing paper. The water pouring out - through the waste-gate had a fall of about fifteen feet. It did not fall directly upon the copper plates, but in such a way as to keep them constantly splashed and wet. The plates had lain where they were found four or five years. Over a pound of amalgam was scraped off them. It would seem that in these striking instances of the unsuspected floating away of the precious metals there is for millmen food for reflection, and for inventors a field of profit and distinction.

Just what becomes of all the quicksilver used in the reduction-works of Nevada is a question which has never yet been fully and satisfactorily answered. Much floats away with the water flowing from the mills; but it cannot be that the whole of the immense quantities used is lost in that way. Quicksilver in great quantities is constantly being taken into the State, and not an ounce is ever returned. When it has been used in the amalgamation of a batch of ore, it is taken to the amalgamating-pans, and is used over and over again until it has disappeared. Whether it may float away with the water used in amalgamating, or is lost by evaporation while in the hot-bath of the steam-heated pans, there must be a vast amount of the metal collecting somewhere, as it is a metal not easily destroyed. In case it is lost by evaporation it must condense and fall to the ground somewhere near the works in which it is used, and if it floats away in the water it must eventually find a resting place on the bottom of the stream in which it is carried away.

It is an axiom among millmen that "wherever quicksilver is lost, silver is lost;" therefore there must be a large amount of silver lost, as we shall presently see. The amount of quicksilver used by mills working the Comstock ores alone averages 800 flasks, of 76 1/2 pounds each; or 61,200 pounds per month. This in one year would amount to 734,400 pounds of quicksilver that go somewhere, and counting backwards for ten years shows 7,344,000 pounds that *have gone* somewhere— either up the flue or down the flume.

The quantity of quicksilver distributed monthly among the mills shows just how much is lost per month. None is sold or sent out of the country in or with the bullion; therefore, if there were no loss, the mills would never want any more quicksilver than enough to give them their first start, as the same lot could be used over and over again, *ad infinitum.*

CHAPTER XIX

THE SOCIAL ASPECT OF THE TERRITORY

Footpads on the "Divide"—Attacking a Dutchman—
Mysterious Disappearances—Search for the Missing—
A Bonanza of Beef—Where Did They Go To?

In 1862-3, with mills running in all directions and mines open and hoisting ore for a distance of a mile or more along the Comstock, Virginia City was a lively place. Where but two or three years before was nothing but a rocky slope covered with sage-brush and scrub cedar, were now to be seen large fire-proof brick and stone buildings, and streets crowded with men and teams.

As all goods were at that time brought across the mountains by teams, and as hundreds of teams were required to haul ore from the mines to the mills, and to bring wood and timber from the hills and mountains, as well as to do all kinds of local freighting, there often occurred most vexatious blockades in the streets. A jam of teams would take place, owing to some accident or to mismanagement on the part of some teamster, and teams rolling in from each side, there would soon be seen a regular blockade. These blockades were of daily occurrence and sometimes lasted for hours. Teamsters waiting for the road to open grew hungry, and producing their lunch-pails sat on their wagons and ate dinner, still waiting patiently for the blockade to be broken. Half a dozen stage-lines were running into the place, and these arrived loaded down with passengers—capitalists, miners, "sports," thieves, robbers, and adventurers of all kinds. Cutting, shooting, and rows of every description became of much more frequent occurrence than at any time in the early days. The stages on all the roads leading to the city were very frequently robbed by masked men, who halted the driver with revolvers or double-barrelled shotguns and called upon him to hand out Wells Fargo & Co's treasure-box. One driver was halted so often and became so well acquainted with the routine of the business, that whenever he happened upon a man with a shot-gun, he went down into the boot of his vehicle for the treasure-box. The usual plan of the robbers, after securing the treasure-box, was to form the passengers in line by the roadside, and while one masked robber stood guard over them with a shotgun, another would search them and relieve them of their coin, watches, and other valuables. After this ceremony they would be ordered on board the stage and told to "go along."

California Co.'s Stages Leaving International Hotel, Virginia City, for California via Donner Lake, 1862, collodion/albumen, attributed to Charles L. Weed (Lawrence & Houseworth). Library of Congress Prints and Photographs Division.

The stages were robbed scores of times, bars of bullion, coin, and all manner of valuables being taken. It was finally ascertained that the gang who did most of this work—indeed, made it a regular business—were men living on Six Mile Cañon, only about five miles from Virginia City. They were ostensibly engaged in mining and had leased a mill, but the bars they produced were those captured in their raids upon the stages. The mill was only a blind. Without it they would not have dared to dispose of their stolen bars. The capture of stagecoaches being considered not quite up to the genius of the gang, they finally took a whole train of cars on the Central Pacific Railroad, and got a spoil of over $50,000. But this was their last exploit. All were soon captured and the greater part of the stolen treasure recovered.

On the ridge between Virginia City and Gold Hill, called the "Divide," and forming the suburbs of both towns, was for some years a place where footpads prowled nightly, and robberies there were of constant occurrence. A belated Gold Hiller would be hurrying to his home when a man would suddenly step out from behind a lumber-pile and tell him to hold up his hands. With a cocked pistol pointed at his head the Gold Hiller, or any other man, uniformly obeyed the order, when he was quickly relieved of his loose change and told to "move on." A footpad would sometimes rob three or four men in quick succession in this way, provided they happened along one at a time. They were quite industrious, and were not the men to borrow or beg while they were able to make a living by the labor of their hands.

On one occasion a Virginian was coming up over the Divide from Gold Hill late at night. He had three twenty-dollar gold pieces in his breeches' pocket, and, happening to be sauntering along with his hands in his pockets, had the coin in his hand. Suddenly a masked man stepped before him and thrusting a pistol into his face, cried: "Hold up your hands, sir!" The gentleman held both hands high above his head, when the footpad searched his pockets and found nothing. The gentleman had closed his hand upon the three "twenties" and held them above his head while submitting to the search. The footpad was evidently much disappointed, as he said: "If you ever come along here again without any money, I'll take you a lick under the butt of the ear. That's what I'll do with you!"

One night a stout young German was passing over the Divide, when he was suddenly confronted by two masked robbers, one of whom placed a six-shooter at his head. The level-headed German just reached out and twisted the pistol out of the robber's hand; whereupon he and his partner in the business of collecting tolls from belated travelers took to their heels, zigzagging and dodging industriously in the expectation that a bullet would be sent after them. Some one asked the young German what put it into his head to go for the pistol. "Py dunder," said he, "I did vant him; because in der spring, you see, I goes to der Bannock country!"

Although few dead bodies were found on the roads, it is supposed that many murders were committed about this time, the majority of the victims being strangers in the country; yet not a few well-known residents of the State have from time to time mysteriously disappeared. Almost every year the remains of human beings are found in old shafts. Inquests are held by the coroner of the county, but the remains are generally so much decomposed that they cannot be identified, and the witnesses summoned can only make mention of the several men known to them who have at various times suddenly and unaccountably disappeared. In one old shaft, when work was resumed on it after the lapse of some years, no less than three dead bodies of men were found. Pieces of rope were found tied about the arms and legs, as though for the purpose of making the bodies up into a bundle convenient for transportation to the shaft. This shaft was located below the town of Gold Hill, a short distance from a road on which there were few houses. Many persons have also, no doubt, accidentally walked into these old abandoned shafts, which everywhere cover the face of the country, in the night or in the winter, when their mouths were covered with drifts of snow. There are many instances of this where persons have narrowly escaped death.

In Virginia City and other Washoe towns many goats are kept by families for their milk. There are hundreds of goats to be seen everywhere on the hills and mountains. The goat is an animal that is fond of caves and caverns. De Foe was right in putting an old goat into a dark cavern, in his "Robinson Crusoe." The goats in Washoe constantly frequent the old tunnels high up on the side of Mount Davidson and other mountains. In many of these tunnels, at a distance of from two hundred to five hundred feet from the mouth, vertical shafts have been sunk, to the depth of from one hundred to two or three hundred feet. It often happens that the goats, in the darkness of the old tunnels, walk into these shafts. Some years ago a man living on Gold Cañon went out to look up a strayed goat. He found the fresh tracks of goats leading into an old tunnel, and ventured in. In walking back along the tunnel in the darkness he fell into a shaft in its bottom. The shaft was about eighty feet in depth, and he would probably have been instantly killed, but that there were at the bottom the bodies of four or five dead goats; as it was, he had an arm and a leg broken.

The man being missed, his neighbors turned out in search of him. They found his tracks leading into the tunnel and went in after him, in Indian file. Suddenly the head man disappeared, he having in the dim light of the place, stepped into the mouth of the old shaft. From the groans heard below his friends knew that he had not been killed, and at once procured a windlass and rope and descended to his rescue, when, to their surprise, they found that they had two men in the bottom of the shaft. The man who last fell in had a leg broken, and by his fall came so near jolting the life out of the man of whom they at first came in search, that when first taken out it was thought he was dead.

In Virginia City, some men who were one day at work in a lumber-yard, concluded it would be a good plan to pile a lot of boards over the mouth of an old shaft that was in a part of the yard, not far from the principal street leading to the town of Gold Hill. After they had commenced the work, one of the men said that as he put down a plank he thought that he heard a groan in the shaft. All listened. After a time another man said he had heard what seemed to be a faint moan at the bottom of the shaft. All again listened, and hearing nothing more were about to go on with their work, when there came up from the bottom of the shaft a deep groan that was heard by all. A windlass was procured, and on descending the shaft a man was found lying at its bottom in an unconscious condition. He was brought to the surface, when it was found that he had a leg broken in two places, and was badly cut and bruised in many parts of his body. He was a man weighing about 180 pounds, and had fallen a distance of over one hundred feet. He proved to be an engineer employed at one of the mills at Silver City, and finally fully recovered. He remembered nothing about falling into the shaft; he only remembered that on a certain day he was in Virginia City and started for home very drunk. From this it was shown that he had been in the shaft three days and nights when found. He stated, that while in the shaft he regained his consciousness for a time, and to some extent comprehended his situation, as, looking about, he saw the walls of the shaft and the light of day at its top. When he recovered he "swore off" drinking— never would drink another drop as long as he lived—and did not get drunk again for nearly a month.

One day a boy about six years of age was lost at Virginia City. His parents and their neighbors searched in vain for the missing child. The police turned out to their assistance, and many firemen and miners joined in the search. Bellringers had been through the city, and every place above ground had been searched. A dog had accompanied the boy when he left home, and this dog was also missing. Finally some one went up on the side of the mountain above town, and entered an old tunnel, in the floor of which was a vertical shaft over one hundred and fifty feet in depth. Calling at the mouth of this shaft, a faint cry was heard below. A windlass was hastily rigged, and a miner descended the shaft, and at its bottom found the missing child with not a bone broken. He had fallen upon the dead bodies of two or three goats that lay at the bottom of the shaft. The dog was also found alive at the bottom of the shaft. The man who descended was almost suffocated when he came to the surface. The air was bad in the bottom of the shaft and the stench from the dead goats almost unendurable. The child was nearly dead when taken out, and was covered with a mass of flies that had insinuated themselves into his mouth, nose, ears, and eyes; but in about ten days the little fellow had fully recovered and was ready for fresh adventures.

Many other instances—scores of them—might be given to show the dangerous character of these traps, which everywhere cover the face of the country, for miles about the principal mining towns, but I shall conclude with the following:

A teamster, stopping at noon two or three miles from the city, unhitched eight yoke of oxen from his wagon, in order to let them graze about among the sage-brush while he was eating his dinner. Although unhitched, they were fastened together in a string by a heavy log-chain which passed through their several yokes. The teamster, seated on his wagon, eating, was astounded at seeing his whole team of cattle, then distant about one hundred yards, suddenly disappear into the ground. In picking along they reached an old shaft, round which those in the lead, had passed, then moving forward had so straightened the line as to pull a middle yoke into the mouth of the shaft. All then followed, going down like links of sausage. The shaft was three hundred feet in depth, and that bonanza of beef still remains unworked at its bottom.

The Comstock range is a region in which a stranger should never venture to wander at night, either on foot or on horseback. Even in daylight, in the midst of a driving snow-storm, a man once rode his horse into a shaft over fifty feet in depth. The city authorities have caused most of the old shafts to be filled up or securely planked over, but scores of open shafts are still to be seen everywhere in the suburbs of the town.

CHAPTER XX

THE MOUNTAIN REGION OF NEVADA
Providing for His Friends—The Sierra Nevada Mountains—
The Ascent of Mount Davidson—An Eclipse—
Going Back to the City—A Majestic Scene

Mount Davidson, of which frequent mention has been made, was originally called "Sun Peak." This was the name given it by the early miners of Gold Cañon—Old Virginia, Comstock, O'Riley, and the other pioneers of the country. It was a very appropriate name, as the towering granite peak reaching far above all others about it is the first to be lighted by the morning sun and the last on which rest his evening rays.

The mountain was given its present name in honor of the late Donald Davidson, of San Francisco, who in the early days purchased the ores of the Ophir and other companies on the Comstock, sending them to England for reduction. On one of his trips to Virginia, Donald Davidson accompanied a party of men to the summit of the mountain. On their return to the town it was unanimously agreed that the tall peak which they had that day scaled should be called Mount Davidson.

Half a score of the hardy miners whose camps were pitched along the lead had accompanied Mr. Davidson up the mountain, and while on their way a number of quartz veins of more or less promising appearance were found. In the evening, while in a saloon, talking over the events of the day, it was thought that it would not be a bad idea to locate some of the ledges they had seen. The charge was then fifty cents per name for record-ing a claim of two hundred feet on a ledge. A man called "Joe Bowers," but probably not the original "Joe" immortalized by the poet, took the lead in making out the notices and arranging for the recording. Joe swore that all the ledges they had seen were immensely rich—millions in them!—and would make the fortune of any man who had an interest in any one of them. As the names were mentioned and written down on the notices, Joe called for "four-bits." This must be put up, in order that it might be handed over to the recorder of the district the first thing in the morning.

Donald Davidson would say: "Well, here is Mr. A., a neighbor of mine in San Francisco, and a very worthy man; suppose we put him down for a claim in this mine?"

"All right, Mr. Davidson," Joe would cry, "all right, sir; put up for him and in he goes!"

"Then there is Mr. B., a friend of mine and a worthy fellow; we might put him down."

"All right, Mr. Davidson," cried Joe, who cared not how long the string of names might be, provided each name were represented in his pocket by a half-dollar, "down he goes!"

All the notices were finally made out, and all the half-dollars paid in. Joe was to attend to the recording the first thing in the morning, but that night he struck a "little game of draw," and to this day those claims have not been recorded—at least not by Joseph.

As the leads upon the side of Mount Davidson have turned out, it was no doubt a fortunate thing for the old Scotchman's "worthy friends" that Joe found his "little game." The height of Mount Davidson above the level of the sea is 7,775 feet, and the altitude of C street, the principal business street in Virginia City, is 6,205 feet. Thus, it will be seen, the peak of the mountain towers to the height of 1,570 feet above the town. As the city stands on the eastern face of the mountain, the sunsets in Virginia are rather early. In winter the sun sinks behind the top of Mount Davidson about 3 o'clock in the afternoon, when the city lies in shadow and it at once begins to grow cold. The altitude of the place is so great that, at any season, when clouds obscure the sun and shut out his rays it rapidly becomes cold. During the summer, however, clouds are seldom seen—weeks and weeks pass without a cloudy day. In order to have the benefit of the sun in winter, until a late hour each day, a Washoe genius once proposed to run a large tunnel through the peak of Mount Davidson. Through this tunnel he pro-posed to bring the light and heat of the sun after it had gone down behind the mountain. As he could not expect the sun to shine directly through the tunnel at all points in his course down to the western horizon, our inventor proposed to set at the western terminus of his tunnel a huge mirror, moved by clock-work, which should pour the rays of the sun in a constant stream through the tunnel. At the eastern terminus was to be placed a large receiving mirror, which should catch the rays coming through the tunnel and throw them to a distributing mirror down in the town, and from this the sunlight would be reflected throughout the town by smaller mirrors placed at proper points on all the streets. Although this grand scheme was much admired, capital—which is proverbially timid—could never be found to begin the work.

There is a grand view from the summit of Mount Davidson. On a clear day the eye reaches hundreds of miles in many directions. The Sierra Nevada Mountains, twenty-five miles away to the west, and extending north and south as far as the eye can reach, form a magnificent panorama of wild mountain scenery, embracing hundreds of tall snowy peaks and dark, pine-clad ridges reaching upwards toward naked granite towers. To the southward along the great range, the peaks are taller and more imposing than those rising along the northern part of its course. To the southward, then, we turn and see at the distance of from forty to seventy-five or eighty miles, scores of massive peaks standing stately and clearly defined against the sky. Seen when robed from head to foot in glittering snow, these peaks present a particularly striking appearance. They may easily be imagined an army of giants marching up from the desert wilds of Arizona in meandering array.

Far away the tail of this procession of the peaks is seen to sweep miles on miles to the eastward, while above the white hoods of the giants forming this lagging curve, is dimly discerned through the haze a hint of heads in the still more distant rear, swinging back to the west and falling, as it were, into the general line of march to the northward. All above, beyond, and about the giant army, looks so settled, calm, and silent that one is awed into all manner of weird imaginings in regard to its motionless march. These mighty peaks are impressive at any time, but when they come before us in procession robed in their trailing shrouds they set us to thinking ponderous, solemn thoughts that we don't more than half like. The view to the eastward is unobstructed for over one hundred miles, and by its vastness and its stern ruggedness is made imposing and grand, though but a region of rocky sterile mountains and broad deserts crested over with salt and alkaline exudations from the sandy and bitter soil.

Far as the eye can range, not a tree, not a house, not a sign of life is seen. All is as dead, and as arid and wrinkled in death, as the valleys and the mountains of the moon. On this side—the east—clinging along the face of the mountain, we see below us Virginia City; turning again to the west, Washoe Lake is seen shimmering almost at the base of the peak on which we stand, its waves washing the feet of the hills that flank the Sierras. Where we stand, on the narrow circle of granite forming the apex of the mountain, is planted a tall flag-staff on which, upon each recurrence of the natal day of the nation, the Stars and Stripes are unfurled. The flag is run up during the night, by a man who is annually sent to the top of the mountain on this errand, and those who turn their eyes toward the peak, on the morning of the 4th of July, will always see the flag of their country floating there through the "dawn's early light."

Top of Mt. Davidson, c. 1890, dry plate/collotype, James H. Crockwell.
Library of Congress Prints and Photographs Division.

On the occasion of the total eclipse of the moon, which occurred on the night of October 24, 1874, it was not only cloudy at Virginia City, but there prevailed a furious and blinding snowstorm. Not a glimpse of the heavens or of the rising moon could be obtained when evening set in. Not to lose a spectacle so grand as a total eclipse of the moon, I determined to make the ascent of Mount Davidson and so reach a point above the clouds. Accompanied by half a dozen friends, I started a few minutes before 8 o'clock in the evening, and, pressing upward through the fast-falling snow, and through the dense cloud-mass, which we entered on the upper slopes of the mountain, at 10 o'clock we reached the topmost peak, and to our delight found that we at last stood above the clouds and the storm.

It was one of the grandest sights ever witnessed by mortals. As far as the eye could reach, on all sides, stretched a level sea of clouds. All the surrounding mountains were shut—all the lower world was hidden; all but the extreme point of the bare granite peak on which we stood, a little island some fifty feet in circumference, with the tall flag-staff standing in its centre. High above, the full moon shone in splendor, and in all quarters of the heavens the stars twinkled brightly. The air was keen and frosty, but we were provided with blanket-overcoats and mufflers.

For some minutes after rising out of the sea of clouds in which we had so long been enveloped, our little party stood at the foot of the flag-staff and gazed on all around in speechless awe. It almost seemed that we had left the world. Our little island appeared to be all that remained of earth. Hundreds of miles on all sides, as it looked to us, stretched a smooth and level sea of pearl. In the distance this appeared to be motionless, but nearer it all moved slowly and majestically from west to east, while, at the same time, a peculiar swaying up and down was seen as it passed along. On and along the crests of these cloud-waves, or rather cloud-swells, were observed to run and faintly flicker such tints as are seen in mother-of-pearl. All this was very beautiful, but with it came a sense of isolation from the world—a feeling of loneliness, that was most depressing. However, as the moon began to enter the shadow of the earth there were so many and such wonderful changes in the appearance of all about us, that our loneliness and littleness were forgotten.

The sea about us, which before had shown only the tints of the pearl, now took on the hue of amber, but still floated past and gently waved up and down as had the sea of pearl. As the obscuration progressed, the more distant portions of the cloudsea changed from amber to brown, and this to black, gradually closing in upon us from all sides, but most from the northward. In our immediate neighborhood all had changed from amber to a deep burnt-sienna tinge. So deep and decided was this tint that at one time, for the space of some minutes, it seemed to pervade the whole atmosphere; our clothing partook of it, and the flag-staff near which we stood looked like a great rod of rusty iron.

During this dark stage a heavy breeze sprang up, and the swells in the vaporous sea surrounding us were tossed far higher than before. At times these billows rolled many feet above our heads, and the eclipse being then nearly total, we were some times, for minutes, left in midnight darkness, and but for the lanterns we had carried up the mountain, and which were standing at the foot of the flag-staff, we could not have seen our hands when held before our faces. But these waves of darkness seldom lasted more than two or three minutes, and we had, from first to last, an imposing and deeply impressive view of the eclipse. It is probable that a total eclipse of the moon was never before observed under precisely such circumstances as was this by our little party, standing on a mountain peak above the clouds. As the eclipse passed off, about the same phenomena were observed above and about us as in its coming on.

Being chilled to the very marrow in our bones, we left the top of the mountain, however, while nearly half the face of the moon was still obscured. Taking a last lingering look at all about us, observing that our cloud-sea was again assuming the hue of amber and that the horizon was widening and brightening in all directions, as the light spread abroad and drove back the brown and the more distant black, we plunged down into the thick cloud-stratum, and, guided by the light of our lanterns, made the best of our way down the bed of a huge gorge in the face of the mountain, and went back into the city. Strange as it may appear to some, we found it much warmer in the midst of the clouds and drifting snow than above on the summit of the mountain. Not one of the party will ever forget that total eclipse of the moon, seen from old Mount Davidson's topmost height, nearly 8,000 feet above the level of the sea.

CHAPTER XXI

THE SIERRA NEVADA MOUNTAINS
How the Fissures Were Formed—Formation of Quartz and Ores—
How the Comstock Vein Was Found—
Disagreeable "Pinching"—Never Discouraged

The Virginia range of mountains, of which Mount Davidson is the principal peak, is separated from the Sierra Nevada Mountains by a series of small valleys, the principal of which are Washoe Valley, Eagle Valley, Steamboat Valley, and the Truckee Meadows. The range can be traced for a distance of about one hundred miles from the point where it diverges from the Sierras, as they trend to the northwest, to where it finally dies out in the Mud Lake region. The average width of the range is about eighteen miles, though it is quite irregular. The great mass of the mountains composing the range is made up of volcanic rocks, the accumulation of several successive outpourings.

On the eastern face of Mount Davidson, about 1,500 feet below the summit, are found the croppings of the Comstock lode. The rock on the west side of the vein—called the "country rock" by mining men, because it is the general rock of the country outside of the lode—is syenite, a rock which forms the mass of Mount Davidson; on the east side of the vein the country rock is propylite, a volcanic rock of much more recent origin than the syenite, (syenite is much the same as granite, and propylite is a rock of a porphyritic character.) Between these two rocks, by some throe of nature, was formed the immense fissure in which lies the Comstock vein—a fissure known to be nearly four miles in length and from one or two hundred to nearly fifteen hundred feet in width. This vast chasm was undoubtedly formed by volcanic action. It is not one fissure, but more properly speaking, a series of rents running parallel with the main opening. The smaller parallel fractures are principally in the propylite or east country rock. It is but natural that they should be in this, as it was the stratum that was lifted up and shattered when the main fissure was formed. In depth, all of these rents will be found to be lost in the principal opening.

After the rending apart of the rocks and the formation of the chasm, there doubtless burst up through the opening immense volumes of hot mineral waters, steam, and gases, from solfataras or hot springs underneath, and these charged the vein with its rich sulphurets and other ores of silver.

Signs of hot springs are seen everywhere on the hills to the eastward of the vein, and hot springs that are still active are found in various directions, at the distance of a few miles, the most remarkable of which are those known as the Steamboat Springs; which, even at this day, are briskly sending up hot water, steam, and columns of heated gases through a fissure over a mile in length, in fact are actively engaged in the formation of a metallic lode.

It is not improbable that the fissure in which the Comstock lode was formed was originally rent by the upward pressure of the confined steam and gases of hot springs formed between the syenite and propylite far beneath the surface of the earth. Be that as it may, the rent was formed, and afterwards was charged with its present mineral contents.

When the rocks were rent apart, fragments from the edges of the chasm—principally from the east or propylite side, the side reared up—fell into the opening, and sliding down the smooth slope of the syenite, blocked the fissure, preventing its closing. Some of these fragments were at least one thousand feet long and from three to four hundred feet in thickness, and many of them were from fifty to one hundred and fifty feet in length, with a proportionate thickness. These still rest in the vein, the ore, quartz, etc. having formed about them.

By the miners these are called "horses." They are generally composed of propylite (commonly spoken of as porphyry in the mines, owing to its inclosing crystals of feldspar and fragments of hornblende), but there are some that came from the west side of the fissure and are syenite.

After the fissure was thus propped open, still other fragments of propylite fell from its roof during the time the vein was filling with its present precious contents, and these are found to be surrounded on all sides by ore of the richest character. The cavities caused by their displacement were also filled with quartz and ore. This makes the east wall or propylite side of the vein very jagged and uneven, while the less disturbed west or syenite wall is quite regular, descending to the eastward at an angle of from thirty-five to fifty degrees, being throughout quite smooth and covered with a heavy coating of clay.

The fragments of rock that fell into the chasm during the time it was being charged with the precious metals, formed each a nucleus about which the quartz and ores collected. In all parts of the vein are to be seen pieces of country rock, from the size of a filbert to many pounds in weight, about which quartz has formed, and with the quartz ore.

After the vein was filled, it appears to have again several times opened, when fresh fragments fell into the newly formed fissures, and were surrounded by quartz and ores by the action of the waters and gases forced up from below. These several convulsions pulverized the quartz and ore previously formed in the vein, leaving it in such a condition that in most of the mines the greater part of it can be dug down with picks.

In most places in the ore-bodies in the lower levels, appearances indicate that while the ore and quartz were in this shattered and pulverized state, floods of hot water poured in upon it and boiled it as in a caldron, and that at the end of this cooking operation it finally settled down, assuming a horizontally stratified position. In this way must have been formed the occasional streaks of clay and the numerous strata of various shades of color and degrees of fineness of subdivision of component parts seen in the ore as it now rests in the vein. It is as plainly sedimentary in form as any gravel deposit seen on the surface. This is not seen everywhere in the lower levels, but in such places as were most subject to dynamical action.

All who have visited the lower levels of the mines on the Comstock lode must have observed, even upon the most cursory examination of the ores, the peculiar stratification of which I speak. The chasm in which is formed the Comstock lode was doubtless at one time a seething caldron, and at the great depths now attained, not only great quantities of hot water are found, but the rock itself is in many places sufficiently hot to be almost painful to the naked hand.

The course or "strike" of the Comstock vein is a little east of the magnetic meridian, about north twenty-five degrees east. The lode crops out in several places along the face of Mount Davidson, throwing up huge piles of quartz at intervals of from three hundred to five hundred or one thousand yards, as it takes its course southward across the "Divide," and through and beyond Gold Hill; also, to the northward, in the direction of Cedar Hill and Seven-mile Cañon. When the ledge crops out it has a first or false dip to the west, but after being followed down it becomes straight, then turns, and takes its regular dip to the east at an angle of from thirty-five to fifty degrees. In the Ophir, when the true dip was first discovered, the vein turned to the east at the depth of three hundred and thirty feet. The croppings of the vein being above and to the west of Virginia City, this eastern dip carries it under the whole length and breadth of the town, and it also passes under the town of Gold Hill, a mile further south in the same way.

The lead follows the curved outlines of the hills on the surface, swinging in at the ravines and bearing out on the points of the ridges, but as depth is attained it will doubtless be found to straighten in the direction of its present general course. The only gangue of the vein is quartz, though, in places, there are found detached patches and masses of gypsum and carbonate of lime. The ore contains native gold, native silver, sulphuret of silver (silver glance), stephanite, chloride of silver, some rich galena and antimony, and a few rare forms of silver in small quantities; also, mingled with the whole mass of the ores, iron pyrites, copper pyrites, zincblende, and a few other minerals.

The early miners began the work of opening their claims along the Comstock by sinking shafts on the croppings and by running short tunnels to pass under these croppings and tap the vein at depths varying from two hundred to six or seven hundred feet. The shafts were mere circular holes precisely like an ordinary well, and a common windlass, rope, and bucket, constituted all there was coming under the head of machinery.

When more water was encountered than could be hoisted out with a bucket, these early miners were at the "end of their string." Those who were running tunnels, however, were not incommoded by the water they tapped during the progress of their work, as it flowed out as fast as it came in.

The Ophir mine was at first worked by means of an incline which followed the dip of the vein to the west. They soon began to be bothered with water and were obliged to set up a small pump, as has already been stated. All of those who had locations on the Comstock, however, were able to find means for the erection of machinery as soon as it was found necessary to use it, though much of the first hoisting and pumping apparatus was too light and was badly arranged. But almost any kind of steam machinery was better than hoisting by the hand-windlass or with the horse-whim.

After starting up with steam hoisting-works, it was not long before a number of companies began to extract ore from the upper series of bonanzas, and these being exhausted, carried their work to lower levels and searched out new bodies of ore. It often happened that when the ore in sight was exhausted, the company was obliged to drift in all directions for a long time before again finding paying ore. In case a level was opened and explored in all parts without finding ore, sinking was resumed in the main shaft, and a new level was opened at a greater depth in the vein. The miners are never discouraged so long as they find a good width of quartz and other vein-matter between the two walls of the lode, as there is then always a chance of finding ore somewhere in the mass. What they do not like, however, is to find the walls coming together—"pinching," as they call it. The coming together of the walls pinches out or cuts off" the vein; yet, even at the "pinch," there is always left a seam of clay, or some such sign, by which the lead may be followed until the pinch has been passed and the vein again widens and becomes ore-producing.

CHAPTER XXII

BONANZA AND BORRASCA

*Sales of Stock—A Day's Vicissitudes—Speculations—
An Infallible Maxim—Mr. Frank's Devices*

There are always some companies in "borrasca"—out of luck; in barren rock—while others are in "bonanza"—in good luck; working large bodies of rich ore. In a year or two, those who are to-day at work in barren quartz may have a rich body of ore, while those who are to-day in rich ore may in a year or two be delving through barren rock in search of a new bonanza.

When a company has for a long time been, engaged in the unsuccessful search for ore, their stock very frequently falls to a very low figure and few care to buy it at all, when of a sudden they come upon a great body of rich ore. A rumor of this reaches the surface, and those who have money to invest buy—"take in"—a few shares at a venture. The officers of the company and their friends in San Francisco—who are daily informed by telegraph of all that is going on in the mine—begin to quietly gather in all of the stock that they can find, and soon the secret is out and the stock at once bounds upward to a high figure. Everybody then becomes wild to possess a few shares of the stock. Men who would not touch it when it was selling for a mere trifle, now rush in and pay the highest prices. Some appear never to think of buying stock until they see the whole community excited about it and recklessly bidding for it; they then rush in and pay the highest figures. It is like piling bricks one upon another till the whole column begins to topple and finally tumbles to the ground. When stock goes down in this way it nearly always goes as far below as it has before been above true merit.

Many men who are good judges of mines make large purchases of stock in mines that are in borrasca—that are out of ore and appear to be out of luck, biding their time for profit. They have confidence in the mine from the position it occupies on the Comstock lode and from its having had rich bodies of ore above. These, they will contend, were never rained down into the mines from the heavens, but came up from the regions below; therefore in the regions below, whence came the rich ore already found, there must be more of the same kind. To find it, say they, is a mere matter of time.

In November, 1870, an immense bonanza was found in the Crown Point mine, Gold Hill, at the depth of 1,100 feet. Four months before the discovery of this bonanza, that is, in August of the same year, the stock of the mine was selling at three dollars per share; in May, 1872, the stock was selling at one thousand eight hundred and twenty-five dollars per share. The same bonanza extended south into the Belcher mine, the stock of which was selling for one dollar and fifty cents per share in September, 1870; in April, 1872, it sold for one thousand five hundred and twenty-five dollars per share. At this time, however, there was a grand stock excitement and the stock of many mines in which there was little if any ore sold at very high figures.

Virginia City Miner, 1867, collodion/albumen, Timothy H. O'Sullivan. Library of Congress Prints and Photographs Division.

The masses had come into the market as purchasers and were blindly buying right and left; they were all industriously engaged in adding bricks to the pile, stocking them up higher and higher, as idiotically strong in the faith that they were building for all time as were the builders of Babel. Finally down went everything in a grand crash. During this excitement there was an increase in the value of the mines on the Comstock, in about two months, of over forty-five million dollars.

It frequently happens that when a company have been a long time in search of ore it is at last found at a time when the officers and leading men have but a small amount of stock in their possession. They then not only keep their strike a secret, but in case of anything leaking out through their men they bear their stock in the market, throwing in all the shares they dare venture for the purpose of breaking down the price in order that they may buy in a great amount at a low figure. Sometimes they succeed in this, but it often happens that the "outsiders" are too well informed in regard to what is in the mine, when there is a general scramble for the stock and it at once goes up with a rush. Not a few persons nearly always make money in stocks by observing the simple rule of buying them when they are down so low that nobody appears to care to touch them, paying for them in full and then holding them for developments in the mines, and it seldom happens that there is not a time within two years when they can sell for twice or three times the price originally paid. If there should be no strike in the mines in which they hold stock there may be valuable developments in adjoining mines, which sends up the price of the stocks of all the mines in the neighborhood.

While work is being done in a mine there is always a probability of something being found, sooner or later. When a company whose claim is

Quartz Mining Works at Gold Hill, 1862, collodion/albumen, attributed to Charles L. Weed (Lawrence & Houseworth). Library of Congress Prints and Photographs Division.

well situated on the lead has been a longtime out of luck not a few will buy stock in their mine, because they consider that it is about time for the luck of the company to change.

The Mexican silver-miners have an aphorism, in the infallibility of which they have unbounded faith. It is as follows: "As many days as you are in borrasca (barren rock), so many days shall you be in bonanza"—rich ore. Such faith have they in this maxim, that in Mexico they frequently go to work in a mine that has ceased to be productive with no other contract or understanding than the simple one that they are to be allowed to work as many days in the "bonanza" as they spend days in finding it. Such a contract as this was once made on the Comstock lode. It was at the time when the upper or first line of bonanzas was opened in the Ophir, Mexican, Gould & Curry, and other leading mines.

Otto H. Frank was at that time superintendent of the old Central mine. He was anxious to find a bonanza in his mine, but found only barren quartz in all of his drifts and cross-cuts.

Some Mexican miners were very desirous of getting into the mine. They "felt it in their bones" that they could find a bonanza. The terms they proposed to Superintendent Frank were simply these: "As many days as we are drifting in search of the bonanza, so many days shall we be allowed to extract ore from the bonanza."

Mr. Frank thought it all over. He had failed in his search for a bonanza; what was proposed by the Mexicans seemed fair enough; he would let them try their luck, anyhow, to get a bonanza.

So the bargain was struck:—"So many days in borrasca, so many days in bonanza."

The Mexicans went to work in high spirits. Mr. Frank also was quite cheerful, as he thought those "knowing cusses" from the mines of Mexico would drift into a big body of ore the first week, when he would step in the week after and turn them all out before they had done more than get a taste of the bonanza. But they didn't strike it the first week, nor the second, nor the third. The fact is they didn't strike it the first month, nor the second, nor the third. Indeed, at the end of six months they had found no bonanza.

Now it was that Superintendent Frank began to be frightened—began to curse all Mexican mining aphorisms and rules and regulations. Should the Mexicans now strike a bonanza, what kind of a bonanza, he reasoned, would it be by the time it came into his hands? In six months those Mexicans would have it completely skinned and gutted. He might as well have no mine. He now began to suspect that the fellows knew exactly where to drift to open out in a bonanza of vast size and incalculable richness—probably nearly all silver—but were only drifting about on the outside of it in order to get more time inside. He began to hate the very sound of those words: "As many days as you are in borrasca, so many days shall you be in bonanza."

Being greatly worried about the bargain he had thoughtlessly made, Mr. Frank went to see old man Meer, an old Castilian who had but one eye, but who was the greatest "ore expert" that ever set foot upon the Comstock—whose one eye bored into the rock further and faster than any diamond drill. He told Meer about the bargain he had made and the fears and suspicions he entertained, asking him to go into the mine, give it a thorough examination, and tell him if there was a bonanza anywhere about. Old Meer went into the mine, traversed all the drifts, cross-cuts, and coyote-holes, boring into the rock at all points with that eye of his.

When they came out and again and stood upon the surface at the mouth of the tunnel, in the broad light of day, Mr. Frank turned to Meer and said: "Well, what do you think?"

Meer uttered only two words, but those two words lifted a great load off Mr. Frank's breast. Old Meer simply said: *"Nada bonanza"* and "no bonanza" it proved.

The Mexicans worked on for another week or two, when they became disheartened and gave up their contract, and with it, doubtless, some portion of their faith in their favorite saying: "So many days as you are in borrasca, so many days shall you be in bonanza." They had toiled more than six long, weary months and the result was—*"nada bonanza."*

Mexican Mine, 1862, collodion/albumen, attributed to Charles L. Weed (Lawrence & Houseworth). Library of Congress Prints and Photographs Division.

CHAPTER XXIII

HOW THE MINES ARE WORKED
Hoisting the "Giraffe"—Deserted Shafts—
Perilous Ways and Dark Places—What They Saw in the Night—
Rather Astonished—Poisoned

When the upper line of bonanzas had been worked out, and the shafts were sunk to greater depths in search of new bodies of ore, they eventually attained such a depth as brought them down upon the barren syenite forming the west wall. The shafts were then deflected from the vertical and passed down along the syenitic foot-wall to the eastward, in the shape of an incline. At length it was seen that these inclines were becoming too long to permit of their being worked through to advantage with the machinery then in use, and company after company moved to the eastward, a distance of a thousand feet or more, and then established a new line of shafts, over which they set up new and more powerful machinery than had yet been seen on the lead. These shafts did not strike the lead until they had been sunk to the depth of one thousand or one thousand two hundred feet, whereas the first line of shafts were either sunk on the lead, or at such a distance in front of the croppings as to tap it at the depth of from two to five hundred feet.

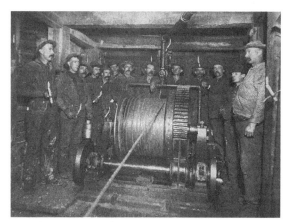

East Incline Hoist, c. 1890, dry plate/albumen, James H. Crockwell.
Library of Congress Prints and Photographs Division.

A third line of shafts had been commenced in 1875, and one of these, which is now being sunk by the Savage, Hale & Norcross, and the Challar-Potosi Companies combined, is nearly a mile east of the croppings. This is intended to be a shaft for all time. It will be of vast size, containing several spacious compartments for hoisting and pumping purposes, and will be supplied with the most powerful machinery that can be manufactured. It will require some years to sink this shaft to a point where it will intersect the vein; meantime the several companies will continue to work through their present shafts and inclines.

The Savage Company are prepared to sink the incline of their present shaft to the great depth of four thousand feet. For this purpose they have set up new hoisting machinery of novel construction and of the most powerful description. The reel on which the hoisting-cable winds is a novelty for the first time introduced on the Comstock lode, and a brief description of it and the cable used upon it may not be without interest for the general reader.

The reel is fifteen feet in length, and at the larger end is twenty-two feet in diameter, while at the smaller end the diameter is but thirteen feet. It is suspended upon a wrought iron shaft about sixteen inches in diameter, the ends of which revolve in ponderous bearings supported by foundations of cut stone reaching into the earth to solid rock. The shell of the reel is covered with thick wooden staves, and the whole somewhat resembles a great tapering cask. Over the staves are securely bolted heavy iron plates forming a strong armor outside of the wooden structure. In this iron armor is a deep groove which, starting at the smaller end of the great conical drum, runs in a spiral manner to the larger end; just as the groove between the threads of a screw is seen to run. In this groove winds the cable as the incline-car ("giraffe") is let down into or drawn up out of the mine.

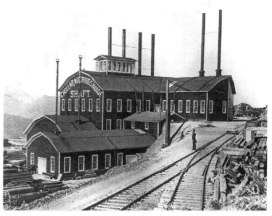

Chollar, Norcross, Savage Works, c. 1890, dry plate/albumen, James H. Crockwell. Library of Congress Prints and Photographs Division.

When the car is at the bottom of the incline, the greater part of the cable is off the reel, and when the hoisting begins it is wound up on the smaller end of the drum, where the engines have greater purchase on the load. As the hoisting proceeds, and the weight to be raised becomes momentarily lighter, on account of the heavy steel cable being wound up, the lifting force is steadily moved toward the larger end of the drum, and each revolution adds to the swiftness of the ascent of the car that is being raised. The cable is round, and is made of the best steel wire. It is 4,000 feet in length, and weighs 25,190 pounds. The upper part, for a distance of 1,500 feet down, is two inches in diameter; for the remainder of its length, 2,000 feet, it gradually tapers till at the lower end its diameter is one and three-quarter inches. The taper is not made by dropping wires in the several strands of the rope, but by drawing each wire (as it is manufactured) slightly tapering for the last 2,500 feet of its length.

The incline hoisting-works stand a short distance from the building in which is contained the hoisting machinery of the vertical shaft, and the cable, after entering the latter building, is carried over a large iron pulley or sheave that is placed over the main shaft. Thence it passes down a compartment of the main shaft a vertical distance of 1,300 feet, when it passes *under* a second sheave and continues down the incline to its bottom.

The car used in the incline runs on an iron track, holds about five tons of rock, and is capable of hoisting (easily) from 480 to 500 tons per 24 hours. The car is made wholly of iron and steel.

When this incline car has been hauled up as far as the bottom of the vertical shaft, that is, to within 1,300 feet of the surface, it there dumps its load by means of a self-acting gate in its bottom. The rock thus dumped from the incline-car is then taken in smaller cars and sent to the surface on cages that ply up and down the hoisting-compartments of the main vertical shaft.

The engines for driving the huge reel, and thus hoisting this iron car or "giraffe," with its load of ore and the 25,000 pounds of cable, are two in number and of 200-horse power each. A precisely similar hoisting apparatus has since been set up at the Ophir mine; indeed, the drawings for this powerful machinery were first made for the Ophir Company. The length and weight of cable at the Ophir is the same as that in use at the Savage mines.

Some of the old shafts opened on and about the first or upper line of bonanzas have quite gone to decay. They still stand, but the timbers in many places, far down in the bowels of the earth, are racked and rotten; while the timbers built up in the mine to support the chambers from which ore was extracted, and set up in the galleries, drifts, cross-cuts, and chutes, millions on millions of feet in all, have quite gone to decay. It is perilous to undertake the exploration of these old worked-out levels. In many places they are caved in every direction, the old floors are rotten, water drips from above, a hot, musty atmosphere and almost stifles the explorer, and in places, the air is so foul that his candle is almost extinguished.

Down in these deserted and dreary old levels, hundreds of feet beneath the surface, are encountered fungi of monstrous growth and most uncouth and uncanny form. They cover the old posts in great moist, dew-distilling masses, and descend from the timbers overhead in broad slimy curtains, or hang down like long squirming serpents or the twisted horns of the ram. Some of these take most fantastic shapes, almost exactly counterfeiting things seen on the surface. Specimens of these are to be seen in most of the cabinets of curiosities in Virginia City. Some of the fungi that grow up from the bottoms of old disused drifts are wholly mineral and are composed of minute crystals of such salts as are contained in the earth from which they spring.

These old, decaying places breed all manner of gases, some of them, as the firedamp (carbureted hydrogen gas), dangerous to human life.

One winter night, in 1874, some of the residents of the western part of Virginia City were startled by seeing what seemed a column of flame fifty or sixty feet in height, shooting up from the mouth of an old shaft near the old upper works of the Ophir Company. It was at first thought that the timbers in the old mine were on fire, and three or four men ran to the spot to see what could be done toward smothering the flames.

On reaching the shaft, however, they found that there was no smell of smoke, and also that the supposed fire was a light unlike anything they had ever before seen, in its weird whiteness and the strange coruscations of its component particles, the light shed about by the flame, the faces of the men were of a corpse-like *palor*. Their clothing and hair also partook in some degree of the same ghastly and unnatural hue. The light came up the full size of the large square shaft, and seen at a distance, as it rose through the falling snow, closely resembled one of the shooting spires of the aurora borealis, and it exhibited something of the same waving and inconstant motion.

Although the men felt creeping over them a sort of superstitious awe, they still had sufficient courage to approach the shaft and gaze into it. A strange sight was there seen. The whole interior of the shaft seemed to be at a white heat, and glowed like a furnace. The timbers on the sides were particularly brilliant. Each splinter, excrescence, or bit of fungus seemed darting dazzling rays that streamed steadily out in all directions. A warm, strange current of air ascended from the sweltering regions below, and there was observed a musty, sickening smell. All of those who looked into the shaft afterwards felt a severe pain in the temples, and two or three were made sick at the stomach.

This strange appearance lasted over half an hour, and before it ended a crowd of a dozen or more miners returning from their work had collected about the shaft. The light died out from the top downwards, and protuberances from the sides of the shaft continued to glow for some minutes after the light was no longer visible at its top. This remarkable phenomenon was undoubtedly caused by the belching forth of a highly phosphorated gas of some kind from the deep, underground chambers of the old abandoned works. The rush of this gas was probably caused by an extensive cave in a place where the timbers had rotted away. One of the men who witnessed the spectacle was of the opinion that the mingling of the gas from the mine with the atmospheric air had something to do with intensifying the light. He observed in the ascending current of pseudo-flame myriads of small particles of some substance of a floss-like texture, which appeared to flash and glow as they darted upward, and which presented in the general column of light much the same appearance as motes moving about in a sunbeam.

In February, 1874, some miners at work in the Utah mine, just north of Virginia City, were all made temporarily blind by certain water or gases which they encountered. They were running a drift at the depth of 400 feet to connect with some old, flooded works. When the end of the drift neared the old works, the water they contained began to be drained off. The water had attained a great height, and the pressure was so strong that it sent streams darting and hissing from every hole and crevice in the rock in which the drift was being run. In places, these streams of water spurted out with as much force as though they had been thrown by a hydraulic pipe.

The water, or the steam and gases from it, poisoned all who worked in the drift. Their heads and faces were so swollen that their eyes were closed, and all were thus rendered blind for some days. A few years before, the same thing occurred in the Savage and the Yellow-Jacket mines, when drifts were run to tap old flooded works in which rotten timbers were soaking. Quite recently, all the miners at work in the Sutro Tunnel were poisoned, and had their eyes closed for some days by the tapping of a shaft which had been filled with water for two or three years. All who are thus poisoned speedily recover by remaining above ground for three or four days.

CHAPTER XXIV

FIREDAMP — A MINE IN FLAMES

Yellow-Jacket Mine in a Blaze—A Scene of Horror—
The Victims Subduing the Flames—The Work of Destruction—
Scenes at the Mouth of the Shaft—On Fire for Three Years—Missing Men

No premature explosion of blasts, crushing in of timbers, caving of earth and rock—no accident of any kind is so much feared or is more terrible than a great fire in a large mine. It is a hell, and often a hell that contains living, moving, breathing, and suffering human beings—not the ethereal and intangible souls of men. It is a region of fire and flame, from which the modes of egress are few and perilous. A great fire on the surface of the earth is a grand and fearful spectacle, but a great fire hundreds of feet beneath the surface of the earth is terrible—terrible beyond measure or the power of words to express, when we know that far down underneath the ground which lies so calmly on all sides, giving forth no sound, are scores of human beings pursued by flames and gases, scorched and panting, fleeing into all manner of nooks and corners, there to meet their death.

A large mine in which are employed from five hundred to one thousand men is of itself a considerable village, though it be a village far below the light of day. In it are more timbers, lumber, and other combustible matter than is found in all the houses of a town of two thousand inhabitants—it contains millions on millions of square feet of timber—in it whole forests have found a tomb.

Besides being built up to a height of from one thousand to one thousand five hundred or two thousand feet, with cribs composed of massive timbers, each crib filling a space five by six feet in size, there are floors of heavy planks, six feet apart, one above another, all the distance from bottom to top. In many places, too, the main timbers are doubled again and so filled with blocks and wedges and braces that all is a solid mass of wood. In numberless places there are stairs leading from floor to floor, and then there are scores of chutes, built of timber and lined with planks, with vertical winzes,

Yellow Jacket Mine. c. 1890, dry plate/collotype, James H. Crockwell.
Library of Congress Prints and Photographs Division.

constructed in the same way, all of which, with the chutes, lead up through the floors from level to level; also numerous drifts and cross-cuts supported by timbers and walled in with lagging (split pine-stuff like staves, but longer), all of which serve as flues to conduct and spread the heat and flames throughout the mine.

The mines of the Comstock have not escaped fires. They have not been, many, but they have been fearful as experiences, and have cost many lives.

The first and most terrible of these fires was that which broke out in the Yellow-Jacket mine, Gold Hill, about 7 o'clock on the morning of Wednesday, April 7, 1869, in which forty-five men lost their lives.

The fire started at the 800-foot level (that is 800 feet below the surface) at a point two hundred feet south of the main shaft, near the line of the Kentuck mine. It was first discovered at 7 o'clock in the morning, though it had no doubt been burning longer, as some of the miners asserted that they detected the smell of smoke as early as 3 o'clock A. M. The night shift (relay) left at 4 A. M. and the morning shift began work at 7 A. M., and it was supposed that the fire originated from a candle left sticking against a timber by men on the night shift. From 4 o'clock till 7 o'clock the only men in the mine were the carmen, but before the danger had been discovered many of the day shift had been lowered into the mines—Yellow-Jacket, Crown Point, and Kentuck.

The first thing done on discovering the fire was to try to get the men up out of the mines. The alarm of fire was sounded, and the fire companies of Gold Hill and Virginia City at once turned out.

Pending the arrival of the firemen with their apparatus, those about the several mines were doing all in their power to rescue the men who were left underground. At first the smoke was so dense that no one dared venture into either of the shafts, but about 9 o'clock in the morning it seemed to draw away from the Kentuck shaft, and men descended on the cage and recovered two dead bodies.'

At the Crown Point mine, when the cage was being hoisted for the last time, some of the men on it were so far suffocated as to fall back and were crushed to death between the sides of the cage and the timbers of the shaft.

Toward noon some of the firemen working at the Yellow-Jacket mine ventured down the shaft to the 800-foot level and recovered three or four bodies of asphyxiated miners.

About the same time, at the Crown Point mine, a cage was sent down with a lighted lantern upon it. It was lowered to the 1,000-foot level, and with the lantern was sent the following dispatch, written on a large piece of pasteboard:

"We are fast subduing the fire. It is death to attempt to come up from where you are. We shall get you out soon. The gas in the shaft is terrible, and produces sure and speedy death. Write a word to us and send it up on the cage, and let us know where you are."

No answer came back—all below were dead.

As soon as it was known that the mines were on fire, and that a large number of miners were imprisoned below, by the dense volumes of smoke and suffocating gases that poured up through the several shafts, the most intense excitement prevailed, both in Gold Hill and Virginia City. The wives, children, and relatives of the lost flocked to the several hoisting works, approaching as near to the mouths of the shafts as they were allowed to come, and, standing there on all sides, their grief and lamentations caused tears to course down the cheeks of the most stouthearted . "Lost! lost! lost!" was the despairing cry constantly uttered by many of the women whose husbands were below.

The Rev. Father Manogue, a pioneer of the country, and several other Catholic clergymen of Virginia City and Gold Hill, moved about among the people and did all that could be done to comfort and quiet the weeping women and children, but even the reverend fathers could find little to say in mitigation of the woes of such an occasion. Many of the poor women, with weeping children clinging about them, stood round the shafts, convulsively clasping and wringing their hands, and rocking their bodies to and fro in excess of misery, yet uttering scarcely a word or a sob—they at first seemed utterly stupefied and overwhelmed by the suddenness and awfulness of the calamity. Turn where they might there was no comfort for them.

At the Yellow-Jacket mine the smoke and gases drew away to the southward, men descended the shaft, and all but one man known to be below at that point were brought up dead.

As the cage containing the dead bodies rose up at the mouth of the shaft there was heard a general wail from the women, who could with difficulty be restrained from climbing over the ropes stretched to keep back the crowd. "Oh! God,! who is it this time?" Some one among them would be heard to say. The dead bodies would then be lifted from the cage, and then borne in the arms of stout miners and firemen outside of the circle of ropes.

As the men passed out with the dead, the women would crowd forward in an agony of fear and suspense to see the faces. "Oh! Patrick!" one would be heard to shriek, when the bystanders would be obliged to seize her and lead her away.

At the Kentuck and Crown Point shafts there steadily arose thick, stifling columns of smoke and pungent gases, generated by the burning pine-wood and heated ores below. No person who stood at the mouth of either of these shafts could entertain the slightest hope that any one of those in the mines could be alive; yet wives and relatives would still hope against everything. In every direction almost superhuman exertions were made to extinguish the fire.

By closing up the shafts and pouring down water, it was thought that the fire might have been extinguished, but to have done so would have been equivalent to saying that all below were dead—and would, indeed, have been death to any that might have been living—besides, the order to close the shafts would have drawn from all present at all interested in the fate of those below such a wail as no one would have cared to hear.

No one could enter the Crown Point or Kentuck shafts, but that of the Yellow-Jacket being cooler, the firemen began to work their way down it, carrying with them their hose and bravely battling with the fire. A long string of hose was attached to a hydrant and carried down to the 800-foot level, where the fight began. It was such work as few firemen in the United States have ever undertaken, and such as none but firemen in a mining country could have done. The miners and firemen battled side by side. The firemen would advance as far as possible, extinguishing the burning timbers, and when a cave of earth and rock occurred, or the blackened and weakened timbers seemed about to give way, the miners would go to the front and make all secure.

The walls of the drifts were so heated that it was very frequently found necessary to fall back, even after the burning timbers had been extinguished, and play a stream on the rock in order to cool it down. In places boiling hot water stood, to the depth of two or three inches, on the floors of the drifts. Steam, fumes of sulphur, and gases from the heated ore and minerals rendered the air so bad that it became necessary to lead in an air-pipe from the main blower above, to enable the men to continue work. When caves occurred, flames and poisonous gases were driven forward upon the men, singeing and partially suffocating them. Their position was one of great peril. Their only means of reaching the surface was through the shaft, and at any moment an accident might happen that would cut them off from this; or the draught might change and overwhelm them with stifling gases before they could ascend to the surface.

The situation below, when the fire broke out, was fearful. The smoke and gases came upon the men so suddenly that, although they ran at once for the shaft, many were suffocated and sank down by the way. At the Crown Point the men so crowded upon the cage at first (a cage holds from twelve to sixteen men) that it was detained nearly five minutes; the station-tender being afraid to give the signal to hoist while so many men were in danger of being torn to pieces. A young man who came up on that cage told me, that as they were finally about to start, a man crawled upon the cage, and thrusting his head in between his (the young man's) legs, begged to be allowed to remain there and go up. He was permitted to keep the place, and his life was saved.

As this cage started up, hope left the hearts of those remaining behind. They were heard to throw themselves into the shaft and to fall back on the floors of the mine. Another young man told me that in rushing toward the shaft, it occurred to him that he might fall into it—all being dark below—when he got down on his hands and knees and crawled, feeling his way until he knew that he was at the shaft. While lying there, three or four men came running along from behind, and pitched headlong into it, to their instant death. At one lowering of the cage, a man who went down from the surface, finding that there were more persons below than could be brought up that trip, generously got off into a drift and put on board a young man who was so far suffocated that he was unable to stand. The man who did this was afterwards brought up unharmed.

The firemen not only went into the burning underground regions cheerfully, but there was strife among them to be allowed to go. To see them in their big hats, ascending and descending the shafts, as they relieved each other, was a novel sight. It was a new way of going to a fire. Although a

Curry Fire Company, Carson City, 1865, collodion/albumen. Nevada Department of Transportation.

stream was kept playing at the 800-foot level of the Yellow-Jacket all day, at 9 o'clock at night it was found that the fire was rising, and a second stream was put on at the 700.

At 2 o'clock, on the morning of the 8th, thirteen bodies had been recovered. Some of these were found in the sump (place in which to collect water at the bottom of a shaft) at the 1,100 foot level where they had fallen from stations above, others were found at the 1,000-foot level, lying in all kinds of despairing positions, just as they had sunk down and died when Overtaken by the poisonous gases.

At 1 o'clock, on the afternoon of the 8th, twenty-three bodies had been recovered. When the fire first broke out, an explosion of gases occurred near the Crown Point shaft, which is supposed to have killed several men in that direction. Wherever the stifling gas swept in upon the men it left them dead. One dead miner was found clasping a ladder with death grip, his head hanging backwards. It was necessary to lower the body with a rope a distance of fifty feet to the bottom of the level. On the 900-foot level of the Crown Point mine, about thirty feet from the shaft, nine men were found in one heap. They had unjointed an air-pipe in the hope of being able to get enough fresh air to keep them alive.

On the morning of the 10th it was evident that the fire had increased to such an extent that no more bodies could be recovered,—that none in that pit of fire could be alive—and at, 11 a.m. the mouths of all the shafts were covered with planks, wet blankets, and earth. At noon, steam from the boilers was turned into the Yellow-Jacket shaft through the air-pipe leading from the blower (a fan revolving in a drum, used in forcing air into the mines) down to the 800 and 900-foot levels, whence it would go wherever it could find egress.

On the 12th, a few more bodies were found, and there was so much fire that the mines were again closed and steam forced into them. Some of the bodies last taken out of the mines were so decomposed, owing to the great heat below, that in order to handle them it was necessary to roll them up in canvas coated with tar. Several bodies were in such a condition that the wives and relatives of the deceased were not allowed to see their faces. They were told to remember them as they had last seen them in life. One woman begged hard to see the face of her husband; then to see his hair. Being shown his hair, she laid her hand on it, and said: "Good-bye, my husband." As she turned away, a little girl she was leading said: "Can't I see my papa?" when the mother fainted.

On the 14th, at 3 o'clock p.m., steam was shut off from the shafts and all the works stopped. Five bodies still remained in the mines. Three days later the shafts were opened and some explorations made. Spots of fire were extinguished, where they could be reached. Almost daily they were able to get into some one of the mines and direct streams of water upon some parts of the fire. At this work men were frequently asphyxiated, and then it was necessary to hasten with them to the surface. On the 28th, another body was recovered, and on the 29th, efforts were made to reach the bodies (four) still remaining on the upper levels of the Kentuck; but some of the men fell down insensible from asphyxia, and the attempt was abandoned.

Thus the miners struggled with the fire, until May 2nd, when it grew worse. The drifts between the Yellow-Jacket and the Kentuck and Crown Point mines were then closed, and the shafts of the latter mines were again sealed. The fresh air thrown into the mines by the blowers was supposed to have given the fire new life.

On May 18th, the Kentuck and the Crown Point mines were opened, and miners descended to the lower levels of both. On the 20th May another body was recovered in the south compartment of the Crown Point shaft, when it was found lying on a scaffold at the 800-foot level, leaving three bodies not yet found. After this the fire again increased and drove the men away from places where they had been able to work. May 24th, it was discovered that the fire was on the 800-foot levels of the Crown Point and Kentuck mines, and the miners finally succeeded in walling it up and confining it to this space.

As late as June 23d, men were occasionally brought to the surface in an insensible condition, and the fire continued to burn in that portion of the mines to which it was confined, for over a year. Nearly three years from the time of the breaking out of the fire the rocks in the 800-foot levels of the Crown Point and Kentuck mines were found to be red-hot. Only fragments of the skeletons of the three missing men were ever found. Their bodies were in those parts of the mines that were walled in and given up to the flames.

CHAPTER XXV

DEATH IN THE MINE

Explosions of Firedamp—How Gas is Formed in the Mines—
Searching for the Dead—What the Giant-powder Did—
The Inquest, and the Dead—Carelessness of the Miners

On the 20th of September, 1873, about 3 o'clock in the morning, a second fire and series of explosions occurred in the Yellow-Jacket mine, by which six men lost their lives and several were seriously injured.

This fire originated in a winze on the 1300-foot level of the mine. The winze was directly over the forge of an underground blacksmith's shop, for which it served as a chimney. The fire seems to have been burning in the wood-work of this winze in a smoldering way, generating a quantity of gas, and when an assistant blacksmith approached with a lighted lantern in his hand, a heavy explosion occurred. A great quantity of smoke rushed up the main shaft and hung in a black cloud over the works. When this was seen, an alarm of fire was sounded on the surface, and soon there were over two thousand persons collected about the mine. Among the wives, children, and relations of those in the mines were enacted the same heartrending scenes as on the occasion of the first great fire in April, 1869. When the firemen reached the works, the fatal mistake was made of throwing water down the shaft, thus driving the smoke and gases back upon the men in the lower levels, and causing the loss of life. This was stopped by Captain

Taylor, superintendent of the mine, as soon as he arrived on the ground.

About this time a man was sent to the old shaft of the mine, some distance above on the hill, to see that all was right there. Doors were shut down over the mouth of this shaft, and while the man was looking to see that these were properly closed, he took the candle from his lantern and held it over the shaft. As he did so, he saw a streak of fire flash along up a post that stood in the middle of the shaft, between the folding doors. Thinking that a quantity of lint on the corner of the post had taken fire, he struck at it with his hat to blow it out. As he did this, an explosion occurred that shook the whole town. A sheet of flame darted from the mouth of the shaft, and the man, who was still over it, hat in hand, was thrown backwards a distance of several feet.

This second explosion, which caused the solid earth to rock, not only added greatly to the terror of those on the surface, but it sent sheets of flame through all the mines as far as the Belcher, a distance of two thousand feet. Men who were in the Crown Point mine at the moment, stated that this fire seemed a solid mass that filled all the space about them, and that it flashed toward and past them as swiftly as lightning. At the same time the concussion which accompanied the flash was so great as to knock them down and drive them along the ground for a considerable distance. These streams of fire did not penetrate into the cross-drifts, but darted straight southward along the main drifts and galleries, owing to which fact, doubtless, several miners who happened to be in cross-drifts, escaped being killed or seriously injured. To add to the terrors of the situation, all of the lights were blown out by the explosions, and the lower levels of the mines were everywhere in total darkness.

Those who lost their lives died from asphyxia, while those who were injured were burned by the sheets of flame that darted through the several mines. The fire burned and stripped the shirts entirely off the backs of some of the men, and those who were touched by any part of the flame lost their whiskers, eyebrows, and the greater part of their hair.

There being several hundred men in the mines, the utmost consternation prevailed when the first explosion occurred, and the smell of smoke and gases—a smell well remembered by the old miners—swept through the lower levels; but the work of hoisting these men to the surface was performed at the several shafts with safety, precision, and almost lightning swiftness. Notwithstanding the excitement that prevailed all about them, the engineers never for a single instant lost their presence of mind. They answered every tap of the signal-bells as promptly, and kept their eyes as steadfastly fixed upon the marks on their cables, as though nothing were wrong below. The cages and "giraffes" were rushed up and down the shafts and inclines with their living freight at a rate of speed which under ordinary circumstances would have been simply terrific. But by no means was this work too rapidly performed to suit the men who were fleeing up from the fiery furnace of the regions below.

It luckily happened that the winze in which this fire raged was surrounded on all sides by solid rock, therefore when the timbers it contained were consumed, the fire died out. The man who at first approached the smoldering winze with his lantern, was found lying dead at a distance of about two hundred feet from it; having been asphyxiated. Men who die of asphyxia in the mines, look like living men if brought to the surface at any time within a few hours after life is extinct. Their cheeks are flushed and roseate, and their bodies are as limp as though they were still alive. With their eyes closed, they appear to be men in a fever, lying in a sound sleep. It is a painless death. Several miners who were brought to the surface in an unconscious state, and who would no doubt have died in a few minutes had they been left in the mine, assert that a sensation of faintness was all they experienced, they did not even remember falling to the ground; but all are very sick after regaining their senses.

As it would have been impossible for the small fire in the winze to have generated such immense quantities of inflammable gases as must have been consumed in the two explosions that occurred during this last fire in the Yellow-Jacket mine, many men are of the opinion that a small quantity of the gas from pine-wood mingled with gases already in the mines, rendered the whole explosive. In this instance some such accidental compound must have been formed. Common air being mingled with the gases probably had much to do with causing the explosions.

On the morning of May 24th, 1874, the hoisting works of the Succor Mining Company, near Silver City, were destroyed by fire, and two miners who were at work in the shaft at the time, lost their lives. The fire was kindled by some cartridges of giant-powder that had been left lying on the boiler. The cartridges did not explode, but simply burned. They were about a dozen in number, enough to have blown the works to atoms, had they exploded. They burned very rapidly, throwing up a fountain of fire. The flames were intensely bright, and wherever the jets struck they set fire to the wood-work. The roof and all that part of the works about the boilers were on fire in an instant.

The only men in the works were the engineer and the carman. Two miners were at work at the bottom of the shaft, five hundred feet below the surface. The engineer and carman shook the cable attached to the hoisting tub, which was at the bottom of the shaft, as a signal for the men below to come up; also, shouted to them, but could not make them understand their danger. Soon the two men were driven out of the building, which was speedily consumed.

Two days later, when the fire in the timbers of the upper part of the shaft had been extinguished, a windlass was rigged and men were lowered to see how things looked below. It was not expected that the bodies of the dead miners would be found, as much earth had caved from the top of the shaft, and its bottom was supposed to be filled to the depth of twenty or thirty feet with broken timbers, rocks, and earth. Contrary to the general expectation, the men had not been lowered a great distance into the shaft before they signaled those above to stop; they then shouted up the shaft that the bodies were found. A large crowd had collected about the shaft, and when this unexpected report came up, the excitement was great.

The bodies of the poor fellows were discovered at the pump station—a recess some feet square in one side of the shaft—to which point they had ascended by almost superhuman exertions. This pump station was two hundred and sixty-five feet above the bottom of the shaft, and the whole of this great distance the men had climbed in their desperate struggle for life, with nothing to cling to but the slight cracks between the timbers walling the sides. Considering the small and uncertain hold afforded by the timbers of the shaft, their climbing to such a height was a feat bordering on the miraculous, and one which could only have been performed by young and active men, as both were. Both men had died from asphyxia. Neither their bodies nor their clothing were scorched.

In the pump station they were protected from the falling brands and beams from the burning building, and there they had remained till suffocated by the deadly gases that settled down into the shaft. The face of one of the men was rosy and as natural as in life, while that of the other, who lay in the outer part of the station, was black and frightfully swollen.

An inquest was held, and the verdict of the Coroner's jury was that the men who lost their lives by the fire, James Billings and James Rickard "came to their death by suffocation caused by the burning of the Succor hoisting-works and part of the shaft, said fire having been caused by the combustion of giant-powder which was kept on the top of one of the boilers, and we strongly deprecate the custom prevalent in many mines of keeping giant-powder on the boilers about the works."

And well they might find fault with this practice of cooking giant-powder on the tops of boilers; also, they might mildly suggest that the custom of thawing frozen giant-powder and nitro-glycerine on stoves and at the forges of blacksmith's shops is a thing not to be encouraged. Several, however, have prospected about until they have found this out for themselves. It is now probably well known in the other world, as a few of those best informed on the point have gone there.

CHAPTER XXVI

DESTRUCTION OF THE BELCHER SHAFT

Progress of the Flames—Descending the Burning Shaft—
Danger—A Cave in the Mine—Deluge of Fire—Courage of the Men—
Still Burning—A Warm Comparison—The Centre of the Earth

About 2 o'clock, on the afternoon of October 30, 1874, the air shaft of the Belcher mine took fire and was totally destroyed. The shaft was not completed at the time of the accident, but went down to a depth of 1,000 feet below the surface. It was twelve by six feet in width, divided into two compartments, and substantially timbered from top to bottom. It had cost between $30,000 and $40,000, and was designed to ventilate and cool the lower levels of the mines—those at the depth of 1500 and 1600 feet.

As soon as the fire was discovered, the miners working below were notified, and all were safely hoisted out of the mine. It being found impossible to save the shaft, all connection between it and other parts of the mine was cut off and the fire allowed to have its way.

The fire was first discovered by persons down in the mine, but it soon made itself manifest on the surface, in the dense volume of smoke of inky

Belcher Shaft, c. 1890, dry plate/collotype, James H. Crockwell.
Library of Congress Prints and Photographs Division.

blackness that rose from the mouth of the shaft and ascended to a perpendicular height of three or four hundred feet. This large column of smoke was one of the grandest sights imaginable. The air was perfectly calm, and the smoke assumed the form of huge balloons rolling upward, one over the other. This ominous cloud of smoke was visible for many miles in all directions and filled the hearts of all beholders with terror. The steam-whistle at the Belcher hoisting works, near at hand, sent forth its long-drawn wail—the fire signal—as soon as the first black puffs of smoke rose above the surface of the ground. Instantly, the whistles of dozens of mills and hoisting works joined in, and the whole air was rent for half an hour with their steady unceasing shrieks. All who saw the awful pall of smoke rise up and hang over the mine, feared the worst, and all who had husbands, fathers, brothers, or friends at work in the Belcher, hastened to the mine.

Firemen from Gold Hill and Virginia, with steamers and hand-engines, soon swarmed the place, but were not allowed to throw water into the shaft—the effects of this had been seen at the last fire in the Yellow-Jacket mine. There were houses to save, all about the shaft, and to this work the attention of the firemen was turned. To attempt to describe the wretchedness and despair of the women and children gathered round the shaft and looking upon the awful column of smoke, would be futile, and to the imagination of the reader may be left their joy on being told that all who had been in the mine were safe upon the surface.

After the great column of smoke had rolled upward from the mouth of the shaft for twenty minutes or more, and when a great crowd was collected about the spot, there came a flash, as of lightning, there was a dull, heavy report, which was heard at the distance of a mile, and a sheet of flame shot upward to the height of nearly five hundred feet.

Instantly, the dark column of smoke was gone—was consumed in the tall pillar of fire. The flame then gradually fell back to a height of about sixty feet, and to this height it continued to rush for over an hour, with a roar that could be heard at the distance of half a mile. Pieces of flaming wood and live coals larger than a man's hand, were shot sixty feet into the air, and fell in such showers that they covered the ground on all sides and rolled by bushels from the roofs of buildings in the neighborhood. At a distance the burning shaft bore a striking resemblance to an active volcano. The draught through it was the same that would be seen on the surface, in a burning chimney a thousand feet in height.

At this critical juncture it was decided to go below and close all of the drifts leading from the burning shaft. The main hoisting shaft and works stood at a distance of one hundred yards from the air-shaft, and in the buildings at this point were collected the miners who had just escaped from the lower levels. Showers of live coals were falling upon the roofs of all the buildings about and over the main working shaft, and a score of men engaged in pouring water over them could hardly prevent them from taking fire. In the hoisting works the engineers stood at their posts awaiting orders. A rope had been stretched about the mouth of the main shaft to keep back the crowd, and within the circle of this rope stood thirty or forty miners, also awaiting orders. The cage was below with two or three officers of the mine, who had gone down to ascertain the situation in the neighborhood of the bottom of the burning shaft. All were anxiously awaiting some news from these men, as since the escape of the miners from the lower levels, they were the first who had ventured back into the underground regions.

Presently a cage—a three-decker—came up and stopped at the mouth of the shaft. On its lower deck stood an underground foreman. As the cage stopped, this official said: "I want eighteen men to go down to the 1,000-foot level with me." The men knew that on the level mentioned was the bottom of the perpendicular portion of the burning air-shaft, but they did not know the situation at that point, nor did they know what they would be asked to do on arriving at their destination. Yet no sooner had the call for volunteers been made than there was a rush of men to the cage.

The lower compartment was instantly filled. The engineer, who stood with his hand on the lever of his engine, dropped the cage till the second compartment stood level with the floor, and this had no sooner been done than it was filled with men. The same was the case when the last compartment came down; indeed there was a quiet struggle among the men for a place on the cage, though few words were spoken. As the six men were taking their places on the last section of the cage, a young man pulled one of them off, and took his place, saying: "No, John, you've got a family."

The men were all brave, determined-looking fellows. The faces of all were calm and firm—not a cheek was pale. While the men were filling the cage, as it hung in the mouth of the shaft. I said to a friend, "Those are all fine, brave men. See! with what nerve they step upon that cage to go down into the burning mine! It may be that some of those men will never reach the surface alive, yet not one shows a sign of fear."

"Very true," said my friend, "but I don't think there is any real danger down there. The fire is confined to the air-shaft, all around it is safe enough."

"Men never go into a mine at any time," said I, "but they are in danger; and when there is anything wrong in a mine the danger is vastly increased—particularly when there is a fire in any of the lower levels."

"Well, but what can happen to these men?" asked the gentleman.

"These men," said I, "will probably come out all right, if no cave shall occur in the burning shaft while they are below; but it will now soon be time for the caving to begin. The timbers must soon begin to weaken."

"Well, what would be the result of a cave in the shaft?"

"It would close up the shaft and suddenly send poisonous gases through the lower levels."

Leaving the shaft and the works, soon after the men had descended on their dangerous mission, 1,000 feet below the surface of the earth, we returned to the town of Gold Hill.

As we entered the main street of the town, we turned and looked in the direction of the burning shaft, half a mile away. No sign of flame was visible, but there rolled up from the mouth of the shaft a great inky cloud of smoke.

"See!" cried my companion, "the fire has gone out! It is all smoke now!"

"There has been a cave in the shaft!" said I, and in less than half a minute the column of flame again darted into the air to the height of sixty or eighty feet, and instantly all the smoke disappeared.

Now let us see what happened in the mine at that time. After the fire broke out in the air-shaft, the draught, which had always before been downward into the mine (contrary to the general expectation when it was made), changed, and rushed fiercely upwards. The draught in the main shaft at the hoisting works, one hundred yards distant, which had before been upward, was instantly changed, and in it there was found a strong downward suction. This allowed the men who went below to approach quite near to the bottom of the burning shaft. They were set to work at tearing out the woodwork and pulling up the car-tracks in a drift connecting with the air-shaft at the 1,000-foot level, preparatory to filling it with a bulkhead of rocks and earth, in order to cut off its connection with other parts of the mine.

While they were at this work the cave occurred in the shaft. When the mass of rocks and earth composing the cave fell down through the shaft— perhaps a distance of five hundred feet— it forced back, down into the mine, and out through the drift in which the miners were at work, a vast tongue of flame as fierce as that from a blow-pipe—forced back upon the men all the heat and flame there was in the lower part of the shaft when it fell.

This deluge of fire lasted but the fraction of a minute, when it was all sucked back into the shaft by the draught, but while it lasted it was fierce as the flames of a furnace. The men working in the drift were naked from the waist upwards, and below wore nothing but cotton overalls. In a moment the flames were upon them, and all were terribly burned, notwithstanding that they threw themselves flat upon the ground. In some instances their overalls were licked from their bodies—turned to ashes in an instant.

Nine of the eighteen men we saw so bravely descend into the burning mine were hoisted out, scarred and crisped; their clothes burnt from their bodies, and the skin peeling off in great flakes, wherever they were touched. One man was brought up dead. He was not found till the next day, when his dead body was discovered at the bottom of a winze into which he had fallen while fleeing before the flames. All of those burned finally recovered, but several not for many weeks. When the first squad of men was disabled, others bravely took their place in the drift, and finally succeeded in completing a substantial bulkhead; thus saving the mine. Though several caves occurred and drove them from their work, none were so disastrous as the first—the mass of rock in the bottom of the shaft doubtless preventing a free outpouring of flame.

Although this fire occurred in October, 1874, in May, 1875, when a new shaft was being constructed, great masses of rocks, still almost at a white heat were encountered by the workmen. These lay at the bottom of the old shaft, and there was no burning timber, charcoal, or fire among them, but they were so hot as to set on fire the timbers the miners were trying to set up in the drift run by them, and in order to work at all it was found necessary to carry a line of hose into the place and play a stream of water upon the rocks.

When we find so small a mass of rocks as can be contained in the bottom of a shaft, remaining red-hot for eight months, should we be incredulous on being assured by men of science that the centre of the earth, once a molten mass of rock, still remains in a molten state after untold ages?

CHAPTER XXVII

WAR IN THE MINE
Smoking out the Enemy—The Early Days of Washoe—
Amiable Miners—The Kossuth and the Alhambra—Causes of Fear—
A Little Mischief—Burnt Rags

Little difficulty has ever been experienced from firedamp, in the mines along the Comstock lode. Firedamp is a gas which is more frequently generated in, and more strictly confined to, coal mines than to any others; yet in a few instances it has been found to exist in mines on the Comstock. It is probably generated by decaying pine-timber.

On one occasion, a mining superintendent of Gold Hill went into an old drift of the Segregated Belcher mine, and while passing along it, happened to lift his candle to its roof, to examine the rock. Much to his astonishment, he set fire to a stratum of carburetted hydrogen (firedamp), which produced a brilliant flash that extended the whole length of the drift. Some miners working in the Gould & Curry mine on one occasion had a similar, but much more lively, bit of experience. On tapping an old drift in that mine quite an explosion occurred, though no harm was done, further than the singeing of the hair and whiskers of the astonished miners.

In the early days of Washoe it occasionally happened that adjoining mining companies drifted into each other's works, far below the surface. On such occasions there was war down in the bowels of the earth. In case pistols and similar weapons were not used, the battles were fought after the Chinese stink-pot plan. Each company sought to smoke the other out. The latest instance in which these underground amenities of the amiable miner were indulged in, was in May, 1874, when the Kossuth and the Alhambra folks ceased to admire each other.

The works of the two companies made an unexpected connection several feet below the surface. As to what passages at arms may have occurred in and about the breach below when it was first opened, those of the surface world are not informed. However, the Alhambra folks presently smelt something burning. They were not long in doubt as to the nature of the fumigation. The odor wafted to them was not that of sandal-wood, neither of frankincense nor myrrh. That which reached them was the hot, pungent, stifling smoke and gas that told of burning pitch-pine. The Kossuth folks had secretly prepared and lighted in a drift of their mine, connecting with the Alhambra shaft, a large bonfire of pine-wood. There being a draught into and up the shaft named, the men working therein soon found themselves in danger of suffocation, and made all possible haste to reach the surface.

The superintendent of the Alhambra mine narrowly escaped losing his life. When he was hoisted to the top of the shaft, some hundreds of feet, he was asphyxiated to the verge of insensibility, and fell back, but luckily caught at the edge of some planks and held on long enough to give those standing near time to snatch him away. Had he fallen to the bottom of the shaft, it would have been certain death, for had he not been dashed to pieces by the fall, the smoke and gases ascending the shaft would have prevented his friends from going down to his assistance, and he must have inevitably perished.

Turning the tables on the Kossuthites was now tried by the men of the Alhambra. They covered the mouth of their shaft with planks and wet blankets, in order, if possible, to force the smoke back into the Kossuth mine. The smoke still appearing to gather in their shaft, several large casks of water were got in readiness, the planks and blankets were raised, and a flood of water turned suddenly down. To what extent this experiment discommoded the Kossuthites was never made public, but the indications were that they received at least a temporary hoist from their own petard, as, shortly after, their numbers above ground were observed to have increased.

During the war, a deserter came over to the Alhambra side and informed them that he had been ordered to drill a hole under the bottom of their shaft, charge it with giant-powder and blow them all to the lower levels of Lucifer's brimstone pit, when they came to work in the morning. Rather than become a second Guy Fawkes, the man threw up his situation;

at least this was his story. The Kossuth folks caused to be published a statement of the affair, in which it was said that their foreman was a second Uncle Toby—he wouldn't harm a fly. As for the smoking business, they had explained to the Alhambra folks the fact that they were about to kindle a little fire to dry their drift, and had told them that in case they found the smoke disagreeable, they could "go aloft."

There is nothing so much dreaded by the miner as fire. When millions of tons of rock begin to settle down he is not frightened. He goes among them when they are being splintered in all directions and are cracking like pistols; coolly puts in double timbers and braces, drives wedges, and builds up sections with rock, for he knows that the settling must be gradual, and that if it is not stopped it can only continue till all the timbers in the place are pressed out as thin as wafers —shortly before which time he will depart. When caves of ore fall from the breasts in a stope, he knows that they only endanger the few men who happen to be under or near them. When the premature explosion of a blast occurs, only those in the immediate vicinity are killed or wounded. But when there is a fire in a mine, the life of every man is in peril.

One great reason why a fire in a mine is so much dreaded, is because there are so few avenues of escape open to the miner. Probably there is but a single shaft (if the mine is connected with no other) and up this, a thousand or fifteen hundred feet, he must go to escape. The smoke and deadly gases may reach the shaft before he arrives, and then he can but sit down and await his death. In case of a fire, there is liable to be a panic. A panic in a church or other building on the surface is always a terrible thing; then what must be a panic in a mine where there are eight hundred or one thousand men, perhaps, all to go up a single shaft a thousand feet, a cage-load at a time? At such times, too, there are explosions of gases which extinguish all of the lights, and the men rushing to and fro are exposed to the danger of tumbling headlong into scores of pitfalls in the shape of chutes, winzes, and other excavations.

All these things being often in the miner's mind give him a wonderful delicacy of nostril. He can scent a fire afar. He knows the smell of burning fuse, of giant-powder, of black powder and of everything with which fire ordinarily comes in contact in a mine, and the scent of these are no more noticed than is noticed the air he breathes on the surface of the earth; but let any unusual substance be ignited and, like the hunted stag, his nose is in the air at once. Let but a splinter of pine be held in a candle, and soon the smell of the burning wood is detected by the miners above and around, and there is a commotion such as is seen when a hive of bees is disturbed— men drop down from, and rush out of, all manner of places where no men were seen before. A bit of burning rag or anything of that nature creates uneasiness.

On one occasion, I was in the 1500-foot level of the Consolidated Virginia mine when a gentleman from San Francisco was getting some samples of ore. These he tied up in small sacks. When he tied up the first he found that he had left his knife above, in changing his clothes. Having no knife with which to cut the string he had tied about the sack, he held it in the flame of a candle and burnt it off. The string was of cotton, and a length of about two inches was consumed in all. In less than a minute afterwards a man from some part of the mine hastily approached, and said to the underground foreman,

"What is burning?"

"Is there anything burning?" inquired the foreman, giving us a wink.

"Yes, sir; there is something burning in this part of the mine."

"What makes you thinks so?"

"Well, I smell it. It's cotton rags or something of that kind."

The foreman then showed the man the cotton string that had been burned off, and he left, giving the San Francisco man a sour look as he departed. Even a dead rat in any close or heated part of the mine annoys the men, and is speedily scented out and sent above. So with everything else from which there can arise the slightest effluvium.

CHAPTER XXVIII

A CHAPTER OF ACCIDENTS

The Adventures of Four Miners—Fixed—A Struggle for Life—
Dangerous Playthings—Exploding with a Scratch—
Those little Copper Cylinders—Loss of Noses and Thumbs

Accidents are of constant occurrence in mines in every part of the world, and the mines on the Comstock lode enjoy no immunity from what appears to be the common lot or prevalent fatality, in this respect. Accidents of every imaginable kind have occurred since the opening of the first mine on the Comstock, still occur, and will continue to occur so long as a mine on the lode is worked.

In the early days, when the miners worked in a primitive way with a hand-windlass, and sunk a small round shaft resembling an ordinary well, they quite as frequently broke legs, arms, and ribs, or were instantly killed, as at the present day. Though men were working in that which was but a straight round hole, only fifty or a hundred feet in depth, they were still able to injure themselves in many ways. They fell out of buckets, or the crank of a windlass was broken, and they went back to the bottom of the shaft "by the run;" a blast exploded while they were yet standing over it; rocks fell out of the walls of their untimbered shafts; or dropped from a bucket as it was being landed at the top of the shaft—in short, they were maimed and killed in ways innumerable and past finding out until the thing had happened.

At the present day, with all manner of safety apparatus, and every avenue to accident seemingly thoroughly guarded, men are wounded and killed the same as before. They are constantly being hurt and killed in new and unheard-of ways—in fact, in every way imaginable. It is a saying in the mines, that these accidents run in streaks; that they occur in groups. When two or three accidents have happened within as many days, you will hear the miners say: "Now, look out, we are going to have a regular run of accidents!" and so it generally turns out. There will often be a dozen accidents within a fortnight, half of them, perhaps, of a fatal character.

More accidents happen to old miners than to men who are new to the business. The old miner sometimes forgets where he is, while "where he is" is just what the greenhorn is all the time thinking about. He is always on the lookout for trouble, and he is always holding on to something that has the appearance of being pretty substantial—particularly when he is in the neighborhood of shafts and winzes; but a man who has worked in the mines for years will walk into a winze or chute in a musing mood, or run a car into the main shaft and be pulled in after it, which is a thing a green hand has never been known to do. Shafts, chutes, winzes, and things of that nature are what he is always looking for, and you couldn't pull him into one of them with any yoke of oxen ever seen in a mine.

Hundreds upon hundreds of accidents have happened in the Comstock mines, some hundreds of them fatal. A large volume would not contain their history. I may furnish a few examples at random—by no means the worst that have happened—in order to give the reader some insight into the nature of the accidents that occur in mines:

In January, 1874, four miners met with quite a thrilling and perilous adventure in the bottom of the main shaft of the Ophir mine. No situation in a sensational play could possibly have been more blood-curdling than that in which the four men found themselves.

They were at work sinking the shaft below the 1700-foot level, and had drilled and charged four holes, all of which they intended to fire at once. All being in readiness, they pulled the bell-rope, striking five bells at the surface, which was the signal for the engineer to lower the cage to the bottom. The signal was answered by the cage coming down to where they stood. They now set fire to the fuses leading into the four blasts in the bottom of the shaft, and then hastened to place themselves upon the cage, when they gave the signal to hoist—this signal being one bell. To their consternation the cage did not move. As each second passed—seconds were long then—they expected to feel the cable taut and the cage start up, but it remained stationary. The fuses were spitting fire and smoke as they burned down toward the powder; still the cage moved not. The signal was again given, but the cage remained as steadfast as before.

The fire was now just boring its way down through the fuses toward the four charges of powder tightly tamped deep in the rock, while the men

Ophir Works, c. 1880s, collodion/albumen, Carleton E. Watkins. California State Library.

were standing helplessly over the fearful spot. One of the men, as a forlorn hope, ran to the charges and wrenched away two of the fuses before they had burned down into the rock below his reach, but when he came to the others he found to his consternation that the fire had passed down into the rock. Rushing back to the cage, he shouted to his companions to save themselves by climbing the cable and timbers.

A fierce struggle for life then ensued. The men scrambled, by means of the cable and the timbers, to get as far up the shaft as possible, each moment expecting the stunning explosion and shower of rocks which they knew must soon come. One of the men, who, it would seem, was completely paralyzed by the terrors of the situation, had hardly made an attempt to move when the explosion came. The three others managed to flatten their bodies against the walls, and screw themselves among the lower timbers of the shaft, and escaped unhurt; but the man below was struck in the forehead, above the right eye, by a small piece of rock which crushed in his skull.

The charges in the bottom of the shaft were usually fired by means of an electrical machine stationed above, but this being out of order at the time, the men took the responsibility of firing the blasts in the manner described, and with the result stated. The trouble in regard to the giving of the last signal was that the bell-rope—one thousand seven hundred feet in length—had got foul on a timber, and no stroke was given on the bell above; thus the engineer knew nothing of the thrilling scene that was being enacted below. Strange to relate, the man who was hurt got well. A surgeon took out a number of pieces of bone, and though a large hole was left in the skull, the man soon regained his senses and complained but little about his injury.

In February, 1874, they had a new blasting experience at the Belcher mine, Gold Hill. They had this experience at the 1200-foot level at a point where a patent drill run by compressed air was being used. It was the practice to drill a number of holes, charge them all with giant-powder cartridges (without any tamping), and explode the whole series at once by means of an electrical battery. On the occasion of the accident, the men on the forenoon shift had fired a number of holes in this way, but one of the holes, it seems, did not explode, the wire thrust into it having slipped out. When the afternoon shift came to work, they supposed this hole was one that had not been finished, and, inserting the drill, began working in it. The concussion of the drill fired the cartridge, and a terrific explosion followed.

At the moment of the explosion there were five men standing about the drill, all of whom were more or less injured. The man who was guiding the drill was struck by a shower of small pieces of rock, which cut his face, and badly cut and bruised his arms and hips, and, in short, peppered him over the whole body. Another man had the bridge of his nose broken, was cut about the head, and had his eyes filled with gravel, and all the others injured were somewhat similarly cut and bruised. Scores of ordinary blasting accidents might be mentioned—accidents that occurred from the premature explosion of blasts; by trying to drill out blasts; by blasts being discharged as the wires from the electrical battery were being inserted; by persons coming unawares upon blasts at the moment of their explosion; and powder and blasting accidents of every conceivable nature—but they can all be imagined.

The caps used in exploding giant-powder and nitro-glycerine are filled with a powerful fulminating powder, and are very dangerous. They explode with the slightest scratch upon their contents. They are about half an inch in length, and their interior diameter is sufficient to admit the end of a piece of ordinary blasting fuse. Persons unacquainted with their uses always appear to be overcome by an ungovernable curiosity in regard to the nature of their contents, the moment they by any means get hold of any of these caps. The first thing they do is to begin probing and scratching in the interior of the little copper cylinders, in order to get out and examine a sample of their contents. It invariably happens that at about the first or second scratch the cap explodes, and the person engaged in prospecting it loses the ends of two fingers and the thumb of the left hand.

In Virginia City and Gold Hill, about one boy per week, on an average, tries this experiment, and always with the same result. In the two towns there must now be scores of boys who lack the ends of the thumb and first and middle fingers of their left hands. On one occasion a boy created quite a sensation in one of the public schools by prospecting the interior of one of these giant-powder caps. The report startled the whole school, frightened the school-teacher nearly out of her wits, and spattered blood and bits of flesh and bone over the faces and books of half a dozen of the pupils. Miners very frequently carry these caps loose in their pockets, often mixed with their tobacco, and thus occasionally get them into their pipes. Several favorite meerschaums have been lost in this way, and the ends of a few noses.

<hr />

CHAPTER XXIX

MINING FATALITIES
Tumbling Down Two Thousand Feet—Blown to Atoms—
A Singular Accident—Automatic Safety—Origin of Accidents—
The Pilgrim in a Coffin—Shuffling Out the "Corpse"

Many miners are killed by thoughtlessly running cars into the main working shafts of the mines, when no cage is standing in the shaft. They probably suppose that a, cage is standing in the shaft ready to receive the car, and, without looking, push it into the open mouth of the shaft.

Accidents of this kind generally happen at the stations of the underground levels. It almost invariably happens when a carman pushes his car into the mouth of a shaft, that he is pulled in after it. The sudden pitching forward and downward of the car, upon the top of the rear end of which he has hold with both hands, causes him to so far lose his balance that he can never regain it, and down the shaft he goes after his car, dashed from side to side against the timbers and planking of the compartments of the shaft into which he has fallen, till the bottom is reached, hundreds of feet below.

The effect of a fall through a vertical shaft 1500 feet in depth is much the same as though a man were shot from the mouth of a cannon and thrown a distance of 500 yards. Mount Davidson stands about 1500 feet higher than

Virginia City, and to fall down a shaft 1500 feet in depth, is much the same as would be a fall from the peak of that mountain (if such a thing were possible) into one of the streets of the town. The body of a man falling a distance of one thousand feet or more, emits towards the latter part of its course, a humming sound, somewhat similar to that heard from a passing cannon-ball of large size.

A few instances will serve to show the effect of a fall of this character upon the human body: A miner who was ascending the Imperial-Empire* shaft, from the 900-foot level, accompanied by six companions, when within one hundred and fifty feet of the surface, spoke of feeling faint. He had hardly spoken before he reeled and fell. As he was falling, his friends caught him by the coat, but as the garment was only thrown loosely over his shoulders, it pulled off, and he fell off the cage and to the bottom of the shaft—a distance of 750 feet. The cage was promptly lowered again and search made for the body, which was found to have fallen into the "sump" or well at the bottom of the shaft. As the sump contained a considerable quantity of water the efforts to fish up the body were not successful, until a good deal of bailing with the hoisting tank (a large tank with a valve in its bottom) had been done.

When the body was at last recovered, it was found to be shockingly mangled. The left foot was pulled off at the ankle joint, the left hand at the wrist, the skull was crushed to pieces, and the bones of the right leg were crushed into small fragments. The face was but slightly disfigured. The left foot was found hanging by the torn tendons, to a timber some 200 feet below where the man fell from the cage. The left hand fell into the sump, and was not found.

Many lives are lost in this way. Men coming up from the heated regions below, when the thermometer indicates a temperature of from 110 to 120 degrees, faint on reaching the cold air at, or near, the top of the shaft. Strangers visiting the mines should always mention the fact to those with them on the cage, if they feel the slightest symptom of vertigo or faintness, as they may then be properly supported.

On one occasion when I was in the Consolidated Virginia mine, a foreman who had gone up with a cage-load of men, some of whom were visitors to the mine, informed us on his return that one of the party just conducted to the surface had made a narrow escape. He said, that just at the moment of reaching the surface, the man fainted, and fell upon the floor of the cage. Had he fallen before, while the cage was in motion, we should probably have had him down with our party at the foot of the shaft,

---

*This is not the name of a single mining company, else it would be as idiotic as it sounds, but the partnership shaft is owned by the "Empire" company and the "Imperial" company—hence the name.

1500 feet below, some minutes before the foreman returned. As our party got on board the cage, I said that a man who felt the slightest degree of uneasiness in the region of the stomach, or of faintness, should at once mention the fact. We were within about 200 feet of the top of the shaft when a gentleman from San Francisco said: "I am beginning to feel sick!" Instantly two or three person took firm hold upon his arms and the collar of his coat, and thus held him until the surface was reached. At the surface he fainted, and a man under each arm carried him into the dressing-room, where he soon revived.

The last time I visited this mine I had but just changed my clothes, and stepped outside of the building, when a miner fainted at the top of the shaft and fell to the bottom.

His head was torn off, his arms and legs were torn off, and all that was left was his trunk, in which not a whole bone remained. The trunk was rolled up in a piece of canvas and brought to the surface, while pieces of his arms, legs, and head were scraped up and sent up in candle-boxes.

In falling, the body bounded from side to side against the walls of the shaft, and, in passing the 1400-foot station, a piece of one of the bones of a leg, with some flesh adhering, flew out of the compartments and fell on the station floor. He was a French Canadian, and had just purchased a lot of trinkets to send home to his wife and family by a friend who was going to leave for Canada the next day.

Just as they were bringing up the remains in the canvas and candle-boxes, this friend arrived to get the trinkets which he was to carry to Canada.

When cages are passing stations, men sometimes put their heads out into the shaft and have them crushed to atoms or pulled entirely off. In June, 1874, a miner was instantly killed by having his head caught by a descending cage at the Crown Point mine. He was at the time in the act of pulling the bell-wire at the station at the 1,000-foot level. As the man went to pull the wire to stop the cage, a friend who was with him turned to a box to get a candle. When he turned again he saw his companion going down with the cage. The cage passed down just below the level of the station, and stopped, having struck the head of the man who had fallen being wedged between it and the side of the shaft. The man left at the station, thinking his friend had gone to the bottom of the shaft, rang up the cage (a double-decker), when the body came up with it, the legs still fast.

In August, 1873, at the Chollar-Potosi mine, a miner ran an empty car into the shaft, and was pulled in after it, falling a distance of 890 feet. In the sump were found floating portions of the shattered car, but the body of the man had sunk to the bottom of the water. By the use of grappling-irons the body, mangled almost out of all semblance to a man, was finally recovered. The whole of the head was gone, down to the under-jaw, both legs and both arms were broken in dozens of places, and, indeed, not a whole bone was left in any part of the body. So torn and mangled was it—so nearly reduced to pulp—that it was found necessary to roll it in a blanket, and lash it to a piece of plank, in order to get it up to the surface. In pulling, the man was dashed from side to side of the shaft, striking against the timbers, now on this side and now on that, tearing all the clothing from his person. Shreds of clothing were found sticking to the shaft timbers in several places. In one place one of his gloves was found lying on a timber, and in another place hung a piece of one of his socks, containing a toe that had been torn from the foot. The pump brought up bloody water for a considerable time after the accident, showing that the whole contents of the sump had been crimsoned.

Although the ingenuity of the many mechanics about the mines is constantly exercised in devising means for the prevention of accidents, and although there are now in operation a great number of useful inventions of this kind, yet men continue to find ways of being wounded and killed never before dreamed of. In all of the leading mines safety-cages are in use; also, safety incline-cars, or "giraffes," and these have saved scores of lives. With the safety-cage or giraffe in use the miners do not fall to the bottom when a cable breaks. The safety apparatus instantly comes in play, and the cage or giraffe is at once stopped, at the point of ascent or descent at which the cable parted.

In all the hoisting works there is a strong cover of latticework over the mouth of each compartment of the main shaft, to prevent men from stumbling or thoughtlessly walking into it.

When the cage comes up the shaft, the iron shield or "bonnet" on its top picks up this cover, and holds it up out of the way, the floor of the cage meantime filling the mouth of the compartment, and guarding it in place of the cover; when the cage descends it leaves the cover behind on the opening through which it passed down, somewhat like the cunning little animal that pulls the door of its hole in after it when it retreats into the ground.

With all these provisions for protecting life and limb, accidents continue, and must ever continue to happen, as there are so many things against which neither the owners of mines nor the miners themselves can guard. In case of a cable parting, for instance, the men who are on the cage are protected by the safety apparatus, but the upper part of the cable is liable to spring backwards and kill the engineer standing at his engine fifty or sixty feet in the rear of the shaft, quite at the opposite end of the building.

A heavy cable of steel wire whipping back in this way, will cut a broad road through the whole length of the ceiling of a building, taking off large joists and beams as though they were so many bars of soap. Huge fly-wheels of many tons' weight occasionally burst asunder, tearing the sides and roof of the works to pieces, killing or wounding all who may be in the way of the flying fragments; boilers sometimes explode, and leave hardly a vestige of the works in which they stood; men are caught in the cog-wheels of the machinery; and, in short, there is no safety either above or below ground.

Below the surface, however, the accidents are most numerous and terrible. In the examples given by means of which to illustrate the fearful velocity attained by the human body in falling through a space of from i00o to 1500 feet, it may be thought that I have selected the most shocking I could find; but such is not the case. It is the usual experience that in falling such a distance, the hand, foot, or head of a man coming in contact with a timber toward the bottom of a shaft, is cut or torn off. It is by no means unusual for the remains of men to be collected at the bottom of a shaft and sent to the surface in candle-boxes; to such an extent are the bodies and limbs of many who fall into shafts rent and scattered. On one occasion of this kind, when the jury of inquest had finished hearing the testimony and were sitting silent round the fragmentary remains, considering their verdict, a man came hurriedly in, with a candle-box under his arm, approached the foreman, and said to him in a reverent tone, "Wait a moment, please—I've got some more of him."

Speaking of undertakers, reminds me of a little story: One night a Virginia City policeman while going his round, found an inebriated "pilgrim" reposing on a bench in front of an undertaking establishment. The officer shook the fellow until he awoke him from his drunken slumber, and then explained to him that unless he found other and less public quarters he should be obliged to escort him to the station-house. The pilgrim sat up, and rubbing his eyes, explained to the officer that he was a stranger in the town; that he had but fifty cents in his pocket, and, the night being warm, he had concluded to sleep out of doors, and save his money to pay for a breakfast the next morning. Not being a hard-hearted man the officer told the fellow that he might finish his sleep, provided he would get up and move out of sight before people were astir in the streets.

Passing the same way, in the course of an hour or two, the officer found that his man had rolled off the bench, and was lying at full length in the empty case of a coffin that was standing at the edge of the sidewalk, close beside the bench. Rousing his "pilgrim" again, the officer told him he must "get out of that!"

"Out o' what?" growled the fellow.

"Why, out of that coffin!" said the officer—though it was only one of those coffin-shaped cases in which coffins are shipped.

"Who's in a coffin?" asked the fellow, evidently becoming somewhat interested.

"Why, you are!" said the officer.

"Not if I know it, I ain't!" said the pilgrim.

"Well, I know it," said the officer sharply," and if you don't get out of it pretty shortly it will be the last of you. Don't you know that if these undertakers get up in the morning and find you snoozing away there, they'll clap a lid on that coffin, screw it down, hustle you out to the graveyard and bury you, then send in a bill and make the county pay your funeral expenses. It's just one of the tricks that our Washoe undertakers like to play!"

Crawling out of his narrow quarters, the fellow rubbed his eyes and gazed at the coffin-shaped case for some time, then said:

"I'd like to know what sort of a dod-rotted set of undertakers you've got out here in this country, anyway, that go and set rows of coffins 'longside the sidewalks, fur to ketch corpses?" and without waiting for an answer, he shuffled away to find safer quarters.

Virginia City Mine Cave-in, 1867, collodion/albumen, Timothy H. O'Sullivan.
Library of Congress Prints and Photographs Division.

CHAPTER XXX

THE TOWNS OF THE BIG BONANZA

The First-born of Virginia City—A Comical Newspaper-Office—
Growing Like Mushrooms—Undermined—
Among the Rubbish-Dumps—Big Loads—"See for Yourselves"

As not much has yet been said in regard to the principal towns of the "big bonanza," I shall now devote a few chapters to Virginia City and Gold Hill, but more particularly to railroads, water-works, lumber-flumes, and other things intimately connected with the growth and prosperity of those towns, and the cheap and economical working of the mines.

To begin, I may say that the two towns, Virginia City and Gold Hill, which were formerly over one mile apart, are now united, and the dividing line cannot be distinguished. The population of Virginia City is a little over twenty thousand, and that of Gold Hill about ten thousand, according to the directory for 1875.

Virginia City, as has already several times been mentioned, lies along the eastern face of Mount Davidson, on a broad sloping plateau, and is surrounded on all sides by rugged hills and rocky mountain peaks. In the early days, these hills were covered with a sparse growth of nut pine-trees—a sort of stunted pine, in size and form of trunk and branches somewhat resembling an ordinary apple-tree—but the demand for fuel for the mines, mills, and domestic uses, swept all these away in a very few years, and even the stumps have been dug up and made into firewood by the Chinese.

Gold Hill is situated at the head of Gold Cañon, on the south side of Mount Davidson, and is shut in by the walls of the ravine, along which stand the principal buildings of the town. A ridge about two hundred feet in height, lies between the two towns, which is known as the "Divide." The Divide is covered with buildings, and is a fine airy location—a place where the "Washoe zephyr" waltzes to and fro at will.

In 1859, there were some scattering nut pine-trees on the sides of the mountains about Gold Hill, but these soon went the way of those about Virginia City, and now all the hills and mountains, as far as the eye can reach, are brown arid treeless. The only covering of either hills or valleys is the eternal and ever-present sage-brush.

This shrub grows to the height of from one to four feet, and its leaves are not green, but of an ashen-grey—much the color and much the same in shape as the leaves of the common garden sage. The botanical name of this shrub is *artemisia tridentata*. Through the scanty covering of sage-brush the rocks everywhere rise up as though they might be the bones of the land peeping through its skin.

Bird's Eye View of Virginia City, 1875, lithograph, Augustus Koch. Library of Congress Geography & Map Division.

The first house built in Virginia City was a canvas structure, eighteen by forty feet in size, erected in 1859 by Lyman Jones, one of the pioneers of the country. Mrs. Jones was the first white woman who lived where Virginia City now stands, and her daughter Ella, was the first white child seen in the camp.

The first white child born in Virginia City was a daughter of J. H. Tilton, one of the pioneer wagon-road builders of the country. She was born on the 1st of April, 1860, and was named Virginia. She still lives in the town in which she first saw the light.

In Virginia City are to be seen as many large and substantial buildings, both public and private, as in any town of like population on the Pacific Coast. The Catholics, Episcopalians, Presbyterians, Methodists, Baptists, and other leading Christian denominations have fine and costly churches in the town, and these are as well attended as the churches in any other land. The Masons and Odd Fellows have fine halls, and both societies are in a very flourishing condition.

There are in the city most of the orders and societies found in other large towns; as, the Knights of Pythias, Ancient Order of Druids, Improved Order of Red-Men, Knights of the Red Branch, Champions of the Red Cross, Crescents, Irish Confederation, Ancient Order of Hibernians,

Caledonia Society, Society of Pacific Coast Pioneers, two Turn Vereins, Miner's Union, Printers' Union, and several similar societies.

In the way of benevolent associations, there are, the Virginia Benevolent Society, Italian Benevolent Society, Hibernian Benevolent Society, St. Vincent de Paul Benevolent Society, and several others. In the city is St. Mary's Orphan Asylum and School (under the charge of the Sisters of Charity), built at the cost of about $100,000, and the St. Vincent Hospital, which cost $40,000 or $50,000. In the town are five military companies—the National Guard, Emmet Guard, Washington Guard, Montgomery Guard, and the Nevada Artillery.

In the several wards of the city are handsome, commodious and comfortable school-houses, and there are several flourishing Sunday-schools, conducted under the auspices of various religious societies.

Knights of Pythias Hall, 1933, gelatin silver, Robert Kerrigan, Historic American Buildings Survey. Library of Congress Prints and Photographs Division.

The city is lighted with gas, is supplied with pure water from the Sierra Nevada Mountains, and has telegraphic communication with all parts of the world.

Two daily papers are published in Virginia, the *Territorial Enterprise,* and the *Evening Chronicle.* The *Enterprise* is a morning paper, and the *Chronicle,* as its name implies, is published in the evening. The *Enterprise* is the oldest newspaper in Nevada. The first number (it was then a weekly), was issued at Genoa, on Saturday, December 18th, 1858. This was the year before the discovery of silver in Nevada, and Genoa was then a town of about 200 inhabitants. The office of publication was removed to Carson City, in November, 1859, and remained there till November, 1860, when it was removed to Virginia City. The office in which the *Enterprise* was first published in Virginia City, was a small, one-story frame building with a shed or lean-to on one side, and was a queerly arranged establishment. The proprietors had the shed part fitted up as a kitchen and dining and lodging-place. Bunks were ranged along the sides of the room, one above another, as on shipboard, and here editors, printers, proprietors, and all hands "bunked" after the style of the miners in their cabins. A Chinaman, "Old Joe," did the cooking, and three times each day the whole crowd of "newspaper men" were called out to the long table in the shed to get their "square meal."

The "devil" went for numerous lunches between meals, and often came flying out into the composition-room with a large piece of pie in his mouth, and the old Chinaman at his heels.

The Virginia City Fire Department contains four fine steam fire engines, one Babcock engine and two or three hand engines, hook and ladder apparatus, and all else required in battling with fires in a town of the size. There are also in various places hydrants, to which hose can be attached and powerful streams thrown, in case of a fire occurring in their neighborhood.

In the business part of the city are many large and substantial fire-proof brick and stone structures. There is a large frame theatre and several halls in which balls and lectures are given. The rooms of the Washoe Club are as fine as those of most similar clubs in large cities, and were fitted

Miner's Union Hall, 1933, gelatin silver, Robert Kerrigan, Historic American Buildings Survey. Library of Congress Prints and Photographs Division.

up at a cost of about $75,000. They contain a library, reading and billiard-rooms, dining-room, and all else required for the accommodation of members. Many fine oil paintings adorn the walls, and the furniture and all the appointments are costly and elegant.

Owing to the fact that the plateau on which the town is built slopes rapidly to the east, buildings that are but three stories high in front, are in places five or six stories in the rear. This configuration of the ground is of great advantage to those who wish to make a display in cellars and basements.

On account of the altitude, the atmosphere is very light and thin, but the climate is as healthful as that of any town on the Pacific Coast. When the town was first settled, for some reason never explained, a notion prevailed that it was a bad place for children—that children could not be reared there; but this was a great mistake. Finer or more robust children can be seen in no town or city in the Union than those of Virginia. They grow like mushrooms. This is probably because they have to contend with but a small amount of atmospheric pressure—there is nothing to prevent their shooting up and expanding in all directions.

It is a well known-known scientific fact that animals, as sheep and deer, found on elevated mountain ranges, have larger lungs than the same species when inhabiting places at or near the level of the sea; therefore the children of Virginia City are likely to be large-lunged and broad-chested when they arrive at maturity. The air being thin and light, it is necessary for those breathing it to inhale it in greater volume than would be required in breathing the denser atmosphere of places at or near the level of the sea, and to

Gold Hill, 1867, collodion/albumen, Timothy H. O'Sullivan. Library of Congress Prints and Photographs Division.

do this, there must be a proper and proportionate expansion of the lungs. Children born in the country provide themselves with a proper supply of lungs without any looking after, but adults sometimes find the stretching of their lungs to the required standard, a somewhat unpleasant operation.

The town of Gold Hill is well supplied with churches and schools, societies of all kinds, fire apparatus, and all else that should be found in a place of its population and business. What has been said of Virginia City in regard to these matters, will apply equally well to Gold Hill. The town has one daily paper, the *Evening News,* contains the works of many of the leading mines of the Comstock, and is a lively, bustling business place—is full of the thunder of machinery and the shriek of steam-whistles. Although but a mile from the centre of Virginia, the temperature of Gold Hill is about five degrees higher, winter and summer, than in the first-named town.

The whole town is undermined, and may be said to stand on a foundation of timbers. The ground worked out underneath the town has, however, been so thoroughly filled in with timbers and waste rock that there is no danger of it caving, though it is immediately but slowly settling. To the eastward of the town, and behind a large hill on which a portion of the town stands, a crevice has opened which is nearly a mile in length, and in places over two feet in width. This shows that the whole place, hill and all, is gradually "subsiding." Both Virginia and Gold Hill have frequently been swept over by great fires, involving a loss of property to the extent of many millions of dollars. The burnt districts, however, have always been speedily rebuilt. The houses destroyed have been replaced with better and more substantial structures, and consequently the towns have improved in appearance by means of the fires they have passed through, though many persons have suffered great loss.

A striking feature of both towns, and one which at once rivets the attention of all strangers, is the immense piles of rock seen in the neighborhood of all the principal mines. In these great dump-piles are heaped the rock and earth extracted in sinking the shafts, running the drifts, and in making other underground excavations. Persons from the Atlantic States, who are in the habit of judging of the depth of a well or other excavation by the amount of rubbish seen on the surface, are greatly surprised at the size of the dumps, and their first question is: "Did all that dirt come out of one mine?" As soon as they see one of these mountains of waste rock, they begin a mental calculation as to the size of the hole left in the ground. It is no small pile of rubbish that comes out of a shaft six feet wide, twenty-two feet long, and from 1,500 to 2,500 feet deep—to say nothing of the *débris* from innumerable drifts, crosscuts and winzes.

The dump-piles of the Savage and Hale and Norcross, mining companies, situated in the southeastern part of Virginia City, are among the largest on the Comstock, the shafts of these mines having been carried down to a depth of nearly 2,500 feet; the waste-dump of the Bullion mine, at the north end of Gold Hill, is also of great size. In many instances, the waste rock hoisted out of the mines is utilized in filling in and leveling the ground sur-

C & C Waste Dumps. 1890, dry plate/collotype, James H. Crockwell. Library of Congress Prints and Photographs Division.

rounding the buildings above the shafts. In this way, acres of level ground are made, and the number of the unsightly dump-piles is much diminished.

J. P. Jones, United States Senator from Nevada, has a residence in the town of Gold Hill, where live his mother and three of his brothers, one of whom, Samuel L. Jones, is superintendent of the Crown Point mine, one of the leading mines of the Comstock. The mother of the Senator, although she might reside in any one of the cities of the Union, prefers to make her home at Gold Hill—is really in love with the wild beauty of the surrounding hills, and the thunder of machinery, and all the sights, sounds, and excitements incident to life in the midst of the silver-mines.

Omnibuses ply between Gold Hill and Virginia City, and soon street-cars will be running between the two towns, and perhaps as far as Silver City, a distance of five miles. Gold Cañon, between Gold Hill and Silver City, is filled with mills, hoisting-works, business houses and residences, and from the place last named to Virginia City, a distance of five miles, it may be said to be one town.

In the early history of the Comstock towns, huge "prairie schooners," laden with goods, merchandise, and machinery, from over the Sierras, thronged the streets. Each "schooner" was drawn by a team of from fourteen to sixteen mules, and each mule was provided with a chime of bells, suspended in a steel bow or arch above the bearskin housings of his collar. A few of these teams sufficed to fill a whole street with music, but it was a kind of music that sounded best when heard at a distance and far up in the mountains. These great teams are now no longer seen. The only big teams are those employed in hauling quartz to mills that are off the line of the railroad, and in similar local freighting.

Many of the wagons still in use are capable of hauling immense loads. In that country they have a way of hitching a second and smaller wagon behind the first, which second wagon is called a "back-action." Often as many as three and four wagons are thus coupled together in a train. In this way twenty-four cords of wood have been hauled by a team of twelve animals; ten horses hauled on one occasion 73,050 pounds of quartz, and on another occasion twelve horses hauled 84,000 pounds of ore a distance of eight miles. Four wagons were used in each instance. These were, of course, unusually large loads, and were hauled on account of there being some bantering between certain team-owners, but the teamsters of Nevada usually haul heavier loads than are hauled elsewhere.

Being in Gold Hill, on one occasion, with two Western farmers who wished to see some of the mills and hoisting works of the place, I was somewhat amused at their anxiety to satisfy themselves in regard to the weight of the loads hauled by the Washoe teamsters. They had been told a good many stories in regard to big loads, and had made many memorandums of the same, but still could hardly credit what had been told them.

Seeing a wagon-load of ore being weighed, they said: "Now we have caught them in the act! Now we shall see for ourselves. They are just weighing that load. Two—four—six horses. We shall now see what is a Washoe load for six horses!"

As the wagon was driven off the scales, I said to the man who had done the weighing: "These gentlemen are farmers from the West. They are curious to know the weight of the load of ore that has just been driven off the scales."

"It weighed just 28,000 pounds," said the man of the scales. The farmers looked at each other and smiled.

Weighing the Load, Gould & Curry Mine, Virginia City, 1862, collodion/albumen, attributed to Charles L. Weed (Lawrence & Houseworth). Library of Congress Prints and Photographs Division.

"You may see for yourselves," said he of the scales; "the weights used, as you see, are still on—count them up."

"No;" said the farmers; "we are satisfied; but it will never do for us to speak of the loads hauled in Washoe, when we get back among our neighbors."

Said the weigh-master, "I'll tell you what is a fact; a team of ten horses, drawing a train of four wagons, hauled a load of ore which weighed over 73,000 pounds along this street on which you stand."

Said the Iowa farmer to the Ohio farmer: "Let us go; we don't want to hear too much!"

The man at the scales then offered to show them a whole bookfull of weights of loads hauled, if they would step into his office; but they had seen and heard enough, and, as they said—"More than we dare speak of at home."

At present, the greater part of the ore that is not reduced near the mines, is exported by rail, and, indeed, the railroad does most of the heavy freighting of the whole country.

CHAPTER XXXI

CONSTRUCTION OF RAILROAD LINES

Travelling in a Circle—Through the Six Tunnels—Crooked Roads—
Side-Tracks and Other Devices—The Way the Iron Horse Goes—
The Men On the Line—Timed by Telegraph

The Virginia and Truckee Railroad, runs from Virginia City to Reno, on the Truckee River, at which point it connects with the Central Pacific Railroad. The length of the road is 52 miles, and it is undoubtedly the crookedest road in the United States—probably the crookedest in the world.

Ground was broken for the road, on the 19th of February, 1869, and in eight months after, it was doing business between Virginia and Carson City—a distance of twenty-one miles.

The heavy work lies between these points—nearly all of the tunnels, deep cuts and sharp curves—and for the greater part of the distance the road was cut through solid rock.

From Virginia City to the Carson River, a distance of 13 miles, the track is a continuous incline. The maximum grade is 116 feet. The maximum radius of curves is 300 feet, and the degrees of curvature amount in all—between Virginia and Carson City—to 6,120; or, in other words, are equal to going seventeen times round a circle. Thus, in traveling from Virginia City to Carson—twenty-one miles—one passes through a sufficiency of curves to carry him round a circle, 360 degrees, seventeen times. This surpasses any "swinging round the circle," political or otherwise, that has ever been done in the United States.

There are on the road six tunnels of an aggregate length of 2,400 feet. All of these tunnels are lined through their whole length with zinc, as a protection against fire. Wood is the fuel used on all the locomotives, and in tugging up the mountain with heavy trains such a Vesuvius of sparks is poured from the smoke-stacks, that without the protection of the zinc lining the woodwork of tunnels would constantly be taking fire.

As I have said, the heaviest work on the road was between Virginia and Carson City. The cost of this section of 21 miles of road was $1,750,000, or about $83,000 per mile, which includes permanent way and graduation—that is, with the track laid, and the road ready for business. The cost of the whole road was about $3,000,000. From Virginia City to Reno, the terminus of the road, the distance in an air-line is 16 1/2 miles, while by rail it is 52 miles. By the wagon-road, over the mountain, the distance from Virginia to Reno is only 22 miles. Over this wagon-road, known as the Geiger Grade, supplies of all kinds, including heavy machinery for the mines, were brought to Virginia, previous to the completion of the railroad;

the hauling being done by teams of ten, twelve, fourteen, and sixteen mules each, attached to huge wagons known as "prairie schooners."

As will be seen, by the distance from Virginia City to Reno in a direct line, the traveler not only swings seventeen times round the circle, in going from Virginia to Carson, but has almost completed a grand circle when he reaches the end of the road and connects with the Central Pacific. He starts off in a southerly direction, and so continues until Carson is reached, when he turns and travels northward until he arrives at Reno.

Crown Point Railroad Trestle, Gold Hill. c. 1890, dry plate/collotype, James H. Crockwell.
Library of Congress Prints and Photographs Division.

At Steamboat Springs, between Carson City and Reno, the traveler who starts from Virginia has traveled forty miles by rail, yet it is but 5 1/2 miles from the place whence he started, Steamboat Springs being situated just back or west of Mount Davidson, on the eastern face of which Virginia City stands. Between Virginia and Carson the only piece of straight road is one little stretch about 5½ miles in length, but between Carson and Reno are found several miles of road tolerably straight. The road does an immense local carrying business. From 500 to 800 tons of ore are daily carried over it to the mills on the Carson River, and return trains bring great quantities of wood, lumber, and timber for use at the mines. From thirty to as high as forty-five trains per day pass over that part of the road lying between Virginia and Carson City.

Notwithstanding the crookedness of the road, trains run over it at a high rate of speed, as the road is kept in perfect order and steel rails are used on the mountains where short curves most abound. So crooked is the road that in places, in going down the mountain with a long train, the locomotive seems to be coming back directly toward the rear car, when directly it gracefully sheers off and heads down the mountain again, the train being thrown into the form of the letter S, reminding one of what the Bible says of the "way of a serpent on a rock."

Gold Hill, 1876, collodion/albumen, Carleton E. Watkins. California State Library. An "S" curve in the Virginia and Truckee railroad tracks is visible in the lower left.

From Reno—over the whole length of the road—come vast amounts of machinery, stores, and supplies of all kinds for the mines and mills, and goods and merchandise for all of the towns along the river and in the mines. Along the road are a great number of side tracks and switches leading to mills and mining works. Some of these are of considerable length and, as more are constantly being constructed, the indications are that the added length of these will possibly exceed that of the main road.

Branch roads, all of a permanent and substantial character, are being built to the shafts of the leading mines, to be used in taking in machinery, wood, timber, lumber, and other supplies, and for sending ore out to the mills. Many of these side-tracks are laid in places where it would be almost impossible to construct an ordinary wagon-road, and to see trains darting out of tunnels, and rushing along the face of almost perpendicular hills, disappearing behind a great tower of rock one moment, and the next coming in sight again and swinging round a second rugged tower, looks somewhat too "lively." All the wonderful engineering required in the construction of these side-tracks, as well as in the main road, was done by Mr. I. E. James, an old resident of the country—the man who has done nearly all of the intricate surveying that has been required in the leading mines on the Comstock lode. Although one of the most modest and unassuming men on the Pacific Coast, with him nothing in the way of engineering appears to be impossible.

Virginia & Truckee Railroad "E" Street Station. c. 1890, dry plate/collotype, James H. Crockwell. Library of Congress Prints and Photographs Division.

After having seen the Virginia and Truckee Railroad, all will say that there is no region so rugged but that a track for the "iron horse" may be found over it and through it in all directions. When engineers, conductors, and other railroad men from the Atlantic States, first begin running on the Virginia and Truckee road they promise themselves that they will make a very short stay, but in a few months they begin to take pride in their ability to run on such a road; they like the excitement of it and consider that those who only run on roads that are straight and level know but little about the beauties of the business—about railroading as a fine art. Although these men run trains down the mountains from Virginia City to Carson River swinging seventeen times round the circle and going at a fearful rate of speed, yet serious accidents very seldom occur. The trains are timed by telegraph and the stations are so numerous that the conductors are always well informed in regard to the trains on the road, and their position.

Surveys have been made for a narrow-gauge railroad from Virginia City to Reno, and thence to the northward, along the eastern base of the Sierra Nevada Mountains. This road will run northward from Virginia—starting out in an opposite direction from that taken by the Virginia and Truckee Railroad, and will pass over some very rough country, but will reach Reno by a shorter *route* than the other road named. The object in building this narrow-gauge road is the tapping of the vast forests of pine lying along the eastern slope of the Sierras.

CHAPTER XXXII

An Engineering Triumph
Spring Business—Tapping the Hills—Dams Constructed—
What Mr. Shussler Did—The Big Water-Pipe—Testing the Siphon—
Great Rejoicings—The Work Completed

Another work that has been of great benefit to the towns along the Comstock, and to all the mining and milling companies in and about the towns, and along the cañons below, was the bringing of an ample supply of pure water from the Sierra Nevada Mountains.

In the early days, when the first mining was done at Virginia City and Gold Hill, natural springs furnished a supply of water for the use of the few persons then living in the two camps. For a time after the discovery of silver, these springs, and a few wells that were dug by the settlers, sufficed for all uses, but as the towns grew in population, an increased supply of water was demanded. A water company was formed and the water flowing from several tunnels that had been run into the mountains west of Virginia City for prospecting purposes, was collected in large wooden tanks, and distributed about the two towns by means of pipes. At length the tunnels from which this supply was obtained began to run dry, and a water famine was threatened. It then became necessary to set men to work at extending the tunnels further into the hills to cut across new strata of rock. This increased the supply for a time, but, at length, the whole top of the hill into which the tunnels extended appeared to be completely drained.

Early in the spring, when the snow was melting, they afforded a considerable supply; but in the summer, when water was most needed, the tunnels furnished but feeble streams and these were much impregnated with minerals, one of the least feared of which was arsenic. The ladies rather liked arsenic, as it improved their complexion; made them fair and rosy-cheeked— almost young again, some of them. The miners did not object to arsenic; as, while it did not injure their complexion, it strengthened their lungs—made them strong-winded, and able to scale mountains. (Every man of them hungered to hunt the wild chamois.) But there were other minerals held in solution in the water—those that caused diarrhoea for instance—that were not so well thought of.

The nearer hills having thus been drained, tunnels were run into such of those further away as were of sufficient altitude to permit of streams from them being brought to the two towns. These tunnels were run for no other purpose than to find water. A hill was examined with a view to its water-producing capacity. It was found that those which rose up in a single sharp or rounded peak were not rich in water. The best water-producers were hills on the tops of which there were large areas of flat ground. That portion of a range of mountains which contained on the summit a large shallow basin surrounded by clusters of hills or peaks was found to yield largely and for a long time, when tapped by a tunnel run under the basin or sink at the depth of three or four hundred feet.

Dams were constructed across the outlets of these basins to hold back the water from the melting snow, in order that it might filter down through the earth to the tunnels. At the mouths of the tunnels heavy bulkheads of timbers and plank were constructed, to keep back and dam up the water where it could be kept cool and pure. Where deep shafts stood near the line of these tunnels, ditches were dug to them along the sides of the hills, and the water formed by the melting of the snow in the spring was let into them. All manner of devices, in short, were resorted to for the purpose of keeping in and upon the hills all of the moisture from snow or rains that fell upon them. Yet one after another these hills failed. When once the tops had been thoroughly drained it appeared to require all of the water that fell on them in any shape during winter to reach down into and moisten them to the level of the tunnels. Finally, there were in all many miles of these horizontal wells. All the hills from which water could be brought, for miles away to the northward and southward of Virginia and Gold Hill, were tapped, thousands on thousands of dollars being expended in this work. When a reservoir of water was first tapped in a new hill there would be poured out a great flood for a few days; this would then fall to a moderate stream and so remain for a month or two, when it would begin to dwindle away. The water from the many tunnels was collected by means of small wooden flumes or troughs, winding about the curves of the hills for miles, and in summer, when most wanted, the sickly streams from the more distant tunnels were lost by leakage and evaporation before having finished half their course to the towns.

Virginia City and Gold Hill were frequently placed upon a short allowance of water, and it was seen that a great water famine must soon prevail in both towns, in case the tunnels that had been run into the mountains were depended upon for a supply. The Virginia and Gold Hill Water Company then determined to bring a supply of pure water from the streams and lakes of the Sierra Nevada Mountains—from the regions of eternal snow.

The distance from Virginia City to the first available streams in the Sierras was about twenty-five miles; but between the Virginia range of mountains and the Sierras, lay the deep depression known as Washoe Valley,—in one part of which is situated Washoe Lake. The problem to be solved in bringing water from the Sierras to Virginia City was how to convey it across this deep valley.

Mr. H. Schussler, the engineer under whose supervision the Spring Valley Water Works, of San Francisco, were constructed, was sent for, and crossing the Sierras he made an examination of the route over which it was proposed to bring the water. He acknowledged that the undertaking was one of great difficulty. To convey the water across the deep depression formed by Washoe Valley would demand the performing of a feat in hydraulic engineering never before attempted in any part of the world. This was to carry the water through an iron pipe under a perpendicular pressure of 1,720 feet. This feat, however, Mr. Schussler said could be performed, and he was ready to undertake it at once.

Surveys were made, in the spring of 1872, and orders given for the manufacture of the pipe. To make the pipe was the work of nearly a year. The manufacturers were furnished with a diagram of the line on which it was to be laid and each section was made to fit a certain spot. When the route lay round a point of rocks the pipe was made of the required curve, and other curved sections were required when the line crossed deep and narrow ravines.

The first section of pipe was laid, June 11th, 1873, and the last on the 25th, of July the same year. The whole length of the pipe is seven miles and one hundred and thirty-four feet. Its interior diameter is twelve inches, and it is capable of delivering 2,200,000 gallons of water per twenty-four hours. It lies across Washoe Valley, in the form of an inverted siphon. The end at which the water is received rests upon a spur from the main Sierras, at an elevation of 1885 feet above Washoe Valley. The outlet is on the crest of the Virginia range of mountains, on the eastern slope of which are situated the towns of Virginia and Gold Hill. The perpendicular elevation of the inlet above the outlet is 465 feet. Thus is brought to bear a great pressure which forces the water rapidly through the pipe.

The water is brought to the inlet through a large wooden flume, and at the outlet is delivered into a similar flume, twelve miles in length, which conveys it to Virginia City. The pipe is of wrought iron, and is fastened by three rows of 5/8-inch rivets. At the lowest point in the ground crossed, the perpendicular pressure is 1,720 feet, equal to 800 pounds to the square inch. Here the iron is 5/16 of an inch in thickness, but as the ground rises to the east and west, and the pressure is reduced, the thickness of the iron decreases through 1/4, 3/16, down to 1/16.

In its course, the pipe crosses thirteen deep gulches, making necessary that number of undulations, as it is throughout its length laid at the depth of 2½ feet below the surface of the earth. Besides these, there are a great number of lateral curves round hills and points of rocks. There was just one place and none other for each section of pipe as received from the manufactory. At each point where there is a depression in the pipe there is a blow-off cock, for the removal of any sediment that may collect, and on the top of each ridge is an air-cock, for blowing off the air when the water was first let in, and at other times when the pipe is being filled. The pipe contains no less than 1,150,000 pounds of rolled iron; is held together by 1,000,000 rivets, and there were used in securing the joints 52,000 pounds of lead, which was melted and poured in from a portable furnace that moved along the line as the work of laying the pipe progressed. Before being put down, each section of pipe was boiled in a bath of asphaltum and coal-tar, at a temperature of 380 degrees. At the first filling of the pipe a stream of water, about the thickness of a common lead-pencil, escaped through the lead packing of a joint, at a point where the pressure was greatest. This struck against the face of a rock, and, rebounding, played upon the upper side of the pipe. The water brought with it from the rock a small quantity of sand or grit, perhaps, but at all events it soon bored a hole through the top of the pipe, and from this hole, which shortly became two or three inches in diameter, a jet of water ascended to the height of two hundred feet or more, spreading out in the shape of a fan toward the top.

When this break occurred, a signal smoke was made in the valley, and the lookout at the inlet of the pipe on the mountain spur shut off the water. Over each joint in the pipe was placed a cast-iron sleeve or band, weighing 300 pounds, and within this sleeve was poured the molten lead which served as packing. In all there were used 1,475 or 442,500 pounds of these sleeves, and but three out of the whole number proved faulty, and failed to sustain the strain brought upon them, and of 12,640 sheets of iron used in the pipe, but one bad one was found. As it would have been a great task to test each section of the pipe by hydraulic pressure at the manufactory, the engineer proposed to bring the whole under the required strain at once, after they were put down. He began the pressure with a perpendicular height of 1,250 feet in the column of water; increased it to 1,550, to 1,700, and finally to 1,850, being 130 feet more than the pipe would be required to sustain when in actual use.

During these experiments, men were stationed at the inlet of the pipe, at its outlet on the summit of the Virginia range, and at various points through the valley, as lookout men. They made their signals by means of a smoke during the day, and a fire by night—a trick learned from the Paiute Indians.

As the water came surging down through the great inverted siphon from the elevated mountain spur, and began to fill and press upon the parts lying in the deeper portions of the valley, one after another the blow-off cocks on the crests of the ridges crossed, opened, and allowed the escape of the compressed air. Compared with what was heard when these cocks blew off, the blowing of a whale was a mere whisper. The water finally flowed through the pipe and reached Gold Hill and Virginia City on the night of August 1, 1873. Early that evening a signal fire was lighted in the mountains at the inlet of the pipe, showing that the water had again been turned on.

As the pipe filled, the progress of the water in it could be traced by the blowing off of the air on the tops of the ridges through the valley, and at last, to the great joy of the engineer and all concerned in the success of the enterprise, the signal fire at the outlet, on the summit of the Virginia range, was for the first time lighted, showing that the water was flowing through the whole length of the pipe.

When the water reached Virginia there was great rejoicing. Cannon were fired, bands of music paraded the streets, and rockets were sent up all over the city. Many persons went out and filled bottles with this first water from the Sierras, and a bottle of it is still preserved in the cabinet of the Pacific Coast Pioneers.

Previous to the laying of this pipe for the Virginia and Gold Hill Water Company, the greatest pressure under which water had ever been carried in any part of the world was 910 feet. This was at Cherokee Flat, California, and was also under the supervision of Mr. Schussler.

In 1875, the Virginia and Gold Hill Water Company laid a second pipe alongside of the first. This has an inside diameter of ten inches. Instead of being fastened with rivets it is lap-welded, and is the largest pipe ever made in that way. As there are no rivet-heads in it to produce friction, it delivers the same amount of water as the larger pipe, namely, 2,200,000 gallons per twenty-four hours.

Previous to 1875, the supply of water was principally obtained from a stream known as Hobart Creek, but, in the year named, the works in the mountains were extended by pushing the supply flume through to Marlette Lake, within the basin of Lake Tahoe, a distance of eight and a half miles, and a total distance from Virginia City of thirty-one and a half miles. In order to reach and tap Marlette Lake it was necessary in one place to run a tunnel 3,000 feet in length under a dividing ridge—the ridge forming the rim of the Lake Tahoe basin. Marlette Lake covers over 300 acres of ground, and in the middle is 30 or 40 feet in depth.

Connected with the works are several reservoirs that hold from three million to ten million gallons of water. Signal fires are no longer necessary along the line of the works, as there is now set up a line of printing telegraph, with numerous stations between Virginia City and Marlette Lake. Marlette Lake lies at an altitude of 1,500 feet above C street, Virginia City, and the water is brought in at such a height above the town that it can everywhere be carried far above the highest buildings, and streams from the hydrants are thrown with great force and effect in case of a fire occurring near them.

There is now not only an ample supply of water in the city for all town and domestic uses, but also for the boilers of the many hoisting works, and for use in the several mills where the ores of the Comstock mines are reduced. The cost of the waterworks was over two million dollars.

CHAPTER XXXIII

How Wood is Cut in the Sierras

The Forests of the Mountains—A Daring Leap—The Rafts on Lake Tahoe— Descending the Flumes—Vanishing Forests—Coal Deposits of Nevada

The Comstock lode may truthfully be said to be the tomb of the forests of the Sierras. Millions on millions of feet of lumber are annually buried in the mines, nevermore to be resurrected. When once it is planted in the lower levels it never again sees the light of day. The immense bodies of timber now being entombed along the Comstock, will probably be discovered some thousands of years hence, by the people to be born in a future age, in the shape of huge beds of coal, and the geologists of that day will say that this coal or lignite came from large deposits of driftwood at the bottom of a lake; that there came a grand upheaval, and Mount Davidson arose, carrying the coal with it on its eastern slope.

Not less than eighty million feet of timber and lumber are annually consumed on the Comstock lode. In a single mine—the Consolidated Virginia—timber is being buried at the rate of six million feet per annum, and in all other mines in like proportion. At the same time about 250,000 cords of wood are consumed.

The pine-forests of the Sierra Nevada Mountains are drawn upon for everything in the shape of wood or lumber, and have been thus drawn upon for many years. For a distance of fifty or sixty miles all the hills of the eastern slope of the Sierras have been to a great extent denuded of trees of every kind; those suitable only for wood as well as those fit for the manufacture of lumber for use in the mines. Already the lumbermen are not only extending their operations to a greater distance north and south along the great mountain range, but are also beginning to reach over to the western slope—over to the California side of the range.

Long since, all the forests on the lower hills of the Nevada side of the mountains that could be reached by teams, were swept away, when the lumbermen began to scale the higher hills, felling the trees thereon, and rolling or sliding the logs down to flats whence they could be hauled.

Saw Mill, Lake Tahoe, 1862, collodion/albumen, attributed to Charles L. Weed (Lawrence & Houseworth). Library of Congress Prints and Photographs Division.

The next movement was to erect saw-mills far up in the mountains, and to construct from these, large flumes leading down into the valleys, through which to float wood, lumber, and timber. Some of these flumes are over twenty miles in length, and are very substantial structures, costing from $20,000 to $250,000 each. They are built on a regular grade, and, in order to maintain this grade, wind round hills, pass along the sides of steep mountains, and cross deep cañons; reared, in many places, on trestle-work of great height.

These flumes are made so large that timbers sixteen inches square and twenty or thirty feet in length may be floated down in them. In a properly constructed flume, timbers of a large size are floated by a very small head of water; and not alone single logs, but long processions of them. Timbers, wood, lumber—in fact, all that will float—is carried away as fast as thrown in. When a stick of timber or a plank has been placed in the flume, then ends all the expense of transportation, as, without further attention, it is dumped in the valley—twenty miles away, perhaps. By means of these flumes, tens of thousands of acres of timber-land are made available, that could never have been reached by teams.

In some places, where the ground is very steep, there are to be seen what are called gravitation flumes, down which wood is sent without the aid of water. These, however, are merely straight chutes, running from the top to the bottom of a single hill or range of hills. In places, they are of great use, as through them wood may be sent down within reach of the main water-flume leading to the valley. Nearly all of the flumes have their dumps near the line of the Virginia and Truckee Railroad, or some of its branches or side-tracks, and in these dumps are at times to be seen thousands upon thousands of cords of wood and millions of feet of lumber.

In some localities a kind of chute is in use, made by laying down a line of heavy timbers in such shape as to form a sort of trough. Down these tracks or troughs axe slid huge logs. When the troughs are steep, the logs rush down at more than railroad speed, leaving behind them a trail of fire and smoke. Such log-ways are generally to be seen about the lakes, and are so contrived that the logs leap from them into water of great depth, as otherwise they would be shivered to pieces and spoiled for use in the manufacture of lumber. Occasionally, in summer, a daring lumberman mounts a large log at the top of one of these chutes, high up the mountain, and darting down at lightning speed, with hair streaming in the breeze, takes a wild leap of twenty or thirty feet into the lake. In one place, in order to obtain a supply of water sufficient to run two lumber-flumes, a tunnel was run a distance of 2,100 feet at a cost of $30,000. This tunnel passed through a ridge, and tapped a lake lying within the basin of Lake Tahoe.

Flume Discharge, 1876, collodion/albumen, Carleton E. Watkins. California State Library.

Yerington, Bliss, & Co., one of the heaviest lumbering firms in the Sierra Nevada Mountains, have built a narrow-gauge railroad from their saw-mills on the shore of Lake Tahoe to the head of Clear Creek, on the first or eastern summit of the Sierras. The road is eight miles in length, and is used in the transportation of lumber from the mills of the company to their large flume at the head of Clear Creek. This railroad passes through a tunnel 500 feet in length, which was the only tunnel and the heaviest piece of work on the road.

Logs are rafted across Lake Tahoe to the mills, from all points. The lake being of great size, and all of its shores and the slopes of the surrounding mountains being heavily timbered, the company have command of a vast area of pine-forests. Through the waters of the lake and its numerous bays, they reach out and up into the mountains in all directions, gathering the pines into their mills, carrying them, in the shape of lumber, up their railroad, and then shooting them through their big flume down over all the hills till they land in Carson Valley.

This is all very well for the company and for the mining companies, who must have lumber and timber, but it is going to make sad work, ere long, with the picturesque hills surrounding Lake Tahoe, the most beautiful of all the lakes in the Sierra Nevada Mountains. Where tall pines now shade all the shores and wave on all the mountain slope, nought will shortly be seen, save decaying stumps and naked granite rocks. But timber and lumber are imperatively demanded, and the forests of not only these hills but of a thousand others, will doubtless be sacrificed.

The rafts of logs are towed across the lake by small steamboats. This rafting is of a novel character. The logs forming the raft are not pinned or in any way fastened together. The steamboat runs up to a bay or other place where logs are lying, and casts anchor. A boat is then sent out which carries a long cable strung full of large buoys. This cable is carried round a proper fleet of logs, as a seine is carried round a school of fish. The steamer then weighs anchor and starts across the lake, towing along all the logs about which the cable has been cast. No matter how rough the lake may be, the logs remain in a bunch, being attracted the one to the other, and clinging together as bits of stick and chips are often seen to do when floating on a lake or stream.

On the side of the lake opposite the mills of Yerington, Bliss, & Co., a man who has a contract for delivering logs in the water ready for rafting, does his "logging" with a locomotive. He has laid a railroad track, some six miles in length, through the heaviest part of the forest, and instead of hauling the logs to the lake with oxen, in the old-fashioned way, rolls them upon low trucks, and hauls a whole train of them away at once, with his locomotive.

At the edge of the lake the track is laid under water for a considerable distance, and the train being run upon this track, the logs are floated off the low cars, and are ready for rafting.

Other large mills besides those of the company named, are engaged in devouring the forest surrounding Lake Tahoe. About five million feet of lumber per month are turned out by the several mills at the lake, and each summer about three million feet of timbers are hewn in that locality. Many of the sugar-pine trees about Lake Tahoe are five, six, and some even eight feet, in diameter; all are very tall and straight.

At a point in the Sierra Nevada Mountains, about eleven miles from the town of Reno, on the Central Pacific Railroad, Messrs. Mackay and Fair have a lumber-flume over twenty miles in length. This flume was built through an exceedingly rugged region, and cost $250,000. It taps a tract of twelve thousand acres of heavy pine-forest owned by the parties named. The land is estimated to contain 500,000 cords of wood, 100,000,000 feet of saw-logs, and 30,000,000 feet of hewn timber; all of which will be brought down to the Virginia and Truckee Railroad, through the flume. A printing telegraph extends along the whole line of the flume, by means of which orders are transmitted to all points.

There are a great number of these flumes reaching up into the Sierras from the valleys of Nevada, and soon it will be necessary to build railroads to haul the lumber up to the heads of these from the California side of the mountains, as has been done by Yerington, Bliss, & Co. No means of transporting wood, lumber, and timber is or can be cheaper than these flumes. When once a plank or stick of wood has been dropped in at the head of the flume it is already as good as at the other end, twenty or thirty miles away. The flumes are far ahead of railroads of any gauge, broad or narrow, as a means of cheap transportation for wood and lumber.

Each season, from 80,000 to 100,000 cords of wood are floated down the Carson River. This wood is cut high up in the Sierras, at the head-waters of the Carson and its tributaries, and is sent down from the mountain slopes for many miles, in flumes of the same kind as those in use for the transportation of lumber. The wood is collected on the banks of the river, ready to be launched at the proper and auspicious moment.

Contrary to what most persons would suppose, the proper time for starting one of these drives of eighty or one hundred thousand cords of wood, is not when there is a big freshet, but at the falling of the stream after a freshet; that is, on the heels of a grand overflow. If the wood be put into the river at a time when its waters are over the banks, it floats away into the flats and out over the valleys, whence it is almost impossible, but at too great cost, to get it back into the channel, and thus it is as good as lost. The lumbermen are for this reason careful not to put their wood into the river while there is danger of there occurring a sudden flood, which would lift it above the banks and scatter it broadcast over the country.

The time for starting the drive is just after the great flood of the season—after the thaw which sweeps the greater part of the snow from the mountains. Then the wood comes down huddled in the channel, and covering the whole surface of the water, for fifty miles or more. At points where there are sloughs or bayous leading out of the river, booms are stretched to keep the wood in the straight and narrow way. French Canadian lumbermen and Paiute Indians are generally employed in making these drives. As the wood must be followed up and kept moving, it is a wet and laborious business.

The time is not far distant when the whole of that part of the Sierra Nevada range lying adjacent to the Nevada silver mining region will be utterly denuded of trees of every kind. Already, one bad effect of this denudation is seen in the summer failure of the water in the Carson River. The first spell of hot weather in the spring now sweeps nearly all the snow from the mountains, and sends it down into the valleys in one grand flood; whereas, while the mountains were thickly clad with pines, the melting of the snow was gradual, and there was a good volume of water in the river throughout the summer and fall months.

The prevailing breezes in Nevada are from the west—indeed the wind seldom blows from any other quarter than the west—which is directly over the Sierra Nevada Mountains. In passing over the fields of snow, on the summit of the Sierras, the breezes are cooled, and the summer weather in Nevada is thus rendered delightful. But when once the mountains shall have been denuded of their timber, all the snow on both slopes will be swept away by the first warm weather of spring—as it is now swept away on the eastern slope—when a marked increase in the heat of the summers in Nevada is likely to be experienced.

Railroads are being pushed, both north and south, along the eastern base of the Sierras, with no other object than to strip the mountains of the forests in which they are now clothed, in the course of time. We may therefore look to see the whole range lying bare in the sun. When this shall come to pass, the Great Basin region to the eastward will be a perfect furnace in summer.

There must come a day when wood will be scarce and dear, and some other fuel must be found. Coal from the Rocky Mountains is now extensively used at Virginia City, but it costs about as much as wood. The problem may be solved in a wonderful deposit of lignite recently opened by the Virginia City Coal Company, and it is to be hoped that the mine will prove to be all that it now promises.

This coal deposit is on El Dorado Cañon, eleven miles from Dayton, ten from Carson City, and seventeen from Virginia City. Such an extensive deposit of lignite as this has seldom been found in any country. There are two strata of it, each fifteen feet in thickness. The first vein was cut at the depth of forty feet, and forty feet below this was found the second stratum, of the same thickness (fifteen feet) as that above. Both veins dip to the southwest, at an inclination of four inches per foot, under a mountain of great size. The company have erected steam-hoisting and pumping machinery, and have sunk their main shaft to the depth of 180 feet, at which point they drifted out until they cut their lower vein, at a point 460 feet distant from the bottom of the shaft. They then followed the stratum back to the shaft, for the purposes of ventilation, and were all the way in coal of an excellent quality. The coal burns well and freely, and must prove of great value as soon as it can be cheaply brought to the several towns where it is needed, as it appears to exist in almost inexhaustible quantities. A narrow-gauge railroad is to be built from the mine to the neighboring towns.

One or two mills have been run with coal, but the cost of hauling it on wagons is too great to make it much more economical as a fuel than the wood and coal already in use.

CHAPTER XXXIV

The "Six Hundred and One"

*A Mysterious Society—Afraid—Led Forth to Death—
The Fate of Perkins—"Another Man Gone"—Kirk's Fate—
Venturing Too Far—"You See He Stayed"*

In the spring of 1871, there sprang into existence in Virginia City, a secret organization known as "Six Hundred and One." It was a "Vigilance Committee" similar to that organized in San Francisco in the early days. The object of the organization in Virginia City, as far as is known, appears to have been the speedy execution of persons guilty of cold-blooded murder, and the banishment of dangerous men from the city.

At the time "601" made its appearance, there were frequent incendiary fires, many murders had been committed, robberies were common, and there prevailed an unusual amount of lawlessness. The idea of those belonging to the organization seems to have been to strike terror to the hearts of evil-doers by the summary punishment of desperate characters who, with little or no provocation, killed peaceable citizens.

"Six Hundred and One" was so quietly and secretly organized that it appeared to spring into existence in a single night. The first that was publicly known of the organization was on the night of March 24, 1871, when Arthur Perkins Heffernan, who, a short time before, had shot down a man in cold blood at the bar of the saloon in the principal hotel of the town, was taken from the County Jail and hanged.

In the morning, when the coroner went to cut down the body of Arthur Perkins, as he was commonly called, there was found pinned upon it a paper on which were the figures "601." This was taken to be the name of the "vigilante" organization, and "601" it has ever since been called. It is supposed to be still in existence, and it is said that meetings are frequently held, in which the "situation" is discussed. The members are supposed to be leading citizens and business men of the town, but just who they are is not certainly known, as they always appear in masks when out on business. Perkins was taken from the jail and hanged, at about 1 o'clock in the morning. The majority of the residents of the city knew nothing of the occurrence until they arose, yet many persons were still on the streets and lingering about the saloons and other places of public resort, and not a few met "601" face to face, greatly to their astonishment.

The meaning of the appearance of armed and masked men in the streets at such a time in the night was rightly guessed by most persons, as soon as they had time for reflection. The members of the organization had quietly taken possession of the armory of one of the military companies of the town, where they armed themselves with muskets and bayonets, drew on their white masks, and suddenly sallied forth.

Their first move was to place a strong guard at the four corners of the streets round the block in which stood the jail. The appearance of these guards at the street corners was the first intimation that the people of the town had that anything unusual was transpiring. Men started to go to their homes, when they suddenly found themselves confronted by a score of masked men, who brought to bear upon them a row of glittering bayonets, and said; "Go back!" Most persons went "back" without a word, but a few wanted to know "what's up!" and "what was the reason they could not pass?" when they were again told to go back or they would "find out what was up!"

Some persons after being thus turned back, went round the block and tried at the next street corner, where they were again met by a glittering array of bayonets and the stern order: "Go back!"

A woman who happened to be scouting about the town at the unseemly hour when the net was drawn about the block, found herself caught in it. She tried every corner and, at each, found a row of bayonets held in front of her. Not a word was spoken anywhere, and this silence and the sight of the arms and masks so frightened her that she galloped about at a very lively rate for a time, then suddenly disappeared, no one knew whither. Some printers also going home from their work on a morning paper, were halted, and their foreman, a fussy, fidgety old fellow, recently from San Francisco, was frightened nearly out of his wits. When he found half a dozen bayonets at his breast, and saw before him the masked faces, he was sure he had fallen into the hands of robbers.

"Don't shoot! for God's sake don't shoot!" he cried. "I'm a poor miserable old printer and haven't got a cent!"

Said a voice: "We know you, you old fool. You only want to go two doors above here. I guess we'll just escort you!" Then turning to the printers, who stood back, heartily enjoying the fright of their foreman, the same masked man said: "Come on boys, you lodge in the same house, I believe!"

Four or five men stepped out and marched the printers within the lines, seeing them to and through their own door.

"Gentlemen, will we be quite safe here?" asked the still anxious foreman, thrusting his head out at the door, after it was thought he was secured within.

"You are safe inside," said one of the masked men, "but if you come out again we'll blow the whole top of your head off!"

The head instantly disappeared.

Every few minutes some belated citizen was halted and turned back, at one or another corner of the beleaguered block, giving him an opportunity of returning to his favorite saloon, telling of the wonder and taking another drink. The armed and masked men at the corners were all that any one saw;

what was going on within the guarded square no one knew, but all were able to make a tolerably correct guess.

Suddenly the heavy boom of a cannon shook the town and disturbed the stillness of the night. Instantly, and as though by magic, the armed and masked men disappeared from the streets, going no one knew whither. The boom of the cannon, which was fired in the eastern part of the city, at an old military post occupied during the rebellion by a provost guard, told that Arthur Perkins was no more.

While the masked men stood on guard at the corners of the streets, Perkins was hanged in the western suburb of the city. It appears that twenty or thirty members of "601" who were within the lines, quietly went to the Courthouse, and, with a crowbar, wrenched open the front door. They then quickly advanced to the private office and sleeping-apartment occupied by the sheriff and a deputy. These officers were surprised in their beds, their weapons were secured, and the keys of the jail and cells taken from them. All the rest was now easily done. Arthur Perkins and a man who, in a fit of jealousy, had shot and wounded his wife, occupied the same cell. When the heavy tramp of the vigilantes was heard in the outer room, Perkins suspected its meaning.

"They have come for me," said he to his companion. "I may as well bid you good-bye; this is my last night on earth!"

When the masked men entered the room in which were ranged the cells, they advanced to that occupied by Perkins, and unlocking the door, said: "Come out, we want you."

The man who was in the cell with Perkins was terribly frightened. He supposed that he, also, was wanted—indeed thought a clean sweep of all in the jail was to be made. He started to march out with Perkins, but was pushed back, one of the men saying: "Go back! we don't want you." These, the man afterwards said, were the most comforting words he ever heard in his life. In his excitement Perkins was unable to get on one of his boots. "Never mind the boot," said one of the vigilantes, "where you are going you will not need boots!"

Perkins was marched by the back way through the Courthouse, was hurried to a point near the old Ophir works, and there, when a convenient timber was found, was hanged. He stood on a plank placed across the mouth of a tunnel and, when the fatal moment came, did not wait for the plank to be pulled from under his feet, but sprang into the air as high as he could leap, in order to fall with as much force as possible and thus end his life quickly and with little pain.

On the 26th of September, 1846, the ship *Thomas H. Perkins* sailed from New York, having on board a portion of Stevenson's regiment of California volunteers. The *Perkins* was commanded by Captain Arthur, and Arthur Perkins

Heffernan was born on the vessel during her passage between New York and Rio de Janeiro. He was named after the vessel and her captain. His father was a corporal in Company F; F. J. Lippite commanding; his mother was a sister of the notorious robber, Jack Powers, who was also at that time a member of company F. A girl was born on the ship *Thomas H. Perkins* about the same time that young Heffernan first saw the light, and it was an understood thing by those on board the vessel that this girl, called Alta California, should, at the proper age, become the wife of Arthur Perkins Heffernan,—an event that never came to pass. Both children were baptized at Rio, at the American Embassy, by the chaplain of the United States' ship *Columbia,* then lying in Brazilian waters.

On the 18th of July, 1871, "601" hanged George B. Kirk, a man who was considered a very bad character, who had killed a man in California, and who had lately been released from the Nevada State Prison. He had received a note (ticket of leave, as these notes came to be called) from "601," ordering him to leave the city. He left, but after being gone some time ventured back. Acquaintances told him that to attempt to remain in the town would cost him his life, but he thought otherwise.

The first night he was in the city he was found at the house of a female acquaintance, and, at about 11 o'clock, he was captured by "601," placed in a buggy, and taken out to the north end of the town, to the Sierra Nevada mining works, and there hanged from the timbers of a flume. Again the cannon in the eastern part of the city boomed, and as the single, heavy shot echoed through the mountains those who heard it said: "Ha! Six Hundred and One! Another man gone!" Had Kirk remained away from the city he would not have been harmed. When he came back in defiance of the order he had received, commanding him to absent himself from the city, the vigilantes found it necessary to make an example of him, as otherwise all who had received "tickets of leave" would have flocked back to the town.

Since the hanging of Kirk, "601" has not found it necessary to "deal with" any others of the desperadoes of the country. A wholesome fear of the organization is felt. All know that a man who behaves himself in even a half-way decent manner is in no danger from the vigilantes.

As the reader may desire to know what the regularly constituted authorities do in the case of an execution of the irregular character of those of "601," I give the verdict of the coroner's jury in the case of Kirk:

"We find the deceased was named Geo. B. Kirk; was a native of Jackson county, Missouri, aged about 36 years; that he came to his death on the 18th day of July, 1871, by being hanged by parties unknown to us."

The morning after the hanging, when Kirk's remains were lying at an undertaking establishment, a man who appeared to be a stranger in the city, observing something of a crowd about the door, approached, and looked in at the body lying in the coffin.

"Man dead?" asked he of a person standing near. "Yes, sir;" shortly answered the person questioned. Fidgeting a little the stranger tried it again: "How did he die?"

"Hung." was the laconic reply.

"Hung! Ah, hung himself?"

"No sir, he was hanged by '601'—by the Vigilantes."

"What did they hang him for?"

"He had been notified to leave town, but after leaving he came back."

"When a man has been notified to leave the town, can't he never come back here again and stay?"

"Yes, sir."

"Yes? Then how is this?"

"Well he came back and"—pointing to the coffin—"you see *he stayed.*"

CHAPTER XXXV

THE WASHOE "ZEPHYR"

An Unpleasant Breeze—"Sleep No More"—A Jackass On the Wing—
Weird Scenes—The Artist's Soul—Light and Shade—
Mountain Scenery—The Giants of the Sierras

The "zephyr" is one of the peculiar institutions of Washoe, and as such is worthy of special mention. At certain seasons—generally in the fall and spring—furious gales prevail along the Comstock range. In and about Virginia City these wind-storms are particularly severe. The city being built on the eastern slope of Mount Davidson, at an elevation of over 6,000 feet above the level of the sea, and the mountain rising abruptly above the city on the west, to the height of about 2,000 feet above the town, fierce whirls and "sucks" are formed in the lee of the mountain.

The prevailing winds of the country come from the west, and from this quarter also comes the "zephyr." It is probably a straight-ahead gale before it strikes Mount Davidson, but upon that towering mass of granite it splits. Currents pass round the north and south sides of the mountain, meet in the city, and waltz about in the shape of whirlwinds of from eighty to two hundred horse-power. To complicate things still more, a third portion of the gale comes howling directly over the peak of the mountain, and plunges down into the town among the whirlwinds, knocking them right and left whenever it encounters them.

It is no doubt this particular and peculiar current of the gale whipping down over the summit of the mountain, that produces the remarkable vertical atmospheric action observable during the prevalence of a first-class zephyr. A breeze of this kind will snatch a man's hat off his head and take it vertically a hundred feet into the air; then, as he stands gazing after it, the hat suddenly comes down at his feet, as though shot out of a cannon, and lies before him as completely flattened out as though it had been struck with a sledge-hammer.

The action of the zephyr is sometimes much the same as that seen in the leathern sucker with which boys are able to lift stones of considerable weight. A furious gust falls upon the flat tin roof of a building, then suddenly bounding upward rips a great hole in the tin. The whirlwinds and winds of all other kinds—for in the same minute, and almost at the same instant, it blows fiercely from every point of the compass—then enter the hole, seize upon the roof, and very soon complete its wreck. A section of tin twenty feet square, may be seen to flap in the air, like the loose sail of a vessel at sea, but with a clashing sound that may be heard a mile away; then, on a sudden, the whole sheet is ripped off, and goes sailing through the air like a piece of paper, landing, perhaps, two or three hundred yards away, and passing over half a dozen houses during its flight.

Of late these "zephyrs" have not been so furious and destructive as in years past. Then the tin on half a dozen roofs was often to be seen flapping in the breeze at the same moment, each section of roofing giving out a roar more startling than would be the combined sheet-iron thunder of a dozen country theatres of average enterprise.

"Sleep! Sleep no more! the zephyr doth murder sleep." After a night of such wild work, the stranger within the gates of Virginia City is likely to make his appearance very early in the morning, red-eyed and wrathy.

I remember to have heard a gentleman who sported a bunch of hair on each cheek, about the size of a coyote's tail, thus express himself one morning after such an elemental carnival:

"Wind! talk about wind! Why, the wind 'owled at such a rate last night that I thought it would bring the bloody 'ouse down about my ears. Blast it! when it 'owls like that a fellow can't sleep, you know! The clark o' the 'otel calls it a Washoe zephyr—zephyr be blowed, it was a bloody gale, you know!"

Not to exaggerate, I may say that one of the good old-fashioned Washoe zephyrs, even in the present condition of the town, not only howls itself, but also makes Virginia City howl, and would make Rome or any other place howl. At times such clouds of dust are raised, that, viewed from a distance, all there is to be seen is a steeple sticking up here and there, a few scattering chimneys, an occasional poodle-dog, and, perhaps, a stray infant drifting wrong end up, high above all the house-tops. Down below in the darkness, gravel-stones are flying along the street like grape-shot, and all the people have taken refuge in the doorways.

Such ripping of signs, threshing of awnings, rattling and banging of iron and wooden shutters—such tumbling about of chimney-pots and sections of stovepipe, is seldom seen or heard in any less favored town.

Out on the Divide, a high part of the city where the wind has a fair sweep (this is generally of nights, when strangers are not likely to see it), the air is filled with dust, rags, tin cans, empty packing-cases, old cooking-stoves, all manner of second-hand furniture, crowbars, log-chains, lamp-posts, and similar rubbish. Hats! More hats are lost during the prevalence of a single zephyr than in any city in the Union on any election held in the last twenty years. These hats all go down the side of the mountain and land in a deep gulch known as Six Mile Cañon—the place where the Johntown Jasons found the first tag-locks of the big bonanza.

After a very severe zephyr, it is said, drifts of hats fully fifteen feet in depth, are to be seen in the bed of the cañon just named. All these hats are found and appropriated by the Paiute Indians, who always go down to the cañon the next morning after a rousing and fruitful gale, to gather in the hat crop. When the innocent and guileless children of the desert come back to town, they are all loaded down to the guards with hats. Each head is decorated with at least half a dozen hats of all kinds and colors—braves, squaws, and pappooses are walking pyramids of hats.

There is a tradition in Virginia City, that in the spring of 1863, a donkey was caught up from the side of Mount Davidson—far up on the northern side, near the summit of the mountain—and carried eastward over the city, at a height of five or six hundred feet above the houses, finally landing near the Sugar Loaf Mountain—nearly five miles away. Those who witnessed this remarkable instance of the force of the zephyr, say that as the poor beast was hurried away over the town, his neck was stretched out to its greatest length, and he was shrieking in the most despairing and heart-rending tones ever heard from any living creature. The oldest inhabitant sometimes tries to spoil this story by saying that what was seen was an old gander, the leader of a flock of wild geese, lost in the storm, and baffled in his attempt to make headway southward against the hurricane. It may be so, but most folks along the Comstock cling to the donkey and sneer at the gander.

Although there is hardly a green spot to be seen in any direction, yet there are, in many places in Washoe, landscapes that will always at once attract attention. From Virginia City, perched as it is, high on the side of Mount Davidson, is obtained a grand view of a vast wilderness of hills, mountains, and desert plains. The eye sweeps eastward over untold scores of hills and valleys to the tall peaks of the Humboldt mountains, distant not less than one hundred and eighty miles. Hill rises beyond hill far away in all directions, each hill exhibiting in all its outlines a stern individuality, and each rearing aloft a rock-crowned and treeless head.

In the interstices of these peaks, each of which stands a dark-browed and sullen Ajax, we catch glimpses of deserts that lie white and glittering, long journeys away, yet we almost feel our eyes scorched as we gaze, by their far-darted shimmer. These spots that so glitter and twinkle, far away through the brown of the hills, are great plains of salt and alkali—deserts more hungry and sterile than the wilds of Sahara. In the view before us we have the "hoar austerity of rugged desolation," yet there dwells in it a grandeur that is almost awful, and a something very fascinating.

Every artist who looks upon this weird and unsmiling landscape feels his soul stirred with a desire to paint it. No man has yet painted it—no man will ever paint it. There is that in it which no cunning in colors can reach—no skill in drawing can express. The only way in which an artist can approach the subject is by painting what he feels, not what he sees. This vast landscape is at all times grand and worthy of study, but when its many moods are evoked by elemental disturbances, it becomes wildly beautiful.

Often in summer several thunder-showers are to be seen in progress at the same moment, far out in the wide wilderness, each separated from the other by a broad belt of blue sky and bright sunshine. While one dark storm-cloud hovers over the city, showering its moisture upon the thirsty earth, another is seen a whole day's journey to the eastward, creeping along some parched desert, with the rain, in slanting columns, pouring upon the white and shining fields of alkali, and still others hang about the mountain peaks in various directions, sending down red bolts of lightning upon their dark granite summits. Away to the northeast the tall, turreted peaks of Castle District rise against an inky sky, each line of their rugged spires distinctly traceable, while to the southeast, looming high above the horizon, are seen, through a shower, the ashen-hued mountains of Como.

To the right of these, and miles on miles further away—far south of the Carson River—stand many tall, purple peaks, here and there one among the highest tipped with sunlight. Eastward, below the level of the city and almost in the centre of the picture, the Sugar-Loaf rears its rounded top, over which, and far beyond, stretched partly in sunlight and partly in shadow, lies the valley of the Carson. A green fringe of cottonwoods, visible along all the river's eccentric meanderings, is the only tinge of green in all the broad land before us. Here and there are seen short reaches in the river that glitter like burnished silver in the rays of the evening sun.

A long table-mountain cuts short our view of the valley and river, but over this mountain we see, spread out like a vast sheet of parchment, the Forty-mile Desert, over which shadows of clouds move as slowly as in early times crawled across the same sands the long trains of weary pilgrims, wearing out the way to the land of gold, over the Sierras. Far beyond, where the cloud-shadows move in black squadrons across the desert sands—quite two days' journey beyond—are reared against the eastern sky the Humboldt mountains, whose white peaks might pass for the tombs and cenotaphs of the giants of the olden times. Some of these are half hidden in patches of dark mist, or veiled by slanting columns of rain, while others stand in the full glory of the sun. But in this scene we have a constant change of light and shade. Peaks that were a moment since sooty-black, suddenly flash up and become golden and brilliant, soon again to resume their dusky robes, while neighboring peaks stand forth clad in the garments of their departed glory.

As the sun sinks lower, night is seen to settle into the deeper cañons, and take shelter behind the lower hills, and the shadow of Mount Davidson goes forth as a giant, and stretches darkness from hill-top to hill-top everywhere.

CHAPTER XXXVI

THE RED PROPRIETORS

The Paiutes and the Other Reds—A Strange Pair—Old Winnemucca—
The Woman Who Made the Indians—The Indians' Ancestress—
The Paiute Brave—Big Injuns

As we have now been a long time among the mines, the reader will probably not object to a little more information concerning the Indians of the country, before making another plunge into the "lower levels" of the Comstock lode.

The Paiute Indians were formerly the owners of all that region in which the Comstock mines are situated; also, of nearly all of the western part of the State of Nevada, though the Washoe Indians held Carson, Eagle, Steamboat, and Washoe Valley, the Truckee Meadows and the country in the neighborhood of Lake Tahoe. The Shoshones owned what is now Eastern Nevada, and they still live in that region.

The Paiutes range nearly up to Oregon, and far south toward Arizona. They have always been great travelers, and as early as in the days of the "Mission Fathers," were in the habit of crossing the Sierra Nevada Mountains and visiting the Pacific seaboard every summer; a journey still taken by many of them each year, as not a few Paiute women are married to Spaniards who own large ranches in the vicinity of Santa Cruz and other towns in the southern part of California.

Originally, it is said, the Paiutes, the Utes, the Pitt River Indians, the Queen's River Indians, and some other small bands, were all Shoshones, but the tribe multiplied rapidly, and at last was spread over such a vast extent of country that one chief could not govern all. They then broke up into large bands that took the names which now distinguish them as tribes.

The Paiutes belonged to the Ute band at the time that the original Shoshone tribe broke up through its own weight and unwieldy size. They settled about the lakes—Humboldt, Pyramid, Carson, and Walker—and were therefore called Pah-Utes; that is, water Utes, "pah" being the word that signifies water among all the Indians of the Great Basin region, Finally, the Utes and Pah-Utes, or "Paiutes"—as the name is now generally, though improperly, written—became separate tribes.

Group of Paiute Indians, 1862, collodion/albumen, attributed to Charles L. Weed (Lawrence & Houseworth). Library of Congress Prints and Photographs Division.

The language of all the tribes in the Great Basin region and far to the northward still retains a sufficient number of the words of the original Shoshone tongue to enable members of any one of the present tribes to make themselves understood by their neighbors. When pressed to go far back into the dim and distant past, beyond the time when they were all Shoshones, the Paiutes have a legend according to which they owe their origin to the marriage of a white wolf and a woman. The white wolf came from the far north, and the woman, who was the daughter of a great chief, came from the south.

The Paiutes, according to the legend, are the descendants of this strange pair. Away north, on the summit of a high bluff on Pitt River, is to be seen a huge white rock which, when viewed from certain points, bears a striking resemblance to a wolf in a recumbent position. To this day, many of the Paiutes point to this rock and say that it is their great father—the father of all the Paiutes—that he never died, but was changed into this rock, in which he still lives. I once told this story to an old and very intelligent Paiute, and asked him what he thought about it. He said: "Who told you this story, Tom or Natchez?" referring to two of the sons of old Winnemucca, the head chief.

"I have heard it from Tom, and also from many other Paiutes," said I.

"O," said he, "it is only a story of times long ago. It was while we were still Shoshones, that this happened. You have heard the story the way the old women tell it."

He then proceeded to say that, a very long time ago, there was a great war between a tribe of Indians living in the north, the name of whose chief was White Wolf, and a tribe living in the south. For years they fought every summer, and many on both sides were killed. Still, the old men would stir up the young men to continue the strife. At last both tribes grew weak and weary of the long war, and at a big council it was arranged that the White Wolf should marry the daughter of the chief of the tribe against which he had so long drawn a hostile bow, and thus all difficulties were settled. The two tribes settled down and lived together, all as Shoshones.

The old Indian then proceeded to give me the true and most ancient tradition that has been handed down in the tribe, in regard to the origin of the Indians living in the Great Basin. He said that the Indians were made by a man and his wife, who came from he knew not where. They made the Indians of clay and something else, taken out of the water, the English name of which he did not know. After the Indian men and women were made, the man made all kinds of animals; as bears, deer, antelopes, buffaloes, rabbits, wolves, and the like. The woman made the birds and the flowers, and all the fishes in the rivers, and the grass and the nut-pine trees, and all the bushes that bear berries.

The man taught the men to make bows and arrows, spears with which to catch fish, and nets for use in fishing and taking rabbits. He also taught them to build and navigate tule (a giant bulrush) boats, for all the country was then covered with great lakes, and the tops of the present hills and mountains were islands. The woman taught the Indian women to make baskets and how to prepare food and do all things proper to be done by women.

After they had done all these things the mysterious pair took their departure, going away to the southward.

"Do you expect them to return some day?" I asked.

"How can I say?" answered the Indian. "They came of their own accord at first."

"Do you hear the old men of the tribe speak of them?"

"Often"

"Do they think the man and his wife will come back?"

"How do they know? They only know that they are gone."

"That is all the old men know?"

"Well, they sometimes say they have gone south to the big water—maybe they live in the big water. Who knows?"

When an Indian begins to say "who knows," he has then told you about all he knows in regard to the point upon which you are questioning him. All the Indian could say was that the pair came and did their work of creation, and then went away to the southward.

This tradition bears a striking resemblance, in many respects, to that of the Peruvians in regard to the appearance among them of Manco Capac and his sister and wife, Mama Ocllo Huaco; also, to the Mexican tradition in regard to the Huastecas, the strange family that came, whence, no one knew, to the mouth of the Panuco River, headed by Quetzalcoatl, priest and lawgiver, and who afterwards disappeared in the direction of Guatemala. The disappearance of Quetzalcoatl is strikingly like that of the pair mentioned in the Paiute tradition. Strange as it may appear, a prehistoric skull was found at the depth of several hundred feet in the Comstock vein which, on being sent to the Academy of Sciences, San Francisco, was found to exhibit peculiarities to be found only in the skulls of the ancient Peruvians, the people to whom appeared Manco Capac and his wife.

What is said in the Indian traditions, about nearly the whole face of the country having been covered with water in ancient times, is undoubtedly true. In all the valleys throughout the Great Basin are to be seen traces of water, and on the sides of the hills water-marks have been left that are visible at the distance of a mile, and can be traced for many miles. In places, there are four or five of these water-marks, showing the gradual subsidence of the lakes. For hundreds on hundreds of miles, on all sides, there was a labyrinth of lakes. The water-marks showing the former levels of the lakes (in places two or three hundred feet above the present level of the valleys) not having yet disappeared by erosion, the date of the subsidence of their waters cannot be many centuries back. The Paiutes and Shoshones have lost nothing by the coming among them of the whites; indeed, they appear to fare better now than in the days when they were in undisturbed possession of the whole land. They pitch their camps in the suburbs of the towns and fare sumptuously every day on the broken victuals collected by the bushel at hotels, restaurants, and private houses, by the squaws. The men, unlike the men of many other tribes, are not above work. They work at sawing and splitting wood, at grading off building-lots, or anything that they can manage—all they want is to be shown money.

It is not unusual to see a Paiute brave marching through a street in Virginia City with a wood-saw and buck under his left arm, and upon his right shoulder an ax—the living exemplification of the dawn of civilization upon barbarism. Thus far, however, he is one of the civilized, and represents "labor" seeking "capital," but with all the implements of peaceful industry borne about him, his pride still clings to the ancient insignia of the "brave" in his tribe. His face is painted in zigzag lines of black, white, and red; a necklace of bear's claws rests on his breast, and an eagle feather decorates his scalp-lock; but instead of bearing a bow and arrows, a tomahawk and scalping-knife, he carries only his saw, buck, and ax, and is only on the war-path to do battle with a wood-pile; therefore is either a peaceful warrior or a warlike wood-sawyer, just as you may choose to consider him. He has, as we may say, beaten his sword into a plowshare, but has not the heart to throw away the scabbard.

Old Winnemucca, the head chief of all the Paiutes, is about 70 years of age, and has but little to say about the "affairs of the nation;" indeed, there is little demand for legislation as the tribe is at present situated. Many years ago the old fellow appears to have turned over business of almost every kind to his nephew, young Winnemucca, then war-chief. Young Winnemucca was in command at the time of the trouble between the Paiutes and the whites, in the spring of 1860. Young Winnemucca never gambled, but old Winnemucca was an inveterate gambler—that is, among his own people. The Paiutes do not gamble with white men. Old Winnemucca has been known to lose all his ponies, all his blankets and arms, and, in fact, everything he possessed, down to a breech-clout, at a single sitting. He is a good-natured, kind-hearted old man, but not a man remarkable for either wisdom or cunning.

CHAPTER XXXVII

WINNEMUCCA AND HIS BRAVES

*On the War-Path—An Interview with the Chief—A White Indian—
Captain Truckee—John's Funeral Oration—The "Princess" Sarah*

At the time the war broke out between the whites and Paiutes, two young Germans were engaged in prospecting at a point in the mountains east of the sink of the Humboldt. They knew nothing of the trouble and started to come into Chinatown.

On reaching a station on the Humboldt River they found the buildings burned, and various articles, such as books and cards, strewn about. The thought then struck them that there was trouble between the Indians and whites. Feeling that they could make no fight, and not desiring to give the Indians an opportunity of blowing their brains out with their own weapons, the young men threw their guns into the river, and poured their powder upon the ground and set fire to it.

After leaving the burned station they traveled on till night, without seeing any Indians; but after they camped, an Indian who spoke very good English came riding up to the fire. He told the young fellows to pack their things and come with him, for should they remain in their present camp they were sure to be killed, as the Paiutes were now at war with the whites.

"Paiute man," said he, "kill um great many white man at Pyramid Lake, get heap gun, heap pony. S'pose white man kill Paiute, Paiute kill um white man!"

The young men thought it best to do as requested, and catching up their mustangs, packed their blankets and equipments, when they announced their readiness to follow their red guide. After an hour's travel they reached a large encampment, and found themselves in the midst of three or four hundred warriors.

Their guide conducted them to a tent near the middle of the camp, which he informed them was "Winnemucca's house!"

Soon the old chief made his appearance and catechized them as follows:

"Where are you from?"

"From beyond the Sink of the Humboldt."

"What were you doing there?"

"Prospecting."

"Did you see many Indians there?"

"A good many."

"Did they beg of you much?"

"A great deal."

"Did you give them anything?"

"All we could spare."

"Did they try to take your grub?"

"No."

"Did they steal?"

"Yes, a little."

"Bad Injuns! bad Injuns! Many white men bad too; many bad men—some white some red! What have you in your packs!?"

"Blankets and grub."

"Have you sugar left?"

"A little."

"Will you sell me two pounds?"

"Yes; certainly—or give it to you."

"No, no! I must pay."

Having measured out the sugar in a tin cup—a cupful for a pound—Winnemucca, on being told the price was a dollar, said it was not enough, and handed them two dollars. He next asked for gunpowder. Being told they had none, he caused their packs to be opened and searched. No powder being found the old fellow looked disappointed.

When first brought into camp, the young fellows were a good deal frightened, but after their interview with Winnemucca, began to feel quite easy in mind. Winnemucca told them that he was only at war with the Californians, and said he had no quarrel with white men who came from the East. The horses of the young men were picketed out with those of the Indians, and they were shown where to spread their blankets. Although surrounded by Indians, they were soon asleep, being very tired.

Late in the night one of the men felt a hand on his head, and awoke. He was greatly terrified at finding that an old squaw with a long knife in her hand had him by the hair, and was about to cut his throat. Before he could make a move, or utter a cry, an Indian lying near, sprang up, pushed the squaw away and then lay down at their heads.

"Hush!" said this man as he lay down.

"I shall speak to old Winnemucca about this in the morning," whispered the man whose throat had been in danger.

"Do nothing of the kind," said their self-appointed guard, "that woman with the knife was one of the old fellow's wives. Say nothing about it."

"Who are you? You speak now like a white man."

Winnemucca (The Giver), a Paiute Chief of Western Nevada, 1880, albumen. Bureau of Indian Affairs.

"I am not only a white man, but am also a countryman of yours. I heard you and your partner speaking together in German last night. Say nothing, I am an Indian now, and have been for years."

The young men were not again disturbed, and in the morning went to Winnemucca and signified their desire to depart. The old chief gave orders for their horses to be brought, and then told them to be sure to travel fast, and not to stop to prospect.

When they had packed up and were about ready to start, Winnemucca gave them a string made of twisted sinews in which were tied a number of knots, telling them that wherever they were stopped by Indians they must show them the string. They were stopped two or three times in the course of the forenoon, but the string operated like magic, as the sight of it instantly changed the countenances of the Indians from the scowl of an enemy to the smile of a friend.

Wherever they were stopped the string was taken from them and one of the knots untied, when it was handed back to them. The Indians would then say, as they left them: "Go straight to Chinatown—travel fast!" In one place, while they were passing through a cañon, they were fired on by a small party of Indians and two or three bullets whistled past them. They halted and called out: "We are from Winnemucca's camp! We are friends!" Two or three Indians then approached, and being shown the pass they exchanged glances, but took the string and undid a knot. They then shook hands, saying; "Now we all heap good friend." As they were leaving, one of them faced about, and said, "Don't tell Winnemucca that we shot at you." In another place they passed a hut that stood near the road, but seeing no one there, except an old woman, they did not take the trouble to show her the pass. In half an hour they were overtaken by three Indians on horseback, who levelled guns at them and told them to stop. On showing their pass they were asked why they did not show it to the old woman; however, one of the braves took out a knot, when all three turned about and went off laughing.

After they had passed the site of Williams' Station, the burning of which, and the killing of the men stopping there, brought on all the trouble, they were again stopped by an Indian who undid their last knot and then kept the string. As the Indian turned to ride away, he began singing in a low tone: "Was ist des Deutschen Vaterland?" and the young fellows said: "There is our countryman again!" They were about to turn back and call to him, but looking in the direction whence he came and in which he was again going, they saw the heads of several Indians and ponies among the willows, on the banks of the Carson River, along which they were now traveling.

Old Captain Truckee, in whose honor the Truckee River was named, was a very intelligent man, and was always a great friend to the whites. He had been a good deal with Frémont and other American explorers, in the capacity of guide, and well understood and appreciated the superior conveniences and substantial comforts resulting from the industrious habits of civilized people. He deplored the ignorance and willfulness of his people in preferring to lead a wandering life—deriving a precarious subsistence from the proceeds of the chase and the spontaneous products of the soil—to settling permanently in their rich valleys and turning their attention to the raising of stock and the cultivation of the soil.

Captain Truckee died in the Palmyra Mountains, in 1860, from the bite of some insect—probably a tarantula. Before his death he gave the most minute directions in regard to his burial. He had in his possession a letter of recommendation from Col. John C. Frémont, speaking of him as being a faithful and efficient guide and a good honest man. He also had other documents of a similar character from other white men, all of which he desired to have placed in his left hand when he was carried to his grave. He had been much about the Catholic Missions in California, and desired to have a cross erected at the head of his grave with his name cut upon it; he also told how deep the grave must be dug, how his head was to be laid, and mentioned particularly that they were to fold his hands on his breast and heap the earth in a mound above his last resting-place.

As the Indians did not know how to do all these things, they asked some whites who were pros-pecting near at hand to come and bury Truckee as he had desired to be buried. All of his instructions were carried out to the last partic-ular. The Indians all loved the old man, and there was great weeping and wailing at his funeral, which was taken charge of by a white man who had long known the old fellow and who was called by the Indians "the white Winnemucca."

At the grave, Captain John, a son-in-law of Truckee, pro-nounced the eulogy. He spoke first in Paiute and then in English, and said:

"A good man is gone. The white man knows he was good, for he guided him round des-erts and led him in paths where there was grass and good water. His people know he was good, for he loved them and cared for them and came home to them to

Captain John in War Costume, Paiute Indian, 1903, dry plate/ albumen, Andrew A. Forbes. Library of Congress Prints and Photographs Division.

die. All know that Truckee was a good man—Paiutes and Americans. He is dead; the good man is gone. All of our people cry, for they loved Truckee.

"I must go to Walker River and see the big Captain there and say to him, 'the good man is dead.' I must go to Pyramid Lake, to Winnemucca, and say to him, 'the good man is dead.' Winnemucca sits in the door of his house and says: 'No sabe, no sabe?' Winnemucca himself is growing old. When he knows the good man is dead, he and the big Captain at Walker River will have a talk and will choose a man to put in his place; but not many are fit to lead in the path where Truckee walked (Captain John was himself chosen). Truckee was much with the white men, he liked their way and learned much of them that we don't understand. He wished to be buried as the white men bury their dead, and the white Winnemucca and the white men his friends have seen it done. I thank him and I thank them—I thank all for Truckee and Truckee's people. Goodbye! I go to Walker River to see the big Captain—" and he at once set out on a run.

Sarah Winnemucca Hopkins, 1883, collodion/albumen, Elmer Chickering.

The Indians who remained packed up their traps, and setting fire to the hut in which Truckee died, they all set out along a trail leading to the northward, weeping and wailing as they went.

One of old Winnemucca's wives (he had three or four) was a daughter of Captain Truckee. This wife was the mother of Sarah, known in Nevada as the "Princess Sarah." She was educated at Santa Cruz, California, at a Catholic Mission, and reads and writes very well, sometimes writing articles for publication in the papers, concerning her people. She was married to a German named Snyder, and lived with him a number of years. Snyder died while on his way to Germany, on a visit, when the "Princess Sarah" married Lieutenant Bartlett, of the United States Army. She lived with him but a short time, when she left him and returned to her people.

When in towns and cities she dresses after the fashion of American ladies, but when with her people generally dons the Paiute dress. Her Indian name is Sonometa—even a prettier name than Sarah. Prince Natchez, a full brother of Sonometa, is heir-apparent to the Winnemucca throne and is now looked upon by all the Paiutes as their leading man—the man to stir up the agent sent to the tribe by the "Great Father" at Washington, and he keeps all the money appropriated for the use of the Paiutes. "Natches" is a name given to the "Prince" by the whites. His folks simply called him "Nah-tze," the Paiute for boy. The Indians have now split the difference and call him "Natchee."

Old Winnemucca wears in his nose a stick some four inches in length, and when he goes to the happy hunting-ground Nachez will no doubt thrust into his nasal croppings this badge of royalty. The name, "Winnemucca," means the charitable man.

CHAPTER XXXVIII

SKETCHES OF INDIAN LIFE

Juan's Spanish Speculation—The Devil's Visit to Earth—
Cooking the Sage—What Was It?—Paiute Theology—
Poco Tiempo—"Plenty Old"—Jim and His Ducks

Shortly after the so-called Indian war I took a prospecting trip into the wilderness lying to the eastward of the sinks or lakes of the Carson and Humboldt Rivers. I had with me two white men, and we roamed through the Indian country for nearly a month. During the greater part of this time we had with us a Paiute guide known as Captain or "Capitan" Juan.

When Frémont passed through the country and took Captain Truckee into his service as a guide, Juan and nine other adventurous Paiute youths accompanied him. When they reached California, these young Paiutes liked the country so well, that the majority of them remained there several years. Juan lived there ten years. He worked upon a ranch and could plow and plant, reap and thresh grain as well as any white man. Then he learned the Spanish language, which he spoke quite as well as the Mexicans generally speak it. He also speaks pretty fair English, but mixed in a good deal of Spanish, when a little excited. He proved a trusty and excellent guide, and we retained him as long as we remained in his country. Captain Juan had seen his ups and downs in the world as well as the rest of us.

One evening when we were all seated about our camp-fire, after a hearty supper, being in a talkative mood, he said: "I was pretty well off once, over in California—I had *fifty dollars!*" He named the amount with an emphasis which showed that he considered the announcement one of considerable importance.

"Indeed!—Had you so much money?" said I.

"O, yes; I was well off—*many ricos!*"

"And what became of all this wealth?"

"Me burst all to smash!"

"Well, that was bad. In kind of speculation?"

"Me not understand spectoolation. What you call um spectoolation?"

"Well, it's when you put your money into something that you expect to make plenty more money out off—like you plant wheat. You plant your money in some speculation to get more money."

"Yes; well, me make one bad plant."

"One bad speculation, eh?"

"Yes; *muy malo*—one *mucho* bad spectoolashe. She was one Spanish spectoolashe. Me marry one Spanish woman. She purty soon got all me money. She say, 'Juan you got-a some money?' Me say, 'No; no, got-a money?' She say, 'Juan, you no ketch-a money you vamose—you git!' Me no like *los senoritas,* Spanish spectoolashe no good for Paiute man—you think?"

"No; very bad speculation. But I suppose you went to work and earned more money for your Spanish wife?

"No; me stop work—heap mad. Me no want no more money—no more senorita. Too much all time want new dress. One night me vamose. Me come over mountains to my people, ketch me one Paiute wife. She no all time want money, money."

"Then you have a good Paiute wife?"

"O, yes; *muy bueno*—muy bonita! Me keep-a her *mucho* well dress,—give her many shirt. She got heap-a shirt Not many Paiute woman get so much shirt!"

"Why, John, you surprise me. How many shirts has she got—twenty?" Juan looked astounded and abashed at this extravagant guessing. He scratched his head, looked at me, then at the fire, and seemed to have some notion of not telling me the exact "quantity" of shirt in which his wife rejoiced. At length he slowly said:

"Well, she got two shirt—two shirt, but all fix up nice—plenty braid, *mucho* ribbon, O, very nice! Twenty shirt no good. What you talk?—me never see one woman got twenty shirt."

Juan one evening told me the story of a wonderful cave in a region far to the northward, where his tribe lived in the days of his fathers—long and long before they came south, and long before the first white men crossed the Plains. This cave was in the side of a great mountain, and when the Evil One tried his hand at creation and began to make scorpions, tarantulas, snakes, horned toads, cactus, deserts and pools of alkali water, the Good Spirit (Pahah) caught him and put him into the cave, closing the entrance with a great mountain. There, far down in the ground, for many hundred of winters the Evil One used to roar and bellow. At times the hills trembled with terror; great rocks were shaken from their beds on the mountains and rolled down into the valleys, and fire came up out of the ground. Some of the mountains burst open, and one—a great one—sank down out of sight and left in its place a broad lake.

The hill rolled off the mouth of the cave at this time and the devil came out and flew away toward sunrise. So large was he that, though he flew more swiftly than a hawk, his wings had not passed over when three sleeps were done. They shut out the light of the sun. There was no moon or stars. The medicine men said there would be no more day till the Evil One was again shut up, for he was very mad and had swallowed the sun, moon, and stars. The medicine men, however, held a council and by burning a great deal of buffalo hair made such a smoke as to make the devil very sick, when he vomited up the sun, moon and a great many stars, and it has been light ever since; but now there are not so many stars as in former times. Since the flight of the Evil One there has been no more groaning in the mountains, and the hills have ceased to tremble.

After the devil left the cave, a great buffalo came and lived in it. This buffalo was larger than twenty ponies, and had horns growing out of his nose. All the other buffalo went into this great cave every winter to see their big chief and did not come back till spring. At last this big buffalo got to be so old and weak that when he went to get a drink at the lake where the mountains had sunk, he stuck fast in the mud. The Indians there found him, and got all round him, and for three days shot him full of arrows and beat him with great stones. Still he was not dead. They then built a big fire on his head, and so killed him. Afterwards, an old man came out of the cave. His hair was as white as snow, and reached to his hips. The Indians called him Taweeta. He never spoke to living man, for he had seen the Great Spirit and had spoken with him, and therefore dare not again speak the language of man.

Taweeta was very wise; he had seen the place where the sun sleeps, and had visited the wigwam where a great black man keeps the thunder in a gourd: he had been allowed to view the happy hunting-grounds, where all who die like men are permitted to live and hunt in peace forever; and he knew the place where winter hides from summer and where the summer has its home.

The white sage on which the herds of Nevada now fatten, was in times past much used by the Paiutes as an article of food. Juan, in speaking of the many advantages enjoined by the Indians since the coming amongst them of the whites, said that in former times they were often almost starved. He said that he could still remember a time, when he was a little boy, when they were obliged to live almost wholly on white sage.

"How did you cook it?" I asked.

"Well," said Juan, "the women cooked it They made soup of it."

"How did they make the soup?"

"Well, they put the sage into a big basket and filled the basket with water, then put in hot stones till it was cooked."

"Did they put in nothing but sage—no meat?"

"Sometimes—s'pose you ketch um—put in some piece rabbit or pish" (fish).

"As you had no spoons, how did you eat the soup—drink it out of the basket?"

"No. All got round basket and dip up with hands."

"Was it good?"

"Yes; good all same hay for cow," said Juan making a wry face.

Juan then explained that in former times when there was a failure of the pine-nut crop and no game could be found, the whole tribe was obliged to subsist on white sage.

The white sage differs from the common sage-brush of the country, which few animals can eat, owing to its extreme bitterness. It sends up a great number of white shoots which become quite tender and nutritious after the fall frosts, when cattle greedily feed and rapidly fatten upon them.

In Nevada this white sage is the principal food of vast herds of cattle that cover not alone a thousand but ten thousand hills—the white sage and the bunch-grass. The bunchgrass is considered to be as good for horses as barley, as it bears a heavy crop of seed. This seed somewhat resembles millet, and is much used as an article of food by the Indians. It is ground on a flat stone, with the seeds of the wild sunflower and other oleaginous seeds, and cakes are made of the meal thus produced. I have seen patches of bunch-grass many acres in extent, that had been cut, bound up in sheaves, and set up in shocks, the same as wheat in a field. This work is done by the squaws, who also sometimes strip the heads of the grass off between two sticks, tied together in the shape of a pair of scissors, throwing the seed over their heads into a large basket carried on their backs.

In regions where deserts abound, on all sides there are always extensive flats on the tops of the mountain ranges where the bunch-grass and other grasses flourish.

In Nevada, no less than four kinds of wild-clover are found. The seeds of one kind are inclosed in a small octagonal burr. In the little valleys on these mountains, flax is found growing wild. It is precisely the same as the cultivated species, except that it is perennial. It is from the fibre of this flax that the twine is made which is used by the Indians in making their nets for catching fish, rabbits, and water-fowl. While all is green and fresh on the summits of the mountains, in the surrounding deserts all is salt, alkali, sterility, and desolation. In the early days, when thousands on thousands of persons were annually crossing the Plains to California and Oregon, hundreds perished because they did not understand the country through which they were passing. In looking for water they always went to the lowest places they could find, as they were in the habit of doing at home in the Eastern and Western States, whereas they should have left the desert valleys and climbed to the tops of the highest of the surrounding hills.

On all of the mountain ranges springs of excellent water are found, and in places, small brooks; but the water sinks in the beds of the ravines and is lost long before it reaches the level of the deserts. The Indians always travel along the tops of the mountain ranges in summer. On their trails are put up signs that tell where springs can be found. These are small monuments of rock, capped with a stone, the longest part of which points in the direction of the nearest spring.

Toward this spring are turned the long points of all the cap-stones on the monuments, until it is reached. Passing by the spring, the index-stones all point back to it until there is a nearer spring ahead, when the pointers are all turned in that direction.

On finding the first monument, after striking the Indian trail, one may thus know which end of it to take to the nearest water. In traveling along a dry cañon, where all was parched and dusty, I have sometimes seen upon one of its steep banks a monument, and, climbing up to it, have found the index pointing directly up the hill, where all seemed as dry as in the ravine below. But taking the direction indicated, it would not be long before a bunch of willows would be seen, and among these a spring was sure to be found. Not knowing the meaning of these little stone monuments, the early prospectors made a business of kicking them over wherever they found them, and so destroyed what would have been a useful thing to them had they understood it.

The Paiutes believe in a heaven and a hell, a good being and an evil being. God, or the Good Spirit, they call "Pah-ah;" the devil or the Evil One, they call "Avea-dagii." Heaven is a delightful place where there is plenty of good water, and abundance of game and droves of stout squaws, to do all the work—no rest for the poor squaws, even in heaven. Hell is one vast burning desert; no water there but that which is red with alkali, and which burns like fire when swallowed. When the bad Indians try to get out of this, and essay to climb the hills to the happy hunting-grounds they are thrust with brands of fire, and so wander back across the burning sands to meet with the same treatment in trying to escape on the other side. Thus they wander forever; always trying to escape, and always thrust back into the burning desert. They have preachers—Paiutes—among them who preach very good Methodist doctrine. They sometimes begin preaching early in the evening and preach all night—telling the Indians that if they lie, steal, and murder, they are sure to bring up in the great desert, "tooroop," when they die.

Among themselves, and at their own games, the Paiutes are nearly all inveterate gamblers. Old and young, male and female, are always ready to bet their last quarter at one of their games. Very few Paiutes will touch whiskey or liquor of any kind. The women are remarkable for their chastity, and are in this respect models not only for the women of all surrounding tribes, but for those of all nations and colors.

Although the Paiutes swarm about the towns no one ever thinks of their stealing anything. On the contrary, the Chief of Police of Virginia City knows a certain man called "Snake Creek Sam" who often brings him valuable information in regard to the movements of rogues who may be hiding or scouting about in the hills. Some of them are a little trickish when it comes to a trade, but there are white men who think it no sin to get the best of a bargain when opportunity offers.

A Paiute on one occasion went about among the residents of Virginia City, selling suckers for trout to such unsophisticated housewives as he could find. One lady thought the fish did not look exactly right for trout, and said: "What makes their noses so long, Jim?"

"Him heap young," said the deceitful Jeems. "Poco tiempo plenty old; no more nose —mout' all same me," and Jim opened his mouth from ear to ear.

Looking upon the open countenance of the red-man, the lady believed him free from guile, and purchased a dozen of his long-nosed trout.

An Indian is always ready to leave any work he may be doing and run after game if any is seen to approach. One day, at Washoe City, a few miles west of Virginia, some men who were stopping at the principal hotel, happened to be out on the veranda, taking a look at the surrounding country, when they saw a large flock of ducks settle down on the further side of Washoe Lake. A Washoe Indian, who was sawing wood near the hotel, also saw the ducks, and told the men that he would go after them if they would get him a gun. In the hotel they found an old United States' musket. This they loaded nearly to the muzzle, and giving it to the Indian, started him for the lake.

The men then went into the balcony of the hotel, and, with opera glasses, watched the progress of the red Nimrod.

He, at length, reached the spot where the ducks had been seen to settle down among the tules—a kind of bulrush from ten to fifteen feet in height.

Presently the watchers saw the smoke dart from the end of the Indian's gun; saw him fall backwards to the ground, then a tremendous roar came across the lake—a sound as though the gun had burst into a thousand pieces. Fearing that the gun had indeed burst and killed the poor devil, the wags began to feel very guilty. They hastened from the house and hurried round the lake to the rescue. When they had gone about half way round they met their Indian coming toward them. There was a long gash across his right cheek-bone, his nose was bunged up, and his face was covered with blood, but he was completely loaded down with ducks.

"Well, Jim," said the wags, who now felt better satisfied with their little joke, "how did you make it?"

"Yes;" said Jim, "one more shoot um—no more ducks, no more Injun!"

CHAPTER XXXIX

CONCERNING "LO" AND HIS FAMILY

A Little Warrior in a Fix—Only a Shrimp—Paiutes in Virginia City—
The Lord and His Lady—How the Little Ones Came—The Early Settler—
Adam and Eve—A Model Parent—An Important Occasion—Sam's Theft

It is said to be next to impossible to astonish an Indian, but on one occasion, while residing in Virginia City, I astonished, frightened, and disgusted a whole flock of the unsophisticated "children of the desert," and with a mere handful of shrimps.

A crowd of Paiutes, numbering over a dozen, male and female, great and small, had come to anchor, squat upon the ground, just off the sidewalk, in front of a fruit-stand (a favorite place of resort with them), and were in the midst of what to them was a great feast. Upon an old shawl, spread in the centre of their circle, was a great heap of half-rotten apples, damaged cherries, soured strawberries, and other offal from the fruit-store in front of which they were squatted. Among the male Indians was Smoke Creek Sam, the Paiute detective, who, with head thrown back, was each moment dropping into his mouth great wads of strawberries, squeezed together, stems and all, of the size of an ordinary codfish-ball.

Some of the little Indian boys and girls were smeared to the eyes with a leathery mess, half strawberries and half dirt, which they scooped up from the common heap, and held to their mouths in both hands.

Even the most comely among the squaws had a brown dab of rotten apple on the end of her nose, which that organ had brought away as a trophy during some one of the frequent visits of her industrious mouth to the deep interior of a slushy pippin.

One hideous old woman had raked a quantity of decayed cherries into her lap, and sat "and munched, and munched, and munched."

Under the vigorous attack of so many diligent hands and capacious and willing mouths, the mound of vegetable garbage was soon swept away.

As I then lacked amusement, I stepped to a market next door, and procured a handful of shrimps. With these I approached the now surfeited group of savages, and began eating, by way of experiment on their nerves.

At first they looked curiously on, and some of the juveniles rose to their feet to have a better view of the new and horrible-looking esculent. At a respectful distance they stood and gazed, as they saw me pull in two and devour the many-legged little monsters, each "little Injun" with lips curled up, teeth set, and nose wrinkled.

The bucks shrugged their shoulders as they saw each fresh "bug" pulled out and eaten, and some of the squaws drew down the corners of their mouths and spat upon the ground with decided emphasis.

The whole party, as though fascinated by a sight so fearful, sat and closely watched each shrimp as it was shucked out and swallowed, the general disgust each moment increasing.

Finally, I held out toward a "brave" of some ten "snows" the few crustaceous specimens remaining in my hand. This incipient warrior was arrayed as to his head, in some Comstock dandy's cast-off "stovepipe" hat, and as to his nether extensions, in a pair of adult unmentionables of bake-oven capacity in the rear.

As my hand approached, his moon eyes rapidly grew moonier, and he began craw fishing, though determined, if possible, to retreat in good order, and with his face to the foe.

At this critical moment I pitched at the budding chieftain the empty shell of a shrimp I had just finished. By chance it alighted upon a lock of hair hanging over his forehead, and there remained for a moment, hanging by the claws, and dangling before his eyes.

The boy gave a yelp, made one grab at the ugly thing, then turned a complete back somersault over the old cherry-muncher. He landed running, but, his "plug" hat being down over his eyes, he soon brought up on all-fours, with his Head between the legs of a passing Chinese wood-peddler, who was so frightened at the unexpected assault in the rear, that he, in turn, came near turning a somersault over the back of the donkey he was driving.

The other youngsters, seeing what had happened, scattered in all directions like a brood of startled quail, while the squaws—lusty old gals, all of them!—hastily snatched up the papooses, which, in their wicker cradles, were lying across their laps, or standing against awning-posts or empty barrels, and deftly slinging them upon their backs, drew the straps across their foreheads, and started up the street at a rolling gallop, the noise of which resembled that of the stampede of a flock of fat wethers when in full wool.

The old hag mentioned as the "cherry-muncher"—probably fearing that a shrimp would be thrown into her straggling locks —hanging with both hands to the dead branch of a cedar, poled herself along in the rear of the stampeders with astonishing agility.

At the distance of thirty yards she halted to get her wind, and seeing that she was not being pursued, faced about. Still grasping her rude staff in both hands, and resting her wrinkled and venerable lump of nose on its top, she stared back at me from under her mop of grizzled hair, like an old witch frightened away from some unholy feast.

Some of the bucks sullenly marched away, casting backward glances from malevolent eyes which plainly showed their opinion of practical jokes, but Smoke Creek Sam stood his ground. He, too, had been outraged and disgusted, but as he had not yet found opportunity to beg a handful of smoking tobacco, he concealed his feelings and deferred his retreat. Extracting the pith of a particularly large and healthy shrimp, I approached Sam with it.

"You no bring um here!" cried he, waving me back with his hand. "No bring um, me say!" "Just try this one, Sam," said I.

"No!" said Sam, decidedly; "glash-hop, purty good; klicket, me eat um; scorpium-bug, heap no good. Scorpium make Injun man high up sick!"

I now saw it all, and was not so much surprised at the astonishment and disgust shown by the whole crowd of redskins. Knowing nothing about shrimps, all supposed that I was eating scorpions, a poisonous reptile very abundant in Nevada, and very closely resembling the shrimp. Seeing me, as they supposed, deliberately devouring scorpions, all thought that the Evil One himself was before them.

The Paiutes are the early birds in Virginia City. Almost as soon as it is sufficiently light for them to see, the squaws are down from their huts on the slopes of the surrounding mountains. The Paiute squaw is the scavenger of the town. When she rolls into the place in the morning, she comes with her gunny-sack over her shoulder, and into this stows all that in her eyes is valuable. She gathers up every little wisp of hay that falls in her way, even to the last straw, as she wants it for the half-starved family pony, staked out in the hills near the camp; looks into dry-goods boxes in search of straw, also for the pony; dives into barrels in front of the markets, for half-rotten fruit, wilted turnips, carrots, and other vegetables good for the family, and as the markets open and the business of the day begins, she manages to secure all the heads and tails of salmon and other fish that are cut up. All this time she has one eye open for fuel—the hills being stripped to the last rotten stick, by the Chinamen, who have even dug all the tree-stumps out by the roots. Bits of boxes, wooden hoops, staves, all that is wood she stuffs into her sack, along with the rest of her plunder.

If the sack is full and a good haul of wood falls in her way, she makes it up into a bundle and places it on her head, and finally, loaded down like a donkey, the frugal housewife climbs the mountain to where her hut is perched, when she makes glad the heart of her lord and master and little ones, with the good things she has brought home to them. Others hang about the kitchens of the town, and collect loads of broken victuals, as there no swine are kept by families, and they have no use for the scraps that are carried from the table.

The male Paiute is not always idle, but he cannot always find a job. The Chinamen swarm the town in search of about the only kinds of work poor "Lo" is able to do. But no man with a fat government contract ever felt himself better fixed, than does one of these ex-warriors when he has fairly settled down at a job of wood-sawing, for which he is to receive one dollar per cord in coin, and board while he is doing the work. This is just the kind of bargain he likes to make with a newcomer, or some other unsophisticated citizen. The kitchen upon which he has thus established a lien is never out of his mind. He is on hand at dawn of day, and from the mountain height on which sits his eyrie, brings the appetite of a tiger. Until he has had his breakfast, his face is ever toward the dwelling of his employer, and ever and anon he is seen to pause with his saw in the midst of a half-finished stick, as he snuffs the odors wafted from the kitchen.

Breakfast over, he begins watching and snuffing for his dinner; dinner over, his mind dwells upon the coming supper. Between meals, he frequently becomes so exhausted that he cannot force his saw through the smallest stick, unless braced up by an occasional cup of coffee, slice of bread, and joint of cold meat.

When the noble red-man boards himself, however, he works like a steam-engine, and loses not a moment until the last stick is done, and he can extend his palm for his coin.

We hear much about the disappearance of the Indian before the march of civilization, and in some quarters predictions are freely hazarded that in a short time he will become extinct— will pass away with the dodo. Whatever may be the case with other tribes, the Paiute has no notion of passing away. He is among the most prolific of *autochthones*. To "increase and multiply" appears to be the first care of the average adult Paiute. It looks somewhat as if he were bound to occupy the land in case his productiveness shall continue. The Paiutes are a remarkably healthy people. They are seldom sick, and few deaths occur among them. The few who die seem to die of old age. There appear to be about one hundred births among them to one death. Hardly a squaw that is over sixteen and under sixty years of age can be seen, but she has a papoose slung on her back, and some of them surpass the wife of the martyred John Rogers in evidences of prolificness. The women do not appear to be much addicted to twins, but the little ones come marching along quite rapidly in single file.

The Paiutes are certainly multiplying more rapidly than any other people in the State of Nevada. Even astonishingly old women among them bear children.

"What shall be done with these people?" will one day be a question in Nevada that must be answered in some way. The women are virtuous, and the men temperate, and so long as they thus remain, there seems to be no likelihood of their dying off.

Among the Paiutes to work is considered no disgrace, and the biggest "brave" is not ashamed to be seen handling an ax or saw—no, nor to be found carrying his child, a thing that would ruin him in almost any other tribe. Their greatest vice is gambling among themselves.

Paiute Indians Gambling at the Wickyup, 1898, Sage Brush Art Co.
Library of Congress Prints and Photographs Division.

All is now well with these children of the desert, as they are not yet so numerous but that the cast-off clothing of the whites suffices for all, great and small, and the cold victuals given away in all the towns is more than enough to feed them; but a time will come when this will not be the case. Then some place must be found, and some provision made for this people.

A well-known old Paiute couple in Virginia City were "Adam" and "Eve." Old Adam was supposed to have been about one hundred years of age at the time of his death, and Eve also was very old.

At the death of the aged couple there was a strange fatality. Old Adam was bitten by a ferocious dog, and after lingering some weeks, during which time he was cared for by the Sisters of Charity, he departed for the happy hunting-grounds. A year later old Eve was attacked and terribly mangled by a savage dog, the sinews being drawn out of one of her ankles by the teeth of the brute. She, too lingered some weeks, watched over and cared for by the Sisters, when she went to join old Adam where the grass is always green and bright waters ever flow.

The old couple seem to have embraced the Christian religion in the early days, at some one of the Catholic Missions in California. Old Adam was very fond of being in and about the Catholic Church in Virginia City, and was never happier than when noticed by Father Manogue, the pastor, with whom the ancient red-man was fond of conversing, in his childish way, upon religious subjects. Whenever grand-children and great-grand children were born to him, "Old Adam" never failed to bring them to Father Manogue, in order that they might be duly baptized. Thus is the name of Patrick and Michael now heard in the Paiute tribe.

About the streets of Virginia is frequently to be seen stalking a thin-visaged, solemn-looking squaw who attracts much attention from her great height and her tremendous strides in walking, The gaunt apparition in female attire is, however, no squaw, but a "buck," a man of the Paiute tribe condemned to wear the dress of a woman all the days of his life, for cowardice exhibited at the battle of Pyramid lake. He is shunned by both the men and women among his people, and therefore, like Baxter's hog, goes in a "drove" by himself. The last time I saw him he had on a new calico dress, of the meal-bag pattern in the skirt, and had a new gingham handkerchief upon his head; still he was not proud. Nothing good, bad, or indifferent is said to him by the Indians, but the white boys about town scoff at him and his face wears a calm, resigned, chronic "sour."

Many of the Paiutes are anxious to have their children learn to read and write, and, in 1875, three little Indians boys were in attendance at the public school in Silver City, the principal of the school taking them in at the solicitation of the father and by way of experiment. In a few weeks they were able to read tolerably well in the first reader. They began with the alphabet and

were very proud of the progress they were able to make. Unlike the majority of white parents, the father of the little redskins thinks it worth while to
visit the school occasionally, to see how things are going. When the stern
old brave visits the school he marches into the institution of learning with
a turkey feather in his hair, his face painted in bright zigzag lines of black,
white and red, and a long double-barrelled shotgun on his shoulder. This
has a business look which is doubtless appreciated by the teacher.

As an object of distraction to the school the "lamb that little Mary had"
would not amount to a row of pins—would be a mere digitless cipher—by
the side of that Indian father in all the full-blown pride of shotgun, war-
paint, and turkey feathers.

The Paiutes have some notion of picking up English songs and tunes.
I one day saw a dusky maiden of perhaps sixteen summers vocalizing in
front of a fruit-store, who evidently felt that she was a long way in advance
of the majority of her tribe. The song she sang was: "I feel, I feel like a
to-morrow morning star, Soo Fly! don't bodda my! Soo Fly!" Her object
appeared to charm a few wilted apples from the keeper of the store, but he
being a native of melodious Italy was not much affected, and even scowled
upon the singer, as though he felt it a duty to discourage and nip in the bud
all talent manifesting itself in such a quarter.

At one time a savior arose for the Paiute people. This was Sam Brown,
the civilizer, an Oregon Indian who had wandered to Virginia City and
who was able to read and write. Sam Brown was a natural born philanthropist—he cared not for himself so long as he could ameliorate the
condition of the aborigine. He desired to see the Indian tribes educated
and civilized, and to this work he was devoted, body and soul. He went
forth among the Paiutes residing in the neighborhood of Virginia and
Gold Hill, and made known to them his plans— told them of the school-
house he would build for the education of their children and how he
should finally have them all residing in houses and working at trades like
white men.

All the Indians were well pleased with what Sam told them; they said it
was "good talk." Sam looked about him for a man fit to be made chief of all
the Paiutes living about the two towns, and finally selected himself as being
the person most worthy to receive that high and honorable position. Soon
after that he one day marshaled all of his people in procession, and with the
American flag proudly floating at the head of the motley throng of men,
women, and children, gaily marched them about the streets of Virginia City.
They were the raggedest lot of recruits ever seen. To observe the dignified
bearing of the old warriors and the grave expression of each countenance, was
ludicrous beyond measure. They thought they were being adopted into the
American nation, and therefore considered it a duty to conduct themselves

in a grave and becoming manner on such a momentous occasion.

The use of a balcony on the principal street in the city was obtained, and from this, Sam Brown and several Paiutes, also one or two white men, addressed the common herd below.

This completed the inauguration of Sam Brown as chief, and he was now ready to begin the work of civilizing his subjects. The first thing in order with Sam was the building of a schoolhouse. He owned a lot somewhere in the suburbs of the town, and on this he determined to rear a proper structure, Sam had worked as a carpenter in Oregon, and felt equal to the task of building the school-house himself, if he but had tools and lumber. However, to the man who is a born reformer and philanthropist, whose soul thirsts continually to improve and benefit his species, no obstacle is so great but that by dint of untiring patience and perseverance it will finally overcome.

Sam stole a chest of carpenters' tools and had made considerable progress in the gradual removal of a lumber-yard, when unsympathetic eyes took cognizance of his philanthropic labors, and, failing to appreciate the purity of his motives, threw him into a prison, the fate, alas! of many great reformers in all ages. Samuel Brown, the civilizer, now abides in the Nevada State Prison, where he has time to consider the vanity of all philanthropic endeavors, and to mourn the obtuseness of the average human intellect in respect to the motives that inspire the soul of the reformer to do noble deeds and undertake arduous labors.

To this day the proposed school-house has not been built and to this day the Paiutes remain uncivilized.

CHAPTER XL

A Visit to the Mines
Above Ground—Suspicious Attacks—How the Cage is Worked—
Great Responsibility—Cages, Reels, and Cables—Comical Disguises

Having rambled far and wide among the Paiute Indians, I shall now ask the reader to accompany me in a ramble far below the light of day, to the underground regions of the silver-mines. During our trip through the lower levels of the mines I shall endeavor to explain all that is seen.

As all of the leading mines in the Comstock lode are opened and worked after the same general plan, a description of one mine will suffice for all. In singling out a mine, a description of the machinery and operations in which shall stand for all, I select the Consolidated Virginia as that in which is to be found all of the latest and most approved machinery, and in which

President Grant Visiting a Comstock Mine, October 1879, albumen, John S. Noe. Library of Congress Prints and Photographs Division. First published nationally in Harper's Weekly magazine, November 1879, as a wood engraving. Left to right: John W. Mackay, Mrs. M.G. Gillette, U.S. Grant Jr., former First Lady Julia B. Dent Grant, former President Ulysses S. Grant, S. Yamada (kneeling), Mrs. J.G. Fair, Nevada Governor John H. Kinkead, and future Nevada Senator James G. Fair.

Geologist Joseph N. Le Conte (center) Visiting a Comstock mine, c. 1905, unknown photographer. Sunset Magazine, February 1906. Entourage includes Southern Pacific Railroad traffic manager E.O. McCormick, Frank Seaman of New York, and Sunset magazine founder James Horsburgh, Jr. of the Southern Pacific Railroad.

President Rutherford B. Hayes (center) Visiting a Comstock mine, September 1880, albumen, John S. Noe. Sunset Magazine, February 1906. Entourage includes First Lady Lucy W. Webb Hayes (center right), Senator Alexander Ramsey (second from left), Commanding General William Tecumseh Sherman (fifth from left), and Major General Alexander McDowell McCook (second from right). Hayes was the first sitting President to visit Nevada.

all operations are conducted in a systematic and scientific manner. It will also be more satisfactory to the reader if he knows that what he is reading applies to a certain mine the name of which is known to him.

In giving a description of the various operations of mining, and of the machinery used, I shall find it necessary in but two or three instances to go outside of the Consolidated Virginia mine. In these cases I shall name the mine in which is to be seen what I am speaking of.

The popular idea of a silver-mine among most persons in the Atlantic

Consolidated Virginia Mine, 1876, collodion/albumen, Carleton E. Watkins. California State Library.

States, appears to be that a deep hole in the form of a common well has been sunk somewhere on the side of a mountain, from the bottom of which is dug the silver ore. As the ore is dug up from the bottom of the shaft, they suppose it to be hoisted to the surface in buckets, by means of an ordinary windlass, or some such rude contrivance. What really is seen at the main shaft or entrance to one of the leading mines on the Comstock lode is very different.

When we approach the main shaft and hoisting works of the Consolidated Virginia Mining Company we find before us a main building of great size, from which extend several large wings. One of these wings is the boiler-house, in which are several sets of boilers, and from the roof arise a number of tall, black smoke-stacks.

Another wing is the blacksmith shop, containing several forges at which are sharpened the picks and drills used, and where is done a vast amount of work of all kinds required in and about the mine.

Then there is the wing in which is the carpenter's shop, where the timbers used as supports in the lower levels of the mine are framed, and where circular saws, run by steam, are used in cutting and shaping the heavy square beams; also, a wing in which is a machine-shop containing a steam-engine which runs planers, lathes, and other machines for working iron. The main building is handsomely finished and painted with fire-proof paint, as are all of the wings. Rows of windows are seen in the several buildings, and from the roof of the main building and some of the wings, arise pipes from which white clouds of steam are constantly puffed.

Sutro Machine Shop, 1862, collodion/albumen, attributed to Charles L. Weed (Lawrence & Houseworth). Library of Congress Prints and Photographs Division.

In the mass of buildings before us we see nothing to cause us to think of a mine. What we have before us more nearly resembles a large iron-foundry or big manufactory of some kind. As we see on the grounds surrounding the buildings a number of immense piles of timber and lumber; in all, an amount sufficient to stock at least half a dozen ordinary lumber-yards, we should be more likely to guess that we saw before us a large planing-mill, or door, sash, and blind manufactory, than that we were approaching the main working shaft of a great silver-mine. Near the main pile of buildings, are detached structures, which are occupied as offices; one being the assay office, where the silver bullion is melted, moulded into bars, and assayed.

Upon entering the main building, we are at once struck by the peculiar style of dress worn by the men we see grouped or moving about. They all wear grey or blue woolen shirts, caps, or narrow-brimmed felt hats, and blue cotton or thin woolen overalls. They are all serious-looking men, and their faces all seem bleached out to an unnatural and unhealthy whiteness. The whole building is floored as handsomely as though it were a church, and all the floors are scrupulously neat and clean. All overhead being open to the roof, forty feet above, and there being no partitions in the main building, the interior presents a most spacious appearance.

Almost the first object that attracts our attention upon entering the place, is the mouth of the main shaft. Toward this we are at once attracted, for the reason that we see rushing up through several square openings in the floor, great volumes of steam. This steam appears to be hissing hot, and rushes almost to the roof of the building. We are surprised to see men coolly ascending and descending the very heart of these columns of steam.

Looking for the first time upon the rolling and whirling clouds of vapor pouring up from the shaft, more than one dandy tourist, who but a few minutes before was very enthusiastic in his talk about exploring the lower levels, has wished in his secret soul that he had never hinted that he had the slightest desire to descend into the dark and dismal bowels of the earth.

Many back down squarely. They suddenly remember that they are subject to vertigo, are threatened with apoplexy; or—which is a very common disease at such times—palpitation of the heart. So many persons visiting the mines, and seeing the mouth of the shafts for the first time, have made serious mention of being greatly troubled with "palpitation of the heart," that the old miner standing near finds it a difficult matter to keep a sober countenance upon hearing that ailment mentioned. Nothing can induce some persons to venture into the steaming shaft after they have taken one good look at it, while proper explanations speedily cure others of their vertigo, apoplectic symptoms, palpitation of the heart, or whatever disease it may be their fancy to affect.

When we inspect the mouth of the shaft more closely, we find before us an opening in the floor about five feet in width and twenty feet in length. This opening is divided into four lesser openings or "compartments," by partitions which run from the top to the bottom of the shaft. Three of these are called hoisting-compartments, as in them the hoisting-cages pass up and down, just as does the elevator in a hotel. The fourth is known as the pump-compartment, as down it passes the pump column, an iron pipe from twelve to sixteen inches in diameter, through which the water is forced up from the bottom of the mine. The pumping machinery is the most pondrous about a mine, and the largest engine in the hoisting works of a mine is always that which drives the pump. The pumping apparatus, balance-bobs, tanks down the line of the shaft, the course of the water from the bottom of the mine to the surface, and the working of the several parts from the surface down, all are too complicated to be explained

Interior Ophir Hoisting Works, 1876, collodion/albumen, Carleton E. Watkins. California State Library.

without the aid of many drawings.

The hoisting-engines, and all the hoisting machinery, are at the end of the building opposite that occupied by the shaft and fifty or sixty feet away. Here we find the alert and keen-eyed engineers constantly at their post by their engines. Before them is a large dial, like the face of a clock. On this dial are figures, and there is a hand like that of a clock, which moves slowly round and tells the engineer exactly where his cage is at all times after it has entered the shaft and passed out of his sight. By watching the hand moving round the dial he can see exactly when his cage is at the 900, the 1,000, 1,200, 1,500-foot or any other station. Besides keeping his eyes upon the dial, he must also keep his ears open for the signals struck upon his bell.

Engine at Gould and Curry Hill, 1862, collodion/albumen, attributed to Charles L. Weed (Lawrence & Houseworth). Library of Congress Prints and Photographs Division.

The bell stands near him and is his only means of communication with those far down in the lower levels of the mine. A man 1,500 feet below the surface strikes a signal upon the bell, and the engineer unhesitatingly obeys it. By means of this bell the engineer receives nearly all his orders. He is told when to start the cage up and when to stop, if he is to stop short of the surface; is told to hoist slowly; that there are men on board; and a great many other things which he understands as readily as the telegraph operator understands the click of his instrument. Each engineer has his bell and knows its sound better than he knows the sound of his own voice.

The hoisting-engines and the engineers who run them, occupy a large platform raised three or four feet above the general level of the floor, and about this platform are placards inscribed:

"NO PERSON IS ALLOWED ON THE PLATFORM, OR TO SPEAK TO THE ENGINEERS WHILE ON DUTY."

The lives of the miners are in the engineer's hands every minute of the day and night. To turn his head to nod to an acquaintance might cost a dozen lives. The man who is trusted at one of these engines is always a man who is thoroughly known and who has a well-established reputation for sobriety, "eternal vigilance," and good qualities of all kinds. In short, he is a man that can be trusted anywhere, and to say that Mr. Jones is engineer at this or that mine is to say that Jones is a man much above the average.

Over the mouth of the shaft stands a frame, made of very large and strong timbers, which is called the gallows-frame, probably from the huge cross-beam it supports. On this cross-beam are fastened the great iron wheels or pulleys over which pass the cables that extend down into the shaft and raise and lower the cages. These cables are not, as might be supposed from the name, round hempen ropes, like the cables of a vessel. The cables used in hoisting from the shafts of mines are flat, like a piece of tape, and are braided of the best quality of steel wire. They are five or six inches in width and about three-quarters of an inch in thickness. As they are constantly exposed to dripping water in the lower part of the shaft, the cables are all kept covered with a coating of tar to prevent their rusting.

Double-decker Hoisting Cages, 1876, illustration.

Near the engine is what is called the hoisting-reel, and on this the cable is wound up or unwound, in raising or lowering the cage, just as a piece of tape would be wound upon a spool. The steam-engines revolve the huge reels, and the cage is let down into the shaft or is hauled up from its bottom just as is required.

The cages work independently of each other. One may be going down while another is coming up, or one may be in motion while the others are standing still. When there is no living freight on the cages, they are often raised and lowered at a frightful rate of speed, but with men on board they are moved less rapidly.

Owing to the intense heat prevailing in many places in the lower levels of the mines, visitors must divest themselves of every stitch of their ordinary attire, as the first step toward their underground journey. This being the case, a comfortable and commodious dressing-room is fitted up in the works.

Hanging upon the walls of this room will be found a great number of clean suits for the accommodation of visitors. A suit for the journey into the lower regions is neat but not gaudy. It consists simply of a pair of blue flannel pantaloons, a grey or blue woolen shirt, a pair of heavy brogans for the feet, and a felt hat, with a narrow brim, for the head. In a suit of this kind even the greatest dignitaries present a very ordinary appearance. A minister of the gospel of meek and lowly aspect, when in his suit of black, becomes such a desperate-looking villain on donning blue woolen pantaloons and shirt, brogans, and felt hat, that you would not meet him alone on a mountain trail for all the wealth of the big bonanza; a pompous railroad president to whom you would almost fear to speak while in his upper-world attire, upon presenting himself before you in lower-level rig looks so much like a sneak-thief that you feel strongly impelled to kick him out of the room.

Fat men have the advantage in dressing for a trip to the lower levels, as nearly all of the pantaloons appear to have been selected for the special accommodation of men of Falstaffian proportions. In thus dressing for a trip into the mine there is always great merriment; each man laughs at his friend, unconscious of the ridiculous, mean, or insignificant figure he himself is cutting.

In the dressing-room will be found a bathtub, hot and cold water ready to hand by the mere turning of the cocks, an abundance of clean towels and all the convenience for taking a bath on coming up from the sweltering lower levels.

CHAPTER XLI

DESCENDING IN THE SAFETY-CAGE
Our Conductor—Downward—Unpleasant Possibilities—
Safety—A Blessed Inventor—The Price of Stock—
Vasquez and His Friends—The Carman

All being clad in the uniform of the gnomes of the silver-caverns, we go out to the shaft. A cage is stopped at the top of one of the compartments of the shaft, and its platform stands just on a level with the floor of the building. The cage is a heavy iron frame with grooves on two sides, which fit upon wooden guides run from the top to the bottom of the shaft. Upon these guides the cage runs smoothly through the whole course up and down the shaft, much the same as an elevator in a large hotel is seen to work.

The cage may have but a single floor or platform, or it may have two or three, upon each of which may be hoisted a car loaded with ore, or on which men may be raised or lowered. Those with two platforms are called "double-deckers," and those with three platforms are called "three-deckers."

One of the foremen of the mine, the superintendent, or whoever is to be our conductor, groups us upon the cage, showing us where we may safely grasp its iron frame for support, and finally all are in position.

The engineer is standing with one hand on the lever of his engine, watching our proceedings. Our conductor turns toward him with a wave of the hand. Instantly we feel ourselves dropping into the depth and darkness of the shaft.

Our first thought is, that between us and the bottom of the shaft—1500 feet below—we have nothing but the frail platform of the cage, and, instinctively, we tighten our grip upon the iron bars of the cage, determined that, should the bottom drop out, we will be found hanging to the upper works of our strange vehicle.

At the first plunge all is dark, but suspended from the cross-bar of the cage, or in the hands of our conductor, we have a lantern or two, and by the light afforded by these, we soon begin to distinguish the sides of the shaft. Our view is very unsatisfactory, however, as all the timbers on the sides of the compartment appear to be darting swiftly upward toward the top of the shaft; just as trees, fences, and telegraph poles seem to be running backwards when we are flying through the country on a lightning-express train.

Our speed is probably not half that at which the cage is lowered when its only load is an empty ore-car, a few beams of timber, or some such freight; but we are not anxious to go any faster. In the early days, on receiving a wink from a foreman, an engineer would drop men down a shaft at such a rate of speed that their breath was almost taken away, but at present, no superintendent on the Comstock allows any such dangerous fooling.

As soon as we have descended a few feet into the shaft, we see nothing of the steam, which, rushing out at its top, had presented so formidable an appearance above. It really amounts to nothing. It is merely the moist, warm breath of the mine coming in contact with the cold air at the surface. It is the same as the steam rising from a spring in winter, or as one's breath blown into the air on a frosty morning. This steam is seen at the mouth of the Consolidated Virginia shaft because it is what is called an "upcast," that is, the draft in it is upward. At the Ophir shaft no steam is seen, as it is a "downcast," the surface air is drawn or sucked in at its mouth. The air that enters the mouth of the Ophir shaft comes out at the mouth of the Consolidated Virginia shaft.

As we dart along down the shaft, we soon begin to pass the stations of the first or upper levels. Our speed is such that we see but little. We get a glimpse of what appears to be a room of considerable size, see a few men standing about with candles or lanterns in their hands, hear voices, and probably the clank of machinery. An instant after, all is again smooth sailing, and we see only the upward-fleeing sides of the shaft. Then there is another flash of many lights, a glimpse of half-naked men, a murmur of voices, and a clash of machinery, and we have passed another station. It is much like running past a railroad station in the night.

Sometimes our conductor is hailed by some one at a station as we dart past. We hear the voice, but distinguish no words. The conductor, however, has understood, and makes answer. As he replies, we drop away from the sound of his voice at such a rapid rate that his words are drawn out into sounds which we can hardly understand, though we are standing by his side. The answer, which is left scattered along up the shaft, is finally gathered in at the station for which it was intended, and is there put together and understood.

When we have descended to such a depth that from one thousand to twelve hundred feet of cable have been paid out from the reel above, we begin to experience quite a novel sensation. This is the "spring" of the cable.

Most persons have observed the very active bobbing motion of a toy ball

Cars Coming Out of a Shaft, 1867, collodion/albumen, Timothy H. O'Sullivan. Library of Congress Prints and Photographs Division. Three miners on the left waiting for their hoisting cage to be lowered, and two ore cars exiting hoisting cages.

suspended from an india-rubber string. The motion of our cage, hanging at the end of the cable, is much the same. The less one has of this peculiar motion the more he enjoys it. When this motion sets in, we at once begin to speculate in regard to the probable amount of "stretch" to be found in a first-class steel-wire cable—how far it may stretch before reaching the breaking point. It may be no more than 500 feet to the bottom of the shaft, but we feel that we do not care to risk falling even that short distance.

However, should the cable really break, there would be no danger, we should not fall. Attached to the upper part of the cage is a safety-apparatus designed expressly to prevent accidents of this nature. At the instant that the cable parted there would be released powerful springs which would throw out on each side of the shaft an eccentric, toothed wheel. These wheels, biting into the guides on each side, would instantly stop and hold the cage, block it fast in the shaft, as the wheels are of such a shape that the greater the weight and downward pressure upon the cage, the tighter they hold. In case of the cable breaking, we should not fall an inch, perhaps not half an inch—thanks to that life-saving invention, the safety-cage!

When the safety-cage was first introduced on the Comstock, I had the

Savage Cage, 1867, collodion/albumen, Timothy H. O'Sullivan. Library of Congress Prints and Photographs Division. A dismantled Savage mine hoisting cage sitting outside in the snow.

pleasure of assisting in making a test of the efficacy of the safety-apparatus at the Savage mine. We attached the cage to the iron cable by means of a large hempen rope.

This done, the superintendent and a gentleman present, who was in search of excitement, got upon the cage, and we lowered them into the mouth of the shaft, which was 1,000 feet in depth. We at the surface, who were conducting the experiment, then asked the superintendent and his companion if they were ready to be "launched into eternity," and receiving an affirmative reply, a brawny-armed miner, standing ready with a big broad-ax, severed the rope at a single blow. The cage dropped less than an inch, we above were all glad the experiment was over.

Had the safety apparatus failed to work, we at the surface would doubtless have all been summoned as witnesses when the coroner held his inquest.

In case of a train of railroad cars getting off the track, we never know where we shall bring up; we may go over an embankment or may be dragged against a point of rocks, but when a cable breaks while we are descending a shaft, we stop exactly where we happen to be when the accident occurs. Thus, as the sailor in a storm at sea pities the poor wretches who are on shore, so may the miner pity those persons above ground who travel on railroads.

In former times, however, previous to the introduction of the safety-cage in the Comstock mines, the breaking of a cable was an accident more dreaded and more dreadful than almost any other. There was no dodging when a cable parted. All who were on the cage must go to the bottom of the shaft. There the cage would be torn to pieces and driven through platforms of plank three or four inches in thickness into the "sump" or well of the shaft, where all who were not killed outright, were drowned.

Whether half a dozen men or a dozen were on the cage, it nearly always happened that all were killed. If any did in any instance escape, it was in such a horribly mangled condition that they were maimed for life. No wonder, then, that the miner every day of his life, and as often as he goes up and down the great shafts, blesses in his heart the inventor of the safety-cage!

We have been a long time in the shaft, though it takes but a very short time to make the actual descent. There is an occasional flash of lights, hum of voices, and clash of machinery, as described above, when the motion of the cage begins to "slow down," and a moment after this is noticed it stops exactly on a level with the floor of the station, 1,500 feet below the surface of the earth. We can hardly realize that we are standing at such a great depth below the upper world and the light of day.

Before us is what is called the "Station."

A "station" is the place of landing at each level of the mine (the levels are generally about 100 feet apart), and it is at the station that the cage stops to take on or let off passengers, to take on cars loaded with ore that are going up, or to put off empty cars that are going down. The station is generally a large and roomy apartment, the walls of which are sealed with rough boards, and the roof of which shows heavy supporting beams. .

It looks not unlike the interior of some of the large, rude wayside-inns seen in places in California on mountain roads. Hats, coats, shirts, and many similar articles are seen hanging upon nails driven into the walls, and two or three large coal-oil lamps fixed in brackets, render the place light and cheerful.

Upon the floor of the station (it has a floor as good as would be seen in most houses), ranged along the walls are seen boxes of candles, coils of fuse, and many other mining stores. There is also a large cask containing ice-water, with a tin dipper hanging on a nail near at hand. The station is a sort of lounging place, where the men who happen to have nothing to do for a few minutes stop to hear the news from the surface. Here there is more chat and sociability than in any other part of the mine. The reports of the sales of stocks in the San Francisco Stock Board are brought to the office of the mine as soon as they are telegraphed to the city, and about the time the reports arrive, you will hear the men at the station anxiously inquiring the price of stocks of the first man who comes down from the surface. The man thus questioned seems well prepared to answer, and gives the prices for the day, of a dozen or more of the leading stocks.

His report doubtless quickly passes through the mine, and soon five or six hundred men away down in the silver caverns, from 1,500 to 2,000 feet beneath the surface, know as much about the price of stocks for the day as do those persons who are walking the streets of the town. Other items of news circulate in the same way; but stocks they are always interested in. Almost every miner owns shares in some mine. There are not a few men working in mines along the Comstock who are worth from $40,000 to $50,000, and some who are probably worth still larger sums. While at work they are earning $4 per day regularly, and can "speculate" just as well as if they were constantly on the streets watching the stock reports.

In some of the stations are to be seen things that one would not expect to find hundreds of feet below the surface. In the Crown Point mine, for instance, the visitor finds on one of the walls of the station at the 1,100-foot level, a handsome little cabinet of ores, minerals, coins, and curiosities of all kinds—all neatly displayed in a suitable case which is provided with glazed doors. On the walls is also to be seen a considerable collection of photographs of actors, actresses, singers, and other celebrities. There is one group that is labelled "Vasquez and His Friends." The "friends" grouped about the notorious bandit are photographs of leading citizens of the town of Gold Hill, a church deacon among the number.

We have all heard about things being played "low down," but it would seem that this joker, at the depth of 1,100 feet, has it down about as low as any man on the continent. The cabinet, and the gallery of celebrities are the property, the care, and the pride of the station-tender of the level named.

A car-track—a railroad track in miniature—is laid through the floor in the centre of the station, which track runs out to the main north and south drift of the mine (it must be borne in mind that the general course of the Comstock lode is north and south), and through the main drift connects—by means of turn-tables—with a great number of cross-cuts and other drifts.

As we stand in the station, cars loaded with ore are regularly arriving from the several "stopes" of the level. These are run upon the cage, the signal to hoist is given to the engineer above, and an instant after, the cage and car, with its load of ore, dart swiftly up the shaft. Perhaps at the same instant a cage comes down the adjoining compartment, bringing with it an empty ore-car. This is at once grasped by a man in waiting, known in the mine as a "carman," and is trundled away to some distant part of the mine, to be again loaded with ore and again whisked up to the surface on the cage.

As there are three hoisting compartments, the arrivals and departures are quite frequent, and the station is really quite a business place.

CHAPTER XLII

BELOW THE SURFACE

Tumbling Down a Chute—Timbering a Mine—
Taking Samples—What the "Giraffe" can Carry—
Gnomes of the Mine—Troglodytes—What is "Sumpf?"

In order that the reader may get a proper idea of the underground works of a mine, I shall now give a detailed description of all that is worthy of special mention. Drifts are openings or galleries from four to six feet in width, and from six to eight feet in height, opened along the course of the vein. They are generally run along one of the walls of the vein, in the "country rock," (rock outside of the vein) as that contains no lime, and therefore stands best, and does not swell and crush the timbers. In some drifts the rock stands without being timbered. The main north and south drift, generally the first reached after leaving a station in a mine, is the highway of the level in which it is opened. It has a car-track running through its whole length, and, in some cases, as in the main drift on the 1,500-foot level of the consolidated Virginia and California mines, contains a double car-track.

The cross-cuts are the same kind of openings as the drifts, but they are smaller and run across the course of the vein—run east and west. They start from the main drift, and are pushed out into the vein and ore-body, if ore-body there be. Pushed out in this way from the main drift at intervals of about 100 feet, they cut through and "prospect" the vein. The progress of the cross-cuts on a new level in a leading mine on the Comstock is always watched with great interest by all the "mining experts," "stock sharps," and mining men generally.

Car-tracks are laid in all of the cross-cuts, and connect with the track of the main drift by means of turn-tables. The crosscuts are pushed through the vein to its opposite wall, in order that the whole of the ground may be thoroughly explored and its boundaries defined. In order to secure a free circulation of air on the level, they are frequently connected at various points by cross-drifts.

Winzes are small shafts sunk from one level to another in the mine. They

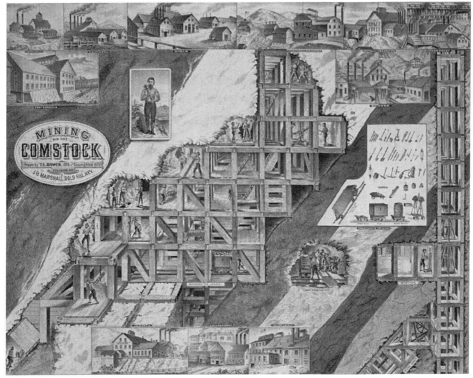

Mining on the Comstock, 1867, lithograph, T. L. Dawes, printed by Le Count Bro's., San Francisco, published by J. B. Marshall, Gold Hill, Nevada. Library of Congress Prints and Photographs Division.

are sunk in any place where they may happen to be required. Some are sunk vertically, but many follow the foot-wall of the vein, and thus go down at an angle of from thirty-five to forty-five degrees. All are of great use for the purpose of ventilation, and those that are sunk at an angle are very frequently properly planked up, and used as chutes through which to send ore or timbers to a lower level. In all mines will be found a great number of these chutes. Sometimes the men fall into them. When this happens they are always to be found at the bottom, on the level below, immediately after. Generally, men are not very badly hurt by sliding through an ordinary chute, yet not a few have been killed by such a fall, and many have had bones broken.

In going down a chute much depends upon the angle of the opening—the steeper, the more danger there is in making the trip. On the surface of the earth all the vertical winzes would be called shafts, and what are called drifts and cross-cuts below would be called tunnels, were they where their mouths came out on the surface. An "upraise" is where the miners begin on a lower level and dig upward toward a higher. While it is going up, it is an upraise, but when it is connected with the level above it is a winze. Should it never reach the level for which it was started it remains an upraise for all time.

Winzes are very often thus made—one set of miners being engaged below at digging up, while above another set are digging down. The progress made by the men below is always much more rapid than that of the men above, as every ounce of dirt loosened at once falls down out of the way.

When the ore-body has been properly opened, explored, and ventilated by means of drifts, cross-cuts, and winzes, the work of extraction is commenced.

The first opening is made on the "track-floor" of the level— the floor on which are run the drifts and cross-cuts wherein are laid the car-tracks— and in the bottom of this opening or chamber are put down the sills for the first "square-set" of timbers.

The timbers, used as supports in a mine are from twelve to fourteen inches square. The posts are six feet, and the caps five feet, in length. The upper ends of the posts are framed in such a manner that the ends of four caps may rest upon each, and leave a mortise in the centre, in which to insert the tenon of the post of the next "set;" on the top of this is a place for another post, and so the work of building up sets goes on to any height that may be required.

As the ore is extracted at the sides of the first set, the same squares of timbers are built up in those places, and there is formed a sort of pyramid of cribs, rising constantly as the work of extracting the ore proceeds. The top sets of this pyramid are secured closely against the ore, by means of large wooden wedges, and the side sets are also wedged up against the ore in the same way, as they are carried up. In this way the mass of ore over-head is supported at all points by the cribs of timbers, except here and there where chambers are being excavated in the ore-body for new sets.

Thus are squares of timbers constantly added, and the pyramid carried up till the ore has been worked out to the level above. If the level above has been worked out, it is already filled with the same square sets as are being built up from below, and the latter rise into their proper places and fit as neatly as the squares on a checker or chess-board.

The sets are six feet in height by five feet in width, and as they rise, floors of strong plank are laid upon each set. Thus there are seen floors some six feet apart from the bottom to the top of the level.

In these floors are square openings as for trap-doors, with short flights of steps leading from floor to floor. The floors are pushed out against the breasts of ore on all sides as the stope is extended. A light blast of giant-powder being exploded in the face of the ore-breast, the mass is shattered, and is then easily pulled down by the picks of the miners.

As the ore is dug down it falls upon the floors, from which it is eas-ily shoveled into the wheelbarrows, by means of which it is carried to the chutes. These chutes lead down to ore-bins on the track-floor, where the cars are loaded which carry the ore to the main shaft and finally up to the surface, and out along a track which leads to the ore-house, from which it is sent to the mills. This is the method of timbering mines that was invented by Mr. Philip Deidesheimer, in the early days of Washoe, when he was superintendent of the old Ophir mine. The building up of timbers in square sets or cribs is found to be exactly what is required, as a cavity of any size, however great, can by this plan be filled up and its roof supported.

In order to still further secure the mine, it is usual to plank or timber

Miners at Work Underground, Virginia City, Nevada, 1867, collodion/albumen, Timothy H. O'Sullivan. National Archives. A miner raking ore from an underground chute into an ore-car.

up a section of four of these square sets, and fill them in from bottom to top with waste rock. Thus is provided a large column of stone reaching up to and supporting the roof of the mine. Such columns are constructed in a number of places, at suitable intervals throughout each level of the mine, and they are found to stand more strain than would all of the timber that could be piled into a level. Being built up of loose rocks they gradually yield for a time, but still stand as firmly in their places as before, whereas a solid column of stone would be crushed into a thousand fragments, and would let down the whole upper part of the mine.

In some mines many blocks of porphyry and other barren rock are found with the ore, making it necessary to do a great deal of assorting, but in the Consolidated Virginia mine there is no work of this kind to be done, at least not on the 1500-foot level, where they are sloping out in the bonanza. There is nothing to do but dig down the rich masses of black sulphuret and chloride ores, shovel them into the cars, and send them to the surface to be taken to the mills, and the same is the case in the California mine.

Samples are taken from each car-load of ore down in the mine, when it reaches the main shaft; at the surface other samples are taken, and at the mills samples are taken of the pulp, every hour, as it runs from the batteries—in short, the ore is sampled everywhere, and at all stages in the handling, from the ore-breasts till it has passed through the mills, and finally appears in the shape of large, shining silver bricks, each weighing a hundred pounds or more. All the samples thus taken are carefully assayed, and the results compared and noted.

An incline is simply an inclined extension of the main shaft, from some convenient point below, or rather at or near the point where the shaft strikes the west wall of the vein. The Comstock lode dips to the eastward at an angle of from thirty-five to forty-five degrees, and as the main working shaft of a mine is always sunk to-a considerable distance—a thousand feet or more—to the eastward of the croppings [*i.e.,* that part of the lode which comes to the surface of the earth], the west wall is not reached until the shaft has attained a depth of from 1,000 to 1,500 feet, depending upon how far east of the croppings it was sunk.

The main incline of a mine is of about the same dimensions as the main shaft, and is timbered in much the same way. In the Consolidated Virginia mine there is as yet no incline, but at the Crown Point mine is to be seen one that is a model in every respect. This incline starts at the 1,100-foot level, from the bottom of the vertical shaft, and goes down with the dip of the vein (at an angle of about thirty-five degrees), to the 1,700-foot level, its present terminus. A track is laid on its bottom, of ordinary railroad iron, and as neither cages nor a car of the usual pattern can be used in an incline, recourse is had to another device. A kind of car called a "giraffe" is used for hoisting through an incline. It has low wheels in front and high ones behind; thus the body of the giraffe stands level, the same as a common ore-car on an ordinary track.

The giraffe is capable of carrying eight tons of ore—more than eight ordinary car-loads. It is lowered down the track to the bottom of the incline, and hauled up to the foot of the shaft by means of a round steel-wire cable which runs upon a reel at the surface.

The cable passes over a large iron pulley at the top of the vertical shaft, and *under* a second pulley of the same kind at its bottom. The cable is also supported by rollers, placed in the centre of the track, as it travels up and down the incline, otherwise its great weight would cause it to drag upon the ground. From the upper side of an incline, stations are made, the same as they are made at intervals along a vertical shaft; drifts are then run, and the work of cross-cutting and prospecting the vein goes on in the same way as when the ore-body is approached by means of a shaft. The giraffe has in front and on the "outside" two seats, facing each other, on which six passengers can ride very comfortably. Sometimes there is hitched behind the giraffe a second car of the same pattern, called the "back-action."

There is not a little of novelty in a ride up an incline on a "giraffe." The conductor of the "train," who is seated by our side, gives the signal for starting by pulling a wire and striking upon the engineer's bell—far away up the incline and up the vertical shaft, and some distance beyond that again in the engine-house—a certain number of strokes. Instantly we start, and soon are darting up the steep iron way at a terrific rate of speed. Lamps are placed at intervals on the sides of the incline; besides, we carry lanterns, and there are lights burning at all the stations. Thus our underground railroad is well lighted up. We have a good view of the track, and can see the rails glistening far ahead of and above us.

We rush up this steep road so rapidly that the posts along the sides of the incline resemble a fine-toothed comb. To look ahead and see before you, and high above you, a hundred yards or more of semi-vertical railroad, up which you are thundering at whirlwind speed, is strikingly the reverse of natural. Going down does not in any way interfere with your notions of the "eternal fitness of things," for it is quite natural for anything that is loose to run down hill, but this fierce darting up the steep iron rails somewhat unsettles you.

Up this queer railroad you are hurled through the caverns of the gazing Troglodytes, till you reach the foot of the vertical shaft, when they transfer you to a cage, and you are shot out at the top, much as the "Red Gnome," in the play, is shot up through the trap in the stage-floor of a theatre.

A giraffe is provided with a safety-apparatus somewhat similar to that on a cage. A large wooden rail runs the whole length of the track. Extending from the side of the giraffe, and almost clasping this rail, are two toothed, eccentric wheels. Should the cable break, these wheels would instantly grasp and clasp the rail, and the greater the weight upon the car the more fiercely they would bite into the wood, and retain their hold upon it. This invention has been the means of saving scores of lives.

The "sump" is the well or hole sunk below the bottom of a shaft, for the purpose of holding the water flowing in from above. In this is placed the "suction" of the pump, and into it is collected the water from all parts of the mine. Although "sump" is now considered an English word, it was doubtless derived from the German word, "sumpf," which means a marsh, pool, bog, or fen. When miners fall down a shaft it is frequently necessary to fish their mangled remains out of the sump with grappling irons.

As some persons may desire to know how sinking can be carried on in the bottom of a shaft where there is a strong influx of water, it may be well to explain the matter. On the end of the pump-column or tube which comes down near to the bottom of the shaft, is a piece of flexible hose, the same as the "suction" of a fire-engine, and this is moved about from side to side in the shaft, always keeping the end of it in the low places where the water collects.

Union Pump Engine. c. 1890, dry plate/collotype, James H. Crockwell. Library of Congress Prints and Photographs Division.

CHAPTER XLIII

CURIOSITIES OF VENTILATION
Draughts and Drifts—Machinery of the Lower-Levels—
Southward Currents—Use of Compressed Air—
Industrious little Engines

The only air-shaft on the Comstock lode worthy of the name, is that of the Belcher Mining Company. In many situations air-shafts do not seem to be required, connections with the main working shafts of other mines serving the same purpose. In some places along the lode are old shafts—sunk in the early days—with which connection has been made, and these often do very good service as air-shafts. The air-shaft of the Belcher Company is sunk at a point about 100 yards to the northward of their main hoisting-works.

The size of the excavation made in the rock is 8x14 feet. This, when timbered up, gives two compartments, each 6x6 in size. Where the rock is hard and perfectly solid the shaft is cribbed with timbers 6x12 inches in size; but where it is soft and inclined to swell, it is timbered in sets; timbers 12 inches square being used. All of this work is done in the most substantial manner possible. From the surface to the 1,000-foot level the shaft is carried down vertically, but from this point it is on an incline corresponding to the dip of the ledge, which is about 36 degrees, and to the east. The portion of the shaft which is carried down on an incline was kept in the west country rock lying back of the ledge. The object in keeping in this rock was to avoid ground that would be liable to swell and then crush in the sides of the shaft.

This shaft is of the same size and is constructed after the same plan as that destroyed by fire, October 30, 1874, by which accident a large number of men were badly burned, and some lost their lives. It extends down to the lowest levels of the mine and will be continued downward as new levels are opened. In excavating the shaft, work was begun at the same time on the surface and down at the 850foot level of the mine—the men below digging upward while those above were sinking.

The shaft is "downcast," that is, the air from the surface of the earth is drawn or sucked down into it and finds its way out through the main working shaft and other shafts connecting with the mine by means of drifts. The first shaft was also a "downcast," but when on fire, the draught was changed, and a column of flame darted upward from its mouth a hundred feet into the air, with a roar that could be heard at the distance of a mile or more. Had not the shaft caved and filled up with rock after the timbers were burned out of it, it would always have remained an "upcast;" at least, so say all the old miners.

Here it may not be out of place to speak of some of the curiosities of ventilation.

The Yellow-Jacket shaft, previous to the great fire in that mine some years ago, had a strong draught downward; the fire changed the draught, and it has ever since remained an "upcast." This is a curious freak of nature which all old miners have observed. When once the change in the draught takes place it is permanent. A curious thing in ventilation— and it is a nut for the scientists to crack—is that everywhere along the Comstock lode the tendency of all currents of air is to the southward—in the same direction that the ore chimneys tend. Here certainly is at work another mysterious force of nature. This tendency of the air-currents to move southward has never been overcome, except in one or two instances, and these exceptional cases will presently be mentioned. There are some queer courses taken by currents of air when once they have descended beneath the surface of the earth, which none of our scientific men have attempted to explain. The commonly accepted theory is that when two shafts are connected by means of a drift, the draught or ascending current of air will be through the higher shaft—the longer branch of the siphon—but exactly the reverse is seen if the short shaft happens to Stand to the southward of the long one.

The air will even go down a shaft and crawl out through a tunnel when that tunnel runs in a southerly direction!

When the Union tunnel connected with the old Ophir mine the air did not draw through the tunnel and pass up and out through the main shaft, but came out of the mouth of the tunnel. When the old Best and Belcher works connected with the Gould and Curry tunnel, the same thing was seen—the air went down the shaft and passed out at the mouth of the tunnel. About the next connection of the kind made on the lead was between the Crown Point and Belcher, at the depth of 160 feet; and the current of air went down the higher shaft, moved southward, and came out at the Belcher. Next the Yellow-Jacket and the Crown Point connected, and the draught was southward to the Crown Point. The Alpha and the Imperial next connected, and the draught went south to the Jacket. When the Gould and Curry and the Savage connected, the draught went south to the Savage. When connection was made between the Ophir and the Consolidated Virginia, the air went south to the Consolidated. The only places I know of on the lead where the air moves to the northward are between the Gould and Curry and the Consolidated Virginia, and between the Hale and Norcross and the Savage, and here it probably would not move north but for strong inducements.

The latest instance of this tendency of currents of air to move southward in mines is seen in the Overman mine. When that mine was connected with the Belcher, the draught was southward, out through the Overman shaft, though it stands much lower than any of the shafts connected with the Belcher mine.

From the facts given, it will be seen that there are some curious things connected with the ventilation of mines, and that it is not altogether impossible that Sutro's big tunnel may draw backwards, when completed.

A great deal of machinery is now beginning to be used on the lower levels of the principal mines on the Comstock. Some years ago steam-engines were set up in the lower levels of some of the leading mines, with boilers, furnaces, and all, just as on the surface. This would not do. The heat of the furnaces, boilers, and steam, added to the heat of the mine, could not be endured by the engineers and others whose duty it was to "stand watches" about the machinery.

A few years since an engine was set up on the 1,000-foot level of the Gould and Curry mine, and steam was conducted to it from boilers situated on the surface. When this engine was started up there was a popping of champagne corks away down there in the bowels of the earth, and a good time was had drinking to the success of the experiment. But it was not a success after all—it wouldn't do. The ground began swelling, the timbers were crushed and twisted, the engine bed could not be kept level three days at a time—it was like a boat in a rough sea, now on this end, and now on that—and the experiment was a failure.

The latest attempt to use steam machinery underground was at the Ophir mine. A boiler and engine were set up on the 1,465-foot level, near the main shaft, up which was extended a sheet-iron smoke-stack reaching to the surface. This engine was used in sinking a winze (situated 365 feet to the eastward) to the 1700-foot level, and also in doing some work on the level last named. The furnace and boiler heated up the level to such a degree that it was "killing" to the men. The boiler still stands where it was set up, but is now used as a reservoir for compressed air.

The introduction of engines and machinery to be run by means of compressed air, was a grand forward stride in the science of mining.

In the Consolidated Virginia and California mines are to be seen at work a number of small engines that are run by compressed air, furnished by two powerful compressors that are constantly in operation on the surface. The air is carried down the main shaft in a large iron pipe, and from this smaller pipes branch off in all directions, and are carried along the roofs of the drifts and cross-cuts, as we see gas-pipes running through buildings in the upper-world.

Thus is the compressed air carried down into all parts of the mine where work is being done. In places we see small engines at work at the top of winzes, where they do all the hoisting, and effect a great saving of both money and muscle. At other points, in passing along a drift, we suddenly come upon a small chamber constructed on one side, and sitting in this we see a "cunning" little engine, industriously at work at running a blower (a machine such as we see in foundries for furnishing a blast to the cupola, where metal is melted), which blower is sending a stream of fresh air through a pipe to men working in some far-away, heated cross-cut or upraise.

There are quite a number of these little engines and blowers in various parts of the mine, and instead of heating they greatly assist in cooling those parts of the mine in which they are used.

As the drifts and cross-cuts are advanced, the air-pipes are carried along their roofs or sides, and are in readiness for use in running the Burleigh drills, by means of which the holes are drilled in the face of the drift where the rock requires to be blasted. The air-pipes being in place in all the cross-cuts and drifts, the Burleigh drill may be moved about from place to place as required, and thus a single drill can be used in several different drifts during the day. When a sufficient number of holes for blasting have been made in one drift, the drill is placed upon its carriage and is moved along the car-track to another, where connection is made with the air-pipe, and it is hammering away again with but little loss of time.

In the Ophir mine a small engine, situated at the winze mentioned above as being 365 feet east of the main shaft, does all the hoisting from the 1,700-foot level, and in a more satisfactory manner in every respect than the same work was formerly done by the old steam-engine. On the 1,150-foot level of the Consolidated Virginia mine a winze was sunk to the depth of 140 feet, with one of these little air-engines, and it could have been sunk to any depth required, but for an influx of water which was too strong to be contended with in that remote part of the mine at that time.

Each year more and more machinery will be run in the mines of the Comstock, by means of compressed air. It is exactly what is needed, as all the air exhausted in the lower levels of a mine is beneficial and is so much ventilation and so much food gained for the lungs of the miners. Compressors, and machinery to be worked by them, are being ordered by all of the leading mines, and are already considered indispensable appliances in modern mining.

Burleigh drills at work. c. 1890, dry plate/collotype, James H. Crockwell.
Library of Congress Prints and Photographs Division.

CHAPTER XLIV

Underground Business Arrangements

*Changing Shifts—A Shift-Boss's Report—Useful Items—
Modern Troglodytes—Shirtless but Hot—Fights and Factions*

In order that the reader may obtain something like a correct idea of
the appearance of the interior of a first-class mine, let him imagine it
hoisted out of the ground and left standing upon the surface. He would
then see before him an immense structure, four or five times as large as
the greatest hotel in America, about twice or three times as wide, and over
2000 feet high. The several levels of the mine would represent the floors
of the building, These floors would be 100 feet apart—that is, there would
be in the building twenty stories, each 100 feet in height. In a grand hotel
communication between these floors would be by means of an elevator;' in
the mine would be in use the same contrivances, but instead of an "elevator," it would be called a "cage."

Our mine, raised to the surface, as we have supposed, would present
much the same appearance as would a large building with the side walls
removed, allowing a full view of all of its floors to be obtained. As we should
see the elevator stopping at various floors to take on and put off passengers
and baggage, so we should see the cage stopping at the several levels to take
on and put off miners or full or empty ore-cars.

Upon the various floors of our mine we should see hundreds of men at
work, but there would be seen between the floors, in many places, a solid
mass of ore, in which the men were working their way up and rearing their
scaffolding of timbers toward the floor above.

Not only would the men be seen thus at work, but there would also be
seen at work on the various floors, engines and other machinery; with,
high above all, the huge pump, swaying up and down its great rod, 2,000
feet in length and hung at several points with immense balance-bobs, to
prevent it being pulled apart by its own weight.

Occasionally, too, we should see all of the men disappear from a floor,
and soon after would be heard in rapid succession ten or a dozen stunning
reports—the noise of exploding blasts.

When blasts are about to be let off in a mine, after the fuses have been
lighted and the miners are retreating to a place of safety, "Fire!" is the startling
cry that is heard from them, as they fall back along the drifts and cross-cuts.
The cry is well understood throughout the mine to mean no more than that
fire has been set to the fuses, and that several blasts will shortly go off.

In the Consolidated Virginia mine, and in all other leading mines, three
shifts of men are employed, each shift working eight hours.

The morning shift goes on at 7 o'clock. Before descending the shaft the men go to the office of the time-keeper, situated in the hoisting works, and give their names at a window which resembles the window of the ticket-office at a railroad-station. These men come up out of the mine at 3 o'clock p.m., and again go to the window of the time-keeper's office, and give their names.

Chamber in C & C mine at the 1,650 foot level. c. 1890, dry plate/collotype, James H. Crockwell. Library of Congress Prints and Photographs Division.

The afternoon shifts go down at this hour—3 o'clock p.m.— giving in their names before descending the shaft. They come up out of the mine at 11 o'clock at night, but do not give their names. If any men are missing, or are taken sick, and do not work, their names are reported by the bosses of their shift.

The night shift go down into the mine at 11 o'clock at night and come out at 7 o'clock in the morning, when they go to the time-keeper's window, give their names, and get their mark for the day's work done. There are three shift-bosses for each level where regular eight-hour shifts are being worked.

When the shifts are being changed the men do not rush promiscuously to the shaft, but form in a line and march up to the cages in single file, just as men are seen to form in line in front of the window of a post-office or at the polls on the occasion of an election. On the levels below, when the men are coming up, they form, in lines in the same way in front of the shaft. No crowding or disorder of any kind is permitted.

The shift-bosses report to the time-keepers the number of men employed on their shift, the number of car-loads of ore, and the number of car-loads of waste rock hoisted during the shift, all of which is placed in a daily report, for which there are, in the office of the time keeper, printed blanks. A carload of ore is calculated to weigh 1,800 pounds, and the number of tons hoisted during the day is also figured up and set down in the blank. The following is one of the blanks used in the Consolidated Virginia—filled up with the exact work of the day on which it is dated—the names given are those of the shift-bosses:

CONSOLIDATED VIRGINIA MINING COMPANY
DAILY REPORT OF ORE EXTRACTED

DATE	NUMBER OF MEN	CARS OF WASTE	CARS OF ORE	TONS OF ORE HOISTED	TOTAL TONS OF ORE HOISTED
MARCH 19TH, 1875					
1,300 STATION LEVEL					
7 O'CLOCK ⎫	17				
3 DO ⎬ WILSON	8				
11 DO ⎭	8				
1,400 STATION LEVEL					
7 O'CLOCK DAN. SKERRY	75	4	54	48 1,200	
3 DO WM. HARPER	78	7	67	60 600	
11 DO JAS. McCOURT	76	5	79	71 200	180
1,500 STATION LEVEL					
7 O'CLOCK JAS. O'TOOLE	63	6	65	58 1,000	
3 DO WM. ODEY	53	3	131	117 1,800	
11 DO RICHD. LEWIS	54	7	117	105 600	281 1,400
HOISTED THROUGH G AND C SHAFT MARCH 18TH, '75	41	26	38	38	38
TOTAL NO. OF TONS					499 1,400

180 TONS TO MILL LUMP
281 TONS TO MINE LUMP

By this report it will be seen that the account of the ore taken out through the Gould and Curry ("G & C") shaft is not handed in until the day after the work is done. The report also shows the number of tons sent to the dump of the big mill, near the mine, and the number sent to the dump of the mine to be shipped to other mills. In all departments an equally exact account is kept of all work done.

In the Consolidated Virginia mine there is a man who is what may be called a general foreman. He has charge of the shaft, the prospecting drifts, and cross-cuts, and attends to the ventilation of the mine and to keeping it clear of water; in short, looks after underground affairs generally.

After ore has been struck in the drifts and the work of extraction begins, this officer turns that portion of the mine over to one of the foremen who superintends the work of extracting the ore.

There is always a day-boss on the 1,500-foot level, and at night his place is filled by a second general foreman of the underground regions, who has charge of everything by night, as the other officer has during the day.

Besides the miners there are employed a great number of timbermen, who look after the timbers and the timbering; the pump man, who takes care of the pumps; the watchmen, who go their rounds, each on his level, to look out for fire and to keep an eye on things generally; and the pick-boy, who goes about through the mine gathering up the dull picks and sending them up the shaft to be sharpened, who carries the sharp picks to the places where they are wanted, who distributes water among the men and who, in short, is general errand-boy in the mine. As may be supposed, his position is no sinecure.

The following amounts of timber, wood, and other mining supplies are used per month in the Consolidated Virginia mine, and, from this, what is used in other leading mines may be surmised: Feet of timber per month, 500,000; cords of wood, 550; boxes of candles, 350; giant-powder, 2 tons; 100 gallons of coal-oil, 200 gallons of lard-oil, 800 pounds of tallow, 20,000 feet of fuse, 37 tons of ice, 3,000 bushels of charcoal, 1½ tons of steel, 5 tons of round and square iron, 4 tons of hard coal (Cumberland), 50 kegs of nails, and a thousand and one other articles in the same proportion. The amount of timbers buried in the mines of the Comstock is almost beyond computation. It is more than there is in all of the buildings in the State of Nevada.

Sierra Nevada Hoisting Works, 1876, collodion/albumen, Carleton E. Watkins. California State Library.

Nearly all the pine forests on the eastern slope of the Sierra Nevada Mountains, for a distance of fifty or sixty miles north and south, have been swept away and buried in the lower levels, or consumed under the boilers of the mills and hoisting works. Already the lumbermen are pushing their way beyond the summit of the mountains, and the demand for timber and lumber is increasing every month, as new levels and new mines are opened.

In a silver-mine it is not all dark and dismal below, as many persons suppose. On the contrary, the long drifts and cross-cuts are lighted up with candles and lamps. It is only the little-used drifts, in parts of the mine distant from the main workings, that absolute and pitchy darkness prevails.

In the principal levels candles and lamps are always burning. When it is midnight above, and storms and darkness prevail throughout the city,

The Tunnel—Gould & Curry Mine, 1862, collodion/albumen, attributed to Charles L. Weed (Lawrence & Houseworth). Library of Congress Prints and Photographs Division.

whole acres of ground, hundreds of feet below in the bowels of the earth, are lighted up; and down there all is calm and silent, save when sounds peculiar to the place break the stillness.

In a mine there is neither day nor night; it is always candlelight. If we go into a mine late in the afternoon and remain below for some hours, a gloomy feeling is experienced when we come to the surface and find it is everywhere night above. We almost wish ourselves back in the lower levels of the mine, for when we are there it seems to be always daylight above.

On the principal levels of a mine we have long drifts, galleries and crosscuts which intersect each other, much as do the streets and alleys in some old-fashioned, overcrowded village—some village seated in a confined place, where encroaching precipices seem to crush it out of shape.

Our underground streets are not wanting in life. As we pass along the highways and byways of the lower levels, we meet with the people of the place at every turn. One mine connects with another, and so we have streets 3 miles long. There are employed in a single mine from 500 to 700 men; a number sufficient to populate a town of considerable size. Men meet and pass us—all going about their business, as on the surface—and frequently a turn brings us in sight of whole groups of them. We seem to "have been suddenly brought face to face with a new and strange race of men. All are naked to the waist, and many from the middle of their thighs to their feet. Superb, muscu-

Gould & Curry Miners. c. 1890, dry plate/albumen, James H. Crockwell.
Library of Congress Prints and Photographs Division.

lar forms are seen on all sides and in all attitudes, gleaming white as marble in the light of the many candles. We everywhere see men who would delight the eye of the sculptor. These men seem of a different race from those we see above—the clothes-wearers. Before us we have the Troglodytes—the cave-dwellers. We go back in thought to the time when the human race housed in caverns; not only far up the Nile, as the ancients supposed, but in every land, at a certain stage of their advancement in the arts of life.

Not infrequently, while traveling along a lonely passage in some remote section of the mine, we are suddenly confronted by a man of large stature, huge, spreading beard, and breast covered with shaggy hair, who comes sliding down out of some narrow side-drift, lands in our path, and for a moment stands and gazes curiously upon us, as though half inclined to consider us intruders upon his own peculiar domain. We seem to have before us one of the old cave-dwellers and we should not be at all surprised to see him cut a caper in the air, brandish a ponderous stone ax, and advance upon us with a wild whoop.

The only clothing worn by the men working in the lower levels of a mine are a pair of thin pantaloons or overalls, stout shoes, and a small felt hat or a cap such as cooks are often seen to wear. Not a shirt is seen. From the head

Savage Mine Miners. c. 1890, dry plate/ albumen, James H. Crockwell.
Library of Congress Prints and Photographs Division.

to the hips each man is as naked as on the day he was born. All are drenched with perspiration, and their bodies glisten in the light of the candles as though they had just come up through the waters of some subterranean lake.

In places, in some of the mines, the heat is so great that the men do not even wear overalls, but are seen in the breech-clout of the primitive races. Instead of a breech-clout, some of the miners wear a pair of drawers with the legs cut off about the middle of the thighs. Something must be worn on the head to keep the falling sand and dirt out of the hair, and shoes must be worn to protect the feet from the sharp fragments of quartz which strew the floors of the levels. One may be well acquainted with a miner as he appears upon the streets, yet for a time utterly fail to recognize him as found attired in the underground regions of a mine.

When about their work in the mine, the miners have little to say, and in going about in the several levels group after group may be passed and nothing said by any one, except some question may be asked by the foreman of the level or the superintendent of the mine, who are the usual guides of those who visit these underground regions.

Underground the men all have their respective levels, and there alone they belong. The miner who works on the 1,400-foot level may not venture down upon the 1,500, nor up to the 1,300. Those who are working on one level of a mine knows no more of what is going on in the level above or below—when there is anything of special importance being done—than they do of the developments that are being made in the mine of another company. The foreman of one level does not intrude upon the domain of a brother foreman. When, for instance, he has shown a visitor through his own level, he conducts him to the next and turns him over to the foreman or "boss" in charge of that portion of the mine.

In small or newly-opened mines this is of course different, as there but little is to be seen, and there is generally but a single officer in charge

No fighting is allowed among the miners while in the lower levels. No matter how angry they may become, not a blow must be struck. The penalty for a violation of this rule is the immediate discharge of both parties to the quarrel.

Comstock Miner, 1867, collodion/albumen, Timothy H. O'Sullivan. National Archives.

It very frequently happens that two men who have had a serious misunderstanding while in the mine, repair to some quiet place when they come to the surface and have their fight out, friends on both sides being present and the rules of the prize ring being observed.

Fights growing out of wrangles in the mines are always thus settled with fists; knives or pistols are never used on such occasions. However, there is much less quarreling in the mines than would be supposed, the large number of men and their various and antagonistic nationalities being considered. The fact that nearly all are members of the same society,—the Miners Union—doubtless has much to do with keeping peace among all the large underground families along the Comstock lode.

CHAPTER XLV

GHOST-HAUNTED SHAFTS
Rats—Unwelcome Visitors—Chasing the Ghost—Cornered

Thus far we have seen only such levels, drifts, and crosscuts as were well-timbered and in perfect order. We will now take a trip through an old upper level, where the ore has all been extracted, and where no trouble is taken to keep the ground up—one of the old upper levels of the Belcher mine, for instance. Here we find about ten acres of worked-out ground which is a regular wilderness.

In this place one sees something of the tremendous weight and pressure of the superincumbent earth. It is a place to make the hair rise erect on the head of any clothes-wearing man who has not been scalped by nature or by art. The large, square timbers are crushed down to half their original height, and are splintered and twisted; chambers originally square are squeezed into a diamond shape, and their roofs almost touch the floor in the centre; solid piles of timber that have been packed into the ground as long as there was room for another stick, are pressed into pancakes; winzes and chutes are "telescoped;" ladder-ways, once spacious, are crushed out of all shape, and now can hardly accommodate a cat—all is confused and shapeless.

This region somewhat resembles the track of a tornado in a timbered country—what is called a "windfall." In places we enter immense caverns where the timbers are gone, and where huge flakes of clay lean far out from the walls, and composedly look down upon us as we tremblingly glide along underneath. One is afraid to sneeze lest he bring these down upon his head. A smell of mustiness and decay pervades the whole place. The whole level is gradually settling down and squeezing together. There is no danger of the sudden caving of any considerable area of ground, but eventually all the timbers will be pressed into a pancake, and the place will be forever closed.

In these deserted levels the paths are circuitous and uncertain, and in threading the labyrinth of fast-disappearing drifts, galleries, and cross-cuts, one must have a guide who passes through them almost daily.

To those not familiar with mines it may appear strange, but the lower levels—indeed, all of the levels—are alive with rats. The miners never kill or molest them, therefore they become quite tame and saucy. As the miners all carry a lunch with them into the mine, the rats live well on the fragments. These rats are really of service, as they devour the scraps of meat and bones thrown upon the ground, which would in a short time create a bad odor in the mine. The decay of the smallest thing in a mine cannot be endured. Should a rat be killed by any accident it must be sent up out of the mine. Should a small piece of cotton cloth be burned in a drift, the miners would smell it throughout the level, and to burn a small splinter of pine would probably cause serious alarm, if not a grand stampede among them, as they would think there was a fire in the timbers of the mine.

In the old upper levels we find as many rats as in any other place. If we sit down upon a fallen timber and converse for a few minutes they will come about us. They think we are miners sitting down to lunch. They come and sit near us on the ends of the timbers, and cock their heads this way and that, as they look inquiringly about. Evidently they do not at all understand it. Why we should be sitting there talking, with no dinner-pails in sight, seems to puzzle them not a little.

There are frequently rats that are the pets of the men working in a particular part of the mine—a rat known to them by some mark, as his having lost a piece of his tail. To this rat they give some such name as "Bobby," or "Tommy," and feed and pet him until he becomes so saucy that he can hardly be kept out of the dinner-pails.

When there is about to be a great cave in a mine, the rats give the miners their first warning. They become very uneasy, and are seen scampering about at unwonted times and in unusual places. The rats first discover that the mine is settling, and they start out in search of a place of safety. It is supposed that in settling, the waste rock and timbers pinch them in their usual holes and haunts, and they are obliged to go forth in search of new quarters, in order to escape being crushed to death. A fire in a mine kills them by thousands. The poisonous gases penetrate to every part of the level, and not a rat is left alive. Sometimes after a fire in a mine they are gathered up on the floors by bushels. In trying to jump across the main shaft, a rat occasionally miscalculates the distance, and falls to the bottom. A rat falling a thousand feet and striking a miner on the head is sure to knock him down. The rat is killed, of course, as he generally explodes wherever he strikes. Dogs are dangerous about a shaft. Some years since, at Gold Hill, a dog fell into a shaft across which he attempted to jump, and killed two men who were at work at its bottom, three hundred feet below the surface.

So many men have been killed in all of the principal mines that there is hardly a mine on the lead that does not contain ghosts, if we are to believe what the miners say.

Some of the miners are very superstitious, while others are afraid, of nothing living or dead, and lay plans for frightening those known to be timid. At times, the miner who is passing through unfrequented drifts in the old upper levels is almost paralyzed by the sudden breaking forth of most fearful groans and shrieks, all ending, perhaps, in a burst of fiendish laughter. These sounds sometimes follow him to a considerable distance, coming from various directions. When a timid man hears these ghostly salutations, he loses no time in making his way to the settled portions of the mine.

The last troublesome ghost was one that haunted the 700-foot level of the Ophir mine, where a miner was killed some years ago. The bells of the engineers and all the signal-bells in the Ophir are worked by electricity. Although there was no one at work on the 700-foot level, troublesome signals often came from there. When the cage arrived at that point the engineer would be signaled to stop. Although confident that there was no one at the level, he could not do otherwise than obey the signal; not to heed it might cost a life.

Next would come a signal to lower to the level below; then a signal to hoist to the top, and the cage which had thus been traveling about would come to the surface with nothing upon it but the car-load of ore with which it started from the bottom of the shaft.

Sometimes there would come from the haunted level a perfect storm of signals, such as no man could understand; then for a day or two there would be no trouble. A man who was set to watch at the level was frightened nearly out of his wits by groans and shrieks, flashing lights, and all manner of fearful things, and swore he would not go there again for the whole Ophir mine. He even went so far as to declare that a ghost crept up behind him and threw its arms about him. All this perplexed the electrician of the mine not a little. One day, therefore, when signals were coming from the haunted level, he took a dark lantern and went down to that point. He had hardly stepped off the cage before he was saluted with an awful groan. Advancing into the drift a blinding light flashed into his eyes, and he heard a low, gurgling laugh that almost froze the blood in his veins.

He had gone down to the level, however, to clear up the mystery of the disturbances at that point, and he determined that no ghost should frighten him away.

He advanced towards where he had heard the laugh, and was again blinded by a flash of light. He then threw the light of his dark lantern before him along the drift, but it was empty. Far away, however, he heard groans, and then a fearful shriek.

Pushing on and flashing his light this way and that, he pursued the ghost. Time and again the light was flashed in his eyes, and the low, mocking laugh was heard, but however quickly he might turn his own light in the direction whence came the sound, he could see nothing. A moment after, the whole mine would seem to be lighted up in the distance, and the laugh would be heard far away.

Did he attempt to advance, the light flashed in his face from some nook near at hand, and a shriek was uttered almost at his side. Becoming desperate, the electrician charged about at random through the level, flashing his lantern in all directions. At length his light fell upon a man just as he was making into the mouth of an old drift. Keeping his light upon the spot, our electrician rushed forward, and pushing into the drift saw his man crouched behind some timbers at the further end. He was cornered at last.

Finding that he was caught, the fellow rose up and coolly said: "Well, *you* don't scare worth a cent!" In his hand the man held the bulls-eye lantern which he had been flashing in the face of the electrician, and he owned to having a confederate somewhere on the level who was similarly equipped, but refused to give his name.

The mysterious signals from the level were now accounted for. This man and two or three other mischievous fellows, who were the only men employed in that part of the mine, had been ringing themselves up and down between the almost deserted levels, and had been frightening out of their wits all who ventured near the haunted 700-foot level. Since the day of the electrician's adventure nothing more has been heard of the Ophir ghost.

CHAPTER XLVI

EXTRACTING SILVER FROM THE ORE
*The Reduction-Works—Working the Machinery—The Batteries—
Preparing the Ore—The Amalgamating-Room—Two Processes*

Having shown the reader what is to be seen in the underground regions of the mines, I shall now proceed to show him what is to be seen in a quartz-mill, explaining the use of the machinery and various processes for the extraction of the silver from the ore. I shall begin with the ore as it comes from the mine, and follow it through the reduction-works until it makes its appearance in the shape of silver bars, stamped with their value, and ready for the mint or the market.

The mills in which the ores of the Comstock lode are reduced, are all built on the same general plan. When the tourist has visited and examined one mill, he has seen them all, both great and small, so far as regards the processes in use for the reduction of the ore. Some mills are more conveniently arranged than others, however, and while in some machinery, is used which is somewhat behind the age, in others will be found in operation in every department machinery of the latest and most approved pattern.

The model mill of the State, and of the world, for the reduction of silver ore, is the new 60-stamp mill of the Consolidated Virginia Mining Company. In this mill is to be found all that is valuable in any mill, and much in the way of machinery that can be seen in no other works of the kind.

In describing a quartz-mill, and the processes used in working the ores of the Comstock mines, I shall, therefore, select the Consolidated Virginia reduction-works as those through which to conduct the reader. The Consolidated Virginia mill stands about 200 feet north-east of the company's main shaft and hoisting-works. The ground was well chosen, there being a considerable incline toward the east, which allowed of a proper and regular descent from the battery room on the west to the room containing the agitators on the east, so that the course of everything is downward, from the time of dumping the ore into the chutes at the top of the mill. The ground was graded out in regular terraces of the proper size for the several

California Pan Mill, Virginia City, 1876, collodion/albumen, Carleton E. Watkins. California State Library.

departments, as the initial step, and in their proper order were reared upon these, foundations for the various kinds of machinery, and the whole covered by one immense building or series of buildings, principally under one roof—a vast aggregation of buildings and machinery.

The battery-room, with ore-bin, etc., is situated on the west side of the mill, and is 100 feet in length by 58 feet in width. Immediately adjoining this, on the east, on a terrace a few feet lower, is the amalgamating-room, containing the pans, settlers, and other amalgamating apparatus. This room is 120 feet in length by 92 feet in depth. East of this, and a few feet lower down, is the room containing the agitators and other apparatus connected therewith. This room is 92 feet in length by 20 feet in width. North of the amalgamating-room is the engine-room, containing the engine and boilers. This room is 92 feet long by 58 feet in width. Near the mill stands a handsome office, 20x30 feet in size; and to the eastward, and distant from the mill some 30 feet, is the retort-house, built of brick, and 20x60 feet in size.

To drive the whole of the machinery of the works there is a compound condensing-engine of 600-horse power. This engine has two cylinders, the first 24x48 inches, and the second 48x48 inches in size. The steam is admitted to the first or "initial cylinder," where it is cut off at half stroke. It then passes into the second or "expansion cylinder," which, being twice the size of the first and having four times its capacity in cubical contents, gives an expansion of eight bulks—twice in the first cylinder, and four times in the second. After the steam has left the expansion cylinder, instead of exhausting in the open air it exhausts into a condenser, where it gains an additional power equal to the atmospheric pressure at the altitude of Virginia. The main shaft from this engine is 14 inches in diameter, and weighs 15,000 pounds. On this shaft is a fly-wheel (which is also a band-wheel and carries the large belt by which the batteries are driven) 18 feet

Omega Mill, 1876, collodion/albumen, Carleton E. Watkins. California State Library.

in diameter and weighing 16½ tons. On the extreme end of the main driving shaft is coupled a shaft 11 inches in diameter, which extends into the amalgamating-room and drives the pans and settlers—indeed, all the machinery except that connected with the batteries. The whole weight of the engine is about 50 tons, and it stands on a foundation of 450 cubic yards of masonry, laid in cement, the weight of which is over 600 tons. There are in this room four pair of boilers, eight in

Nevada Mill. c. 1890, dry plate/albumen, James H. Crockwell. Library of Congress Prints and Photographs Division.

all, each of which is 54 inches in diameter, and 16 feet in length. All of these boilers can be used simultaneously, or each pair can be run separately—just as may be required. From the floor of the engine-room to the ridge of the roof the distance is 50 feet. The west side of this, and of some of the adjoining rooms, is formed by a stone wall 22 feet in height. In these walls there are in all, 4,000 perches of mason-work—all trachyte rock. The smoke-stacks of the boilers are four in number, and each is 42 inches in diameter and 90 feet in height. In this room are two large steam-pumps for use in feeding the boilers, or to be used for fighting fire, if need be; each being supplied with hose of sufficient length to reach to any part of the building.

About 28 cords of wood are used per day—10,080 per annum. This wood is brought to the mill from a side-track of the Virginia and Truckee Railroad, on a truck which holds exactly one cord. Thus is the wood

Distributing Room, 1862, lithograph, plate from a Gould & Curry Silver Mining Company stock prospectus. California State Library.

Battery Room, 1862, lithograph, plate from a Gould & Curry Silver Mining Company stock prospectus. California State Library.

measured as it is delivered. The truck dumps the wood into a chute, which carries it down into the boiler-room, and it is landed just in front of the furnaces, where it is wanted.

We will now return to the west side of the mill and ascend to its extreme top, even above the roof. Here, above the roof, comes in a large car-track, leading directly from the main shaft of the hoisting-works at the mine. This track is 278 feet in length, and is housed in for its entire length. It is handsomely finished off, contains windows its whole length, is painted a light brown color, and strikingly resembles a ropewalk.

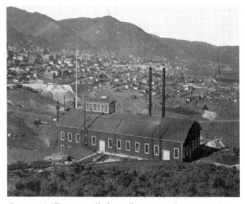

When the cages bring to the top of the shaft the cars loaded with ore, a carman is standing ready, who takes the car from the cage and pushes it before him over an iron track to the chutes which lead down through the roof of the mill

Bonanza Mill, 1876, collodion/albumen, Carleton E. Watkins. California State Library.

into the huge ore-bin below. This car-track, and the long building covering it, are supported upon a strong trestle-work constructed of large square timbers, and rising forty-four feet above the surface of the ground in the highest part. To keep the stamps supplied with ore requires one car-load to be sent out from the shaft every five minutes during the day and night. Although the cars were at first pushed out over the track by hand, they are now made up into trains of ten, and are hauled by a mule from the hoisting-works to the mill.

The ore, on being dumped into the chutes at the top of the mill, descends to the centre, from each side. The chutes have in their bottoms what are called "grizzlies"—iron bars placed three inches apart so as to form a screen—through which the fine ore drops into the bin below, while the coarse rock rolls on down and is dumped on a floor above the ore-bin, and about its centre, where stands the rock-breaker.

The rock-breaker is a heavy piece of machinery, which in appearance,

Gould & Curry Reduction Works, 1867, collodion/albumen, Timothy H. O'Sullivan. Library of Congress Prints and Photographs Division.

and the principle upon which it works, not a little resembles a huge nut-cracker or lemon-squeezer. It is the same kind of machine that is used in some cities for chewing up rock for macadamizing streets, and which is known as a "masticator."

The coarse rock being crushed in the rock-breaker is carried into the ore-bin by a chute. In the main chutes above are what are called distribut-

Interior of Buckeye Quartz Mill, 1862, collodion/albumen, attributed to Charles L. Weed (Lawrence & Houseworth). Library of Congress Prints and Photographs Division.

ing chutes, which are chutes that carry the descending ore far away from the centre of the bin. But for this arrangement, all of the ore would fall in the middle of the bin, which is no feet in length.

In the battery-room are ranged in a row, north and south through the building, six batteries of ten stamps each, or sixty stamps in all. Each , stamp weighs 800 pounds. Each set of ten stamps works independently of each other set, and can be stopped and started at will by simply moving a sort of brake or clutch. The whole of the stamps and the apparatus connected therewith, are driven by a belt from the main fly and band-wheel (mentioned above), which belt is 24 inches in width and 160 feet in length. This runs the counter-shaft in front of the batteries, and from the pulleys on this countershaft there are belts 14 inches in width and 60 feet in length which run each battery of ten stamps.

The main belt, which drives the whole of this machinery, runs at the rate of 3,600 feet per minute.

From the ore-bin the ore descends into the Tulloch self-feeders, one of which machines is required for every five stamps, or twelve in all. These do the whole work of feeding. The ore is not touched by anyone after it falls into the bin. Two men are able to keep watch over all the feeders supplying ore to the whole sixty stamps. The feeder is the invention of James Tulloch, of California, and is a very valuable laborsaving apparatus. The feeders are self-regulating, the motion

Empire State Mill, 1876, collodion/albumen, Carleton E. Watkins. California State Library. Located down Six Mile Cañon near Sugar Loaf Mountain.

of the stamps in dropping, operating them. When there is too much ore in the battery, the tappet of the stamp does not fall sufficiently low to strike the end of the rod attached to the feed-table, and no more rock enters the battery for a time; but as the rock is worked out, the feeder again begins to operate. In most of the mills the ore is still fed into the batteries, with shovels, by men known as "feeders." When the feeding is done by hand, the amount of ore reduced in a given time, depends much on the men who

do the work. They must put under the stamps all the ore they can crush, and no more. This must be done constantly throughout the twenty-hours for weeks and months.

In the Consolidated Virginia mill, the mortars—the huge iron boxes in which the stamps work—do not discharge the pulp or pulverized ore in front, as is usual, but at one side. This gives free access to the mortars in front for the purpose of putting in new shoes and dies. The "shoes" are

Pacific Mill, 1876, collodion/albumen, Carleton E. Watkins. California State Library.

the heavy blocks of iron or steel fastened to the lower end of the stamp. It is the shoes that fall upon and crush the ore when the stamp is dropped by the cam which raises it. The "dies" are much the same in shape and size as the shoes, and are fitted into the bottom of the mortar in such a position that one is exactly under the point where the shoe of each stamp strikes. Thus it is between the "shoes" and "dies" that the rock is pulverized.

Nevada Mill Stamp Room. c. 1890, dry plate/collotype, James H. Crockwell.
Library of Congress Prints and Photographs Division.

A small stream of water is constantly running into the battery among the ore, which water, being strongly churned and agitated takes up and floats all of the finer particles of ore. Across the face of the mortar, just in front of the dies, are the screens, made of the best Russian sheet-iron, punched full of small holes. Through these holes the water and the finely powdered ore pass into a sluice or trough running to the settling-tanks in the amalgamating-room, where the ore, now in the shape of fine sand, is deposited, to be finally shoveled out and placed in the amalgamating-pans. The finer the screens the smaller the quantity of ore that can be put through a battery in a given time.

The roar of Niagara is as a faint murmur compared with the deafening noise of sixty stamps, all in full operation. In the battery-room, and indeed throughout the mill, the noise is such that it is almost impossible to converse. Every word must be shouted into your ear at the top of the speaker's voice, and in a tone that would be audible at the distance of a mile in the open air. There is little talking done in the battery-room; except when ladies visit the works; then you can see that their lips continue to move, and the presumption is that they are talking right straight along.

Just in front of the battery-room, but having its floor some feet lower, is the amalgamating or pan-room, 92x120 feet in size. Into this room comes the pulp as it runs from the batteries. The pans stand in two long lines, running east and west, and back of the lines of pans are the settling-tanks, while in front of them are ranged the "settlers," a

Savage Works Mill, 1867, collodion/albumen, Timothy H. O'Sullivan. Library of Congress Prints and Photographs Division.

Carson River Mills. c. 1890, dry plate/collotype, James H. Crockwell.
Library of Congress Prints and Photographs Division. Plate from *Souvenir of the Comstock* showing the C.C. Stevenson, the Eureka, the Brunswick, the Vivian, the Mexican, and the Morgan mills.

large kind of pan into which the pulp passes from the pans proper—the amalgamating-pans. On each side of the building, over the settling-tanks, are sluices bringing the pulp (mingled with water) from the batteries. Each sluice brings the pulp from thirty stamps, and supplies one row of settling-tanks—there being spouts leading from the sluice to each tank. There are seventeen of these settling-tanks, and when the pulp has settled in them till

California Pan Mill, Interior, 1876, collodion/albumen, Carleton E. Watkins. California State Library.

it is of the consistency of thick mortar, it is shoveled out upon a platform which runs alongside the row of amalgamating-pans. There are sixteen pans in each row—thirty-two in all—and each pan is five and one-half feet in diameter, and holds a charge of 3,000 pounds of this pulp.

In the bottom of the pans are thick plates of cast-iron called "dies," while revolving upon these are the mullers, which are furnished with other thick plates of iron called "shoes." It amounts to much the same thing as the shoes and dies in the batteries, except that in the latter the ore is pulverized by percussion, while in the pans it is done by a rotary motion—by grinding.

When the charge of pulp has been shoveled into an amalgamating-pan, a certain quantity of water is added to thin it to the proper consistency for working, when the mullers are set in motion, and the work of grinding the ore in the pan begins. The pans have covers and double bottoms, and when they are at work, steam is not only let into the pulp, but also underneath, between the two bottoms.

After the pulp has been thus heated and ground for two and a half hours, there is placed in the pan 300 pounds of quicksilver, and it is run two and a half hours longer—five hours in all. Besides the quicksilver, there is put into the pan with the charge a certain quantity of salt and sulphate

Nevada Mill Pan Room. c. 1890, dry plate/collotype, James H. Crockwell.
Library of Congress Prints and Photographs Division.

of copper; also, when thought necessary, soda and some other chemicals are added.

The foundation of this method of working silver-ore is the old Mexican patio process. When Americans came to engage in the working of silver ores, upon the discovery of the Comstock lode, they found the Mexican plan of working too slow, and they began to study, in order to make improvements in it. In the Mexican patio process the pulverized ore is made up into a thick mortar on a floor of planks or stone (which is the patio), when salt and sulphate of copper are added and mixed in, and the pile of mortar is built up in the shape of a mound, and allowed to heat and sweat.

After a proper time has elapsed the mound is pulled down and spread about, when quicksilver is sprinkled upon and well worked into the mass, and it is again made up into a mound-shaped pile, to heat. This pulling down and building up, spreading about, and airing, is several times repeated, and the whole operation lasts a number of days, when finally the mass of mortar is washed and the quicksilver and amalgam secured. By placing the pulp, or mortar, in large iron pans, heated by steam and stirred by machinery, we see that the time of bringing the ore to the metallic state, is reduced from five or six days to as many hours. The principle involved in the two processes—pan and patio—is essentially the same.

On a platform below the amalgamating-pans, stand eight settlers, one for each pair of pans. The settlers are each nine feet in diameter, and five or six feet in depth. Into the settlers, at the end of five hours, the contents of the pans—quicksilver and all—are drawn. The pulp, quicksilver, and the amalgam (silver and quicksilver combined), remain in the settler about two hours, during which time the quicksilver and amalgam are drawn off through a pipe, at the bottom of the settler, and run into strainers, one of which stands in front of each settler, and all of which are provided with iron covers that are kept locked.

The silver separates from the ore while in the amalgamating-pan, being changed from the chloride and sulphuret to the metallic form, by the action

Pan Mill, Six Mile Cañon, c. 1890, dry plate/collotype, James H. Crockwell. Library of Congress Prints and Photographs Division. A small pan mill powered by water from a stream.

of the salt and sulphate of copper. As soon as it has assumed the metallic form, it unites or amalgamates with the quicksilver, but both in the pan and in the settler it is still mingled with the earthy matter of the ore from which it was produced.

It is first seen freed from this gross and earthy matter—pulverized rock, principally quartz—when it passes from the bottom of the settler through the iron pipe into the top of the strainer. Then it is mingled with nothing more base than quicksilver.

The strainers are bags of heavy canvas suspended in strong boxes, covered, as has been mentioned, with iron lids, somewhat funnel-shaped, and perforated with holes through which the quicksilver and amalgam may pass to the straining-bags—where we will leave them for the present.

CHAPTER XLVII

Assays of the Silver Bullion
How Quicksilver Vanishes—Charging the Retorts—
Ladling out the Molten Silver—How Assays are Made—Results

The water and pulp discharged from the settlers runs through sluices to the lowest part of the building, where, some eight or ten feet below the level of the floor of the amalgamating-room, stand the agitators, four in number. These are huge tubs, having in them revolving rakes or "stirrers," and here is caught whatever valuable matter may have passed through the settlers.

Twice in twenty-four hours, the heavy matter collected in the bottom of the agitators is cleaned out and placed in four small pans and two settlers that stand in the same room to be re-worked. Finally, the pulp leaves the agitators and, carried by a quantity of water to float it, passes out of the mill in a trough or flume , through which it flows eastward to a considerable distance from the mill, when it reaches what are called the "blanket sluices," the working of which will be described further on. In speaking of the pans and settlers, I have described but one row or set. The two rows, one on the north and the other on the south side of the large room, are exactly alike. Each row of pans has its row of settling tanks, settlers and amalgam strainers. To these strainers, in which we left the amalgam and quicksilver, a few minutes since, we now return.

While in the strainers a great quantity of the superfluous quicksilver mingled with the amalgam drains off, and flowing through pipes, is conducted to a large receiving-tank under the floor of the room. After it has thus drained till no more quicksilver will flow from it, the amalgam is removed from the ordinary strainers and is taken to the hydraulic strainer.

It is now a pasty mass of fine particles of silver, held together by quicksilver, and when pressed between the fingers gives out a peculiar squeaking sound. Although we may be unable to start a single globule of quicksilver from a lump of this amalgam by pressing it beneath our fingers, yet it is far from being as dry as it may be made by pressure. In this state it is placed in the hydraulic strainer, a heavy cylindrical cast-iron vessel, a good deal resembling a mortar—such as bombs are fired from. Over the "muzzle" of the "mortar" is fastened, by means of bolts and screws, a lid of iron through which enters an iron pipe. This pipe is then connected with a water-pipe, and water under several hundred feet of pressure is turned into the strainer. The pressure exerted upon the amalgam in this strainer amounts to 150 pounds to the square inch.

When taken out the amalgam has changed color and looks much less bright than before; one would think that but little quicksilver now remained in it, yet three-fourths of the mass is still quicksilver. Though strained and pressed as thoroughly as possible by ordinary methods, amalgam yields but one-sixth or one-seventh in silver bullion when retorted, whereas by the hydraulic strainer the yield is one-fourth.

The quicksilver pressed out by the hydraulic strainer is also conducted to the large receiving tank under the floor of the room. From this tank it is pumped up by powerful patent machinery—a pump having valves which are india-rubber balls [Toy balls of india-rubber, such as children play with may be used when those furnished with the pump are not at hand]—and goes to the distributing tanks. There are two of these tanks, one standing above each row of pans. Each distributing tank feeds eight quicksilver bowls, and each bowl supplies two pans, all by means of pipes. Thus, it will be seen, the quicksilver is in constant circulation. It passes through the pans, settlers, and strainers to the main receiving tank, from which it is pumped up into the distributing tanks, from these flows into the quicksilver bowls, thence passing into the pans again. So it goes on constantly circulating until it is worn out and lost.

The loss in quicksilver by grinding the "life" out of it in the pans is very great. In the eight mills of the Consolidated Virginia Mining Company— mostly mills of from ten to twenty stamps each—the loss in quicksilver amounts to between $60,000 and $70,000 per month. Much of this loss is occasioned by grinding quicksilver in the pans five hours, when it should only be subjected to this destructive process two and a half hours. The intention is to have quicksilver in the pans but the length of time last mentioned, but in drawing off their contents into the settlers a considerable quantity remains behind in the interstices of the dies in the bottom of the pans, and is thus subjected to the two and a half hours of grinding given the first charge of pulp, previous to the putting in of the usual dose of 300 pounds of quicksilver. Many millmen and amalgamators are experimenting for the purpose of, if possible, devising means by which this extra grinding of quicksilver may be obviated.

Through the whole length of the amalgamating-room, between the two rows of strainers, a car-track is laid upon the floor and on this runs the amalgam car, made wholly of iron, and capable of holding two tons of amalgam. When told that this car, so insignificant in size, holds two tons, we get some idea of the great weight of the amalgam. The car takes the amalgam from the hydraulic strainer and conveys it to the retort-house, standing about 30 feet from the main mill building.

The floor of the amalgamating-room is eight or ten feet above the level of that of the retort-house, and when the car, with its load, has reached the end of the car-track in the amalgamating room, it is run upon a hydraulic elevator by means of which it is quickly lowered to the level of the track running to the retorts.

The retort-house is built of brick and is 24 x 60 feet in size. It contains six retorts, capable of retorting five tons of amalgam per day, but the amount retorted daily is but from two to two and a half tons. The retorts are cast-iron cylinders about six feet in length and eighteen inches in diameter, placed horizontally in brickwork, each having under it a small furnace. The row of retorts closely resembles a row of little steam boilers.

In charging the retorts they are about half filled with the amalgam, which looks more like grey mud than silver or any other metal. It is very

Retorting and Smelting Room, 1862, lithograph, plate from a
Gould & Curry Silver Mining Company stock prospectus. California State Library.

cheap-looking stuff. Although one cannot see a single globule of quicksilver in it, yet it is about three-fourths quicksilver. You can squeeze no quicksilver out.

Upon the application of gradual but intense heat, the mercury separates rapidly from the silver, which from the retort-house is taken' to the assay-office. All mining companies do not do their own melting and assaying. It is only a few of the leading companies that can afford to have assay-offices of their own.

The assay-office of the Consolidated Virginia Mining Company is a large and handsomely constructed building standing a short distance south of the main hoisting works. It is divided into a number of rooms, in which are the several departments of the business. In the melting-room are six furnaces ranged in a row in which are placed the melting-pots, which are made of plumbago. These pots are capable of holding 300 pounds of silver each, but the quantity melted is generally from 220 to 230 pounds, sufficient to make two large bars or "bricks," as they are commonly called.

After the silver is thoroughly melted it is well stirred up, and the dross which rises to the surface is skimmed off. The pots are then lifted out of the furnace, and the molten silver is poured into iron moulds which form the bars, weighing a little over 100 pounds each.

When the pots of molten silver are lifted out of the furnace, a small quantity of the liquid mass is taken from the surface in a little ladle.

The silver thus taken out is thrown into water, when it scatters, and spreads out in a thousand fantastic shapes. Some of these sprays of silver resemble butterflies, flowers, or the leaves of plants—all are very bright and beautiful. They are called "granulations" and it is from these particles of silver that the assays are made by which the value of the bar is known.

As the molten silver is poured from the pot, in moulding the second and last bar, the little ladle is dipped quite down to the bottom of the pot and a small quantity of the liquid metal is taken out and thrown into cold water, as was the first. The resulting granulations are assayed, and the two assays must agree exactly, or all is to be done over again before the bars can be stamped with their value in silver and gold, All of the Comstock bullion contains a considerable percentage of gold. This percentage varies in different mines. Thus in the Belcher bullion it is often as high as 50 per cent., while in the Consolidated Virginia bullion it is as low as 10 per cent.

On an average there are melted, moulded into bars and assayed at the Consolidated Virginia assay-office from 500 to 600 pounds of bullion per day.

In making an assay of the granulated silver, a French gramme in weight is taken. This is wrapped up in a thin sheet of pure lead—lead which contains no silver—when it is put into a cupel, made of bone ashes, and the whole is then placed in a muffle-furnace. In the great heat of this furnace both lead and silver are soon liquefied, when the lead is absorbed by the cupel, carrying with it whatever base metal there may be in the gramme of bullion. The "button" left at the end of this process of cupellation is weighed, when is ascertained the weight in fine metal—gold and silver.

The bullion is now hammered out till it forms a thin sheet, when it is placed in an annealed glass flask, called a matrass, and strong nitric acid is poured over it. The flask is then placed in a sand-bath (a sort of oven, the bottom of which is covered to the depth of an inch or more with hot sand) and the flattened button is boiled in the acid until all the silver in it is dissolved. The gold which remains in the bottom of the flask in the form of a fine powder, is collected in an unglazed porcelain crucible. The crucible is placed in a warm place until the gold has dried; when it is put into a furnace and annealed— heated until the particles unite and form what is called "matte."

It is then removed from the crucible and carefully weighed. The weight of this matter shows the gold contained in the button, and the loss in the weight—that which was dissolved out of the original button by the action of the nitric acid—represents the silver. The bars being next accurately weighed, their value is determined from the amount of gold and silver found in the sample of one gramme taken from the silver of which the bars were moulded. The calculations here required are much facilitated by the use of very comprehensive tables of values for all degrees of fineness of silver and gold—a species of logarithms. Thus, for instance, when silver is 900 fine, an ounce of such silver is worth $1.16.36, and when gold is 900 fine an ounce of it is worth $18.60½. This is seen at a glance by referring to the tables; and the same is the case no matter what the degree of fineness of the metal may be.

The scales used in assaying are wonderfully delicate and sensitive. The smaller ones will weigh a piece of hair only an inch in length, from the human head. There is a separate room in which the weighing is done and the calculations made. All in this room is as heat and clean as in the finest parlor. In another room are the muffle-furnace and sand-bath, and in still another the furnace where the assays are made, also a still for distilling water. In ore assays, 200 grains of finely powered ore are placed in a small earthen crucible; a proper quantity of flux is added, and the whole is then placed in the furnace and melted. After the mass has remained in the molten state a sufficient length of time, the crucible is taken out and allowed to cool. When cold it is broken by a blow with a hammer, and the button deposited by the ore is found at its bottom. This button is then assayed in the same way as the granulations taken from the melting-pot, and from the result the value per ton of the ore is calculated.

In the Consolidated Virginia assay-office from sixty to eighty assays of ore, tailings, and slimes are daily made. The finished bars of silver have stamped upon them their weight, fineness of gold and silver, value in gold and in silver, and the total value of the bars. They are then ready to be sent to one of the United States' Mints to be coined, or to be shipped to Europe, China, or Japan, and sold. The total cost of the Consolidated Virginia reduction works was $350,000.

CHAPTER XLVIII

SALOON BIRDS

Big Eaters—Recognizing Murphy—A Nice Little Supper—What he Did with his Gun—"A Devil of a Time"—"A Nice Agreeable Gentleman."

As the reader has been kept for some time in the "lower levels," and amid the roar of the machinery of the mills, I shall now give a few chapters illustrative of life in Virginia City, and along the Comstock lode.

In Virginia City are found many odd, curious, and reckless characters. It would be strange, indeed, if such were not the case, in a city having a population of over twenty thousand souls, composed of adventurers from every land, all attracted thither by the great richness of the mines and the abundance of money. Hundreds of thousands of dollars being paid out on the first of every month to the miners and the workmen employed in the many mills, there have been attracted to the Comstock range hundreds of gamblers of all grades, and men of all kinds who live by their wits. There is always a small army of men who haunt the saloons and gambling rooms, and by begging a good deal and stealing a little, and playing all manner of tricks and dodges, manage to pick up a precarious subsistence. There are in Virginia City about one hundred saloons, all of which have their customers. The majority of these saloons are what are called "bit houses;" that is, drinks of all kinds and cigars are one bit—twelve and one-half cents. The dime, however, passes as a "bit" in all of these houses.

The money in circulation is wholly gold and silver coin, and the smallest coin in use is the bit, ten-cent piece—sometimes spoken of as a "short bit," as not being twelve and one-half cents, the "long bit." There being no smaller change in use than the dime, the bit passes for the half of twenty-five cents.

Thus, whenever a customer throws down a quarter of a dollar in payment for a drink or a cigar, he gets back a dime, and so has paid fifteen cents for his "nip" or smoke. The new twenty cent pieces, of which Senator Jones, of Nevada, is the father, will, however, cure this little ill. In the "two-bit," or twenty-five cent saloons, everything is twenty-five cents, even the same drinks that are sold in the bit houses for ten cents; as lager beer, soda water, lemonade, cider, and the like.

There is really but one hotel—kept after the plan of hotels in other places—in Virginia City. The people of the town eat at restaurants and have their rooms at lodging-houses. It is on the European plan, except that a restaurant is seldom found in the same building as a lodging-house. Those who live in lodging-houses patronize that restaurant which best suits them. Restaurants and lodging-houses are, therefore, even more numerous in the town than saloons.

International Hotel, 1890, dry plate/collotype, James H. Crockwell. Library of Congress
Prints and Photographs Division. This is the third, and largest, incarnation of the
International Hotel: the first was moved to Austin, Nevada (still extant); the second
was destroyed in the city-wide Great Fire of 1875; and the third destroyed in a 1914 fire.

The grand army of men who live by their wits are always at war with the restaurant keepers. Of late, however, the latter have formed an association for their mutual protection, and furnish each other lists of all swindling customers, which makes it no easy matter for one of the "dead beats" to get a "square meal," unless he first "puts up" his coin. These fellows cannot now rove from house to house as in former times.

Some years ago a restaurant keeper had a number of, these customers, who were eating him out of house and home. One day he seriously remonstrated with one of his patrons. He told him that unless he and others like him paid up, the house must close.

Said the restaurant man: "Here, now, it has been two weeks since I paid my meat bill. If I don't pay up this week the butcher will shut down on me, and I can get no more meat. Don't you see, I shall be obliged to close my house!"

"O, no!" said the customer, "don't close your house. Keep her open. We'll all stay by you. If you can't get any meat, we'll play you a string on vegetables!"

Even some such customers as pay are a terror to the restaurant keeper. When the check-guerrilla is eating his semi-weekly square meal, the landlord paces the room wringing his hands—eyes red, face flushed, brows corrugated, general aspect venomous in his walk—as steak after steak disappears—he eyes his customer in a malignant, yet helpless manner. In case of fifteen or twenty such customers arriving in one day, the restaurant keeper generally goes out into his back yard and cuts his throat.

Pat Murphy had the name of being the biggest eater on the Comstock range. He was a very good sort of man, and tried his best not to make his appetite conspicuous, but it was a thing that could not be concealed. In order not to be too hard on any one man, Murphy was in the habit of changing his boarding place quite frequently. On one occasion a new restaurant was opened, and nearly every morning the patrons of the place would ask the landlord if Pat Murphy had not yet come to board with him. The landlord would say that he had seen no man of that name. Finding that the "sports" who were boarding with him continued daily to ask if he had yet seen Murphy, the landlord began to feel that he should like to know something about him. He asked what kind of man Murphy was, and how he would be able to recognize him in case he should come to the restaurant.

"Never mind about how he looks," said the sports, "you will know him when he comes."

One morning a tall, gaunt, middle-aged man came edging into the restaurant, and meekly took a seat. The landlord rather liked the appearance of the new customer, and at once went to take his order.

"Landlord," said the man, "let me have a porterhouse steak and onions, some liver and bacon on the side, six fried eggs, a bit of ham, a Jarman pancake, some fried pertaties, a cup of coffee, and a couple of doughnuts, and—if ye have them—a couple of waffles." When the sports came in to breakfast, the landlord said: "He has been here—I've seen Murphy, the man who eats."

Many of the emigrants from the older states arrive in Washoe with exaggerated notions and with eyes and ears open for strange things of all kinds. Being well aware of this, a Comstocker who dropped in at a chop-house where about a dozen newcomers had just settled in a flock, at two or three adjoining tables, concluded to have some fun with them. Seating himself near them, the Comstocker roared: "Waiter, how long does a man have to sit here before you come to take his order?"

"All right, sir!" said the alert waiter, who was well acquainted with the customer, and saw that he was up to some kind of mischief. "All right! What will you have, sir?"

The emigrants all turned to take a look at the man of stentorian voice, who spoke so authoritatively.

Straightening himself up, and speaking even louder than before, the Comstocker cried: "Give me a baked horned toad, two broiled lizards on toast, with tarantula sauce—stewed rattlesnake and poached scorpions on the side!"

Without the slightest hesitation or the least sign of astonishment, the waiter called out to the Chinese cooks in the kitchen: "Baked horned toad; two broiled lizards on toast, tarantula sauce; stewed rattlesnake and poached scorpions. Very nice and well done, for Mr. Terry!"

There was then a great buzzing among the emigrants as they laid their heads together, and many curious side glances were shot at that most incorrigible of jokers, Bill Terry. Even after Bill's breakfast had been placed before him—his real order having been given on the sly—the emigrants were unable to make out what he was eating, though they nearly twisted their necks out of joint with glancing over their shoulders at his table.

The white sage which grows in great abundance throughout Nevada, is not only useful as a food for cattle, but from it has been manufactured a hair restorative—a wash for making hair grow on bald heads. One day Bill Terry happened to be seated opposite a stranger at a table in a restaurant, when the stranger—who was a side-whiskered, lisping man who showed a good deal of the dandy in his dress—attracted the attention of "William" by opening a conversation as follows:

Stranger.—"Deah me! this is disgusting!" Holding up his knife and gazing fixedly at its point. "This is either the second or the third hair that I have found in this buttah!"

Bill Terry—"You've not been here long, I judge?"

Stranger—"No sir; I arrived here yesterday morning."

Bill Terry—"I thought so, otherwise you would not complain of hairs in the butter."

Stranger—"Not complain of hairs in the butter? You suppwise me, sir! How could I do otherwise?"

Bill Terry—"Those hairs, sir, are just as natural to Washoe butter as butter is a natural product of milk. They are just as good and just as clean as the butter."

Stranger—"Impossible!"

Bill Terry—"Not at all, sir. All our butter comes from the great valley of our State where flourishes that most nutritious and truly wonderful plant, the white sage. On this white sage our cattle feed and fatten. The plant has many virtues. It is of an oleaginous nature and is good in lung diseases, and from it is also manufactured a most wonderful and very popular hair restorative."

Stranger—"Ah, yes; I've heard something of the kind."

Bill Terry—"Well, then, sir, in a country where all the cows feed on the white sage, do you think it likely that the butter will be bald-headed."

Promontory is a new place out on the Central Pacific Railroad. Out there they have no "Hotel and Restaurant-keepers' Mutual Protection Association," as they have in Virginia City. The place is too small and scattering for the advanced ideas that rule in the more metropolitan towns. A Comstocker went out to Promontory to prospect and look around for a time. He stopped at the principal hotel, which stood at the edge of the town. Our Comstocker liked the looks of things. The landlord seemed a very agreeable and friendly sort of man, and he thought he would stop and board with him a while.

When dinner was ready the landlord took a double-barrelled shot-gun from behind the bar, and, stepping out in front of his house, fired off one of the barrels.

The Comstocker, who had followed him to the door to see what was up, said to him: "What did you do that for?"

"To call my boarders to dinner," said the landlord.

"I see," said the Comstocker, "but why don't you fire off both barrels?"

"Well," said the landlord, "you see I keep the other to collect with."

Having but a few "short bits" in his pocket our Comstocker, after getting his dinner, concluded to shoulder his carpet-bag and jog along. Speaking of short bits: A "hoodlum" went into a cigar store in Virginia City one day, and after getting a "bit" cigar, laid a dime on the counter and picked up a twenty-five cent piece which he saw lying there, saying as he walked off: "Just the change!"

The astonished shop-keeper gazed at the lone bit, then at his box of cigars, and then in the direction taken by the young sharper. At last he said: "Veil, now, how dat vas? Dat vas make der right schange, sure; but it look to me like it vas make emde wrong vay somehow. Veil, de next time what dare comes a bargain like dese, I make der schange mineselfs. Ven effery fool what come to der store make schange, it soon schpiles der piziness!"

The saloon-keepers as well as the keepers of restaurants have some very amiable gentlemen to deal with occasionally, but more frequently such as are "on the beat."

One evening a tall wild-looking fellow rushed into a first-class saloon apparently in a terrible state of excitement. Throwing his hat on the counter he said to the bar-keeper: "There'll be the biggest row here in about a minute that ever you saw! Give me a drink quick!"

The bar-keeper set out the bottle, and while the fellow was helping himself, looked under the bar to see that his six-shooter was all right and his club handy.

Leaving his hat on the bar, the fellow ran to the door, looked out, then rushed back and said: "Yes; in less than half a minute there'll be a devil of a time here! Give me another drink, quick!" And seizing the bottle he helped himself to another rousing horn. He then took up his hat and was coolly marching away, when the bar-keeper called after him: "See here you fellow there! What's all this about a row? Do you know you haven't paid me for those drinks!"

"There you go!" said the fellow.

"Well, and there you don't go until you pay for your drinks. Come back here or I'll give you a taste of my club!"

"There you go again! Didn't I say there'd be a fearful row here in about a minute? I knew it; and there you go!"

The bar-keeper now saw the point and said: "Look here, you can come back here and take another drink if you like, but I wish it distinctly understood, my good fellow, that this is to be the last 'row' you ever raise in this house!"

A man one day sauntered into a two-bit saloon and called for a drink of whiskey. The proprietor of the place was behind the bar and set out the Bourbon bottle. When the man had drank he threw a ten-cent piece on the counter and started off.

"This is a two-bit house, sir," said the proprietor, in a tone which showed that he felt some pride in the establishment.

"Ah!" said the customer. "Two-bit house, eh? Well, I thought so when I first came in, but after I had tasted your whiskey I concluded it was a bit house."

Some of the customers of the saloon-keepers are not only fellows of infinite jest, but are also men of such an agreeable disposition that it is pleasant to have them around.

"Do you know Mr. Popper?" asked a saloon-keeper of one of his customers.

"I've heard of him," said the customer, "but I don't know that I ever met him."

"No;" said the saloon man. "Well, you ought to make his acquaintance.

He's a nice agreeable gentleman. I never saw him until night before last when he came in here about 12 o'clock and took a drink. He is a man who makes himself at home with you at once. Why he had hardly been in here five minutes before he drew out his six-shooter and began shooting holes through the pictures, the lamp, and other little notions about the place, just as familiarly as though he and I had been boys together. Nothing cold and distant about him! He's a charming fellow!—charming!"

There is nothing at which these agreeable gentlemen are more likely to take a shot, than a large and costly mirror. A mirror is generally the first thing that attracts their attention when they are inclined to be sociable and good-natured, though a lamp, suspended in the middle of a room, very frequently draws their first fire. Sometimes two or three marksmen take a hand in the sport. Then it's right jolly.

Probably as preparatory to a more public performance, half a dozen men went one night to a pistol gallery to practice. To snuff a candle with a pistol or rifle has always been a great feat among crack shots. These men were not only going to snuff the candle, but each man in turn was to hold the candle while the other snuffed it. At the first fire the man who held the candle got a bullet through his left hand. Although the wound was of a very painful character, he insisted on having his shot. He got it, and put a bullet through his friend's arm just below the elbow. After this the party did not feel that enthusiasm for candle-snuffing which previously animated their bosoms. They concluded that they were not candle-snuffers.

CHAPTER XLIX

SOME VERY QUEER CUSTOMERS
A Trifling Accident—Blazer and His Friends—
A Little Misunderstanding—"Couldn't Drink Alone"—
"I'll Bring in the Rabble"—The Deacon Sent For—
Resurrection!—"Awful Big Gooses."

ut on the Divide, in the extreme southern part of Virginia City, they do much better shooting than that mentioned in the last chapter— also, much worse. Out there, one morning, a man fired six shots at his brother-in-law and missed him every time, though the practice all took place within the bounds of a small door-yard. During the afternoon of the same day some men at a saloon were discussing the morning's shooting, and all agreed that it was scandalous—was a discredit to their end of the town, and to Washoe. That to shoot at a man six times, and not hit him, was shameful. After awhile, with these things occurring, it would go abroad that a Washoe man could not hit the side of a barn.

After much more talk about the disgraceful affair of the morning, a man from Pioche—a lively camp in the eastern part of Nevada (they kill a man there every week or two) bantered a Comstocker, whom he knew to be a fine shot with a pistol, to go out into the back yard with him and do some shooting, just to show the "boys" how it should be done.

In the saloon—which also was a grocery-store—was a box of eggs, and the Piocher proposed, that they each shoot two eggs off the bare head of the other, at the distance of ten paces, the one missing, to treat the crowd. The Comstocker was determined not to be bluffed by a man from the other end of the State, so to the back yard all hands adjourned. Each man used his own six-shooter. The Comstocker first "busted" his egg on the top of the Piocher's head, and the feat was loudly applauded by all present.

It was then the Piocher's time to shoot, and an egg was produced to be placed upon the head of the Comstocker, but when he removed his hat, there was a general laugh, as the top of his head was as smooth as a billiard-ball.

For full five minutes all hands tried to make an egg stand on the smooth pate of the Comstocker. It couldn't be done. The Piocher then taunted the Comstocker with having gone into the arrangement knowing that he was safe. The latter told him to set up his egg, and it was all right—he was there. The Pioche man stood contemplating the bald pate before him for a time, then turned, and went into the saloon. A moment after he came out with a small handful of flour, which he dabbed upon the bald head of the Comstocker, and then triumphantly planted in it his egg, fell back ten paces, and knocked it off. The Comstock man then told him to set up his second egg and shoot at it, as he didn't want to have his head chalked twice during the same game. This was done, and the wreck of the second egg streamed over the Comstocker's pate.

The Piocher now stood out with his last egg on his head. The Comstocker raised his pistol and fired. The Piocher bounded a yard into the air, and the egg rolled unscathed from his head.

"I've lost!" cried the Comstocker. "Let all come up and drink. By a slip of the finger, I've put half the width of my bullet through the top of his left ear!" and so it proved upon measurement.

All Washoe men, however, do not stand fire so well as this pair of egg-shooters. On one occasion a "sport," of herculean frame, and wearing a huge black beard that gave him a most ferocious appearance, cheated a miner out of four or five hundred dollars in a game of draw-poker. As he made his last losing, the miner saw the cheat, and demanded the return of all the money he had lost. The big gambler laughed in his face. The miner, who was quite a small man, left the place wearing an ugly look. Some of those present, who knew the miner, told the big sport that he had better leave, as his man had gone off to "heel himself," and there would soon be trouble.

But the big man was not alarmed—he was not going to be frightened away. He sat in a chair in a rear room of the saloon, near an open window, his head thrown back, and his legs cocked up. He didn't care how many' weapons the miner might bring.

"Why, gentlemen," said he, "you don't know me!—you don't know who I am! I'm the Wild Boar of Tehama! The click of a six-shooter is music to my ear, and a bowie-knife is my looking-glass—" Here he happened to look toward the door, and saw the miner entering the door with a shot-gun, when he said: "But a shot-gun lets me out!" and he went through the window behind him, head first.

A very different sort of man from the "Wild Boar of Tehama" was Blazer. Blazer was a man who never felt himself at peace except "when at war." He would leave his dinner any day, if he thought he could find a fight. When unable to "mix" in a "muss" of some kind, he was the most miserable dog alive. A week without a battle, and he began to think there was nothing in the world worth living for.

Although Blazer seldom won more than one fight out of ten, it was all the same to him. He rather enjoyed a good pommelling.

One night some of Blazer's friends—because they were his enemies—happened to be passing through a part of Virginia City called the "Barbary Coast," on account of its being the roughest and worst place in the town—the "Five Points" of the place. As Blazer's friends were passing through this region of blood and robberies, their attention was attracted to a "shebang" near at hand, by a terrible uproar within its doors. There was a smashing of glass, a crashing of chairs, bottles, and tumblers; fierce yells, bitter curses, and, in short, a fearful commotion.

Thinking one of the voices heard above the din had a familiar sound, Blazer's friends entered the place. As they pushed in at the door they saw Blazer surrounded by half a dozen "Coasters," who were giving it to him right and left. Blazer's nose was flattened; one eye closed; his upper lip laid open, his face covered with blood, and his clothes nearly torn off his back. A clip under the ear sent him to "grass," when those nearest him began jumping upon him and kicking him in the ribs. His friends rushed to his rescue. The breath was completely knocked and kicked out of poor Blazer, and he lay stretched senseless on the floor.

Some water dashed in his face revived him. Recognizing his friends, he smiled as amiably as was possible, with his distorted upper lip, and huskily whispered: "Boys, it's gorgeous! I've struck a perfect paradise!"

Somewhat of the same pattern as Blazer was the youth encountered on this same "Barbary Coast" one night by a policeman whose beat was among the "dives" in that region.

"Where was that row just now?" said the policeman. The question was addressed to a wall-eyed young hoodlum, who, with hands thrust nearly to his knees in his breeches pockets, lounged against a lamp-post.

"Ro-o-ow?" listlessly drawled the short-haired youth. "I hain't seen nuthin' of no row."

"You hain't?" said the policeman, eyeing the young gentleman over.

"N-o; I hain't!" reiterated the fellow, with a sneering Bowery drawl. "Do yer sup-pose I'd be a loafin' here if ther' was any row a-goin? Not much!"

"I was told down street," said the policeman, "that there was a regular row in one of the shebangs up this way. Now I want to know where it was—do you understand?"

"Wa-all, I dunno, but I guess maybe ther' mout a bin a little misunderstandin' or sumpthin' o' that sort in at Broncho Sail's saloon. 'Bout a minit or so ago I seed Wasatch Sam roll out 'er thare and seed him spit out some feller's ear, as he went 'long by here; but I don't reckon there's bin any pertickler row—hain't seed nuthin' o' none."

The same policeman one night heard a sound of scuffling in a Barbary Coast "dive" and ran in to see was what going on. As he entered the place, he saw two men struggling upon the floor. The uppermost man arose from the prostrate and bleeding form of his antagonist as the policeman approached, and said: "I'm a quiet man, a man who wouldn't harm a fly, but when I'm crowded too far, I will remonstrate!" where upon he spat out the nose of the man who was lying on the floor.

Curious characters are frequently encountered in towns of the silvermines—queer customers from all parts of the world. A few drinks generally bring out the peculiarities of these men. One day an odd-looking, wiry old chap, evidently from some ranch in the Sierra Nevada Mountains, and apparently a man rich in flocks and herds, made his way to the bar of one of the first-class two-bit saloons of Virginia City. His "keg" was evidently "full" to overflowing, yet he was still athirst. Cocking one eye upon the bar-keeper and the other on the array of bottles before him, he thrust his right hand deep into his breeches' pocket and there stirred up a stunning jingle of coin. Turning to a gentleman standing near, the little old man said: "Stranger, excuse me, but will yer jine in a drink?"

"Please excuse me, sir," said the gentleman addressed, "I've just drank."

"Stand another, can't yer?"

"No; I'm much obliged. I don't wish to drink."

Turning to another gentleman, the old fellow said: "Take a drink, sir—with me?"

"No, sir; I thank you, I've just been to dinner," and this man turned and walked away.

The little old man of the mountains looked annoyed and irritated, and turning from the bar, he walked across the saloon to where three or four gentlemen were conversing together: "Gentlemen," said he, "you must excuse me, I'm a stranger here, but I never like to drink alone. Now, will you oblige me by all comin' up and takin' a drink at my expense? I'm one of your sociable kind, and never like to go in a drove by myself."

Thinking the old fellow had drank about as much as was good for him, all declined the proffered treat. This exasperated the old chap. Jerking his cap off his head and slapping it against his thigh, he broke loose with: "Well, now, this beats my time! Not a man in this room that will drink with me! Damme! I'll go forth into the street and bring in the rabble! I'll be like that old rancher down in the Valley of Galilee, that the Bible tells of. He was one of my kind. When he had a frolic he wanted to see things whiz!"

"Which of the old patriarchs was that?" asked a gentleman present, who thought it might be worth while to draw the old fellow out.

"I'm not much of a biblist," said the old man, "but I mean that jolly old cock that lived somewhere down in Galilee or Nazareth. The old gentleman, you know, that gave the big blow-out when his oldest gal got married. You recollect he killed a lot of oxen, and sheep, and calves, and goats, and had a tearin' barbacue, invitin' all the neighbors for miles round. But devil a one came near the house. All too durned hightoned! Then what does that old chap do but git up on his ear and swear the thing shall be a success. So he sends his hired man out to gather up all of the old bummers and deadbeats, the lame, halt, and blind, sayin: 'Bring 'em all in, and we'll have a regular tear—the big blow-out of the season!'

"Then the hungry and thirsty old bummers and guttersnipes all came charging in from the back alleys, and tumblin' up from the lumber-yards, and they piled in and they made it hot for that lunch, and whiskey, and lager-beer, and they fiddled and danced till they all got blind drunk and broke up in a row. But the gal had a stavin' lively weddin' after all!

"Now that's the kind of man I am. Ef *you gentlemen* won't drink with me, damme, I'll go out and bring in the rabble and we'll eat up all the free-lunch, drink ourselves disorderly, and have a reg'lar weddin' feast right hyar!"

This little oration had the desired effect. All in the room shook hands with the old chap and took a drink with him, when he exultantly exclaimed, bringing his fist down upon the counter, as he emptied his glass: "Damme, you don't know Old Sol Winters down hyar; but he's a pretty big Injun when he's at home, up in Orion Valley!"

Another curious old 'coon was "Old Taggart." Old Taggart is dead. We planted him under the sod in 1874. Where the soul of Old Taggart has gone to, nobody knows. Old Taggart was a good sort of man, but had his "ways." Old Taggart didn't fear death. As he lay on his death-bed, he was conscious, calm, and serene to the last. Said he toward the close:

"During these many years I have thought it all over, and I am ready to take the chances."

Being what is called a "pious" woman, Old Taggart's wife was a good deal disturbed by the thought of seeing her husband die without having "experienced religion." She worried the old man a good deal toward the last on this account.

Old Taggart said: "Wife, I'm as sorry for all the bad things I have done during my life, and as much ashamed of all the mean things, as any man could be."

Still the old lady wanted to see him "experience a change of heart." So she sent for Deacon Dudley to come and talk to the old man. The deacon came, and, seating himself by the bedside, turned to the sick man and told him about the wonders and the glories of heaven. He told him all about the New Jerusalem, where the streets are paved with gold, and where angels "touch the soft lyre and tune the vocal lay." He then asked Old Taggart if he didn't think he'd like to go up there.

"No;" said Old Taggart, "I don't think I should feel at home in the kind of place you tell about."

"But, my dear friend," said the Deacon, "you are at the point of death— you should not talk in this way about heaven!"

"Well, Deacon, I'll jist die and trust to the Almighty. I'll jist settle down wherever he puts me. I don't know nothin' about the lay of the land in 'tother world myself, but I'll chance Him."

"I'm surprised, my good friend, to hear that you don't want to be one of that heavenly band that sit before the throne, playing on golden harps, and singing praises forever and forever!"

"Me play on a harp, Deacon?" said Old Taggart, smiling faintly.

"Yes; upon the wondrous golden harp!" briskly replied the Deacon.

"There," said Old Taggart, doggedly, "I don't want to go to that part of heaven. The Lord will give me a place out in some of the back settlements, like. He'll find a place for me, I'll be bound!"

"It's wicked to talk as you are doing," said the Deacon. "You have the worst ideas about heaven of any man I ever saw!"

"Can't help it, Deacon," said Old Taggart, "its all nonsense to talk about me playin' a harp. I tell you plainly, Deacon, that I don't want to go among the musicians up there. It wouldn't suit me!"

"This is absolutely sinful!" said the Deacon.

"Can't help it," said the old man, "can't help it! It's no use of talkin'; I'll die my own way, and trust to the Almighty. I've a notion that when Old Taggart comes to Him, He will make him comfortable somewheres up there in the kingdom."

Here Old Taggart gave a gasp or two, and was dead. He has probably found a place "up there."

Then there was Old Daniels, a queer old fellow who lived at Gold Hill. Old Daniels would sometimes get so drunk that he didn't know whether he was dead or alive. Very late one night some wags found Old Daniels lying in an alley so much intoxicated that they at first thought he was dead. They got a hand-barrow and carried him out to the graveyard. They there found the grave of a Chinaman that had been opened in order that the bones of the defunct might be sent back to China. The old shattered coffin of the Chinaman still lay beside the open grave, and alongside of the coffin they laid Old Daniels.

The wags then secreted themselves near the spot in order to see how the old fellow would act when he came to his senses, for he was sleeping like a log. They were obliged to wait a long time—till very weary of it—but about daylight, when the air began to grow cold, Old Daniels began to toss and tumble uneasily, and presently was fully awake. He arose to a sitting posture and began a deliberate survey of his surroundings—the empty coffin by his side, the open grave, the tombstones all round.

"The day of resurrection!" said he solemnly, then took another survey of the graveyard. "Yes;" said he, "the day of resurrection, and I'm the first son of a gun out of the ground!"

In the early days, a Frenchman brought to Nevada half a dozen camels, which he placed on his ranch, on the Carson River, a few miles below Dayton. The climate and the herbage of the country appear to be well adapted to the requirements of the animals, and they have thriven and increased and multiplied until the herd now numbers about forty, of all ages. These camels are used in packing salt from the deserts, for carrying wood, hay, and freight of all kinds, and they carry quite as large loads as do the camels of Arabia. They are not allowed to be brought into the streets of Virginia City during daylight, for the reason that they frighten mules and horses, and cause dangerous runaways. Mules cannot endure the sight of them. Of nights, however, the camels come into town and pass along the back streets.

One moonlight night, as the animals were solemnly stalking along an unfrequented street, a pair of Teutons, who had probably been enjoying themselves at some festival until a late hour, turned into the street through which the camels were passing: "O, Sheorge," cried one of the men, to his companion, "yoost see dem awful big gooses!"

The other took one look, and said: "Mine Gott, Levi, we petter run home quick. I dinks dare coomes der raisurrection!" and both took to their heels.

CHAPTER L

ORIGINAL CHARACTERS
A Fuddled Pillar—Philosophical Advice—
"Don't Git Married"—Mr. Jones's Guest—
The War-hoss of the Hills—Something of a Fighter—
Beating a Retreat—"Jim Cartter or the Devil"

Occasionally persons not usually found training in the ranks of the festive throng of Comstockers are out until the "wee sma'" hours, and meet with adventures quite as strange as was that of the two Germans who encountered a herd of camels at a time when they supposed that there were no animals of the kind nearer than the desert of Sahara.

One of the pillars of the church, a powerful exhorter and a liberal disburser of psalmody before the Lord, went astray one Fourth of July night, and even got into a German dance-house before his patriotism was fully expended. However, he recollected himself presently, and took his departure. As he was meandering along the street, with his hat resting in a style of graceful bravado on his left ear, he was met by a policeman who knew him and advised him to get home.

"Home? No, sir!—no sir!" cried the exhorter. "Live while you live. Life is short, sir; we are like flowers of the field, sir—lilies of the valley. Let us not be proud nor puffed up, for we are all worms of the dust! I'm not proud, sir—nozur! I've been among the daughters of the Teuton, sir, even among the cunning dancers whose feet are beautiful on the mountains—whose feet twinkle as alabaster in the waters of the Jordan—also have I been among the sons of Jubal, even such as handle the harp, the fiddle, and the psaltry. I have danced even as David danced, and drank wine even as Noah, when he began to be a husbandman. But tell it not in Gath, publish it not in the streets of Virginia!" The policeman—a "son of Belial," the fuddled pillar called him—now began to talk very plainly, and the godly reveller caught a glimpse of the error of his ways, and changed his tune.

"Woe is me!" cried he, "how could I dare to burn incense unto Baal and walk after strange gods! Silver spread into plates is brought from Tarshish, and gold from Uphaz, but who shall be able to keep shekels of silver, wedges of gold, or rings of jasper from these greedy Delilahs—Delilahs not to be appeased with hair, whose hands a whole wig would not stay! For the mountains I will take up a wailing, and for the habitations of the wilderness a lamentation. I flee from the daughters of the Teuton; they are as black as the tents of Kedar. How can I face that good woman, Hanner?—bone of my bone and flesh of my flesh—for in the day that I see her face will there come, that selfsame day, a blowing of trumpets, a breaking of seals, and a pouring out of vials! No, sir; don't talk to me or wrestle with me, even as the angel wrestled with Jacob at the ford of Jabbok; whither thou goest I cannot go; whither thou lodgest I cannot lodge. I'm the speckled bird of the mountains of Gilboa—a hungry pelican in the wilderness, sir! I go to the unsealing—to the breaking of seals, and the blowing of trumpets—yea, I go to face Hanner!" and the "speckled bird of Gilboa" spread its wings and took its zigzag flight to meet the good Hannah, mighty blower of trumpets, breaker of seals, and out-pourer of vials before the Lord.

These matters—churches and pillars of churches—bring up the "old French Doctor," of Virginia City, who was one of the oddities of the place. Whole volumes of his curious sayings might be given. The old man is now dead, but he is still remembered and quoted along the Comstock by those who knew him in life. The old doctor—for a wonder—had been to church, and came away delighted.

"Ah, my dear boy," said he, "I have to-day listen to one ver' excellent narratif by ze reverence preacher. It was about David and Nasan. You see Nasan he vish to make to David one grand reproof. So Nasan he come to David one day, and tell to him one ver' long, big sheep story. He fool David—Nasan do—wiz ze story of ze sheep and ze big rich man zat steal ze sheep of ze poor man, till by and by David become ver moche interest in ze narratif—become ver' much enrage wiz ze rich man. Wiz zat, and precisement at zat moment, Nasan he jump up on ze top of a bench and he proclaim to David: 'Zou art ze man! I see ze wool in you teef!' Ah, my boy, zat was one gran' reproof—one ver' big what you call sell, on Monsieur David—eh?"

"Uncle Pete," the curb-stone philosopher, always had his "say" on all topics of the day, and he also looked after the welfare of such of the rising generation as fell in his way. His disciples were generally of the genus "hoodlum." Propped at ease against a favorite lamp-post, with one of these before him, he would say: "Young man, don't you go to strivin' for a big name, or frettin' yourself to make a mark in the world. It's all wanity and wexation of spirit. Study to become a philosopher. Look at me! Life has no terrors for me; yet I toil not, neither do I spin. To live without care is my philosophy. That's a motto to live up to. All else is wanity. What does a man get by doin' things, makin' inwentions and the like? Nuthin.

"Look at Christopher Columbus! What does he get for the trouble he had in discovering America? He gits called a swindler and a imposture. He had all his trouble for nuthin', for they have found out that he wasn't the feller that discovered America after all. It was some Laplander—one of them fellers away up north. But he never said nuthin' about it until lately. The next generation will find out that the Laplander was a humbug.

"What does William H. Shakespeare git for the trouble he had in writin' them plays o' his? He gits busted out intirely. They now say there never was no sich man as William H. Shakespeare, and I believe 'em. No one man could a-done it.

"What was the use of William Tell shootin' old Geyser? He run a big risk of passin' in his own checks, and now they say there never was no sich man. He'd better staid up in the mountains and prospected.

"See the life that Robinson Crusoe led on that 'lone barren isle,' as the song says, and now they say there never was no Crusoe.

"Young man, don't you never try to discover America, nor the steam-engine, nor the cotton-gin, nor the telegraft—as old Moss did—'cause you'll find out when its too late to be of any benefit to you that it wasn't you at all, but some other jackass that died before you was born, and don't know whether he ever done anything or not. Lead the life of a philosopher, young man. Get all you can out of the world, and never do nothin' for the world—then you are ahead of the world and are a true philosopher!" The disciples of Uncle Pete are many and promising.

The inebriated individual who took his friend by the button and read to him the following lecture on matrimony, was also something of a phi-losopher: "Now, don't get married, Afferd —don't git married! If you git married yer gone up the flume—busted out. You won't be married a week 'fore yer wife'll put on her worst shoes and stick 'em rite up on the stove under your nose. When she gits all the clothes she wants, she'll have a sick sister down to San Jose; wants two hunerd fifty dollar go see'r poor sisser. Goes; sisser dies; father-in-lor straitened sirkstances; wants two hunerd fifty more—bury poor sisser. Goes into hunerd fifty dollar wuth mournin', then wants more money to come home on. Comes home'n calls you nassy, dirty, drunken beas'—don't you git married, Afferd—don't!"

This man should have had a dog such as that owned by the ranchman on Truckee Meadows. This rancher once brought his dog to Virginia City. The dog rode into town by the side of his master on a load of potatoes. He was not a pretty dog. He was a tall, gaunt, shaggy-haired, wild-eyed, brin-dle beast of unrecorded pedigree. When the wagon halted in town some men who were lounging in the neighborhood began to remark upon the ungainly appearance of the countryman's dog.

"Fellers," said the owner of the animal, coming to the front, "that air ain't a purty dog, I know—he's like me, makes no pertentions to nat'ral beau-ty—but he's jist the durndest knowenest dog what ever wore har. Now, he's got more instink, that dog has, an' more savey, an' pen'tration into human natur, right in that ugly old cabeza of his, nor can be found in the heds of a whole plaza full of eddicated town dogs—poodles and sich.

"Now, that's what I pride in him fur—his reg'lar human sense. I tell yer, fellers, he's jist the durndest dog out! Now, ef I come home from town perfectly sober (when I've left him to see after the ranch), it would do your hearts good to see that dog show off what a sense of appreciation he's got of me. Fellers, his gorgeous tail then stands aloft; he skyugles about; he runs on afore me, a-scrapin' up the yearth with his hind feet, sendin' the chips a-flyin'; he holds up his head and barks in a cheerful, manly tone of voice, escortin' me forward, and feelin prouder'n ef he'd holed a woodchuck!

"But let me come home full of tangle-leg, sheep-herder's delight, and tarant'ler juice, and that is the durndest shamedest dog above ground. He jist takes one look at me and he knows it all. Down goes his tail, he lops his years, hangs his head, squats his back, and slinks away, and crawls under the barn—acturly ashamed to be seen about the primises for fear somebody'll find out I own him!"

Just previous to the Senatorial contest which resulted in his election, the Hon. J. P. Jones had the following funny adventure in Virginia City with a man who came to hire himself out as a "fighter:"

Mr. Jones and several friends were in one of the first-class saloons, sipping their wine, smoking and chatting, when a rather strange-looking customer entered the place, and, sauntering up to the group, began the operation of "eying over" the gentlemen composing it.

He was a man of middle age and medium height, with arms dispro-portionately long, great, spreading hands, and knotty fingers. His angular, ungainly form was poorly and scantily clad, and he was topped out with a curious little bullet-head, set upon a very short allowance of neck. From the sides of his little, round head stood leaning out two great pulpy ears, and all that appeared on his face in the way of beard was a jet-black stubbed moustache. This seemed to have been planted a hair at a time with a peg-ging-awl and hammer, the latter coming down on the defenseless nose as each bristle was inserted, and so intimidating said organ that it had ever since remained crouched out of sight behind the hairy stockade. A large, livid scar described a semi-circle round one of his projecting cheekbones, and passing down entered the corner of his mouth, giving to the feature an ugly upward hitch on that side. Wobbling his little, glittering grey eyes over the party before him, until said orbs rested upon the rotund form and rosy face of Mr. Jones, he pulled off the hirsute ten-pin ball which he would have called his head, a scrap of hat, and making an awkward bow, said:

"J. P. Jones, I believe?"

"That is my name, sir," said Jones.

"Correct," sententiously observed the strange visitor.

"Do you want to see me?" said Jones.

"About three minutes, and in private, if you please."

Mr. Jones led the way to a large private room in the rear of the saloon.

"Mr. Jones, sir, you don't know me," said the fellow, "but when you lived in old Tuolumne, I war also in that part of Californey—in the adjinin' county. Mr. Jones, I'm the 'Taranterler of Calaveras;' I'm a war-hoss of the hills and a fighter from hell!"

"I don't dispute your word, sir," said J. P., "but how does your being 'war-horse of the hills' concern me?"

"I'm here to tell you. Here, now, you are goin' into this here contest, and it's liable to be a very lively one. About 'lection day it'll be all-fired hot. Now what you'll need will be a good fighter; a feller to stand up, knock down, and drag out for you; a man what can go to the polls and knock down right an' left—wade through everything!"

Mr. Jones said he had not thought it would be necessary to have such a man at the polls on election day.

"Oh, but it will!" cried the man of muscle. "You see you don't know about them things. I'll manage it all for you."

"So you want me to hire you as my fighter?"

"Jest so!"

"What would be your price from now till after election? You see as I've never yet had occasion to hire a fighter, I don't know much about the value of such service.

"Well, I couldn't undertake the job short of $1,000; there'll be lots of work to do."

"Ain't that pretty high?"

"Of course its a considerable sum, but thar's a terrible rough set over here. These Washoe fellow are nearly hell themselves, and they are more on the cut and shoot than is healthy. You see $1,000 is no money at all when you calkerlate the risk. I'm liable to be chopped all to pieces, riddled with bullets, and either killed out and out or crippled for life. You see $1,000 is no money at all."

"Well, come to look at it in that light, I don't know but your price is reasonable enough."

"Cheap! of course it is. I rather like your style or I wouldn't undertake the job at that figger. Come –is it a bargain? Am I your man, at the figger named?"

"Well, not so fast. If I am to have a fighter, I want the best that is to be had. I don't want a fellow that will be kicked and cuffed about town by every bummer. I am able to pay for a first-class fighter, and I won't have anything else!"

"Ain't I a fighter?" rolling his eyes fiercely and thrusting first his right, then his left arm, straight out from the shoulder, ducking his head comically about and poising himself on one foot; "will anybody kick and cuff me? me, the war-hoss of the hills; the Taranterler of Calaveras? Not much!"

"Have you ever whipped anybody?"

"Ever whipped anybody? Me—have I ever whipped anybody? Ha! ha!

ha! You make me laugh. Next you will be asking if I was ever whipped. Show me your man—show me your men—for I ain't perticular about 'em coming one at a time. Bring 'em on, and I'll whip all that can stand in this room in one minute by the clock!"

"Well," said "J. P.," "I think you'll do; but, as I said before, I want the best man in the country. My fighter must be a regular lightning striker. Now I have another man in my eye. He is something of a fighter. Has a graveyard of his own of considerable size. It lies between the pair of you. The best man is the man for my money."

"Damn your man! Bring him on. Damn me, I'll devour him! Show him to the Taranterler!"

"Remain here two minutes and I'll bring him in."

Now, before coming into the room with the fellow, Mr. Jones had observed James N. Cartter—commonly known on the Pacific Coast as Big Jim Cartter—sauntering around the saloon. As is well known to everybody in this city, and pretty generally throughout the towns and cities of Nevada and California, Jim Cartter is a powerfully-built man, standing over six feet in his stockings, a man who is "on the shoulder" and who is at home with either knife or pistol, as more than one grave can testify. Calling to Cartter, Mr. Jones briefly made known the situation and invited him in to interview the "war-hoss of the hills."

This was as good a thing as Cartter wanted, and into the room they went.

"Here," said Jones, as they entered the room, "is the man. Nobody will disturb you here, and after all is over the best man is the man for my coin."

Jim waltzed into the room with his hat standing on two hairs and a wicked smile playing upon his features. Said he:

"Is this the blessed infant that has come to eat me up? Is this the Calaveras skunk that has come over here to set himself up as 'Chief?' Move back the chairs!"

With this Cartter began to wriggle from side to side in the effort to "shuck" himself of the long-tailed black coat he always wore, and in so doing he displayed on one side that famous old white-handled, sixteen-inch bowie-knife, his constant companion, and on the other the but of a navy revolver.

"So this is the lop-eared cur of Calaveras who comes here to set up as a fighter? Move the chairs to the wall!" cried Cartter still wriggling at his coat.

"Mr. Jones," cried the mighty devourer of men, "Mr. Jones this man is a friend of yours. I can't fight any friend of yours. With any friend of yours I am a lamb; I could not harm a hair of his head!"

"No friend at all. He is a fighter like yourself. Besides, what has friendship got to do with a transaction involving $1,000? I want the best man I can find. If you whip this fellow I hire you as my fighter. That's all there is about it."

"That's fair and business-like, you skunk!" cried Cartter. "Peel yourself and waltz out here!"

"Mr. Jones," said the "war-hoss of the hills," in a mild conciliatory tone, "I am satisfied that this man is a friend of yours. You might insult me and banter me and tear me all to pieces, but against a friend of yours I'd never lift a hand. Now your friend is of the right stripe; I like his looks. Thar's no use of two good men a-fightin for nothin, so I'll tell you what you best do. You give him $500 and me $500 an' we'll work together. The two of us could chaw up the town—we'd be a terror to it."

"No," said Jones, "you won't do. You ain't game, you—"

"He's a dunghill!" chipped in Cartter.

"I can't fight in a room," said the fellow; "I have never yet had a fight in a room. I don't like it."

"I guess you're not struck after it anywhere!" said Cartter.

"It is rather close to fight in a room," said Jones. Then turning to the fellow, whose eyes were still wandering in the direction of Cartter's coat-tails, he handed him a twenty-dollar gold piece, saying; "Take this: I hire you for my open-air fighter. You are never to fight for me except in the open air and where there is a good chance for you to run."

"Thank you Mr. Jones," said the fellow, pocketing the coin and making for the door. "Thank you, and if I ever see a show to put in a lick for you I'll not forget to do it."

"Provided you have a chance to run," sneered Cartter.

Turning as he was passing out of the door, the fellow said:

"It's all very nice, Mr. Jones, but that is either Jim Cartter or the devil, and you can't ring him in on me!"

CHAPTER LI

THE "HEATHEN CHINEE"
A Strange Mixture of Duties—Wicked Mongolian Tricks—
'Melican and Chinaman Compared—A Ghostly Difference—Restless Spirits

As a rule the miners have no very exalted opinion of geologists, mineralogists, and other scientific persons who come into the country and claim to be able to tell all about each lead and stratum of rock, from the earliest ages down to the last Presidential election.

In 1874, after a State Mineralogist had been elected in Nevada—it was just previous to the transit of Venus—a Comstocker gave the following information in regard to the duties of the newly-elected officer, they not being very well understood by the majority of the people:

1. He will calculate all eclipses of the sun, moon, and larger stars, as soon as he is reliably informed that any have occurred, sending in to the Board of Alderman on the following Tuesday evening his diagnosis, in order that it may be duly referred to the Committee on Fire and Water.

2. He is to discover earthquakes and provide suitable means for the extermination of the same; also, for book-agents, erysipelas, corn doctors, cerebrospinal meningitis and the Grecian bend.

3. He will be expected to foretell cloud-bursts, and to cause them to burst by degrees.

4. He is to guard the State against irruptions of the grasshopper, and must at suitable intervals, put up petitions for the putting down of the potato-bug.

5. When Venus transits he is to go up to the top of Mount Davidson, the day before, provided with a shot-gun and other nautical instruments with which to stop her, if, in his opinion, what she does on that occasion is liable to have a bad effect on any of the leading interests of this State—particularly the anchovy-fields and the bologna marshes.

6. In case of an aurora borealis he will let it take its course—the same with comets and measles.

7. In the spring, when the farmers have sown their cereals, he is to go down into the valleys and reduce the atmospheric pressure, in order that the grains may sprout without painfully straining themselves in swelling; also, in the fall he will perform the same duty, so that the pumpkins and cabbages may grow with less effort.

8. He will assist the Fish Commissioner in the introduction into our State of the alligator and other improved breeds of shrimps; will splice out short rainbows, cure warts free of charge, and furnish antidotes for hare-lip, nightmare, corners in stocks, twins, and Beecher-Tilton at the same price—sending his bill in to the Board of County Commissioners.

9. In case of foreign invasion, by the Paiute Indians, or any other intestine foe, he is to so alter the boundary lines to our State, so as to throw the part containing the war into California—reserving, of course, our right to the free navigation of the waters of Lake Tahoe.

10. Should he at any time discover in any part of the State indications of milk-sickness, female suffrage, poison-oak or choke-damp, he will forthwith proceed to make an assay of the same, and, having extracted the cube root, will deposit it among the archives of the Pacific Coast Pioneers; with a recommendation to the mercy of the Court.

11. When a man is bitten by a mad dog, he is to kill the dog first—the same if the dog bites anybody else.

12. When not otherwise engaged, he is to keep our cows from giving

bloody milk; cause the water to run up hill in the Virginia City sewers; bag the surplus of all "Washoe zephyrs" for use in the lower levels of the mines; clip the ears of black-and-tans; cause the sun to shine on cloudy days; vaccinate for fits; have the moon shine on dark nights, and cause all the leading mines on the Comstock range to pay monthly dividends every two weeks.

In the eastern suburbs of Virginia City is situated the Chinese quarter of the town, commonly called "Chinatown." In this Chinese quarter live several hundred Mongolians of both sexes and all ages and conditions. In their part

of the town they have stores of various kinds, shops, and markets, gambling-dens, a joss-house, where they worship their gods, and all other establishments required by them either for business or pleasure. In their part of the town these people live much as they would at home in China.

Many of the men are employed as servants in families in the city, generally in the capacity of cooks. In most of the restaurants, Chinese cooks are also employed. Many of them are laundrymen, and the town is full of wash-houses. There are several Chinese-physicians in the city,

China Town, 1876, collodion/albumen, Carleton E. Watkins. California State Library.

some of whom are frequently consulted by white persons. Among the residents of Chinatown are a great number of wood-peddlers. During the summer months they collect wood among the hills surrounding the city, often scouting out several miles. They get wood where a white man would see nothing that he would think of attempting to convert into fuel. For many miles in all directions about the town they have dug up and hacked to pieces the stumps left by the white men who first denuded the hills of their sparse covering of cedar and nut-pine.

The Chinese wood-peddlers are a feature of the town in winter. They are to be seen on every street, patiently plodding along behind the donkey on which is piled their stock-in-trade. They utter no cry in passing along the streets, but expect to be called by those who want wood. The common price is one dollar for a donkey-load, but when the weather is very cold and stormy, or when a storm is imminent, if you say: "How much-ee, John?" John, with a knowing look from his weather eye, in the direction of the approaching storm, glibly says: "One dolla quarty!" If the storm is very bad he probably says: "One dolla hap!" The price of wood goes up and down with the mercury.

John also understands the art of piling wood. He cuts his sticks very short and piles them up to a great height. While he is trading with you he keeps the head of his donkey turned toward you, so you have but an end view of the commodity in which you propose to invest. To the casual observer this manoeuvre of the Mongolian may seem to be mere accident, but it is pure cunning and is one of the tricks of his trade. Turn his donkey about broadside and view your load of wood edgewise, and it is not much thicker than a trade dollar. Take a rear view, and you find that the rotten ends of all the sticks of the load are pointing in the direction of the donkey's tail. When you see John approaching you he seems to have a monster load on his donkey, but when he is opposite there is little of it but "ragged edge." Take what appears to be quite a little "jag" of wood, as seen on the donkey, and when it is tumbled off, and lies on the ground, half of it seems to have disappeared—such is their cunning in piling it on their donkeys.

The Chinese are a curious people and have curious notions on all subjects. They are like Europeans in nothing. They are very superstitious, and believe in ghosts and all that sort of thing, yet they sometimes act as though Satan himself could not frighten them. As showing their notions in regard to funerals, death, and a future state, I am able to give the ideas of a very intelligent Chinaman, of the name of Wing Lee.

On the 29th of June, 1875, at 11 o'clock at night, there occurred in Virginia City an explosion of nitro-glycerine by which ten or twelve persons lost their lives, three buildings were torn to pieces and then totally destroyed by a fire which broke out in them. The explosion occurred in a room occupied by General J. L. Van Bokkelen, in a large brick building. The General was agent for a giant-powder company, and at the time of the explosion was known to be experimenting, with a view to the invention of an explosive that should be far more powerful than anything known; but nobody knew that he was conducting his experiments in the heart of the city, until after the mischief had been done. What it was that blew up was never exactly ascertained, but it was known that he had in his room a considerable quantity of gun-cotton saturated with nitro-glycerine. He also had in his room a pet monkey, and by many it was supposed that the monkey having seen the General experimenting, tried his hand among the chemicals. Man or monkey, the explosion killed ten or twelve persons, and destroyed property to the value of nearly $200,000. Among those killed were several leading citizens, and the funeral procession on the occasion of their burial was one of the largest and most imposing ever seen in the place.

It was while this procession was passing through the town that the Chinaman referred to above gave me his views in regard to such matters. What he said can only be given in his words. Said he: "Suppose some big lich (rich) Chinaman die; Chinaman no get newspaper all same 'Melican, so he family send-ee some letter to everybody come bury. Everybody be belly glad for cause one big lich man die; he all heap come—two, tlee (three) thousand maybe—all glad get heap eat-ee. Put many mat on ground; 10 o'clock morning all begin eatee pake (pork) and licee (rice); all belly glad, heap eat-ee.

"Now all people, everyone, he get tlee (three) piec-ee white cloth—two yard-ee long, hap (half) yard-eewide. One piec-ee he tie 'bout he head; one piec-ee 'bout he waist, one piec-ee on arm—all white; no black same 'Melican man. Now, all go to take dead man; all go foot, no wagon, no horse-ee, all go foot. Big lichmanhe get one big housee make on top big hill; housee all stone. Put he in he housee he sleep well, all set up in he chair make in stone; all he fine dress put on, all he diamond, all he watch-ee, all he chain—everything same one live man. Then he git all fasten up by heself in he housee; then he family hire one man watchee every nightee all time, so no man he come dig. So everybody he go home belly glad, for because he got one big dinner, tlee piecee good clothee—all Chinaman belly glad when one big lich Chinaman dies. Poor Chinaman, put he in one hole like 'Melican, all in mud—no big dinner, no clothee. Some big lich Chinaman he funeral cost-ee ten, twenty thousand dolla.

"One dead Chinaman he all same one live Chinaman—he heap eat all time, he come back to he hous-ee, to he bed, he walkee in house all same like when he no dead. Suppose you no put some pake (pork), some licee (rice) on he grave he come back in dark nightee, talkee in your ear, he pinch you toe. Dead Chinaman heap hungry, all same one live Chinaman—heap want eatee.

"Chinaman no likee git bury this countlee—he no git good feed—likee be take back he own countlee to he father, he mother, he sister, he brother, so he git feed—no likee die here. You say 'Melican man no come back when he die?—me no sabe why—Chinaman he come back, sure. Dead Chinaman all same live Chinaman.

"One 'Melican man he die on one bed; two nightee more you put one live 'Melican sleep same bed—no good! You put one live Chinaman in one dead Chinaman bed, dead Chinaman he makee some d—d hot for live Chinaman—you bet! Dead he all same live Chinaman—Chinaman he never all dead: You know one Chinaman two, tlee year 'go, he git kill down Chinatown? Well, he heap come back—many Chinaman see him—you bet.' He lookee all blood; he say all time: 'Oh! oh!' and all time he say: 'You go catchee that one man what he kill me!' He come walkee up and down belly much. One time he no come one hap (half) year; all other time he come every week. When dead Chinaman he come back some people he much flaid, put-a blanket on he head; some people heeno flaid, talkee to dead Chinaman: 'What matter? You no sleep well?' Some Chinaman no got good eye, no can see dead Chinaman; he only can hear dead man walkee, maybe talkee. Me hear belly good, me no got good eyes—no see dead Chinaman.

"Dead Chinaman all the same like one live Chinaman! Las' year one Chinaman git die here in this town, git bury over China bury-ground. Nex' night he come back he say to one man: 'Me no can sleep; my one leg he crook up, me belly (very) sore.' But that one man he will no go straight he leg, so he go to some other several Chinaman and all time say: 'Come fix me leg.' Well, when they can no do other way some Chinaman go dig up fix he leg; he sleep belly well, he come back no more. Dead Chinaman he not get plenty eat, he come back, sure—you bet! Dead Chinaman all same like one live Chinaman!"

CHAPTER LII

CHINESE OPIUM-DENS

How They Smoke the Drug—Babel—Street-Scenes in Virginia City—
Voices of the People—Hard Cash—The Grasshopper Man

In Virginia City, as in all other places where there is a considerable Chinese population, are found opium-dens. These are sometimes on the first floor, but are generally in a cellar or basement. We will take a look at one not in any building: it is a subterranean opium-den—a cave of oblivion.

In the side of a little hill in the eastern part of the Chinese quarter of Virginia City is to be seen a low door of rough boards. An open cut, dug in the slope of the hill and walled with rough rocks, leads to the door. The boards forming the door and its frame are blackened by smoke, particularly at the top, for the den has neither chimney nor flue. The surface of the hill forms its roof. All that is to be seen on the outside is the door and the walled entrance leading up to it. Not a sound is heard within or about the place. The cave of the Seven Sleepers was not more silent. But gently pushing the door, it opens—opens as noiselessly as though hinged in cups of oil.

At first we can see nothing, save a small lamp suspended from the centre of the ceiling. This lamp burns with a dull red light that illuminates nothing. It seems more like a distant fiery star than anything mundane. Though at first we see nothing but the lamp, gradually our eyes adapt themselves to the dim light, and we can make out the walls and some of the larger objects in the place. A voice says: "What you want?" Looking in the direction whence proceeds the inquiry, we see a sallow old Mongolian seated near a small table. He is the proprietor of the den. "What you want?" he repeats. We feel that we have no business where we are, but to speak the truth is always best, therefore we simply say, in pigeon-English: "Me comee see your smokee saloon." The old fellow settles one elbow on the table before him, and makes a remark which appears to be the Chinese equivalent for "Humph!"

Before this taciturn dispenser of somnial drugs are a number of little horn boxes of opium, several opium-pipes, small scales for weighing, with beam of bone, covered with black dots instead of figures; small steel spatulas, wire probes, and other smoking-apparatus.

We now observe that two sides of the den are fitted up with bunks, one above the other, like the berths on shipboard. A cadaverous opium-smoker is seen in nearly every bunk. These men are in various stages of stupor. Each lies upon a scrap of grass mat or old blanket. Before him is a small alcohol lamp burning with, a blue flame which gives out but little light— only enough to cast a sickly glare upon the corpse-like face of the smoker, as he holds his pipe in the flame, and by a long draught inhales and swallows the smoke of the loved drug. These fellows are silent as dead men, and seem unconscious of our presence. Occasionally, at a sign, the proprietor arises and furnishes the customer a fresh supply of the drug. The peculiar sweetish-bitter odor of the burning opium fills and saturates the whole place—one can almost taste it.

While the majority, lying upon their sides, and propped on one elbow, are calmly inhaling their dose, a few appear to have had enough. These lie with their heads resting upon short sections of bamboo, which serve this curious people as pillows, and move no more than dead men. The eyes of some are wide open, as in a fixed stare, while those of others are partially or wholly closed. If they have any of those heavenly visions of which we are told, they keep them to themselves; as, save in a few somniloquous mutterings, they utter no sound. The door is gently opened, and a gaunt, wild-eyed Mongolian slips stealthily in. The old man at the table merely elevates his eyes. The newcomer steps out of his sandals and, making no more noise than a cat, crosses the earthen floor of the room and creeps into a vacant bunk. The boss of this cavern of Morpheus now raises his elbows from the table, takes up a pipe and its belongings, sleepily lights one of the small alcohol lamps, and then places the whole before his customer. The old man then returns to his table and sits down. Not a word is spoken.

Thus the business of the cavern goes on, day and night, and this is all of opium-smoking that appears on the surface, tales of travelers to the contrary notwithstanding. What shapes may appear to the sleepers, or what flight their souls may take into interstellar regions, we know not. To a looker-on it is all vapid, vacuous stupefaction.

Not a few white men in Virginia City—and a few women—are opium-smokers. They visit the Chinese opium dens two or three times a week.

They say that the effect is exhilarating—that it is the same as intoxication produced by drinking liquor, except that under the influence of opium a man has all his senses, and his brain is almost supernaturally bright and clear. An American told me that he had been an opium smoker for eighteen years, and said there were about fifty persons in Virginia City who were of the initiated. In San Francisco he says there are over five hundred white opium smokers, many women among them.

During summer, men who have for sale all manner of quack nostrums, men with all kinds of notions for sale, street shows, beggars, singers, men with electrical-machines, apparatus for testing the strength of the lungs, and a thousand other similar things, flock to Virginia City. Of evenings, when the torches of these parties of peddlers, showmen, and quack doctors are all lighted and all are in full cry, a great fair seems to be under headway in the principal street of the town—there is a perfect Babel of cries and harangues.

The man with the electical-machine, for instance, leads off with:

"Who is the next gentleman who wishes to try the battery? It makes the old man feel young, and the young man feel strong. Remember, gentlemen, that a quarter of a dollar pays the bill. Try the battery! Try the battery! Bear in mind that there can be nothing applied equal to it, as it is one of nature's own remedies. A quarter of a dollar places you in a position to have your nervous system electrified. The small sum of one quarter of a—Try the battery, sir? The small sum of one quarter of a dollar pays the whole entire bill. Who is the next man to try the battery? Try the battery! Try the battery and improve your health while you have the opportunity. Who is the next man that wishes to—Try the battery, sir? Try the battery! Try the battery! Purifies the blood, strengthens the nervous system; cures headaches, toothaches, neuralgia, and all diseases of the nervous system. Can be applied to a child six months old as well as to a full-grown person. Try the battery! Try the battery! Re-e-emember, gentlemen, that the ema-a-all and tri-i-fling sum of o-one quarter of a dollar pays the whole entire—Try the battery, sir? Try the battery! Try the battery! Can regulate the instrument to suit all constitutions. Try the battery! Re-e-member that electricity is life. It is what you, each and every one of you, require, and it is utterly impossible for yon to live without it. Try the battery! Try the battery!"

The soap-root tooth-powder man next starts in with his little talk:

"Gentlemen, I have here three little articles, and I start out by telling you that they are all three humbugs. But starting out with this proposition that they are all humbugs, I only do so in order that before I get through I may [Try the battery!] disprove said proposition to your entire satisfaction. I will first show you a little article called [Try the battery! Try the battery!] the California Soap-root Tooth-powder. Years ago, gentlemen, about 75 miles northeast of Waterville, in the State of California, I saw the Indians [Try the battery!] washing their clothes with this root. I examined it and found [One quarter of a dollar pays the entire bill!] it was a wonderful production of nature, gentlemen. I found that It [Makes the old man feel young, and the young man feel strong!] grew in abundance in the mountains. I procured a quantity of it and took it to [Try the battery, sir?] San Francisco, when I began to [Try the battery!] to try [Try the battery!] experiments with it The result was, gentlemen, that I produced this beautiful article which [Purifies the blood, strengthens the nervous system, and improves your general health!] instantly removes all stains from the teeth and [A quarter of a dollar pays the whole entire bill!] leaves the breath pure and sweet. [Try the battery!]"

The German ballad-singer now comes to the front:

"Lauterbach hab' i mein' Strumpf verlorn,
Ohne Strumpf geh' i not hoam,
Geh' i halt weider auf Lauterbach,
Kauf' mir an Strumpf zu dem oan.
 Tillee leari, oiko, hi oiko, hi oiko!
 Tillee oiko, oiko. Tilli oi-i-oi-oiko!
 Tillee leari—[Try the battery!] hi oiko!
Z' Lauterbach hab' i mein Herz verlorn,
Ohne Herz kann i not [Try the battery!] leb'n."

Clem Berry (Scipio Africanus) now takes the field:

"Only two dollars, gentlemen, takes you to Reno by this splendid Concord coach, landing you there at 6 o'clock in the evening, when you may [Try the battery!] sleep till the train arrives [Seventy-five miles northeast of Weaverville, in the State of California, where I saw the Indians—] from the East, when you [Try the battery!] get aboard [which removes all stains from the teeth] at the same time as the passengers by the Virginia and Truckee Railroad [Tillee oiko, hioiko!] and [Try the battery!] are perfectly fresh—[Oi-ioi-oiko!]"

The spotted boy, dwarf, and big snakes now loom up, and we hear that:

"This wonderful spotted boy was captured in the wilds of Africa [Seventy-five miles northeast of Weaverville—] with his strange companion [Lauterbach], the huge boa constrictor, which you see [Try the battery!] him handle with the greatest possible [Hioiko!] freedom [without causing the gums to bleed]. And here is the wonderful little Fairy Queen, 18 years of age, and only thirty-one inches in height.

She was born [Ohne Strumpf] in Grand Rapids, [Seventy-five miles northeast of Weaverville], Wisconsin; has a thorough education, and possesses [A splendid Concord coach!] the [Small sum of one quarter of a dollar] graces and manners becoming a [Lauterbach] lady of the highest [Hioiko!] standing in society."

All hands round:

"Get right aboard here, now, and at 6 o'clock I'll land you at Reno, seventy-five miles northeast of Weaverville, in the wilds of Africa, where I saw the Indian thirty-one inches in height, born at Grand Rapids, try the battery and take all the stains out of the wonderful spotted boy, who only eats once in four months, and sheds his skin twice a year. Having been educated in a convent in Milwaukee, geh i' not hoam to try the battery, when the big white snake eats the little girl across the way you'll get a drink for a bit, and see the sea-lion try the battery free, up in the mountains this wonderful Lauterbach soap-root climbs a tree and then hangs by the tail, tilee leari, oiko hi oiko! which purifies the blood, strengthens the nerves of the spotted boy, cleanses the teeth, and does not fear to encounter either the lion or the tiger, being able to regulate the instrument to suit all constitutions."

In Virginia City, as well as in all the towns and cities on the Pacific Coast, gold and silver coin is the only money in circulation. There are now in circulation at least two American coins almost unknown in other parts of the Union—the trade-dollar and the twenty-five cent piece—as their coinage was not authorized until after greenbacks became a legal tender, and had taken possession of the Atlantic States to the exclusion of all coin, except copper and nickle.

The trade-dollar was coined for our trade with China and Japan. It was coined expressly to supersede the Mexican dollar in the countries named. It contains a trifle more silver than the Mexican dollar, and the Chinese were not long in ascertaining this fact. Now the American trade-dollar is in great demand both in China and Japan, and the old Mexican dollar is thrown completely into the shade. The Chinese and Japanese are great lovers of silver, and the American trade dollar, being pure silver, is preferred by them to the coin of any other nation. The end—the final fate—of the trade-dollar, however, is inglorious. It is sent to India by the Chinese for the purchase of opium. In India they are sent to the Calcutta mint and are there made into rupees, stamped with the value on one side and on the other outlandish heathen characters. Thus the silver of the big bonanza fills the opium-pipe of the Chinese mandarin. The amount of American silver sent to India to pay for opium is very great.

The Chinese in Nevada and in all other towns on the Pacific Coast industriously gather trade-dollars which they send to the head men of their companies in San Francisco, by whom they are shipped to China. Persons who have but lately arrived from States where no coin is seen, are astonished at the abundance of silver in Virginia City, and delighted to be in a place where they may once again hear the almost forgotten jingle of gold and silver; though I once heard a New York lady say: "I never saw such a place. I hear nothing but the jingle of money from one end of the town to the other. The people all go about jingling their money as though on purpose to show that they are able to pay their way!"

To the impecunious new arrivals—the weary and tattered immigrants—this jingling of coin must be still more aggravating.

A gentleman in Virginia City one day told a story about slipping a silver half-dollar into the gaping coat pocket of a grasshopper sufferer who was gazing hungrily in at the window of a restaurant. The man continued looking at the good things displayed in the window for some time, devouring them in imagination, then, heaving a sigh, turned away. As he was moving off, however, he carelessly, and through force of habit, as it were, put his hand into his pocket. Bringing forth the silver coin the instant his hand came in contact with it, the fellow gazed upon it with a face which wore a look of astonishment comical to behold. Finally he seemed to conclude that it was all right, the Lord had sent it, when he retraced his steps to the restaurant and soon was seated before that which was probably the first square meal he had faced in some days.

A Comstocker, who heard this story told, relates that he concluded he would experiment a little in the same direction. If half a dollar had power to so astound an impecunious immigrant, he would try the effect of a trade-dollar. Procuring a bright, new trade-dollar, he sallied forth in search of a subject. He had not travelled far until he saw before him a young man of most rueful countenance—an undoubted grasshopper sufferer. The man was leaning against a lamp-post on a street corner, his face elongated, his mouth standing negligently open, and his half-closed eyes gazing wearily up among the fleecy clouds, as though he were wishing himself dead and taking his ease as an angel, far away in the realms above.

The Comstocker saw that here was his man, and, passing near the dreamer, slily slid the trade-dollar into the capacious pocket of his butternut coat, then taking up a position a few paces distant, awaited developments. He had not long to wait. Soon, in shifting his position, the grasshopper man mechanically placed his hand in his pocket, and, as was to be seen by the general awakening of his features, was not a little surprised to find something where he had supposed there was nothing. When he brought out the big bright dollar, his eyes almost started from their sockets, and he looked as though about to fall down in a fit of some kind. However, after a gasp or two he appeared to recover somewhat, and glancing curiously, and in a bewildered sort of way, at all standing near him, started across the street, carefully fobbing the dollar as he went.

By the time he had gone half across the street, he appeared to change his mind. After gazing back and scratching his head for half a minute, he returned to the post and taking up his old position, spread open the pocket of his coat to its fullest extent. He had concluded to set it again.

CHAPTER LIII

How Fortunes are Made and Lost
Bulls and Bears—Doings of the Brokers—On a Margin—
"Pussy-Cat Wilde" and "Bobtaile"—Going Up!—Dealers and Dabblers

During the prevalence of a big stock excitement, times are lively along the Comstock range. Virginia City then hums like a Brobdignagian beehive. All who failed to make fortunes on the occasion of previous excitements in stocks are going to do better this time. They have seen how these things work, and this time are going to sell when they can do so at a fair profit. They don't want the last cent: they will give some one else a chance to make something.

This is the way they talk at the start. As soon as there is a marked advance in stocks, however, they will be heard to say: "As soon as I can double my money I am going to sell." In three days from the time of their making this assertion, stocks have taken such a "jump" that they could sell and double or more than double their money. Everybody is saying, however, that they are not selling for half what they are worth; that they will sell for twice or three times present prices before the end of another month.

The men who were intending to sell whenever they could double their money cannot think of doing anything of the kind as things are now looking. Instead of selling they become excited, put up their stocks (which they had probably bought and paid for "out and out") as a "margin," then put in all the money they can raise besides, and buy as many shares of their favorite stocks as they can in any way manage to secure. Stocks still go up, and each day these dabblers will be found counting their profits. They have invested largely in the low-priced stocks of "outside mines"—mines in which nothing of value has yet been, found, but mines in which, all are saying, grand developments are liable to be made at any time—mines, in short, which in dull times are generally designated as "wild-cat." The masses—the servant girls, chamber-maids, cooks, hostlers, washerwoman, preachers, teachers, hackmen and draymen—are wildly and blindly buying these low-priced stocks, and from day to day they are going up "with a rush," and everybody is getting rich.

Our men who only "went in" to make a fair profit, now tell you that they made yesterday $10,000; to-day they have made $15,000, and in a week or two they will say that they are worth a quarter of a million, half a million or a million of dollars. But they are not going to sell yet: no, indeed—the rise has only commenced. Pretty soon stocks fall off a little. Never mind, to-morrow they will do better. To-morrow they are still a "little off," as is said when stocks are going down. The next day they are rather "soft," which is the same thing as a "little off." However, that is all right. Our dealers—amateur speculators— have some points, given them by a friend who is on the inside. A development is about to be made in a favorite mine. The "bears" are trying to break the stock; but they can't do it; no, sir!—impossible. Too much merit in the mines at this time. All will be up and "booming" in a day or two, Next time you shall see them go higher than they have yet been seen.

Our men who started in to make a fair profit might yet sell and double their money—much more than double it—but they are not going to do anything of the kind. They are going to wait till "things take a turn." The "bulls" will soon make a grand rally, and when things go up again our men will sell. They admit that they should have sold when their stocks were all up before, but, never mind! they will go to the same figures again in less than a fortnight, when they will be sure to sell.

There does come a "spurt," and for a day or two there is a cheering improvement in prices along the whole line. Faces brighten and everybody talks of all stocks going higher than ever.

All at once everything is again "soft;" the next day "softer," and the next decidedly "off." It is then said that some one in the "bear" interest has been telegraphing to the "Bay" (San Francisco) a pack of lies about the mines, and the "bears" "below" (at San Francisco) have made use of these lies to get up a "scare." Never mind! the scare will be over in a day or two.

But stocks still go down. Then it is said that some big dealer is "unloading" and there is talk of a "crash." Still-our men who started in but to make a "fair profit" do not feel like taking thousands, when they might a short time before have taken tens of thousands of dollars. They still hold on, saying that even though one or two big dealers are unloading, the big men among the bulls will "stand in" and take all the stocks that are offered. Also, they will have some points from a friend "on the inside" and developments are about to be made in one or two of the mines that will make all who have sold "very sick" particularly those bloodless demons who have "sold short." The "shorts" will have a merry time of it when they come to "fill."

Thus matters stand, when suddenly there comes what looks very much like the beginning of a "crash." The "bears" are all diligently crying, "stand from under." Many persons become frightened, and throw their stocks upon the market. Down go prices and soon "soft" is no name for it. The masses—the tinker and tailor, the preacher and the teacher, the hostler and the waiter—rush in to try to "save themselves" and there is seen a grand and unmistakable crash. Brokers are calling on all sides for "margins" to be "made good," and men are rushing about trying to raise money to "put up" in order to prevent their stocks being sold at less than cost.

They perhaps raise the money required, and for a few days breathe again, when there is a further decline in stocks, and the brokers are again sending notes to their customers telling them that if they do not put up more money they will be sold out. Sooner or later there comes a time when the customer can raise no more money, and his stocks are thrown into the market by the broker—in whose hands they remain—and are sold. Thus ends the grand speculation.

Our men, who at the start were resolved to be content with a fair profit are generally found among the number of those who are sold out, when they are heard to say that if they ever have another such chance to make money they will not hold on for the last cent. They have said the same thing year after year ever since the opening of the Comstock mines. But whenever there is a grand upward movement in stocks they never fail to become excited and try to buy about ten times as much stock as they can pay for. In this way they lose all except what they may have happened to purchase at a fair price in a mine of real merit.

Persons who purchase mining-stocks on a "margin" pay their broker, as a rule, one-half the market value of the stock so bought. The other half is advanced by the broker, the customer paying him interest on the amount at the rate of two per cent, per month. The broker also receives one per cent commission on all sales and purchases made for the customer. Stocks are nearly always bought and sold in the San Francisco Stock Board, the broker in Virginia City telegraphing to his agent "at the Bay" to buy or sell such a number of shares of a certain stock, and the bill for this telegraphing is paid by the customer.

In case of a decline in the price of the stock purchased, the customer must pay in to the broker enough money to make him secure for the amount he has advanced, taking into account the current price of the stock. Should there be a further and continued decline, the customer must continue to put up money, in order to make his broker safe. If he is unable to do this his broker sells him out—*i.e.,* takes care of "number one."

From this it will be seen that the broker who does a strictly commission business—who is not himself a dabbler in stocks—makes a very soft thing out of it. Sometimes, however, stocks drop so rapidly that the broker cannot sell in time to save himself. This is generally when the customer has been allowed to buy stock on the presumed value of the stocks he already has in the hands of his broker, putting up stocks that have advanced at their current value as a margin on which to purchase still other stocks, and so running his purchases up on the compound-interest principle.

When a broker calls for money to make margins good, "mud" is the slang word used among dealers in stocks, by which to designate the money so demanded. One frequently hears a man -who is a dabbler in stocks cursing his luck, the condition of the market, and all else, concluding with: "And here is my broker calling for more mud!" When the reports of the sales of stocks are received from San Francisco and prices are a "little off," one hears some person who has read the news sing out: "More mud, boys!"

The demand for "mud" often causes very long faces to be seen on the streets—to many it means ruin. Yet men will continue to buy on margins, taking all the chances, and stretching what ready-money they have as far as the broker will allow them to go. Provided men buy on a margin at a time when stocks are very low and then shortly after comes a grand excitement, they are liable to make a little fortune with a very small amount of capital, but to buy in this way at a time when everything is high is dangerous business and the demands for "mud" are likely to be very numerous.

The following letter received in Virginia City, from a Frenchman, in San Francisco, shows how he first became acquainted with this dreadful word, "mud" and how he relished the thing itself:

SAN FRANCISCO, CAL. APRIL U 1875.

Monsieur—By zee advice of one goot friend who informed me zat he be on zee inside, and who make for me zee negoziazione, I have procure some time past on what you call "on zee time," many share of zee Bobtaile. Zee prix zat time be fortee dollare on monnie d'or des Etats-Unis; bote I buy on zee time and not pay zee prix. My friend on zee insides tell me Bobtaile one ver fine bargain for fortee dollare. Ah ha! Bobtaile one ver fine compagnie! plenty mashine pour work; grand nombre d'employes; Superintendent un salaire plus grand, je suppose! all ting ver fine. Me buy? Vraiment, oui! He—mine friend who repose on zee insides—express himself of zee mine wis moche enthousiasme. "Zee mine be one merveille de la nature; zee works, un chef-d'œuvre de l'art!" Je suppose to purchase be une chance rare. I purchase, but now, pretty soon—le diable! Zee brokaire man use zee expression to me, as follows: "More mud." At zee first I not ver well comprehend. Sans doubte it be une expression, ver mysterieuse—zis exclamation: "More mud." So many five, seex time have he, zee brokaire, desire of me some leetle more mud, zat now I mus make one grand sacrifice pecuniaire. It be now become scandaleuse! Parbleu, c'est horrible, cette "mud!" For me to communicate wis my brokaire—bah! it was one grand plaiser, Of de mine, des minerals I be plenty sick. Under de circonstances I read no more wis enthousiasme of—"Les compagnie's certificat d'incorporation;" "la Pussy Cat Wilde, objet: Operations dans l'Etat de Nevada, etc."— "Les directeurs sont: Bill Tubb, Sam Hobb, Jack Dobb, etc." "Capital social, \$45,800,000,002; divise en 56,000,000,000,000,000 actions." Vraiment oui!—"More mud!" Pretty soon you hear one crash financial,—I gone bust—me! No more do I eat me my dennaire a de la restaurant du Poodle Dog, rue Duponte, but wis circomspection admirable I betake me to la cote de Barbarie, to zee Hell Kitchen— zee cuisine de l'enfer. Parole d'honneur monsieur, I be ver moche perplex wis zee stoke, prices, He viggle up, he viggle down all zee time. Vill you have zee complaisance to inform me how soon he vill viggle high up and remain to pass some time up dare? "Mud!" le diable!—zee word have for me un signification sardonique!

Your tres-humble and tres-obeissant servant,
PIERRE EDOUARD OUDIN.

In the winter of 1874-75, owing to the wonderful developments made in the Consolidated Virginia and California mines, there was a grand stock excitement throughout the towns of the Pacific Coast. San Francisco and Virginia City, however, were the two great centres of this excitement. As the vast and astonishingly rich deposits of ore in the California mine began to be drifted into and opened to view, the stock of the company rapidly and steadily advanced from about fifty dollars per share to nearly one thousand dollars. Consolidated Virginia stock advanced in about the same ratio, as in the mine of that company the width and richness of the ore was far beyond anything that had ever before been seen on the Comstock lode. In the Ophir mine, the next north of the California, large and rich bodies of ore were being opened, and the stock of that company advanced with almost bewildering rapidity. Persons who happened to have twenty, fifty, or one hundred shares in either of these mines suddenly found themselves rich. The investment of a few hundreds of dollars had brought them thousands, and the investments of thousands brought them tens of thousands of dollars.

The great strike in the "bonanza" mines started up the stocks of all the adjoining mines, and, indeed, of all the mines along the Comstock range. The stock of mines that were rich in "great expectations" only were as eagerly sought for and as briskly dealt in, as were those in which ore was already being extracted, for many said: "It is just as well for us to double our money in a stock that costs but one or two dollars per share as in stocks that cost from one to five hundred dollars." And many did double and more than double their money in such stocks; indeed, in some instances they sold for five or ten times what their stocks cost them.

Every day there is a morning and an afternoon session of the San Francisco Stock Board, and the reports of the sales are telegraphed to Virginia City, Gold Hill and other Nevada towns as fast as the stocks are called. Thus, as soon as the Stock Board is in session and business begins, reports of sales begin to arrive in Virginia City and are placed in the windows or on the bulletin-boards of the various stock-brokers of the town, where all interested may see them. Therefore during a big stock excitement the bulletin-boards are the centres about which are seen large crowds of anxious dealers—and nearly everybody in the city dabbles more or less in stocks, women as well as men.

On very critical occasions, either when stocks are rapidly rushing or when they are rapidly "tumbling," then is a grand charge made upon all the bulletin-boards as soon as it is known that the reports have arrived. Dry-goods clerks—yardstick in hand and scissors peeping from vest-pocket—come running out bare-headed and bald-headed to catch a glimpse of the bulletin; bar-keepers in their white aprons come; bare-headed, bare-armed, and white-aproned butchers smelling of blood, come; blacksmiths, in leather aprons and hammer in hand, flour-dusted bakers, cooks in paper caps, cobblers, tinkers, and tailors all come to learn the best and the worst. The miner on his way to or from work, carrying his dinner-pail and candlestick, halts for a moment to see how fares his favorite stock, the teamster stops his long string of mules opposite one of the centres of attraction and, thrusting his "black snake" under the housing of his saddle-mule, marches to the board to read his fate. Ladies linger as they pass the groups at the bulletin-boards and try to catch some word of hope, or ensconce themselves in the nearest shops, and hence send messenger-lads to bring tidings of their favorite gamble.

Even the Chinese dabble in stocks. Some of these are able to read the reports for themselves, while others ask white men to tell them the price of the stocks in which they are dealing. There was an old fellow who, for a long time was dealing in the stocks of the Belcher and the Segregated Belcher mines. The Belcher he called the "big Belch," and the Segregated Belcher the "little Belch." Crowding his way up to a bulletin-board he would say to some bystander: "How much-ee to-day catch-ee big Belch?" Being told, and finding the stock up, he would say: "Bully for big Belch!"

Next he would ask: "How much-ee to day catch-ee little Belch?"

Finding that stock a "little off" he would say: "Belly bad! belly bad! Little Belch too much-ee all time, bust me up!"

In passing the bulletin-boards one catches scraps of conversation like the following: "Didn't I tell you so? I have said so all the time." "I saw a man this morning who is thoroughly reliable, and he says"—"Yes, it may be a buy, but, confound it, I get sold so often!"—"I knew they would all be up to-day"— "Now you raise the money; I tell you it is just as I say. I have points that"—"Dealing in stocks with these rings is just like playing poker with a man who knows both hands"—"They have it awful in the"—"They haven't got an ounce afore in the"—"I shan't sell yet. Stocks have only begun to go up." "I wish I had sold yesterday." "Well I have laid up my treasures above, where the bulls and bears can never come."—The last speaker is generally a newspaper reporter or some other such holy person, who is seen standing aloof from the ungodly worshippers at the shrine of Mammon.

The amount of "stock talk" heard in every saloon, public-house and shop, and on every street, is at times enough to render an easy-going Granger from one of the eastern or middle States, to whom it is all Greek a raving maniac or a driveling idiot. The sidewalks on C street, the principal business street of Virginia City, are generally so thronged that it is a difficult matter to pass along them, except at the same slow pace at which the mass of the pedestrians is moving; therefore at times when there is an excitement in regard to stocks there are frequent blockades in front of the offices of the brokers, and persons wishing to pass are obliged to take to the streets. At times the police are obliged to clear passages through the throngs, as men become so interested in their stocks as to have neither eyes nor ears for anything else, and ladies and children find them* selves unable to pass.

CHAPTER LIV

Curious Speculations in Stock
Old Joe's Disaster—A New Excitement—Sharp Doings—
"The Greatest Buy On the Lead"—A Lady's Speculation

Then there is a grand upward movement in stocks, and all is excitement among the dealers, from the big operator worth millions, down to the little curbstone broker whose fortune is yet to be made, early and reliable information in regard to what is going on in the lower-levels is valuable and is always in demand.

On the Comstock there is a class of men, for whom there is no distinctive name, whose business it is to find out all that can in any way be learned in regard to the condition of the mines, and report the same to the dealers in stocks by whom they are employed. These mining reporters, they might be called—as a class, are shrewd and eternally vigilant. They must always keep their employers, who are generally in San Francisco, well informed in regard to the condition of the Comstock mines at all times when a "strike" is anticipated or reported in any particular mine; it is expected of them, by hook or by crook, to ascertain exactly in what part of the mine it was made or is about to be made. If made at all, they are to find out the value of the strike, probable extent of the body of ore found, its richness, direction, and many other things not easily ascertained.

When a strike is reported made in a mine and all its gates and doors are closed, the strictest secrecy enjoined on all the workmen, and admittance refused to all "outsiders," then is the time for the mining reporter to display his genius or give up his trade. By bribing workmen or by getting a man of his own into the mine to work, or in some other way he must find out what he wants to know.

On one occasion a rich strike was reported in a leading mine. Every avenue to the lower-levels was closed against the outside world. The superintendent was exceedingly closemouthed and mysterious; the miners were reticent and unbribeable—nothing could be learned in regard to the strike, though strike there was, as all felt convinced. The gatherers of mining news scouted about the surface works, watching everything and making mental notes of all that occurred which appeared to be indicative of a rich body of ore below. Nothing, however, of the slightest value could be bored, pumped, or gouged out of anybody or anything, and finally all the news-gatherers but one drew off and gave it up as a bad job. One man still lingered, day after day, all eyes and ears. The superintendent came and went, and he was none the wiser for having seen him.

At last a bright idea struck him. The superintendent came to the mine, and, as usual, went down into the lower-levels. Our man remained loitering about the works until he came out—lingered until he had seen him take off and throw aside his muddy boots, his clay-besmeared overalls and shirt, and till he had finally taken himself off. Watching his chance, the hungry reporter of mining news darted into the dressing-room, and with his jack-knife scraped from the boots, overalls, felt hat, shirt, and everything, all the mud, clay, and earth sticking to them. Of this and the loose particles of ore found in the pockets of the shirt, he made a large ball, which was composed of a general average of the bottom, top and sides of the drift run into the new deposit; he had a little of everything the superintendent had touched, and this ball he had carefully assayed. By the result obtained he became satisfied that a strike of extraordinary richness had been made. He immediately telegraphed to his employers in San Francisco to buy all of the stock they could get. They bought largely, and made an immense profit, as the stock soon went up from a few dollars to high in the hundreds.

At the time of the big excitement in 1875, a fine, motherly-looking old lady came up to Virginia City from Reno to see about the "big bonanza." She had in her pocket twenty shares of California stock which she had bought when it was selling at $30. At the time she made her trip to Virginia the stock was selling for over $600 per share. Her son accompanied her on her trip of inspection. Leaving the cars at the depot, mother and son walked down the railroad-track to a point where could be obtained a good view of the Consolidated Virginia hoisting-works, the big mill of that company and of the Ophir works. Some men of whom they inquired told them that the ground they saw between the Ophir and the Consolidated Virginia, was that of the California Company, and was principally bonanza.

On hearing this, the good old lady wiped her spectacles, placed them astride of her venerable nose, threw back her head, and long and carefully surveyed the lay of the land between the two sets of hoisting-works. This done, she took off and folded up her glasses, put them into their case, and carefully deposited them in her capacious pocket. She then brought forth her reticule, opened it, took out her stock, found it all right, replaced it, and drew the string as tight as her trembling fingers would allow of her doing. She then said to her son: "George, give me your arm. Let us go home—it will go to $1,000."

Nat Codrington was one of the unlucky speculators. He was always complaining about William Sharon, the great mining millionaire. Whenever things went wrong with Nat, "Uncle Billy"—as Nat affectionately called Mr. Sharon—was at the bottom of the business. When Nat bought stock it was sure to go down at once, then he would say: "That's Uncle Billy, he's turning the crank again!" As soon as Nat sold short on a stock, up it would go, and he would say: "Well, Uncle Billy's at it again—grindin' of 'em the other way this time!"

As long as he could, Nat responded to the calls for "mud," but his pile of filthy lucre was not like the widow's cruse of oil, and at last it became a thing of the past, and Nat ceased to take even his former feeble interest in "Uncle Billy's" crank-turning.

The last seen of Nat he was off for California. The iron had entered his soul and he had reached the seventh level of despair. No more mining—no more mud-eating stocks for him. "Yes," said Nat, "I'm off for the pastoral regions, where the woodbine twineth and the dissolute grasshopper sitteth on the mullin stalk and assiduously raspeth his stridulous fiddle."

Old Joe Staker is one of a class to be found both along the line of the Comstock and in San Francisco, on those streets where speculators in stocks most do congregate. Old Joe probably never owned the shadow of a share in any mine on the Comstock lode, yet he is always in the thick of every excitement, and claims to have shares in all the big mines.

In 1875, Old Joe was in his element. His is a very sympathetic nature, and when California was booming up toward $1,000 per share, Old Joe was rushing about, ever in the midst of the *mêlée*—was ever with those who were drinking and rejoicing.

Later in the season, when there had been a crash along the whole line—when all stocks, good, bad, and indifferent, "tumbled"—Old Joe was to be found in the midst of the mourners, drowning his sorrows at every opportunity. He did not, however, at all times find those who were losing their thousands each hour by the fall so liberal as had been those who had been winning at the same rate by the rise, nor were they so good-natured, and Old Joe frequently found himself elbowed out altogether.

One day half a dozen groups had given him the shake. He was exceedingly thirsty—his throat as dry as a lime-burner's shoe.

While he was disconsolately roving from saloon to saloon in search of a sympathetic being with whom to shed tears, he encountered a dilapidated-looking individual just arrived from the great West—a Kansas sufferer, in short. Old Joe heard something of this man's story of the ruin wrought in the West by the grasshopper, and at once froze to him with his story of losses in stocks. After three drinks together—the grasshopper man appeared to have a thin stratum of greenbacks left in his wallet, toward which Old Joe cocked an occasional eye—after about three drinks it was settled by the pair that grasshoppers and bonanzas were two of the worst plagues by which the world had ever been devastated. As more drinks were taken, grasshoppers and porphyry and bonanzas and beanstalks became fearfully mixed. At a late hour they were still mingling their tears and toasting each other. "Here's hoping," said the grasshopper man, "that yer cornstalks may always bear three full (hie!) ears and a nubbin!" "And here," said Old Joe, "is death and confusion to all (hie!) brasshoppers and gonanzas!"

Old Joe then encircled the neck of his new-found friend with his left arm, and said in his most kindly tone: "Now, ef you was perfee'ly des (hie!) destitute and I was perfee'ly des (hie!) tute, you'd soak everything you had for (hie!) me, and I'd spout everything I persessed for you; (hie!) wouldn't we?"

The opening of the big bonanza at the north end of the Comstock occasioned a grand rush of prospectors to the northward of Virginia City, a region which had, strangely enough, never been prospected.

There had been some surface-scratching done in that direction in early times, and some shafts had been sunk to the depth of fifty to one hundred feet, but no regular scientific prospecting had been done. Claims were taken up in all directions, first-class shafts begun, machinery set up, and buildings of all kinds erected. In a few months quite a village was built up, to which was given the name of North Virginia. This place is about two miles north of Virginia City, and in case of the continuation of the Comstock lode being found in that neighborhood will be likely to be a place of considerable importance. Some excellent "prospects" are being found in the shafts that are being sunk in that direction, and the owners of several mines are confident that at no distant day they will find a big bonanza on their part of the lode.

At the time these claims were being located there was almost a revival of the scenes of early days. Men were out in the night staking off ground and posting notices, and there was a good deal of claim-jumping, with some fights, going on. Men were seen bringing pieces of rock into town as specimens from their mines, and these were passed from hand to hand and commented on, much as when the miners first began to roam the hills. Even the colored population, who seldom trouble themselves about mines, caught the infection and went out prospecting and locating mines—became experts on ore. One of these coming into town with a big chunk of rock in his hand met a friend whose eyes began to dilate at what he thought might be a lump of solid silver. Said the—

First Expert—"Wha—what yer got thar?"

Second Expert—"Look at dat, sah! Dat's out'en de Day of Jubilee mine. Boy, I tell yer dat's gwine to be a mine. Wha—what you say, now, dat's gwine to pay at de present prices of deduction, hey?"

First Expert—"Fore de Lord, I doesn't know! Gwine to pay, think?"

Second Expert—"Gwine to pay? *gwine to pay?* Now you makes me laugh. Jes look at dat rock, Edward Arthur—look at dat side of it! See de pure chloroform dat's percolated all ober it! Now ax me ef dat rock's gwine to pay. Look at de formation and de stratification! Ax me ef dat rock's gwine to pay! Why, you see you doesn't know de fust principles 'bout dem oldah prefatory periods when dis here yearf was a multitudinous mass, floatin' roun' in a chaotic hemisphere; time o' de propylites an jewrasic periods. Your ignorance perfectly affixes me."

During the stock excitement on the Comstock, in 1872, a shrewd operator in stocks found himself in possession of an immense number of shares of Alpha mining-stock—many more shares than he cared to hold. He was a man who was and still is considered one of the sharpest operators on the lode. A word or even a hint from him was worth a whole mint of money. One day this "stock-sharp" said to his wife: "My dear, how much money have you got?"

"I have $6,000," said the wife. "Why?"

"Put it all into the Alpha," said her husband. "Ask no questions, but buy all the Alpha you can get. Be careful, however, not to mention to a living soul that I told you to do this."

The wife faithfully promised that she would "not even breathe the name of the mine." As soon as her husband was out of sight, she put on her hat and shawl and hurried away to the house of her married sister and gently murmured into her ear the news that Alpha was a "big buy." That night the brother-in-law, Mr. Hornbeck, knew that there was a big speculation in Alpha; his folks and the Doolittles next heard of it, then the Turners, and Homers, and Huffs, and Howards—all the relations of the speculator's wife, and the relations of their relations, were in possession of the grand secret in about three days, and about the fifth day all the bosom friends of all these knew that Alpha was going to "boom sky-high" and all were buying Alpha right and left.

Being in such great demand, the stock did "boom," sure enough. All the time it was booming, and the wife's relations were going for it, our shrewd manipulator and deep observer of human nature (feminine), was quietly feeding it out to them at the highest figures—not only to them, but to hundreds of others, for by this time about half the population of Virginia City had been confidentially informed that Alpha was the "greatest buy on the whole lead."

Just what was to happen in the mine no one knew—no one pretended to know—but the grand head authority—away back so far along the line of knowing ones that few in the front ranks knew his name even—could not be mistaken. The general idea was that a grand development was about to be made in the mine. Some went so far as to say that a big strike had been made in one of the drifts on the lower-level of the mine months before, but that the drift had been boarded up for reasons best known to the officers of the company. This bit of news, it was said, had come out through one of the miners who was of the secret shift engaged in the drift when the rich ore— "almost pure silver," some now began to assert with a considerable degree of positiveness—was struck.

All at last being loaded down with the stock, and no new buyers coming in, Alpha began to tumble. The Homers and the Huffs and the Howards became frightened and began to sell. The stock then tumbled more rapidly than ever, and the Hornbeck's and Doolittles and Turners became panic-stricken and threw their stock upon the market, when from $280 per share it finally went down to $42 and stopped there dead and fiat.

One day, soon after this low price had been reached, our stock-sharp said to his wife: "By the way, my dear, how did you come out with that

Alpha stock of yours? You sold, I presume, while it was up?"

"Why, n-no, dear," hesitatingly answered his better-half, "I thought from all I heard that it would go to $500 and so I held on to it and have got it all yet."

"Well, well," said the husband, "did I ever hear the like in my life! Got all of your stock yet? Tut! tut! then you've lost your $6,000! Well, dear, don't mind it. Here is a check for $6,000; take it, and don't you ever again try speculating in stocks. You don't understand it, my dear—indeed you don't!"

CHAPTER LV

HOLIDAYS AND FUN

Romantic Scenery—A Curious Freak of Nature—Lake Tahoe—
Hank Monk—He Couldn't Tell a Lie—Practical Joking—The Summit

The people of the land of the "big bonanza" do not toil always and without ceasing; but, as in other lands, give some time to pleasure and recreation. There are a number of places of summer resort to which all may flee for a few weeks each year during the hot weather of July and August. Most popular among these is Lake Tahoe, situated high among the grand scenery of the Sierra Nevada Mountains, and distant but thirty-five miles from Virginia City. No land can boast a more beautiful sheet of water than Lake Tahoe, and its surroundings form a fit setting for such a gem. Donner Lake, also in the Sierra Nevada Mountains, and situated but a few miles north of Lake Tahoe, is almost as popular as the latter, though it is much smaller. Its surroundings are, however, grand and picturesque, turn which way we may.

There are, besides, Webber and Independence Lakes, which are in the same neighborhood, and which are easy of access. In Hope Valley on or near the summit of the Sierras, where many pleasure-seekers go, there is found fine trout-fishing in all the brooks, and excellent quail and grouse-shooting everywhere among the hills. Indeed, for those who have the time and means to spend a few weeks in the bracing atmosphere and amid the wild and picturesque scenery of the mountains, there is no lack of attractions. The man of meditative disposition, who is weary of the bustle and strife and the noise and crowds of towns, will wander along by himself and be happy in many and many a place away up by the tall peaks in the grand solitudes, where whispers from heaven seem to come down through the pines.

Lake Tahoe lies one mile and a quarter above the level of the sea, and is surrounded on all sides by most romantic and picturesque mountain scenery. The lake is about thirty miles in length from north to south, and from eight to fifteen miles in width. It lies partly in California and partly in Nevada. Its waters are of extraordinary purity and clearness and, in places, have been sounded to a depth of over two thousand feet.

There are several fine bays around the lake, the largest and most beautiful of which is that known as Emerald Bay, which is over two miles long. This bay is about four hundred yards wide at its mouth, but rapidly widens inland. It is completely landlocked and is surrounded with timbered

Emerald Bay and Eagle Cañon, 1862, collodion/albumen, attributed to Charles L. Weed (Lawrence & Houseworth). Library of Congress Prints and Photographs Division.

hills, many of which are covered with rugged and picturesque rocks, which tower among and above the pines, and other evergreen-trees. There are some small islands in the bay which add much to its beauty, and on all sides are to be obtained fine views of immense rocky cañons. Eagle Cañon contains some vast piles of rocks, with clumps of pines scattered here and there among them, and a whole day might be spent in rambling through it without exhausting its many beauties. Cave Rock, on the eastern shore of the lake is a huge pyramid of granite which occupies a very picturesque position and which contains on one side a cavern of considerable extent. In the neighborhood of this rock tall and beautiful pines are seen quite down to the shore of the lake.

The view from what is called Rocky Point, on the eastern shore, looking toward Cave Rock is also very fine. Another fine view in the direction of Cave Rock is obtained from the Sierra Rocks. The view to the northward from

Cave Rock, 1862, collodion/albumen, attributed to Charles L. Weed (Lawrence & Houseworth). Library of Congress Prints and Photographs Division.

Sierra Rocks, toward Rocky Point, is one in which are found several pictur-esque tree-covered points of rocky land, extending far out into the waters of the lake. Indeed, there are new beauties to be found in all directions.

Zephyr Cove, also on the eastern shore of the lake is a most romantic spot and the scenery is such as to set the artist thinking of his pencils the moment he enters the little bay. The Shakespeare-Rock, plainly visible from the Glenbrook House, on the southern shore of the lake, is so called on account of there being in the rugged outlines of its face a striking resemblance to the features of the immortal poet. All who visit the lake desire first of all to see this rock. Like many other things of the kind, there is much in the position from which it is viewed, and not a little in the imaginative powers of the person viewing it. The water of the lake is so transparent that pebbles on its bottom can be distinctly seen at the depth of fifty or sixty feet. When out upon the water in a boat during a time when it is perfectly calm,

Zephyr Cove, 1862, collodion/albumen, attributed to Charles L. Weed (Lawrence & Houseworth). Library of Congress Prints and Photographs Division.

one seems suspended in mid-air. It is not easy to swim in the waters of the lake. Owing to the great altitude and consequent decrease of atmospheric pressure, the water is much less dense then the water of a lake or stream at the level of the sea. On account of this lack of density and buoyancy, the bodies of persons drowned in the lake never rise to the surface. Many have been drowned in Lake Tahoe, but a body has never yet been recovered.

Leaving the lake and rambling off into the surrounding country, much that is grand and romantic is to be found. From the western summit is to be had a magnificent panoramic view of the lake and the valley or basin in which it is situated, with all the surrounding mountains. The tourist may extend his rambles above Lake Tahoe to Fallen Leaf Lake, one of the most beautiful little lakes in the mountains. Cascade Lake and other small lakes will also be found worthy of a visit. About the shores of Lake Tahoe will frequently be encountered the huts of the Washoe Indians. They are generally found in some romantic spot, and, with their uncouth occupants, add not a little to the picturesqueness of the region. Some of the old saw-mills are also of a rather unusual style and will attract the attention of the tourist and the artist.

At "Yank's Station," on the Placerville road, a short distance from the shore of the lake, is to be seen a most singular freak of nature to which the name of "Nick of the Woods" has been given. It is a large knot in a crotch of a cedar-tree, which forks a few feet from the ground, but it looks like a work of art. It startlingly resembles the head of an old man. In looking upon this marvel of nature we can very easily imagine it to be some hoary-headed old sinner thus wedged into the crotch of the tree and imprisoned for all time on account of some grievous offense committed about the time that he was thus placed in the stocks. So natural and perfect is this head of an old man, and such an expression of patient suffering is seen in every feature of the face, that many persons will not believe that it is wholly the work of nature until after having closely examined it. "Yank's and all of the other stations along the Placerville road, were places of much importance during the early days of Washoe, when all the machinery and supplies of every kind came over the mountains on wagons.

When the teamsters stopped at night or noon, the road in front of the stations at which they halted would be blockaded for a great distance, and it looked almost as though all the teams in California were crossing the Sierras in one grand caravan. Now, since the completion of the Central Pacific, and Virginia and Truckee Railroads, the travelers on the old mountain-roads are few, and nothing of the old life and bustle is seen at the once famous stations. Even the old Lake House, at Tahoe, though it was built of good pine-logs and was very warm and substantial, has given way to more stylish structures. Times are changed and few but pleasure-seekers are now seen on the old road where once the sounding "blacksnake" awoke the echoes far and wide among the hills.

The tourist who wishes to see as much as possible of the mountains may go to the Big Tree Grove, Calaveras county, California, from Lake Tahoe, by taking what is called the Big Tree Road. On this road he will find many beautiful valleys, and much romantic scenery at an elevation of from seven to nine thousand feet above the level of the sea. At Lake Tahoe there are large and well-kept hotels at several points, two or three small steamboats and a great fleet of sail and row-boats, with fishing-tackle of all kinds, as trout abound in the waters of the lake. Tourists from the East who desire to visit the lake while on their way to California can do so very conveniently by leaving the Central Pacific Railroad at Reno and taking the cars of the Virginia and Truckee Railroad to Carson City, a distance of thirty-one miles, thence by stage to the lake, a distance of fourteen miles.

Nick of the Woods, 1862, collodion/albumen, attributed to Charles L. Weed (Lawrence & Houseworth). Library of Congress Prints and Photographs Division.

On this stage-line (Benton's) from Carson to Lake Tahoe will be found Hank Monk, one of the best known and most famous stage-drivers of the Sierra Nevada Mountains. He it was who gave Horace Greeley his memorable ride across the Sierras on the occasion of his visit to California. Mr. Greeley was anxious to reach Placerville as early in the evening as possible, as he was expected to make a speech to the people of the town, and once or twice expressed a fear that he should be behind time. Monk said nothing, as he was then on a long up-grade. At length the top of the mountain was reached, and Monk started on the down-grade at a fearful rate of speed. Mr. Greeley bounded about the coach like a bean in a gourd, and soon became greatly alarmed. He thrust his head out at the coach window and tried to remonstrate, but Monk only cried: "Keep your seat, Horace, I'll take you through on time!"

Mr. Greeley then remained quiet for a time, when he again became alarmed as they whirled at lightning speed around some short curve in the road, and out would come his head, and again Monk would shout: "Keep your seat, Horace."

It is safe to say that the philosopher never took a wilder ride, than that in the Sierras with Hank Monk for his driver.

Monk, in common with all his tribe, hates the sight of one of those ponderous specimens of architecture in the trunk-line known as the "Saratoga bandbox." On one occasion a lady who was stopping at the Glenbrook House, Lake Tahoe, had a "Saratoga" of the three-decker style at Carson City, which she wished brought up to the lake. The trunk was about as long and wide as a first-class spring mattress and seven or eight feet high. The lady had managed to get it as far as Carson by rail, but the trouble was to get it up into the mountain. Monk had two or three times promised to bring it up "next trip," but always arrived without it. At last he drove up in front of the hotel one evening, and, as usual, the lady came out on the veranda to ask if he had brought her trunk.

Like the immortal Washington, Monk cannot tell a lie, and so he said: "No, marm, I haven't brought it, but I think some of it will be up on the next stage."

"Some of it!" cried the lady.

"Yes; maybe half of it, or such a matter."

"Half of it?" fairly shrieked the owner of the Saratoga,

"Yes, marm; half to-morrow and the rest of it next day or the day after."

"Why, how in the name of common sense can they bring half of it?"

"Well, when I left they were sawing it in two, and —"

"Sawing it in two! Sawing *my* trunk in two?"

"That was what I said," coolly answered Monk. "Two men had a big cross-cut saw, and were working down through it— had got down about to the middle, I think."

"Sawing my trunk in two in the middle!" groaned the lady. "Sawing it in two and all my best clothes in it! God help the man that saws *my* trunk!—God help him I say!" and in a flood of tears and a towering passion she rushed indoors, threatening the hotel-keeper, the stage-line, the railroad company, the town of Carson, and the State of Nevada with suits for damages. It was in vain that she was assured that there was no truth in the story of the sawing—that she was told that Monk was a great joker—she would not believe but that her trunk had been cut in two until it arrived intact; even then she had first to examine its contents most thoroughly, so strongly had the story of the sawing impressed itself on her mind. Monk's "Saratoga" joke is still remembered and told at Lake Tahoe, but the ladies all say that they can't see that there is "one bit of fun in it."

Just here I may say that when at Carson City, by taking the cars of the Virginia and Truckee Railroad to Virginia City, the "big bonanza" and all of the big mines, and mills on the Comstock lode may be seen and explored. The distance is but twenty-one miles.

In passing down the Carson River by rail, the tourists will see a number of water-mills that are at work on silver ores, and after leaving the river, and beginning the ascent of the mountain to Virginia, he will see many miles of the crookedest railroad in the world. Were these wonderful silver-mines in Chili and Peru, all Americans who found themselves anywhere within five hundred miles of them would visit and examine them, even though obliged to bribe a dozen squads of guards in order to attain their object; but being here on American soil, where they may be reached in a ride of three hours by rail from the main line of travel, few take the trouble to visit them. Ladies, as well as gentlemen, may visit and explore the mines, even to the lowest of the lower levels.

Travelers may leave the Central Pacific Railroad at Reno, take the Virginia and Truckee Railroad and run up to Virginia City, examine the mines and mills, return to Carson City and take the stage-line to Lake Tahoe, cross the lake on a steamer, then take another line of stages, nine miles, to Truckee, on the line of the Central Pacific again, when the journey to San Francisco may be resumed.

In passing by stage from Carson City to Lake Tahoe a fine view will be obtained of the huge lumber-flume of the Carson and Lake Tahoe Lumber Company, which is twenty-one miles in length and through which seven hundred cords of wood, or half a million feet of lumber or mining timbers can daily be delivered at Carson from the eastern summit of the Sierras. The altitude of the eastern summit is 7,312 feet; of Lake Tahoe, 6,220 feet; and of the western summit, 7,315 feet; consequently the lake lies in a basin about 1,000 feet in depth.

At the north end of the lake, near Tahoe City, stands the mountain selected for the Lick Observatory. This astronomical observatory is to be built with money donated for the purpose by James Lick, a San Francisco millionaire, and on it is to be mounted the finest and most powerful telescope that can be manufactured in the world. At Truckee, on the Central Pacific Railroad, the altitude is 5,860 feet; at Summit Valley, seventeen miles further west, it is 6,800; and ten miles beyond, at Cisco, it has decreased to 5,950. Here is the great snow-belt on the summit of the Sierras. It is here that snow falls to such a depth as to almost cover up the houses, and here it is that the people travel on Norwegian snow-shoes in winter, when they travel any other way than by rail.

About Cisco the snow appears to fall to a greater depth than at any other point on the mountains. It is a very difficult matter to keep the track of the railroad open at this place in winter, and at times the trains are almost buried in the snow. The snow-banks are frequently so high on both sides of the track that even the smoke-stack of the engine is hidden when a train passes along.

CHAPTER LVI

TERRIBLE STORY OF THE DONNERS
Donner Lake—Lost in the Snow—A Horrible Scene—
What Became of the Donners—The Sulphur Springs—The Golden State

On his arrival at Truckee, the pleasure-seeker will do well to spend a few hours in the examination of the beauties of Donner Lake, a lake much resorted to by the people both of California and Nevada, and a perfect little gem. Those who are afraid to venture out upon the broad waters of Tahoe, will be quite at ease on Donner.

From the town of Truckee, Donner Lake is reached in traveling a distance of but two miles, over an excellent carriage-road. The lake is about three miles in length and from a mile to a mile and a half in width. It is shut in on all sides by lofty and picturesque mountains. To the south and west these are very imposing—mountain piled on mountain. While the mountains to the southward are covered to a considerable extent, in their lower ranges, with pine, fir, spruce, and other evergreen trees, those on the west, toward the summit, are principally bald and barren piles of granite; though there are scattering pines clinging in places where their roots find a hold in the crevices of the rocks.

The track of the Central Pacific Railroad passes along the face of the mountains on the south side of the lake, hundreds of feet above its placid waters. From the lake the trains are seen moving along the sides of the great cliffs, where they seem to run on a track laid in the air or to cling to the rocks "by their eyebrows," as an old "mountain man" once suggested, on looking up at the trains. At numerous points along the track there are snow-sheds which greatly interfere with the view of the lake from the cars, yet in many places picturesque glimpses of it are obtained, and of the mountain scenery in all directions.

Through the bare granite mountains walling in the lake on the west, passes a tunnel, into which it is a relief to see the trains plunge as they dart through the last of the snow-sheds and glide round the last of the cliffs.

From the top of the great mountain through which passes the railroad-tunnel, is obtained a grand and comprehensive view of Donner Lake and all its surroundings. The valley in which the little sheet of water lies is so small that, seen from above, it presents much the appearance of the crater of an extinct volcano. At each end, east and west, are seen dark groves of small pines, a few acres in extent, and these, with the waters of the lake, occupy all the level land in the basin.

To the eastward of the lake, days of mountain climbing distant, rise the snowy peaks of the eastern summit of the Sierras, glittering in the sunlight and dimly seen; to the westward, on the western summit, rises Donner Peak, crowned with black and rugged rocks, necked with patches of snow, and tufted here and there with a few scattering and stunted pines. The water of Donner Lake is as clear, cold, and sweet as that of any mountain-spring. At the lake are good hotels and both sail and row-boats for the accommodation of visitors. Those who are lovers of the sport so lauded by good old Isaak Walton, will find an abundance of trout in the small brooks putting down from the mountains. The lake has an outlet at the east end which forms a stream of considerable size, called Little Truckee River. This unites with the main Truckee River, which is the outlet of Lake Tahoe. There is good trout-fishing in the Little Truckee, which is a bright and rapid stream.

It was on the banks of the Little Truckee, in the groves of pine at the foot of the lake, that occurred the horrible Donner disaster, some years before the discovery of gold in California.

The unfortunate Donner party, numbering seventy-six souls, principally emigrants from Illinois, reached the Sierra Nevada Mountains, October 31st, 1846, a month later in the season than was safe at that time to be found in such a region. That year the winter snows set in about three weeks earlier than usual, and with unusual severity, and in a few days fell to the depth of several feet.

When the snow began falling, the train had crossed what is known as the eastern summit of the Sierras, and had entered Summit Valley, in which lies Donner Lake. The train was pushed on through the storm until the foot of the lake was reached. Here the snow fell so rapidly, day and night, that it was soon several feet in depth, and it was impossible to proceed; indeed, so great was the fall of snow that the cattle and horses of the train were soon buried beneath it in all directions about the camp.

The emigrants then built a number of log-houses in which to winter, and moving into these from their wagons, began a season of suffering unprecedented in the history of the Sierras, where many men have perished in the snow. Though many individuals and small parties have lost their lives in these mountain's, as a horrible scene of suffering, starvation, and death, the disaster which befell the Donner party stands alone in the history of the Pacific Coast.

The stumps of the trees cut by the party still stand, and are from fifteen to eighteen feet in height, showing the great depth to which the cabins and all in the camp lay buried. At first the unfortunate people lived on the cattle they were able to dig out of the snow, but there came a time when no more of these could be found, and then the pangs of hunger began to be felt in the dreary camp. It was seen that unless relief could be obtained from some quarter, all must soon die of starvation.

In this emergency a Mr. Reed, a man of iron frame, provided with a scanty stock of such provisions as could be gathered in the huts of the castaways, struggled through the snow till he had crossed the western summit of the Sierras, when he made his way as speedily as possible to the village of Yerba Buena, now San Francisco; the first place where he could look for relief. Here he made known the perilous position of his friends in the mountains. As soon as his story was heard, a meeting was called, provisions were contributed, and a relief-party was organized. When the relief-party arrived at the camp on Donner Lake and entered the cabins of the unfortunates, forty persons were found to be still alive and were rescued. Thirty-six were dead, and the snow formed for them a winding-sheet.

When the relief-party started on their return from the cabins, they were obliged to leave behind Mr. Donner, a farmer from Illinois, who was very ill; also, his wife, who refused to be saved if her husband must be left behind. Keysbury, a German, for some reason for which no satisfactory explanation has ever been given, was left behind with the Donners. These three persons were left to winter in the camp, such provisions as could be spared by the relief-party being given them. What passed in the lone camp during the dark and dreary months that followed, will never be known.

In April, a party, under General Kearney, was sent out to bring these persons over the mountains. On entering the camp, only Keysbury was found alive. The party found the body of Mr. Donner in a tent, where it had been carefully laid out by his wife. Nothing could be seen of Mrs. Donner, however. Old Keysbury was found reclining at his ease upon the floor of one of the cabins, calmly smoking his pipe, and apparently engaged in watching the smoke-wreaths as they curled upward. He sat near a wide fireplace on the hearth of which blazed a fire, on which hung a camp-kettle, found to be half filled with human flesh. Near at hand stood a bucket partly filled with blood and pieces of human flesh, while pieces of human flesh, fresh and bloody, were strewn about the floor.

Old Keysbury himself presented a most repulsive appearance—no ogre or ghoul, feasting in his den, could have been more hideous. His beard was of great length, and spread in tangled strings over his breast, his hair in a great, matted mop, hung about his shoulders and stood out over his eyes, while the nails of his fingers had grown to such a length that they resembled the claws of a wild beast. He was ragged to an indecent degree, exceedingly filthy, and as ferocious as he was filthy. When confronted in his den and discovered in the very act of indulging in his cannibal feast, he roused up and glared upon those who approached as though he were a hyena.

After some trouble he was secured and was then charged with having murdered Mrs. Donner for her flesh and money. He stoutly denied the charge, but a rope having been placed about his neck and one end of it thrown over the limb of a tree, the old fiend began to beg for his life, and, being released, showed where he had hidden a portion of the money. In pity of his miserable condition—he appearing not wholly in his right mind—and in view of the apparent fact that he was driven to the deed by the pangs of hunger, Keysbury's life was spared, but he was driven forth from the society of his kind, and became a wanderer on the face of the earth, spurned and avoided wherever he became known.

A young son and daughter of the Donners were rescued by the first relief-party. They were carried over the deep snow that lay in the mountains, on the backs of men. When these children reached San Francisco they excited universal sympathy and in order to do something toward giving them a start in the world, they were granted a 100-vara lot each. Many years afterwards, when the village of Yerba Buena became San Francisco, and a great and rich city, these lots became the subject of a lawsuit of much importance. The remains of the Donner cabins were to be seen until a few years since. In some of the cabinets of the curious, in Virginia City, are bones collected at the old Donner camp, about the sites of the decayed cabins, and some of these may even have been gnawed by old Keysbury.

At no great distance from Virginia City, there are in several localities hot springs, all of which possess medicinal virtues and are much frequented by persons afflicted with rheumatism and kindred disorders. The most wonderful of all these are the Steamboat Springs, in Steamboat Valley, on the line of the Virginia and Truckee Railroad, about midway between Reno and Carson City. The springs are situated on a low mound, about a mile in length and six hundred feet in width, formed of rocky incrustations deposited by the mineral waters. Running north and south through this low ridge are several large crevices from which arise columns of steam, heated air and gases.

Early in the morning, when the air is cool and calm, as many as sixty or seventy columns of steam may be seen rising along the ridge, many of which ascend to the height of over fifty feet. Far down in the crevices, which are over a foot in width, may be heard the surging of billows of boiling water. At the sides and ends of the crevices are a great number of boiling springs, some of which spurt water to the height of two or three feet above the surface. A strong smell of sulphur pervades the atmosphere, and pure sulphur is found in many places along the line of the large crevices.

At times, some of these springs spout water to a great height. In 1860, one about the diameter of an ordinary well, threw a column of hot water three feet in diameter to the height of over fifty feet. This spring was intermittent. After spouting steadily for an hour it would suddenly cease with a sound as of a great sigh, as the direction of the internal force changed and the water seemed sucked back into the regions below. The eruptions of this spring occurred once in about eight hours. After the water was sucked back into the ground, a hole about nine feet in depth was seen, the bottom of which was covered with sand. The withdrawing of the water through this sand appeared to be the cause of the sighing sound heard at the end of each eruption.

When a grand season of spouting was about to begin, a heavy rumbling would be heard below, there was a hissing sound at the bottom of the well, bubbles came up through the sand, and presently boiling water surged in. This water would rush, foaming and hissing, to within two or three feet of the surface, when it would suddenly withdraw with a great sigh. In about a minute the hissing and rumbling would again begin, and again the water would rush almost to the top of the well. When this had been three or four times repeated, the preliminary performance—notes of preparation, as it were—had ended. A rumbling much louder than anything before heard began, the ground for many rods about the spot was violently shaken, and on a sudden, with a great roar, a huge column of water darted into the air. Had this spring continued these eruptions, it would have been one of the lions of the country, but after a season of activity in the Spring of 1860, it became closed up, and has since been one of the tamest springs along the line. In 1862 a spring for a time spouted water to the height of fifty or sixty feet, through an orifice about three inches in diameter.

In June, 1873, the then proprietor of the Steamboat Springs and hotel, lost his life in one of the springs. He was engaged in the erection of a new bath-house over a large pool of boiling water, some five feet in depth, for use in giving steam baths. Timbers for the foundation had been laid across the pool, and the man walked out on one of these 10 arrange a cross-timber, when he slipped and fell into the scalding water. The water was so deep as to reach nearly to his neck, and so hot that eggs could be cooked in it in two minutes.

When he fell into the pool, he was either so much frightened or felt such pain that for a time he seemed in a manner paralyzed, and did hardly anything toward trying to make his escape. He was in the spring at least half a minute before he got out, which he at last did principally through his own exertions, though a man who was working near the place ran to his assistance and lent him a helping hand when he had reached the bank of the pool. When his clothes were taken off, the greater part of the skin slipped from his body. He was literally cooked alive, and lived but a short time.

At certain seasons of the year, many of the millionaires of the Comstock are to be found rambling in California, taking their ease in that land of sunshine and flowers. Los Angeles, Santa Barbara, and other places on the sea-coast are much frequented by those who are weary of the eternal sameness and the light and dry atmosphere of the mountains, and who wish to find some pleasant place in which to rest and recuperate. Said an enthusiastic Comstocker, who had just returned from a visit to the "Golden State": "California, sir! It is the land of the palm, and the banana! Look abroad on her vine-clad hills, sir! Beautiful! Observe her glorious gardens—gardens such as were not in Eden—the propped trees of her orchards; her fields of golden grain; her giant eucalyptus; and see, towering over all and overshadowing all—with one hand resting on the peaks of the Coast Range and the other on the summit of the Sierras—her hoodlum! Beautiful, sir, beautiful!"

CHAPTER LVII

TRACES OF THE TRICKSY MINER
A Neat Little Game—What Doubting Thomas Found—
"Doctoring" a Tape-line—Devices of an Honest Man—
What a Stockholder Found

Now that we have had a ramble among the lakes and the valleys of the Sierras, and are rested and recuperated by reclining under the tall pines, and breathing the cool air of that region of eternal snow, we return once more to the mines and the miners. A few chapters on the tricks of miners, and their characteristics, good and bad, may prove of interest to readers residing in regions purely agricultural.

The "honest miner" is sometimes a little trickish. Should he find that he has made a bad bargain in taking a contract, he will sometimes resort to "ways that are dark" in order to "play even." A trick of rather an original character was some years since successfully played by some roving miners who had taken a contract to extend a certain tunnel at Virginia City, a distance of ten feet. The tunnel already extended a distance of five or six hundred feet, and in exceedingly hard rock. The miners, four in number, contracted to drive the tunnel forward ten feet, at $30 per foot, but soon found they would make nothing at this price, owing to the extreme hardness and stubbornness of the rock.

When they took the contract an officer of the mine caused a hole to be drilled in the rock, and a wooden plug inserted just even with the face of the tunnel. The plug was shown the contractors as their starting point—the point from which they were to advance the work a distance of ten feet. All this was quite satisfactory, but when the men began work they soon found that they had undertaken a very unprofitable job—a job that would not pay their "grub."

As soon as they became fully aware of this, the men began to consider how they might best find their way out of the trouble into which they had involved themselves. That way they were not long in hitting upon. They drew out the wooden plug which had been placed in the rock as the mark from which they were to start, then putting a blast in the hole, blew it out, completely obliterating all trace of the place where it had been drilled. They then measured back from the face of the tunnel a distance often feet, good strong measure, and drilling a hole in the rock drove into it the plug. This done, the four men took their ease about town for some days—about the length of time that would have been required to do the work—when they waited upon the officer from whom they had taken the contract and informed him that they were ready to receive their pay: also, putting in a great deal about the hardness of the rock and the very poor speculation the job had proved. The secretary, if it was that officer, hunted up a tape-line and went out to the tunnel with one of the men to measure the work.

Mr. Secretary found the peg all right. Placing the end of his line upon it, he measured back to the face of the tunnel and found the distance to be ten feet, good and strong. The honest sons of toil received their $300, immediately slung their blankets across their shoulders and "lit out" in search of a new camp and another profitable contract.

The trick was not discovered until a "doubting Thomas," a member of the company—some days after the money had been paid—called for a measurement of the tunnel from its mouth back to its face. The whole tunnel was then found to be exactly the same length, to an inch, as before the last contract was let. The language of the members of the company who were present when this last measurement was made, as they groped their way out of the tunnel, was such as would be discountenanced in any Sabbath School in the land.

"Doctoring the tape-line" is a trick that strolling miners have sometimes been known to perform, when the opportunity was found. This operation is simple enough. All that is to be done is to get hold of the foreman, superintendent, or whoever is likely to measure the work; and cut out a few feet. The line is then neatly sewed together again. In order to succeed in this game it is necessary for those playing it, to "doctor" the line a few hours before their work is to be measured—at night, for instance, when they know their work is to be measured the first thing in the morning.

A mining superintendent, on the Comstock range, one day said to me: "I had my tape-line 'doctored' the other day, and, confound the fellows! they got away with their trick nicely."

"How was that?" I asked.

"Well, I had let a contract to some boys who came along to sink a small shaft to the depth of 50 feet. One morning they told me the shaft was finished, and asked me to go out and measure the work.

"One of the men got into the bucket and was lowered into the shaft, holding the end of the line, which was reeled off as he descended. When he got down he held his end of the line on the bottom of the shaft, and, looking at my end, I found the shaft exactly 50 feet in depth. I paid the men their money, and they left. In a day or two I had occasion to measure something—a stick of timber—and was astonished to find it much longer than it looked. Overhauling my tape-line, I found that just six feet had been cut out of it and the two parts neatly sewed together again. I knew then that my shaft was exactly 44 feet deep, and, I tell you, I never was more ashamed of anything in all my life!"

In 1861, a miner who had been out on a prospecting expedition, upon his return to Silver City, the place whence he started, showed several business men of the town some very fine specimens of ore taken, as he said, from a lead he had discovered in the foothills of the Sierras, a few miles below Carson City. He proposed to put the names of the business men down in his notice of location, informing them that all he asked of them was a trifle monthly to be used in the purchase of provisions, powder, fuse, and other supplies. He was ready to do all the work, provided these things were furnished him. As the specimens shown contained a considerable percentage of gold and silver, a number of men allowed their names to be used, and agreed to be assessed for the amount that would be required in pushing the proposed mining enterprise. This was in the fall of the year. From the time of perfecting the arrangement for working his claim, and all through the winter, the miner was punctually at hand every month for his assessments. He reported the work progressing favorably, and brought specimens of ore that showed steady improvement; each month the ore was just a little better than the last.

The men who had been taken into the company by the honest miner, paid the assessments willingly and smilingly; each man expecting at no distant day he would be able to sell for several thousand dollars that which cost him but a few dollars per month.

About the middle of the winter the assessment was more than doubled, but none of the stockholders found fault with this, as the miner informed them that his tunnel had attained such a length that he had found it necessary to hire two assistants, to help about the blasting and wheeling out of the earth. As it would have looked a little mean to have found fault with the miner about the manner in which he was doing the work, after he had as good as given them their shares-in the mine, all spoke well of the plan of rushing along the work by hiring assistance.

All went on swimmingly until late in the spring, the honest miner appearing punctually on the first day of each month for his regular assessment. As it was no unusual thing at that day to locate as many as fifteen or twenty men in one claim, each man being set down in the notice for 200 feet of ground, the assessments, when they were all gathered in, amounted to quite a snug little sum. Finally, when the snow was all gone from the hills, and wild-flowers began to bloom in the little valleys on the side of the mountains, the honest miner came no more for his assessment. The stockholders wondered, yea, marveled greatly at this—the man had heretofore been as true to his time as the planets in their course. They began to think some accident had befallen their honest friend—feared he might have been hurt by a cave in the tunnel, There were some, however, who held other views. "If this man was hurt by a cave," said these, "his assistants would most assuredly have come up to Silver City and made known the fact." Their idea was that their man had suddenly drifted into a bonanza of immense richness and that he was going to manage in some way to cheat them out of their share.

Finally, one of the party holding this opinion volunteered to spare sufficient time from his business to go and look after the mine, which, by the way, was called the "Royal George." He arrived in the neighborhood in which the mine was understood to be situated, and after two days of inquiry at last found a man who said he could point out the Royal George location. This man led the way to a rugged hill and in its side, where there was a small streak of decomposed granite, pointed out a little open cut, such as any man of ordinary industry might dig in half a day. The stockholder thought his guide mistaken: "Where was the tunnel, where the dwelling of the men, the ore-dump and the rest of the works?" The guide, however, pointed to a notice posted on the trunk of a small cedar, a short distance above the cut; and proceeding thither, the stockholder read the name of the claim—the Royal George—and below it his own name and the names of fifteen or twenty of his business friends as the locators of—"this silver lode or lead, with all dips, spurs, angles and variations."

During his journey back to Silver City, the stockholder had plenty of time in which to swear, and he doubtless made the most of the opportunity. It was afterwards ascertained that the honest miner who was the discoverer and original locator of the Royal George, never went near the claim after making the location, but was all the fall and winter engaged in cutting wood on a ranch he had taken up in the Palmyra Mountains, many miles away, and quite in a different direction from the region in which was located the Royal George. The assessments collected were sufficient to keep the honest fellow in provisions, to enable him to hire some assistance, and, indeed, to keep his wood-ranch running very nicely until he found a purchaser at a good round sum—good wood-ranches being at that time in, brisk demand.

CHAPTER LVIII

THE PARADISE OF BOGUS MINERS
"Me Ketch 'um There"—Doings of the Roving Miner—
The "Goddess of Poverty"—The Bully Honest Miner

In the early days the roving, prospecting miners who swarmed the country were given to tricks of all kinds. Not being able to "salt" quartz veins as easily as they had salted the placer-mines of California, where they frequently planted gold in the gravel, to the taking in and undoing of Chinamen and greenhorns, they often showed rich specimens of ore obtained from mines on the Comstock, and, pretending that they were obtained in some wild region in distant mountains, soon had about them men of capital from San Francisco and other cities, who were only too glad to accommodate them with loans of from $20 to $50 or $100.

These men were always about to return to the place wherein was situated their "big finds," but were able to find no end of excuses for not going at once. They must have money with which to pay up their landlords before leaving; they must have money with which to procure a proper outfit, and when this had been given they pretended to have discovered that they were being watched—that there were parties dogging them day and night for the purpose of following them out into the mountains and crowding in and gobbling up the lion's share of the "big thing" discovered.

Thus these pretended prospectors, who probably never went outside of the town, would linger and delay, living on the fat of the land. They carried a memorandum book of considerable size, in which they could be induced, after much persuasion, to place the name of a man of means as one whose good fortune it would be to have a share in the wonderful silver discovery when the mine came to be duly located. Once he was thus fairly hooked, the man of money was never to refuse the jolly prospector any favor, was always to stand ready to hand out any sum that might be called for, from a four-bit piece to a double eagle; otherwise, the prospecting man might bring out that little stub of a pencil which he always carried in his vest pocket—with which he was to be seen figuring most industriously, as though trying to estimate the millions in his mine—and at a single sweep scratch out the name of the moneyed man and his chance for an interest in one of the biggest things of the age. This kind of game the pretended prospector would play till found out by all with whom he had dealings, when he would find it necessary to start business afresh in some other camp.

In the early days the Indians were supposed to know the whereabouts of many rich mines, and men were ready to follow wherever they might lead. A man who always had an eye open for the main chance, one day saw a Paiute Indian strolling about Virginia City with a piece of very rich silver ore in his hand. He at once secured that Indian's undivided attention by enticing him out to a vacant lot.

Would Jim tell where he found the ore? Well, Jim might tell. Could he find the place again? O yes; Jim could find the place, sure. Was there more ore of the same kind in the place Jim had seen? Heap more. Finally, Jim agreed to point out the place in consideration of his receiving a big red blanket and two new shirts. Jim then led his white acquaintance up the side of the mountain to the dump of the Ophir Mining Company, and pointing out a great heap of ore said: "Me ketch um there. You see, heap plenty more all same. Injun man heap good, he no lie!" It was a fair transaction, still the white man was not happy.

The paradise of the roving class of miners for many years was the gold-fields of California. There was his "happy home," the place where he roamed and howled—when he felt inclined to howl. Put him in a gulch where there was free water, water for the use of which in his mining operations he was obliged to pay no man a cent, and he asked nothing more—except that the distance to the nearest place where grub and grog could be obtained should not exceed six or eight miles; just a nice Sabbath day's journey for him.

The real simon-pure, "honest miner" was pretty apt to "peter" (fail to pay, become unproductive) a short time before his mine had "petered," as he laid by treasure with which to tramp away in search of fresh fields. In case of his becoming "dead broke," he often had a hard time of it with the dealers in grub and "tarantula juice," for if he had not "played them a string" some of his friends of a feather had, and in order to get trusted it was necessary for him to do big talking and show big prospects. It was not so in the "days of '49," for then all had money, or if they had not, no man was refused credit for provisions, as those who had no gold to-day were liable to have thousands to-morrow. In the days of the roving class to which the "honest miner" belongs, however, many of the diggings were of the kind spoken of by the Chinaman, who said that in his claim you "wash 'um one pan, catch 'um one color."

When silver was discovered in Nevada, there was a grand rush of the roving miners of California to the Comstock range, but they did not like the hard work requisite to insure success in quartz-mining, and it was not long before the majority of them made their way back to their old haunts in the foothills of California, where they could find patches of ground in which to use their rockers and sluices. While they remained in Nevada, these were the fellows who carried memorandum books and talked of wonders in distant wilds, big things they had found, but had not yet fully appropriated.

I shall conclude my account of the honest miner by giving "A Tribute to the Goddess of Poverty," by George Sand, and a parody on the "good goddess," in which I shall try to do justice to the "honest miner."

Tribute to the "Goddess of poverty"

Paths sanded with gold, verdant heaths, ravens loved by the wild goats, great mountains crowned with stars, wandering torrents, impenetrable forests, let the good Goddess pass through—the Goddess of Poverty! Since the world existed, since men have been, she travels the world, she dwells among men; she travels singing, and she sings working—the Goddess, good Goddess of Poverty! Some men assembled to curse her. They found her too beautiful, too gay, too nimble, and too strong. "Pluck out her wings," said they; "chain her, braise her with blows, that she may perish—the Goddess of Poverty!"

They have chained the good Goddess; they have beaten and persecuted her; but they cannot disgrace her. She has taken refuge in the soul of poets, in the soul of peasants, in the soul of martyrs, in the soul of saints—the good Goddess, the Goddess of Poverty! She has walked more than the Wandering Jew; she has travelled more than the swallows; she is older that the egg of the wren: she has multiplied more upon the earth than strawberries in Bohemian forests—the Goddess, the good Goddess of Poverty! She always makes the grandest and most beautiful things that we see upon earth; it is she who has cultivated the fields, and pruned the trees; it is she who tends the fields, singing the most beautiful airs; it is she who sees the first peep of dawn, and receives the last smile of evening—the good Goddess of Poverty! It is she who carries the sabre and gun; who makes war and conquest; it is she who collects the dead, tends the wounded, and hides the conquered—the Goddess, the good Goddess of Poverty!

Thy children will cease, one day, to carry the world on their shoulders; they will be recompensed for their labor and toil. The time approaches when there will be neither rich nor poor; when all men shall consume the fruits of the earth, and equally enjoy the gifts of God. But thou wilt not be forgotten in their hymns—oh, good Goddess of Poverty!

Tribute to the "Honest Miner"

Two-bits to the pan on the bed-rock, bed-rock pitching, nuggets loved by the dead-broke, great chunks of gold in the ground-sluice, fine dust in the boxes, oceans of free water, hardest granite rim-rock, let the Honest Miner pass through —the bully Honest Miner!

Since "indications" have existed, since miners have been, he tramps the mountains, he dwells in brush-shanties, he packs his blankets, he whistles as he works his rocker—the Honest Miner, the bully Honest miner! The grub dealers assembled to curse him. They found him on his muscle, too strong, too much sinew, too handy with his six-shooter.

"Seize him by the coat-tails," said they; "roll him in the mud, let into him with pick-handles, that he may be knocked into a cocked-hat, that he may kick the bucket—the Honest Miner!"

They have kicked the bully Miner; they have ducked him in the ditch, but they can't make him pungle. He has fallen back on his "dig," swears by the soul of a beggar, by the soul of a Chinaman, by the soul of a Digger, by the soul of a nigger he has nary red—the Honest Miner, the bully Honest Miner! He has out-packed the Dutch peddler; he has travelled more than a candidate for Congress; he is older than Washoe butter; he is younger than the beef; he has drunk more cocktails than there are shares on the Comstock—the Honest Miner, the bully Honest miner!

He it is that makes it hot for the free-lunch tables; it is he that bucks at *monte;* plays draw-poker; fights the tiger; patronizes the Hurdies; sings like a "Washoe canary;" it is he who sees the first peep of dawn—through the bottom of a tumbler—through the same cocks his eye on the last smile of evening—the bully Honest Miner! It is he who carries the pick, pan, and shovel; who digs about croppings; who picks up "indications," pounds them in a mortar, and "salts" the "prospect"—the Honest Miner, the bully Honest Miner! Thou wilt, one day, cease to carry sacks of "specimens" on thy shoulders; thou'lt go into thy last "prospect hole; "six feet will be the extent of thy last claim on earth; the stakes bearing thy last "notice" will be no further apart—six feet only; but six feet is a big "interest" in the "Eternal lead," if properly "recorded;" the "pay-streak" there is broad, the bullion pure—no base metal. Every miner claiming on this lead shall find pay, even unto the farthest "extension." Honest Miner, we shall think of thee as we halt and read thy last "notice." So long as thou art remembered, thou shalt not be forgotten—oh, bully, Bully Honest Miner!

CHAPTER LIX

PAY-DAY AT THE MINES

Among the Employees—Miner's Union—Labor and Capital—
A Heavy Pay-list—Where the Money Goes to—"Steamer Day"

The majority of the miners at present working in the silver mines of Nevada are honest in the true and best sense of the word, and are the most charitable men, as a class, to be found on the continent; and the same will apply to the owners and officers of mines.

The money annually donated by the miners of the leading mines on the Comstock must aggregate a very large sum. When a brother miner is accidentally killed it is not at all unusual for the men of the mine in which he worked to make up a purse of from $1,000 to $1,500 for his widow and orphans.

A small sum is generally given at once—say, two or three hundred dollars—then on the first of the next month, which is always pay-day in the mines, each man, as he receives his wages, leaves in the hands of the officer who is "paying off" from one to two dollars, to be given to the person to be assisted. There being in the leading mines from five hundred to eight hundred or one thousand men, a large sum is in this way speedily raised. Each man gives cheerfully and as a duty, for he does not know but that on the next pay-day his brother-miners may be giving a share of their wages for the support of his own widow and her children.

When men are hurt in the mines the companies always render them assistance and they are also assisted, if long disabled, by their comrades. There are three Miner's Unions, one at Virginia City, one at Gold Hill, and the third at Silver City, the object of which is the protection of the interest of the working miner and the keeping up of wages to the standard of four dollars per day—eight hours. These Unions have handsome and commodious halls in which they hold regular meetings, and, thus far, the principal officers and leading spirits of the several organizations have been men of such honesty of purpose and have shown such fairness in all of their demands that there has been no trouble between miners and mine-owners.

These Unions always have money with which to assist the distressed in case of emergency. The excursions of the Unions, and balls and benefits of all kinds, are always very liberally patronized by all classes of citizens, and thus, when their treasury has been depleted by some calamity in the mines—as a fire—large sums of money are speedily placed in their hands.

The relations existing between the miners and the superintendents are generally very cordial. The men are always respectful and obedient and the superintendents by no means haughty or austere in their intercourse with their men, conversing as freely with a miner upon all subjects, when conversation is in order, as though he were a millionaire. The same may be said of the foremen of the mines, most of whom have been raised from the ranks, as also, have not a few of the superintendents. The miners always have it as an incentive to good conduct and the acquiring of skill and knowledge in mining, that they may one day be promoted.

Most superintendents take a good deal of pride in their men —in having men who are industrious, skillful and reliable in every emergency—and

Gold Hill Miner's Union Hall, 1940, gelatin silver, Historic American Buildings Survey, National Park Service. Library of Congress Prints and Photographs Division.

they not infrequently take an interest in the pecuniary affairs of those who are found to be deserving, lending them a helping hand occasionally and always advising them as well as they are capable of doing, when their advice is sought in regard to any little investments they may think of making.

The miners in return take a considerable degree of interest and feel a certain pride in a mine in which they are at work—in the richness of its ores, the power and perfection of its machinery, and, in short, in all connected with it. As sailors are proud of belonging to a first-class ship, so miners are proud to be able to mention a first-class mine as that in which they are employed. In short, thus far the relations of miner and mine-owner have been all that could be desired, and there seems to be no danger of any trouble in the future, as it is generally conceded that the miner who risks his life in the mines and toils in the sweltering lower levels should receive at least four dollars per day.

The mining superintendents themselves lead no easy life, as they make daily visits to the mines in their charge, descend into the lower levels, and pass through and inspect all manner of dangerous and disagreeable places. Often they are in the lower levels for hours at a time, and sometimes are obliged to descend into the mine three and four times in one day.

As a rule the superintendents of the mines on the Comstock lode are men much above the average in understanding, culture, and education—men of marked ability and such as would be leaders in any line of business in which they might engage—captains among men, as it were. The foremen are men of much the same class as the superintendents, but are generally less prominently before the public. Their time is spent in the mines among the men, and though they do not labor with their hands, they have by no means an easy time of it, as they must be almost constantly on their feet, and are obliged to climb and crawl into all manner of dangerous and difficult places. When anything is going wrong in a mine—ground settling, and timbers giving way, a fire or a rush of water—they have little rest until all is again secure.

But for the better wages and the honor of the position, the ordinary miner has a more desirable place in a mine than that occupied by a foreman, as he has nothing to do but work his shift, of eight hours, when he can go home and leave care behind—he has no responsibilities, nothing about which to worry. To do an honest day's work is all his care.

The engineers, station-tender, pump-men, and the watchmen on the lower levels, all occupy positions to which are attached grave responsibilities, the lives of their fellow workmen being constantly in their hands. The miners receive their pay—$4 per day—regularly every month, from the first to the third day of the month. Pay-day is a happy day with the men. They go to the office of the-time-keeper as they come up out of the mine, at the change of shifts, and "get their time" for the month—that is they get a slip of paper on which is an account of the number of days they have worked during the month.

With this they go to the office of the secretary or head-clerk of the mine where they form in a line, as lines are sometimes formed in a post-office or at the polls on an election day, and each man in his turn receives his wages.

Over half a million dollars are paid out on the first of every month along the Comstock, to miners, mechanics, and others who are employed in and about the mines. The monthly payrolls of some of the leading companies are as follows: Consolidated Virginia, $90,000; Crown Point, $90,000; Belcher, $65,000; Ophir, $33,000; Savage, $22,000; Chollar-Potosi, $25,000; Hale & Norcross $20,000; and a long list of companies whose pay-rolls amount to from $10,000 to $15,000 per month. Even at mines where they are merely sinking a prospecting-shaft, from ten to fifteen men are employed and there is paid out per month in the shape of wages from $1,500 to $2,000—as mechanics, carpenters, blacksmiths, and engineers, receive from five to seven dollars per day.

Besides the money that is paid out monthly to the men about the mines, the wages of the men employed in the many mills about Virginia City, and Gold Hill, and along the Carson River amount to a large sum. There may be added to this the wages of the men employed on the Virginia and Truckee Railroad, over which ore is sent to the mills, and lumber, timber, and wood are brought to the mines; also, the men employed in the saw-mills and in other branches of the lumbering business in the mountains are paid monthly, and all this money is expended in the towns along the Comstock.

Such large sums paid out every month to working men—who scatter it broadcast in the land—causes money to be quite plentiful in all the towns. In case of business being a little dull toward the close of any month, merchants, shopkeepers, and others do not grumble. They merely say: "Never mind, the pay-days are near at hand!" It is not as in agricultural communities, where when a bad crop is made all must wait for another year before good times can be expected.

Besides the money paid out every month in the shape of wages, dividends are paid each month by such companies as are in a sufficiently flourishing condition to thus gladden the hearts of their stockholders. The Consolidated Virginia alone pays $1,080,000 per month in dividends.

In many kinds of business the persons employed are paid every week, and the merchants, and business men in general, square all accounts of transactions among themselves every Monday; hence Monday in Virginia City is sometimes jocularly termed "steamer day," as corresponding to the old "steamer day" of San Francisco—the day when the steamer sailed for New York, and when all business men were expected to make good all their coin contracts.

When the miners receive their wages the first business of the unmarried men is to pay the rent of their lodging room, and the next is to pay their bill at the restaurant, while the married men settle their bills at the meat-markets, the grocery and provision stores, and the dry-goods stores. Happy is the man who can square up every month and have a few dollars to put by for a rainy day. Some, as in every country, are always behind, but the most miserable of the miners are those who gamble. Much of the time they are working to pay for a "dead horse," for when they have lost their wages they borrow as long as they can find friends to lend. But whether gambled away or judiciously and economically expended, the money paid out each month to laboring men makes lively times for a fortnight or more—all have coin jingling in their pockets, even check guerrillas and thieves.

CHAPTER LX

The Hottest Place in the Mine

Secrecy—"Booming" Stock—Adventures of a French Count—
Left in the Dark—Making it Hot for Him—Rescued—Polite to the Last

"Curbstone brokers" and many other dabblers in stocks rely a good deal upon "points" obtained from miners, in regard to what is going on in the lower levels of the mines. It probably happens once in a while that a miner gives some friend on the "outside" early news of a rich strike in the mine in which he is employed, but it is generally on condition that the "outsider" purchase and carry for him a considerable amount of the stock of the mine.

In order to keep himself well informed in regard to the mines, in this way, the speculator must not only have a man in each mine but must have a man on nearly every level of each mine, as the miners are not allowed to ramble about at will in the lower levels of any of the leading mines. To fee a man on each level of half a dozen mines, even, would be a very expensive means of obtaining early information.

As the miner who is merely receiving a fee occasionally for such "points" as he may be able to furnish is desirous of receiving a "price" as frequently as possible, he is somewhat addicted to the manufacture in a dull time.

Men working in a large and strictly-regulated mine have little opportunity of knowing when a development has been made at a particular point in a mine, or anything about the value of any body of ore that may be encountered.

When a cross-cut is being run at a point where it is thought that ore will be found, the work is carried on by what is called a "secret shift." This shift is composed of the oldest and most trustworthy men in the mine—men who will work for weeks in a drift that sparkles with native silver and yet remain as mute as the same number of oysters, when above, circulating among those of the surface-world. These secret shift men generally find their silence profitable. They are helped to a few shares of the stock at the low figure at which it is probably selling when the ore is found, and pocket whatever advance there may be in the stock when the nature and extent of the new development have been made known. The men working on a secret shift are not sworn to secrecy, and it is seldom that they are even pledged—they know why they are selected, and what is expected of them. When a secret has been divulged and the guilty person cannot be discovered, every man on that shift is discharged, and not one of them will again be employed on a secret shift in any mine until the real culprit has been found. Men working in any kind of place in the mines are very cautious about telling what is going on underground, as any valuable information given on the surface is soon sown broadcast, and is not long in reaching the ear of the superintendent, foreman, or some other officer of the mine, when it is quickly traced to the man who brought it up from the lower levels. This being the case, many of the men, when "pumped" for "points," invent some story of a rich development at some paint in the mine where all is country rock or mere barren porphyry. These stories circulate as rapidly as the others, but a quiet smile is all the attention they receive from the officers of the mine—they, at such times, remain mute and neutral.

During the great stock excitement in 1872, a gentleman who had several thousand dollars that he desired to invest in stocks, cultivated the acquaintance of a man who had the appearance of being a miner, and soon gave him to understand that in case he could give him any points in regard to what was going on in certain mines, they would invest and divide the profits. The man thus "approached" was a miner, but was out of employment, was at work in no mine on the lead. However, he was willing to do something. He saw that the gentleman in search of points was a stranger in the town, and felt that a good thing to do would be to take him in. Therefore points were promised. In a day or two the alert miner made his appearance at the hotel of the stranger, and beckoning him out, furnished him a big point in regard to a grand development in a certain Gold Hill mine, and a large number of shares were at once purchased.

This was just at the beginning of the excitement, and the next day there was a considerable advance in the price of the stock. The man of points said the newly-discovered ore-body was improving. Day after day the stock continued to rise, and the pseudo-miner swore it was the richest thing he ever saw in any mine on the Comstock. He seemed greatly excited, and was not made easy in mind until he had sworn the gentleman to secrecy, saying that if even a whisper in regard to the strike got abroad he would lose his place—would almost be kicked out of the mine.

What the fellow said about the strike seemed to be gospel truth, as the next day after he had described the appearance of the silver-caverns in which he was daily delving, the stock went up like a rocket in the San Francisco Stock Board.

"Aha!" cried the gentleman, "they have found it out already down at the Bay!"

For two or three days the stock "boomed"—for every stock was just then booming—then it began to go down a little and "see-sawed" for a day or two. As soon as the latter symptom became manifest, the well-informed miner came to his stranger friend wearing a long face and told him to sell at once. The gentleman was inclined to think that by holding on a day or two the stock would go to a higher figure than it had yet reached, but on hearing this the miner came out with another great secret, and the stranger was again sworn. The ore-body had pinched out in porphyry, and in cross-cutting through what at first appeared to be a vast body of immensely rich ore, it had been found a mere shell, all the rest was barren quartz. Hearing this, the gentleman sold at once, and the pair of speculators divided over $6,000 profit. The joke of the whole affair was that no work was being done in the mine whose stock they had been dealing in, nor had a pick been struck in any part of it for over two years.

Some of the pranks of the miners are quite amusing. The following is an instance: At the time that the 1,400-foot level of the Crown Point mine was being opened, and while it was boiling hot, a Frenchman, a stranger and a very suave and enthusiastic young man withal, called at the hoisting-works and asked permission to descend and examine the lower-levels. The foreman was very busy at the time, and would have refused the request had it been preferred in language less polite or manner less eager and earnest. But, seeing the man's soul in his eyes, and that he was almost trembling with excess of desire, he thought it would be positive cruelty to deny him the favor he craved. After some hesitation, with the Frenchman's pleading eyes still fixed upon him, the foreman said it was not a proper time for admitting visitors; that he was particularly engaged at the moment and could not accompany him; yet, some miners being about to descend to the lower levels, he might, if so inclined, go down in their company. The little Frenchman was delighted. It was just the arrangement that suited him, and he was profuse in his thanks.

Leaving the native of "sunny France" for a moment, the foreman advanced to where the workmen were preparing to descend the shaft, and told them he was going to send a Frenchman down with them to see' the lower levels, and that one of them could bring him up after he had satisfied his curiosity. Being somewhat vexed at having to send the man down at all, the foreman added to his other instructions: "And, confound him, put him into the hottest hole you can find!"

"All right, sir," cheerily answered the men.

The Frenchman was told to get aboard the cage, when down he was sent in the same clothing in which he came to the mine—coat, hat, and all. Now the miners in whose hands the Frenchman had fallen, were all fellows of "infinite jest"—ready for any kind of deviltry. They considered that in the parting words of their foreman—"Put him into the hottest place you can find," they were given permission to play the Frenchman almost any trick their humor might suggest.

On arriving at the 1,400-foot level, while moving about lighting candles, the plan hit upon for "doing" their French friend was whispered among the miners. They showed their man about for a time, greatly to his delight. He admired everything; yet he could but exclaim occasionally: "Begar zee atmosphere which exist here be fearful intemperate!" At length the miners informed the visitor that they were about to conduct him to the most interesting point in the mine—to the most advanced drift, the place in which all the hopes of the company were centered. They honestly stated that the place was very hot, but if he could stand the heat he should see a spot the eye of no "outsider" had yet viewed, but which many would give thousands of dollars to behold.

"Oh," cried the Frenchman, "it will be one grand plaisir! I sail be ver delighted! Nossing could be more agreeable. Bote, now zat I sink of it, I would prefer zat I have leave me coat at zee surface."

The miners led the way to a long drift, in the end of which had been bored a deep drill-hole, from which flowed a stream of water so hot that eggs had actually been boiled in it in a few minutes. All of the rock forming the walls of the drift was so hot that to place the naked hand upon it was painful. The crowbars and drills lying back near the face of the drift were so hot that they could not be handled.

Into the very end of this drift the miners led the enthusiastic little man, and began showing him the ore there to be seen. Soon the perspiration poured in streams from his face and a small rill ran from the end of his nose. He opened his vest and clutched at his necktie to get air, but still he was not utterly discouraged. Said he, rubbing the water from his eyes: "How ver true it is for you gentlemen vich vork in zee mines what is observe in zee Bible, in zee curse to the first parent—'In zee perspiration of you forehead sail you eat of zee loaf of bread!'"

About this time, in some unaccountable way, all of the candles at once went out. Pitchy darkness prevailed. The miners charged their French friend to stand perfectly still and they would go out and re-light their candles. The poor devil only said:

"Veil, veil, ziz is to me incomprehensible and must be one chance extraordenaire for all zee candaile to become extinguish so very instantaneous. Je suppose it was one accident. Make all zee dispatch vich is possible. Zee heat of zee atmosphere is indescriptible!" Soon after this little scene in the drift, Sam Jones, superintendent of the mine, came along through the level with a lantern in his hand. Much to his surprise, he found several men standing in the dark before a drift, the mouth of which they had carefully closed with "logging" and pieces of boards.

"Hello!" cried he, "what are you all doing here in the dark? And why is the mouth of this drift closed?" No one volunteered a remark, each waiting for the other probably.

"Have you seen a young Frenchman on this level?" asked the superintendent, "the foreman above tells me he sent him down here."

Now some one *had* to speak.

"Yes;" said one of the men, "he is here."

"Here! Where?"

"Back in the end of the drift."

"What in thunder is he doing there?"

"Waiting for a light, I think."

"In the devil's name! what trick is this?" cried the superintendent. "Don't you know that the man is an ex-count and a big French banker—a man of note?"

"Can't help that. The foreman told us to show him the hottest place in the mine, and we're a-showin' it to him—and makin' it as hot for him as we know how."

In an instant the superintendent had torn away the planks and logging, and was making his way back, lantern in hand, to where the poor devil of a Frenchman was roasting—literally roasting, for the whole drift was as hot as a furnace seven times heated, and the man was more dead than alive. Elevating his lantern, to get a view of the foreign gentleman, the superintendent found him standing with coat and vest across his arm, and collar and necktie in his hand. He was wilted till as limber as a dish-rag.

"Ze Cod on 'bove be praise," he cried, "zat you have come! I am just on zee point to expire. Zee distemperament of zee place have increase immediatement after you retire in more as ten-fold progression." Then, wiping the blinding perspiration from his eyes, he surveyed Mr. Jones for a moment in surprise. "Ah! pardon me monsieur," he cried, "I have not first zee plaisir to behold you before. I mistake you for zee gentlemen who have depart wis the purpose to re-enlight zee candaile. Excuse me zat I trouble you wis zee narration, bote we meet here wis one leetle accident, sare; one leetle accident which have, how you call it? exterminate, estinguis' zee entire of the candaile, sare."

"I am sorry that anything so unpleasant should have occurred," said the superintendent, "and I assure you, sir, I shall look into this matter."

"You are too kind, monsieur—too kind! I assure you sare, zat I have remain here until zis moment in parfaite tranquilety; bote now, sare, I vill depart, if you please. Vill you have zee complaisance to put me on zee machine, and elevate me to zee surfaice immediatement? My God, sare, I expire wis zee heat! Elevate me, monsieur, wis dispatch—wis all dispatch. I vill not remain for zee gentleman who have go wis zee purpose to re-enlight zee candaile. Some ozzaire time I vill make zem my apology."

In all haste the superintendent led the way to the main shaft, the polite little Frenchmen hurrying after, saying: "Yes, some ozzaire time I moos make to zem my apology." They were soon aboard the cage, and, a minute after, at the noo-foot level. Here the superintendent was obliged to stop a few minutes, but told the Frenchman that if he would get off and wait, they would go up together on the next cage. But to this the half-dead man would not listen. He stuck to the cage like grim death, and said:

"Let zee machine continue to ascend up, if you please, sare, I vill be elevate on zee surfaice promptment—wis all despatch, sare."

The superintendent then sent a trusty miner up with the roasted ex-count. When daylight was reached the little fellow was himself again.

"Ah!" cried he, "how ver' beautiful is zee cool air, zee light of zee glorious sun, and all of God's work, how grand! I have make one terrible experience; bote I would not have miss him, sare, no, not for many dollaires!"

He then tried to make the man who came up the shaft with him accept a five-dollar gold piece. Not succeeding in this he made him go with him to the nearest saloon and get a glass of beer. Not satisfied with this, and the men below again coming into his mind, he paid the barkeeper for two buckets of beer, telling the miner with him that he wished it given to the men who went to light the candle.

"I have," said he, "been ver impolite to come away before zee return of zee gentlemen who have gone to re-enlight zee candaile. Veil, zat was one ver curious accident and bring to me one ver terrible experience of zee discomfort of zee heat at zat place of remarkable interest."

Although the French count doubtless suffered terribly while shut up in the drift, with boiling water and heated rock all about him, his "discomfort," after all, was not much greater than was that of the miners who played him the trick while drinking the beer he sent them—though their torture was of a different kind. Most amply, yet most innocently, had the Frenchman avenged himself.

CHAPTER LXI

UNDERGROUND BATTLES
The Beginning of Trouble—The Contest—Fighting Interests

In the early days of Washoe, fights between rival claimants of mining ground were frequent, and often stubbornly contested and bloody. These fights sometimes occurred upon the surface, sometimes far down in the bowels of the earth—one company having broken into ground claimed by another with a drift or a tunnel. On such occasions the rival companies armed and fortified underground as well as upon the surface.

Sometimes a company tried to smoke their rivals out, and in this they generally succeeded, but were, in most instances, themselves smoked out as well, by their own bonfires and stink-pots. Of late years, however, most difficulties in regard to the ownership of mining property have been settled in the courts. Men at last began to realize that battles with guns, pistols, and knives settled nothing; no matter how many lives were sacrificed, matters had to be brought before the proper tribunal at last. Yet a little of the old warlike spirit is occasionally manifested even at the present day.

The last mining fight, of any importance, on the Comstock lode, occurred at the Justice mine on the evening of Saturday, October 3, 1874, which resulted in the death of five men in about as many minutes.

It may be of interest to give the particulars in regard to the last affair, as it will serve to illustrate the manner in which these battles in the mines are fought, and show in what way they are sometimes brought on. The fight occurred at about 6 o'clock in the evening, at what is known as the Waller's Defeat Shaft of the Justice mine, situated on Gold Cañon, between Gold Hill and Silver City. The battle was between two factions of the Justice Mining Company, contending for possession of the mine. There had for some time been trouble among the trustees of the company, and on the day of the fight the president of the company appointed a new superintendent and instructed him to take possession of the mine.

It was the talk that the old superintendent would not give up the mine, and there were rumors during the afternoon that a fight might be expected, and many were talking about going down to the Justice to "see the fun." Finally the brother of the newly-appointed superintendent, as a deputy, and accompanied by a number of men, went down to the mine, and had a talk with the foreman in charge about taking possession of the works, foreman said he was ready to give possession whenever the other came with proper authority, but as things then stood he would prefer to hear from his superior, the old superintendent, before doing anything.

Meantime the newly-appointed superintendent was in Virginia City looking for the old superintendent, in order to show him the dispatches he had received from San Francisco, instructing him to take possession of the mine; but he failed to find him and left the city. About this time the old superintendent, who was in Virginia City, sent a note to his foreman at the mine instructing him to give the newly-appointed officer possession of the works at both shafts—the old Justice and the Waller's Defeat Shaft.

Before this note reached its destination and before the two superintendents—the old and the new—had met, the men themselves had precipitated the fight. There were with the deputy superintendent twelve men who were to be used in holding possession of the two shafts in case of their being given up by the men in charge. All of these men were armed with pistols, and some of them had been drinking enough to make them feel inclined to have things go about as they wished. They grew impatient on account of the delay in giving possession of the works and presently left the Justice shaft, and started for the Waller's Defeat, two or three hundred yards distant.

The deputy superintendent had started to go to Gold Hill, when, looking back, he saw his men moving in a body toward the Waller's Defeat Shaft. Fearing trouble, he turned and hastened after them. When he overtook them they were close to the building over the shaft and were still advancing. It was well understood that there were in this building several armed men, and he ran before his men and tried to induce them to halt.

At the same time a voice from the hoisting-works over the shaft commanded them to stop. It was now growing dark, and the persons in the building could not be seen. As the deputy was still trying to keep his men back, two of them pushed past him and advanced toward the building. One of these raised his revolver as he moved forward, and instantly a volley was fired from the building. Three men fell, two of whom died on the ground, while the third, who was shot through the spine and abdomen, lived but a few hours.

A short parley now ensued. The deputy superintendent told those within the building that he desired to have a talk with them; to tell them what he wanted to do. He said that such work as they were having must not go on; that he did not come there to have a battle with those in possession of the works. He then asked if he might enter the building. A voice said he might come in, if he came alone; but if another man attempted to follow him they would fire on the whole party. The deputy then advanced to the building, and had just raised his foot to step into the door when those inside fired, and he fell dead in his tracks. One of his men ran up to bring away his body and received a charge of buckshot in the breast that laid him dead beside the deputy. During this time several shots were fired into the building by those on the outside, but without effect. After these scattering shots there was an entire cessation of hostilities on both sides, and outside parties—persons not belonging to either faction—were allowed to approach and carry away the dead.

A gentleman who was on the ground through the whole affair, considered the advance of the deputy's party as being very ill-advised, and quite against the wishes of the deputy himself, as that gentleman did all in his power to keep his men back. Much rashness and hot-headedness was exhibited on both sides. It was said that the reason the deputy was fired on was that as he advanced to the door of the works some of his men moved forward behind him. The dead were carried to a small cabin near at hand, and when they had been decently composed, with handkerchiefs tied over their heads and under their chins, they presented a ghastly spectacle, as they were still in the clothes in which they fell, all of which were soaked in blood. Their shirts were open, and the wounds of those shot in the breast were exposed to sight. To stand in the little cabin, twelve by fourteen feet in size, and see the whole floor covered with dead bodies, one seemed to be on the edge of a field whereon had just been fought some great and bloody battle.

The news of the fight brought not less than a thousand persons to the spot, but all gave the building over the Waller's Defeat shaft a wide berth. All was dark and silent as the grave within the building. This stillness and darkness seemed ominous. No one wished to venture near it, as all said it was quite certain that the men within would not be taken alive. A guard was placed about the works and all night men armed with muskets patrolled before and around the building.

When daylight came a cautious advance was made, and finally the building was entered. Not a man was found within it. All had escaped some time during the previous night, probably immediately after the last shooting, and long before the guard was set. Though no men were found in the building, there was found a Henry rifle, a double-barreled shotgun, three revolvers, and a smaller pistol, together with several powder-flasks and a quantity of ammunition; also, about one hundred cigars, and two demijohns partly filled with whisky—"fighting whisky," no doubt. An inquest was held by the coroner of Storey County, and the following verdict found:

"We the undersigned jurors, summoned by Coroner Homles of Storey County to make due inquiry into the cause of the deaths of William Kellogg, Michael Riley, John Brown, Michael Cain, and W. D. Shifiett, on being duly sworn do find that the true names and ages of deceased were as follows: Michael Cain, a native of Ireland, aged 35 years; W. D. Shifiett, a native of Virginia, aged 47 years; W. P. Kellogg, a native of New York, aged 42 years; Michael Riley, a native of Ireland, aged 37 years, and John Brown, a native of Pennsylvania, aged 37 years: and we do find that they came to their deaths at Waller Defeat shaft of the Justice mine in Gold Hill, Storey County, Nevada, on Saturday October 3, 1874, from gunshot wounds inflicted by the hands of parties to us unknown."

Four men were arrested on suspicion of being concerned in the shooting, but these were finally discharged by the grand jury, and so ended the last mining battle on the Comstock lode.

The men who were in the Waller's Defeat building, and handled the guns, were not regular miners such as work in the lower levels, but belonged to a class that generally toil on the surface at about ten dollars per day, taking "fighting interests" in mines that are in dispute, or hiring out keep possession of property that has more than one claimant. In former times they were a class of laborers that were in brisk demand.

CHAPTER LXII

THE WEALTH OF THE WORLD
Mines of Ancient Days—The Yield of American Mines—
Humboldt's Curious Calculations—Varied Fortunes—
The Plum in the Pudding —Value of the Different Levels—
Searching in the Dark

Silver was known to the ancients as far back in the dim and distant ages of the past as any record extends. It was undoubtedly one of the first metals mined by mankind. In writings, both sacred and profane, mention is made of silver in the earliest ages of the world.

Gold being a metal that is found native, and silver being very frequently found in the native state, these were doubtless among the first metals with which the primitive races of mankind became acquainted. Native silver being found mingled with various ores of silver, it was probably not long after the metal became known and valued that men conceived the idea of smelting these ores and thus obtaining a larger supply of the metal than was yielded in the native form. In the Bible frequent mention is made of silver, from the very beginning. Silver was more highly prized than gold by all the primitive peoples of the earth. Even the sacred writers speak of it with gusto. To this day we find that savages and semi-civilized nations prefer silver to gold. It is the case with the negro tribes of Africa, the Indians of the American Continent, and with the nations of China and Japan. The human animal must be educated up to a just appreciation of gold, but silver by its brilliant white lustre and flash in the light of the sun recommends itself to him as soon as its sheen strikes his eye.

All metals were no doubt first extracted from their ores by smelting, yet it appears that the process of extracting silver from its ores, and gold from its matrix, by means of quicksilver was not unknown to the ancients. Pliny and Vitruvius speak of quicksilver being used for this purpose. In ancient times, if Pliny is to be believed, the art of mining was well understood, as he speaks of silver-mines being worked to the depth of a mile and a half. If this be true, our modern mines have little to boast of. To have done such mining the ancients must have possessed hoisting and pumping machinery, or their equivalents, with appliances for ventilation equal to if not surpassing any known to the mining engineers of the present age. There is every evidence that silver-mines were worked in many countries in the Old World at a very early day, and not a few are still being worked, in regard to the date of the discovery and opening of which there is no record. All that is known is that they seem to have always been worked.

Fuller, in his treatise on silver-mines, says:

"Wherever in any part of the world silver-mines have been worked they are worked now, unless for some unexplainable cause, such as the lack of machinery, the existence of war, the invasion of Indians, etc. We know of no silver-mining regions in the world that have given out. Mexican mines, worked by the Aztecs before the conquest, are still worked as profitably as ever; the old Spanish mines opened long before Hannibal's time, are still worked with enormous profits; the South American mines have constantly yielded their wealth for more than three hundred years, and are as productive as ever; mines in Hungary, that were worked by the Romans before the Saviour's time, still yield abundance of ore; the silver-mines of Freiburg, opened in the eleventh century and worked continually ever since, yield their steady increase. So in Norway, Sweden, and Russia, and indeed wherever silver-mines have been opened, we believe without exception, they continue to be worked at the present day, and generally are more productive than at any time in their past history. For permanent and rich returns, silver-mining has no parallel in any other business."

In regard to the yield of the silver-mines in Spain in ancient times little can now be ascertained. By many persons the Spanish peninsula is regarded as the Tarshish of old, and through such traditions as have come down to us it is quite certain that Solomon drew much of his wealth from the Spanish mines at the time it is said, "it was nothing accounted of, for the King made silver to be as stones in Jerusalem."

Among the fabulous stories of the ancients in regard to the silver-mines of Spain is that of Diodorous, who relates that the shepherds of the Pyrenees set fire to the forests in the neighborhood of their camps, when by the burning of the fallen timber the minerals of the earth were fused and the molten silver ran upon the ground as water in a brook. Among the modern silver-mines of Spain are those of Sierra de Almagrera, which were discovered and opened in 1839, and which in 1845 gave employment to eight thousand miners. The most important silver-mines in Spain at the present time are those of Hiendelaencia, which were discovered about thirty years ago and which have been productive ever since —their average annual yield for twenty years was 31,577 pounds troy. The whole silver yield of Spain is at present about one hundred thousand pounces troy per annum.

In Germany, the silver-mines discovered in the Hartz mountains and at Freiberg, Saxony, in the tenth century are still being worked as vigorously as fiver. Much of the silver-ore worked in Germany is of no better quality than is thrown away on the Comstock as "waste rock." In Norway and Sweden silver-mines known before the discovery of America, are being worked. The mines of Sala, Westmania, which are yet being worked were known and worked over 500 years ago. The Cero de Pasco mines, Peru, discovered in 1630, from which no less than five million pounds of silver wore taken out in forty-three years, are still productive. The famous mines of Potosi (Cerro de Potosi), Bolivia, formerly included in the territory of Peru, discovered in 1544, are said to have yielded $1,200,000,000. The total annual yield of Bolivia at present is about 450,000 pounds.

The Zacatecas mines, in Mexico, were opened in 1548, and the mines, of Guanajuata in 1558. The principal mines of Mexico are those of Guanajuata, Catorce, Zacatecas, and Real del Monte. The yield of the Mexican mines since the conquest of the country by the Spaniards, up to 1860, amounted to $2,039,100,000. The following is the yield of some of the older silver-mines of Mexico and South America: Sierra Madre mines, $800,000,000. Veta Madre, $235,934,636; Rio Grande, $650,000,000; Royas, $85,421,015; Valencia, $31,813, 486; Santa Anna, $21,347,210; Biscania, $16,341,000. These are, in most instances, not single veins, but mining districts in which there are numerous veins of various sizes and degrees of richness. They are groups of parallel veins. The Veta Madre, of Mexico, is however, situated much the same as the Comstock lode of Nevada. It fills a similar fissure and is in a similar formation. Although other mines in Mexico contain much richer ores, the Veta Madre (Mother Vein), has been more extensively worked than any other mine in that country. It has been steadily worked for over three hundred years, yet during the three centuries there has been taken from it but little more silver than has been taken from the Comstock during sixteen years.

Humboldt says the silver sent to Europe from Mexico and South America, from the discovery of the New World by Columbus to 1809, would make a solid ball eighty-three and seven-tenths Paris feet in diameter; at the present rate of production the Comstock lode alone should roll up a tolerably large ball, as in sixteen years it is estimated the yield of the vein has been $220,000,000, or an average annual yield of $13,750,000. This is a good showing when we consider that our people did not know what the silver-ore was when they found it, and that during the first two or three years after they began working the ores much time was spent in trying experiments with all kinds of processes, and with machinery of an inferior character.

In 1874 the yield of the Comstock mines was $21,940,123.96; in 1874, it was $22,242,274.95; and for 1875 it will be much greater.

According to recent estimates the total silver product of the world from 1850 to 1875 was $1,025,000,000 and the Comstock mines are now yielding one-tenth of the entire amount produced in the world. The latest estimates of German and American authorities give the total product of all the gold and silver-mines in the world, from the year 1500 to 1874, as follows: Pounds of silver—364,000,000, valued at $8,175,000 000. Pounds of gold—17,000,000, valued at $6,450,000,000. Total pounds of gold and silver—381,600,000; valued at $14, 625,000,000. These figures are probably not very exact. It is a hard matter to get the exact yield of even such mines as are worked by regularly organized companies, and almost impossible to get figures at all where gold is being rained from placers.

It would not be of general interest to trace the progress of mining events on the Comstock year by year from the discovery of silver up to the present writing. It is sufficient to say that in 1862-3, up to which time operations on the lode have been pretty fully described, there began to be an abundance of tolerably efficient mills, and hoisting-works that were sufficiently powerful to do the work at the depth to which the shafts of the principal companies had then been sunk. Even as late as 1866 the greatest depth which had been attained in any mine on the Comstock lode was 923 feet. This was in the Chollor-Potosi mine. The Gould & Curry were then working at a depth of 900 feet, Belcher, 850; Bullion, 800; Hale & Norcross, 783; Savage, 614; Ophir, 547, and other leading companies at a depth of from 500 to 600 feet. Ever since the setting up of the first steam-hoisting and pumping machinery on the lode, and ever since the starting of the first mills for the reduction of the ores extracted, improvements have been made and still continue to be made. The mills and hoisting-works at present in operation would astound the miner and millman of 1862-3, though he doubtless flattered himself that the mills and hoisting-works of that day had attained a degree of perfection beyond which there was little room for improvement.

During these years there were numerous changes in the fortunes of the companies along the lode. Some that had rich ore upon the surface had worked down to the bottom of their deposit and had found themselves in clay or barren porphyry, while others who had started in with no ore on the surface, as the Hale & Norcross and some others, found themselves in "bonanza" at the depth of six or seven hundred feet; and when ore began to grow thin with these last the first companies, by drafting east from the point where their pay pinched out in clay and porphyry, had again found ore and in larger and richer bodies than at first. Thus the bonanza and luck shift, and will probably so continue to shift as long as the mines are worked. It never but once happened—which was in 1865—that so many mines were at once in barren as to depress business and cause a feeling of distress in regard to the permanence of the mines.

No sooner had some of the more timid taken their departure, however, and raised the cry that the country was "played out," than longer and richer bodies of ore began to be found than ever before. Those who had run away then came back, bitterly regretting the want of faith which had caused them to leave just at a time when a fortune might have been had for a mere song. In 1862, the Reese River mines, 150 or 200 miles east of Virginia City, were discovered, a rush to these occurred, and the town of Austin was built up; then came the White Pine excitement, and the towns of Hamilton and Treasure City were built; afterwards Eureka and Pioche were built by the discovery of rich mines in their neighborhood. The camps named still flourish, though they have their "ups and downs"—are sometimes in "bonanza" and sometimes in "borrasca."

It may be well just here to explain these words. Both are Spanish. "Bonanza" signifies prosperity, success—that all is well. At sea it is used by sailors when the weather is fair and they are sailing with a fair wind—when all is well with them. Among miners it means that they are working in a body of ore, that they are in luck, and all with them is prosperous. "Borrasca" means just the opposite of "bonanza." At sea it means tempestuous and dangerous weather, bad fortune—all going wrong; among miners it means that they are in barren rock, that they are in a bad streak, out of luck. Among miners, borrasca is suggestive of long faces, sad hearts, and empty pockets, while bonanza shows us faces wreathed in smiles, hearts that are merry, and purses that are plethoric. Along the Comstock the mining companies are sometimes in bonanza and sometimes in borrasca. So long as they are in the great fissure, however, and have a good width of "vein-matter" they are not utterly cast down even though they may be drifting in barren rock—they are liable to run into ore at any time and often do so when such good fortune is least expected. Some have compared the vein-matter of the lode to a great pudding into which has been stirred raisins, currants, and plums; sometimes you find a currant, sometimes a raisin, and sometimes a plum, while again you are blessed with nothing better than the matter of which the mass of the pudding is composed.

To multiply examples would be tedious, but an example or two will probably not be out of place. Although there is ore in the Crown Point mine, Gold Hill, at the depth of 900 feet, their first great bonanza was not found until they had attained a depth of 1300 feet. This was a magnificent body of ore, and yielded many millions of dollars. The very rich ore was confined to a space about two hundred feet in length lying just north of the line of the Belcher mine, but the vein contained a considerable amount of low-grade ore for a distance of about 350 feet further north. Finally, in 1873, they had worked down through this rich deposit to the 1400-foot level and there started a cross-cut east in search of ore. When this cross-cut had passed through the west clay wall of the vein a deposit of very rich ore was found some feet in width. Passing through the cross-cut next encountered, a streak of white and almost barren quartz about two feet in width, and beyond this reached ore worth from $45 to $75 per ton. This body of ore proved to be twenty-four feet in width. The cross-cut being continued east across this suddenly struck a solid wall of porphyry. The whole face of the cross-cut was in this barren rock, and it was at first thought that the east wall of the ledge had been reached, but after passing through a few feet of porphyry a very large body of ore assaying from $250 to $600 per ton was reached. As the mine continued to be worked this search for ore was repeated at intervals, and thus far the search has never been in vain. In 1875 ore was being extracted everywhere from the 900 down to the 1,500 feet level, though much of that obtained in the upper-levels was of low-grade, yet too rich to be left behind.

In May, 1873, in the Belcher mine, adjoining the Crown Point on the south, was found the continuation of the same rich deposit worked on the 1,300-foot level of the last mine named. Afterwards, other bodies were found at a still greater depth, and to the eastward, and so the work of sinking and searching for new bonanza still goes on, while at the same time ore is being extracted from those already found. In the Savage, Gould & Curry, Hale & Norcross, Chollar-Potosi, Yellow-Jacket, Imperial, Empire, Overman, and a score of other mines this is the work which is constantly going on.

Gold Hill, Overman New Shaft, 1876, collodion/albumen, Carleton E. Watkins. California State Library. Watkins's portable darkroom wagon is partially visible in the lower left.

Some persons will no doubt think that if there is a deposit of ore in a mine it should be found in a short time and with but little trouble, but miners can see no further into the ground than persons who have their homes and business on the surface. Place a man in the bottom of a shaft one thousand feet in depth; then tell him to drift off and find a body of ore, and he is much the same as a man groping about in a dark cellar. He knows which way to go to reach the vein, but when once he is in the vein he may almost touch that of which he is in search without finding it.

If mining men knew the exact spot in which the rich deposits are located, it would be an easy matter to sink a shaft or run a drift to tap them. Thus it happened that it was fourteen years after the discovery of silver, and the Comstock lode before what is now known as the "Big Bonanza,"—the chief of all the bonanzas—was found. For fourteen years men daily and hourly walked over the ground under which lay the greatest mass of wealth that the world has ever seen in the shape of silver ore, yet nobody suspected its presence. The ground on the surface presented the same appearance as the soil in other places in the same neighborhood, and roads were dug in it, houses were built upon it, and all kinds of things were done on, in, and about it without anybody thinking any more of, or about it, than of any other ground in the town.

CHAPTER LXIII

FLUCTUATIONS OF FORTUNE

*The Comstock Mines—Hidden Treasure—A Great Sensation—The
Excitement Increases—Panic— A Millionaire's Advice*

What are now known as the "bonanza mines" are in great part made up of small mines that were located to the southward of the Ophir soon after the discovery of silver. The big bonanza lies in the Consolidated Virginia and California mines, and its northern extremity extends into the Ophir, as is supposed; it is also thought that it will be found to extend into the Best and Belcher, which is the first mine south of the Consolidated Virginia.

The north end of the vein is divided into claims at this point, as is shown

Longitudinal Section of the North End of the Comstock Lode.

NORTH	
Sierra Nevada	2,657 ft.
Union Consolidated	600 ft.
Mexican	600 ft.
Ophir	675 ft.
California	600 ft.
Consolidated Virginia	710 ft.
Best & Belcher	224 ft.
Gould & Curry	921 ft.
Savage	768 ft.
SOUTH	

in the accompanying diagram.

The California mine contains 600 feet on the length of the ledge, and is of whatever width the vein shall prove to be, as the owners have a right to follow it, wherever it may go. It consists of the original California of 300 feet to which has been added by purchase the Central mine No. 1, containing 150 feet; the Central No. 2, 100 feet, and the Kinney ground 50 feet. There are 900 shares to the foot, or 540,000 shares in the whole mine.

The Consolidated Virginia mine contains 710 feet of ground along the lode, and is made up of the Dick Sides ground, 500 feet, and the White & Murphy ground, 210 feet. There are 108,000 shares in the mine. The Ophir, which lies next north of the California mine, contains 675 feet and is divided into 100,800 shares. In 1874, 600 feet were taken off the north end of the Ophir and, incorporated as a separate mine, which was called the Mexican. The Mexican contains 108,000 shares.

The bonanza mines are situated in the northeast part of Virginia City, and many buildings stand on the ground under which they lie. Small bodies of paying ore were found in some of the mines composing the California mine in the early days, but they were soon worked out, and for a number of years the ground lay idle. In the Dick Sides and White & Murphy, the two mines from which was formed the Consolidated Virginia, very little ore of any kind was found on the surface or even at the depth of three or four hundred feet, and these claims had also lain idle several years before they were purchased by Messrs. Mackay & Fair and their associates Messrs. Flood & O'Brien, of San Francisco. However, on what is now the Consolidated Virginia ground, a shaft had been sunk to the depth of six or seven hundred feet from the bottom of which had been run a drift of considerable length.

Ore was first found in the Consolidated Virginia, in March, 1873 at the time when Captain S. T. Curtis (in 1875 superintendent of the Ophir) was in charge. The ore then found was a body about twelve feet in width, which was encountered at the depth of 1,167 feet below the surface in a drift run from the corresponding level of the Gould & Curry mine. At the same time two other bodies of ore—the largest seven feet in width—were found, which yielded assays averaging $60 per ton. At this time their present main shaft was down 710 feet, and was being sunk at the rate of three feet per day.

In October, 1873, the main shaft had reached the 1,167-foot level and in drifting southeasterly a distance of 250 feet a very rich deposit of ore was reached—the top of the big bonanza, in fact. The work of breaking out and regularly extracting ore from this body was commenced October 16, and by the 29th a chamber had been opened in it from six to nine sets of timbers in width (the sets are five feet apart each way) and four floors or sets in height, with solid masses of ore in sight on all sides. A drift had then been run lengthwise through the ore a distance of one hundred and forty feet, while the nine sets of timbers showed it to be fifty-four feet in width. Although all this wealth was in sight in the mine, the people of the town, walking over and around the mine knew nothing of it. What was in the mine was only known to those at work there, and to the officers of the company. I had the satisfaction of being the first "outsider" to descend into the mine and inspect the deposit in regard to which—the mine being closed to visitors—there had been a thousand surmises, favorable and unfavorable. I took samples from all parts of the ore-body and had them assayed. The highest assay obtained was $632,63 per ton, and the lowest, $93,67,—seven samples being tested. Thus it will be seen that even the top of the bonanza was wonderfully rich.

The company continued to explore this body of ore in all directions, running drifts and cross-cuts through it, sinking winzes upon it and making upraises. They followed it down to the 1,200, the 1,300, 1,400 and to the 1,500-foot levels, with the same rich ore everywhere. Although people knew in a general way that there was an abundance of rich ore in the mine, they did not get excited about it, nor did they trouble themselves much about it in any way, further, perhaps, than to say: "Well, I am glad to hear that the Consolidated folks have a big body of ore; it will be a good thing for the town." The mine did not attract more attention than many others, until in October 1874, when the work of opening out on the 1,500-foot level was begun. The ore then found was of such extraordinary richness, and the ore-body appeared to be of such unprecedented extent that people began to talk about it, and then some few began to visit and examine it, all coming to the surface greatly astonished at what they had seen. The reports in regard to the great wealth in sight in the mine, brought to the people of the upper world by scores of reliable men and capable mining experts, soon caused not a little excitement, and everywhere in the streets persons were to be heard talking of the wonderful wealth that was being developed in the Consolidated Virginia mine. Day after day the excitement grew as the reports came from the visitors to the mine that the cross-cuts had been advanced fifty feet, seventy-five, then one hundred feet into the big bonanza and still no signs of getting through it were seen. The cross-cuts still contained in a solid mass of ore of the richest description and each day found them advancing in the same, even after they had gone one hundred and fifty and two hundred feet.

At this time no cross-cuts had been made into the California ground, but the most northerly cross-cut in the Consolidated Virginia was but a few feet from the California south line, therefore this would serve very well to test that portion of both mines. All who comprehended the situation being now confident that the great body of ore which was slowly being explored in the Consolidated Virginia must extend far northward into the ground of the California Company, the stock of said company was soon in brisk demand. As drifts extended southward from the Ophir mine into the California and they encountered rich ore in two or three places, it was considered certain that a mass of ore extended all the way from the Consolidated Virginia to the mine first named, a distance of six hundred feet. Although the stock of the California was but $30 or $40 per share in the beginning, it finally reached $750, for the old shares —afterwards increased five for one.

At this time, although there were no cross-cuts in the California section of the bonanza, there was a main north and south drift extending from the Consolidated Virginia mine to the Ophir, through the west-country rock, and, from this, cross-cuts had been started, and at no distant day reached the ore.

As the progress of these cross-cuts in the rich ore of the bonanza was made known from time to time the excitement gradually increased until it reached fever heat, both in Virginia City and San Francisco. Never were the people more fairly treated on the occasion of any big strike on the Comstock lode than they were by the Consolidated Virginia and California Companies during the time the big bonanza was being opened and explored. All who desired to do so were allowed to descend into the mines and see for themselves what was being done. Often there were such crowds of visitors as to very seriously interfere with all underground operations. There were times when for days together the miners did not do more than two or three hours work on a shift, so frequent were the interruptions caused by persons visiting the drifts and crosscuts that had penetrated the ore-body. One party had no sooner been shown through the two mines than another arrived. All were allowed to dig into and examine the ore, to carry away samples for assays, and, in short, to try whatever experiments they chose in order to satisfy themselves in regard to the value of the deposit.

The men who visited the lower levels and made themselves most familiar with the developments thereon, were the men who purchased more freely, and those who were experts in mining matters were those who were most astounded at the great richness and vast extent of the body of ore opened into. These men bought on their judgement while the mercurial masses bought at random, and under the influence of contact with persons as much and as blindly excited as they themselves were

It was the coming in of the multitude, as, indeed, it always is, that sent not only the stock of the bonanza mines, but also all other stocks rushing sky-ward with rocket-like celerity. When the people start in *en masse* to buy stocks they—to use a very elegant illustration—shut their eyes and rush in like a hog going into battle. They exhibit startling vigor, activity, and enthusiasm, for a short time, but the moment they stop to "get their wind," that moment they are in a fit condition for a panic. The least thing now startles them, and they take wing and are off like a flock of pigeons; or, to carry out the simile, turn tail with a snort, and make for the canebrakes. As many of these unusual dealers in stocks have bought at the highest figures, and on margins to a ruinous extent taking all manner of desperate chances, a panic among them speedily demoralizes the money-markets, and persons who have made their purchases with the best of judgement lose, as all stocks are driven as much below as they were before forced above their real value.

In the time of a grand panic the coolest of persons and men of best judgment are forced to sell their stocks in self-defense, or because it is, as they say, "business" to sell when it is plainly to be seen that the tendency of prices is irresistibly downward; and in this way the crash is made still more complete and sweeping. Men no more take into consideration the real value of a stock at a time when there is a crash in the market than they do when the market is unduly excited and everything is going up with a "rush." The condition of the mines is not taken into consideration on the occasion of a panic. Rich developments in the mines undoubtedly are the prime cause of an advance, and this advance is generally such as is justified by the mineral wealth brought to light until the people "rise up in their might" and take a hand in the business, after which time no man can say what will happen.

As the masses purchase without knowing anything of the mines except what they have heard, so they sell in spite of all that may be told them. Having never seen or examined the mines into which they have bought, when a panic occurs they are more ready to believe that there are no mines at all than to believe that they still exist and remain the same as when they made their purchases. Thus at the time of the panic, in 1875, there was actually a vast deal more ore in sight and the mines were looking better than at the time that the highest figures were reached—that was daily being brought to light the existence of which had formerly only been surmised. Men, however, were not dealing in the big bonanza as it existed in Nevada, but as it appeared on California street, San Francisco. They had lost their interest in the mines and were thinking only of their money.

At the time of the panic men who had seen and examined the great bodies of ore developed in the Consolidated Virginia and California mines, not only held on to their stock but continued to purchase as long as they had money—buying more and more as the stock receded, and in this way some of even the best informed "came to grief," as, looking only at the mines and not at California street, they bought on margins, and the call of the brokers for "mud" soon distressed them and forced them to make ruinous sacrifices. In speaking with Mr. John Mackay, the mining million-aire and one of the principal owners in the bonanza mines, about this time

(February, 1875), he said to me: "We have not yet fairly started in upon the California. It will require steady work for at least six months to show what that mine really is."

In regard to the Consolidated Virginia (then yielding at the rate of $1,000,000 per month), he said: "Some persons think that the stock has already sold for more than it is worth. The truth is that it has never yet sold for one-half of its value; but all this will be seen in good time. People will see it after a while."

Speaking of the crash in stocks, Mr. Mackay said; "It is no affair of mine. I am not speculating in stocks. My business is mining—legitimate mining. I see that my men do their work properly in the mines, and that all goes on as it should in the mills. I make my money here out of the ore. Had I desired to do so, I could have gone down to San Francisco with ten thousand shares of stock in my pocket, and, by throwing it on the market at the critical moment, I could have brought about a panic and a crash, just as has been done. Suppose I had done so, and had made $500,000 by the job—what is that to me? By attending to my legitimate business here at home I take out $500,000 in one week."

Mr. Mackay, indeed, troubles himself very little with the ups and downs of the stock-market or with the chicanery and wirepulling of the stock manipulators. As he says, he is content to see that all goes well in his mines and mills, and, as it were, scoops his coin directly from the lower levels into his pockets. He wants to make no money by engineering crashes in stocks which ruin thousands on thousands of industrious and worthy persons. During a short conversation with him, Mr. Mackay repeatedly said: "My business is square, legitimate mining, I make my money here from the mines—from the ore itself. Both here and in San Francisco," continued he, "persons are constantly coming to me, or writing to me, to ask—'What shall I buy?' I say to all that come to me—'Go and put your money in a savings bank,'"

Indulging in a quiet laugh, at this point, Mr. Mackay said: "You should see some of them stare at me when they hear this advice. They evidently consider me a strange kind of mining-man. But in speaking so I mean just what I say, and my advice is good. I never advise people to buy mining-stocks of any kind."

In this Mr. Mackay is right. He can never know what jobs may be put up by the "stock-sharps" to break the price of almost any stock on the list, merit or no merit. By giving no advice he escapes all reproach, and pursues the even tenor of his way, digging his dollars out of his mines, regardless of the fluctuations in stocks and the machinations of the "manipulators."

CHAPTER LXIV

THE RICHEST SPOT IN THE WORLD

The Grand Gallery—Glittering Caverns—
The World's Greatest Treasure-Store—
"Ventilation"—A "Horse" in the Mine

As by this time the general reader will have heard as much as he will care to know about excitements in stocks, crashes, the tricks of the manipulators, and the troubles of the manipulated, I shall now turn to the Big Bonanza itself.

A description of a trip down a deep shaft being given elsewhere, I shall with the reader's permission, drop at once to the bottom of the shaft of the Consolidated Virginia mine, landing among the miners at a station 1,500 feet below the surface of the earth, on what is known as the "1,500-foot level."

Although many bodies of ore that have yielded millions of dollars have been found on the great lode, here has at last been discovered what appears to be the heart of the Comstock. At the point where the big bonanza was found the fissure in which is formed the Comstock lode is of unusual width. Measuring, from the country-rock (syenite) on the west to the east country rock (propylite), the distance is from one thousand to one thousand two hundred feet. This space between the two country-rocks represents the width of the fissure, and is filled with a "vein-matter" or gangue composed of quartz, clay, and porphyry. In this gangue has been formed the ore. As the vein-matter or gangue appears to be the "matter" of the ore, in order to produce so great a deposit as is seen in the Consolidated Virginia and California mines, an immense mass of it was required. In a place where the fissure is narrow and the vein-matter is pinched, no great breadth of ore may be looked for—it will be in proportion to the vein-matter.

As we have seen, the Consolidated Virginia folks reached the crest of the subterranean silver-mountain in 1873, at the depth of 1,167 feet, but it was not until in the fall of 1874 that they began to open out on the 1,500-foot level, running crosscuts into the mass of ore that produced an unprecedented sensation among the mining men of both Europe and America.

Leaving the station into which we dropped with the cage from the hoisting-works, standing 1,500 feet above, we advance a few steps eastward along a broad gallery, the sides and roof of which are composed of a mass of heavy timbers and thick planks, when we reach the main north-and-south drift, which is the great highway of the mine. It is a grand gallery, nine feet in width by about the same in height, and over one thousand feet in length. It extends through the whole length of the California (600 feet) to the Ophir mine. From the Ophir to the north line of the Consolidated Virginia it was made of double height in order to carry a great volume of air; as the air, fresh and pure from the surface, is drawn down the Ophir shaft and passing through that mine enters the great main drift which it follows through the California and the Consolidated Virginia to the shaft of the mine last named, where it ascends and again mingles with the atmosphere of the upperworld. In passing from shaft to shaft, however, this air has been turned from its direct course in various places (by means of doors closing drifts and cross-cuts) and carried to where it has refreshed and given life to many miners digging down the ore in the breasts of the several heated stopes.

Crossing this thoroughfare of the 1500-foot level and advancing a few steps further to the eastward, we reach the vast deposit of ore known as the "Big Bonanza." Cross-cuts pass through the ore, east and west, and cross-drifts from north to south, cutting it into blocks from fifty to one hundred feet square, as the streets run through and divide a town into blocks. It is indeed a sort of subterranean town, and is more populous than many towns on the surface, as it numbers from 800 to 1,000 souls, and nearly all are voters.

Passing to the south end of the bonanza, to the place where it was first crossed by a drift, we find it to be one hundred and forty-eight feet in width—all a solid mass of ore of the richest description. Here a large stope is opened, and we see the miners at work in the vein, blasting and digging down the ore. They are working upward from the floor of the level, and as they progress they build up square sets of supporting timbers in the cavities or chambers cut out in extracting the ore from the bonanza. Even here, well toward its south end—as far as explored—the ore-body is by no means small, being over nine and one half rods in width! This is not a mixture of ore and worthless rock, but is a solid mass of rich silver-ore which is sent to the mills just as it is dug or blasted down—ore that will pay from $100 to $300 per ton. As thirteen cubic feet make a ton of ore, we have here for every block of ore three feet square from $200 to $600 in pure silver and gold.

We may take our stand here, where the miners are digging out the ore, and for a distance of seventy-five feet on each side of us all is ore, while we may gaze upward to nearly that height to where the twinkling light of candles shows us miners delving up into the same great mass of wealth. On all sides of the pyramidal scaffold of timbers to its very apex, where the candles twinkle like stars in the heavens, we see the miners cutting their way into the precious ore—battering it with sledge-hammers and cutting it to pieces with their picks as though it were but common sandstone. Silver-ore is not—as many may suppose—a bright and glittering mass. In color the ore runs from a blueish-grey to a deep black. The sulphuret ore (silver glance) is quite black and has but a slight metallic lustre, while what is called chloride ore is a kind of steel-grey, with, in places, a pale green tinge—the green showing the presence of chloride of silver. Throughout the mass of the ore in very many places, however, the walls of the silver-caverns glitter as though studded with diamonds. But it is not silver that glitters. It is the iron and copper pyrites that are everywhere mingled with the ore, and which, in many places, are found in the form of regular and beautiful crystals that send out from their facets flashes of light that almost rival the fire and splendor of precious stones. There are also often found in the mass of the ore great nests of transparent and beautiful quartz crystals that are almost as brilliant as diamonds. Many of these crystals are three or four inches in length. Some of the nests of crystals are of a light blue color, and then they may be classed among the precious stones, as they are amethysts. Some of these are almost as handsome as the precious amethyst. The miners always like to find these nests of crystals, as they indicate life and strength in the vein.

On the 1,500-foot level the bonanza extends into the Consolidated Virginia ground over three hundred feet. How much further it may extend in that direction on the levels below remains to be ascertained. The "chimneys" of ore, or bonanzas, everywhere on the Comstock have had a southward inclination, in addition to dipping eastward with the vein. The dip of the vein is to the east, at an angle of from 30 to 45 degrees, while the inclination of the chimneys of ore to the southward is at an angle of from 60 to 75 degrees. This southern dip or inclination will, as many suppose, carry the southern part of the bonanza into the Best & Belcher ground at a certain depth. To reach the Best & Belcher the ore must pass entirely through the lower-levels of the Consolidated Virginia mine. At the depth of 1,700 feet a drift has been run southward into the Best & Belcher ground from the Gould & Curry, and the work of cross-cutting commenced. Even at this depth it is not unlikely that they will tap the bonanza.

Gould & Curry Miner, 1867, collodion/albumen, Timothy H. O'Sullivan. Library of Congress Prints and Photographs Division.

Two hundred feet north of the bonanza we have been examining (the stope at cross-cut No. 3), another stope has been raised (on cross-cut No. 1) toward the 1,400-foot level, and here large quantities of rich ore are being extracted. Crosscut No. 2, about half way between the two stopes mentioned, shows the bonanza to be three hundred feet in width, all of this great distance being a mass of rich ore, and ore that can be sent to the mills without assorting. Think of a mass of silver-ore over eighteen rods in width! In many places a vein of ore three feet in thickness is considered large, and in California veins of gold-bearing quartz that are only from one to six inches in thickness are profitably worked. Compared with such deposits the bonanza is not a vein at all but a field, a district of ore!

No such breadth of silver-ore has ever before been found in any mine in the world. The silver-bearing veins of Europe are but a few feet in width, and to speak to a German miner of a mine in which the breadth of ore was measured by rods would cause him to suppose that he was talking with a crazy man. Even in the richest mines of Mexico and South America they have never had any such astounding width of bonanza. Then they have always been able to keep up their ground with single timbers—posts and caps—which they could not have done with bodies of ore more than a few feet in width. On the Comstock hardly one bonanza has been found that could have been worked by timbering with posts and caps. In order to work the ore-bodies of the Comstock it became necessary to invent a new and special system of timbering.

In this broadest part of the bonanza we find at work a great number of miners, but they are so distributed that we see but a few in any one spot. They work on separate floors, and floor above floor they are digging down the ore. The pyramids of timbers rise to the height of fifty or seventy-five feet, and, as all the heated air of the level ascends to the highest point, it is very hot where the upper gangs of men are at work. In addition to the natural heat of the mine, coming from the heated rock and hot water, the flame of the hundreds of candles and lamps does much to heat the limited atmosphere of the level; besides, the air is vitiated by the breathing of so many men. Candles and lungs rapidly consume the oxygen contained in a given amount of air. In order that the miners in the upper part of the stope may work in something approaching to comfort, there are here small blowers which send up to them through tin tubes a supply of fresh air. Without fresh air from the surface men can no more work in a mine than they could work under the sea in a diving-bell, were no air sent them. These blowers are all driven by small engines run by compressed air, there being in constant operation on the surface two powerful air-compressors that force air down through mains, under a great pressure, for the supplying of the Burleigh drills and the engines in various places on the several levels of the mine.

Besides the air-engines that run the blowers in this part of the mine there are other engines, driven by compressed air, that hoist all of the timbers to the men working in the upper part of the stopes. Nothing is done by hand that can be done by machinery. As the miners always work upwards in extracting ore, there is little heavy handling of the ore itself after it is dug out of the breasts. It is sent down to the floor of the level in chutes, which land it in bins, from which it is drawn out through gates into the cars which convey it to the main shaft, up which it is hoisted to the surface.

In the centre of this part of the bonanza we have on each side of us a width of over nine rods of silver-ore that will mill from $100 to $250, and in many parts of which ore is found that assays five or six hundred dollars. Not only have we this mass of ore on all sides of us, but it also extends to a great height above. On the 1,400, 1,300, 1,200, and the 1,167 foot levels men are at work as we see them here. From the level last named, when the ore was first found, in 1873, they have followed it up to the 1,000-foot level and even above. Fifty feet below the level on which we stand, or on the 1,550-foot level, a long drift has been run through rich ore toward the Ophir mine, and from this drift a number of cross-cuts have been run into the bonanza. On this 1550-foot level a winze has been sunk to the depth of over two hundred feet, all the way in excellent ore. This shows the bonanza to extend, at least, to a depth of over 1,750 feet. Near the stope on cross-cut No. 1, about the California line, is seen some of the richest ore found in the great bonanza. At this point comes in what is called a "horse," which is a huge mass of propylite (generally spoken of as porphyry in the mines), which tumbled into the vein from the upper or hanging wall at the time of the formation of the fissure. This "horse" crowds the ore into a smaller space, and the ore-body is here only about twelve rods in width, but the greater part of it is immensely rich—such as will yield from $300 to $600 per ton.

Here are frequently found deposits of stephanite, or silver in the form of crystals. This is almost pure silver. In the places where the stephanite occurs there are frequently found nests of pure, malleable silver in the shape of flattened wires that look as though they had been pulled in two, and in springing back after breaking had coiled up against the pieces of ore on which they are found. Some of these wires have the lustre of metallic silver, but the greater part are blackened as though by the fumes of sulphur. Some of the smaller and finer wires on being unrolled and straightened out are found to be a foot or more in length, and often have several branches, when they somewhat resemble sea-moss, or some similar vegetable production. The old Mexican mine was particularly rich in specimens of this kind. In that mine they were found in a kind of yellow clay in the crevices occurring in the mass of the ore.

Free gold, in glittering spangles, is also very frequently found in the places where the rich deposits of black sulphuret of silver, and native silver occur. A large percentage of the value of the ores of all the mines on the Comstock is in gold. In many instances the bullion extracted is fifty percent gold. In that part of the bonanza through which passes the line between the California and the Consolidated Virginia Companies, it is an easy matter to find ore that assays from $1,000 to $5,000 or $10,000 per ton, but this is, of course, only in places where the strength of the vein appears to have concentrated.

At the time that the first cross-cut (No. 1) was run through this part of the bonanza, at a point about fourteen feet south of the California line, a chamber about ten feet square was opened (at a point marked "winze down to 1,550" on the map) the walls of which were a solid mass of black sulphuret ore flecked with native silver, while the roof was filled with stephanite, or silver in the form of crystals. This was one of the richest spots found in that part of the bonanza, and the masses of ore taken out were almost pure silver. Many magnificent specimens for cabinets were taken from this chamber and parts of the mine adjoining, some of them little else but stephanite and wires of native silver. The whole cross-cut through this part of the mine showed an average assay of $600 per ton. Bottom, top, sides were all the same. Look where you might you saw but a solid mass of black sulphuret ore mingled with the pale green ore containing chloride of silver.

Two mining superintendents were one day discussing the bonanza, when *one* of them said to his brother silver-hunter: "Supposing the Almighty to have given you full power and authority to make such a body of ore as you pleased, could you have made a better than this?"

"I don't know that I could," said the other, "but I should have made it still bigger."

"Well," said the first speaker, "you have more cheek than any man I ever saw!"

CHAPTER LXV

AGGREGATED WEALTH

*A Fortune in One Foot—Future Prospects—What Yet Remains—
Undiscovered Bonanza—Figures Before Facts—Facts After Figures—
Distribution of the Wealth—Its Influence*

In the California ground the bonanza extends through to the Ophir, the next mine north, and by the cross-cuts run into it every one hundred feet, it is shown to be—as far as explored—from one hundred and fifty to two hundred and fifty feet in width, and everywhere are found the rich chloride and sulphuret ores. At the present writing (August 1875,) no ore has been extracted from the California, except that taken out in running drifts and cross-cuts. The ground, however, as far as developed, has been laid off in large blocks by means of drifts and cross-cuts, therefore is ready to be mined whenever it is necessary to extract ore for reduction, which will be whenever the company's new mill is completed.

In the California ground are found the same nests of stephanite and other extraordinarily rich ores as are seen in the Consolidated Virginia mine. While these form no large part of the bonanza, they are sufficiently large and numerous to very materially swell the average value of the deposit. (The Consolidated Virginia Company extracts five hundred tons of ore per day. This is the average daily yield from all parts of the mine—from the 1,500-foot level, and from the levels above. Although much of the ore from the upper levels is of low grade, yet the whole averages $100 per ton in the mills. The yield of the mine has regularly been $50,000 per day, or from $1,500,000 to $1,600,000 per month ever since the work of reaching ore from the bonanza began. Much of the ore on the 1,500-foot level is too rich to be economically worked alone by pan process, therefore it is mixed with poorer ore from certain parts of the upper levels. Much more than 500 tons of ore per day might be extracted were it necessary, but that is all that is required to keep the mills of the company in operation.

Opened as it now is, there can easily be extracted from the California mine as many tons of ore per day as are being taken out of the Consolidated Virginia, and ore that will average even higher, as the upper levels of the California are all intact. There is not the slightest doubt that when the California mill shall be started up, these two mines will produce $3,000,000 per month, or $34,000,000 per year; and not for one or two, but for many years—ten years at least, in which time would be extracted $360,000,000. A single foot of ground taken out across the whole width of the bonanza in its widest part would contain a fortune for any man of moderate desires. Should we go into the centre of the Consolidated Virginia ground and take a slice from the bonanza 250 feet in width and extending one level below and two levels above the 1,500-foot level we should then have a section of ore 300 feet long, 250 feet in width, and one foot thick. This would contain 75,000 cubic feet, and containing thirteen cubic feet to the ton would weigh a trifle over 5,769 tons, which at $100 per ton would amount to $576,900 for a single slice of the bonanza one foot in width. By continuing to cut off such slices until we had reached the California line—say 230 feet—we should have in all $132,687,000.

At a time when the Consolidated Virginia mine was much less extensively developed than at present, Mr. I. E. James, a mining engineer who has been engaged on the Comstock for many years, made an estimate of the ore contained in the mine at the time. He took from the working plans of the mines the actual length of each drift and the cross-cuts measured by sections, and measured all triangles separately. The winzes were measured no lower than they had been sunk, and in no place did he estimate ore which had not yet been opened. The amount of ore thus found was 20,669,500 cubic feet. The usual calculation is thirteen cubic feet of ore to the ton, but in order to make ample allowances for "horses" and waste rock two feet were added and fifteen cubic feet reckoned to a ton, giving 1,377,966 tons, which at $100 per ton amounts to $137,796,600, and at $200, as many estimate, the average of the ore in the bonanza proper, would amount to $275,593,200. Mr. James G. Fair, superintendent of the mine, puts the cost of milling and mining at $17 per ton, but calling it $18, it cost to mine and mill the number of tons mentioned $24,803,388. Subtracting this from the gross amounts at $100 and at $200 per ton, and dividing the product by the number of shares in the mine,

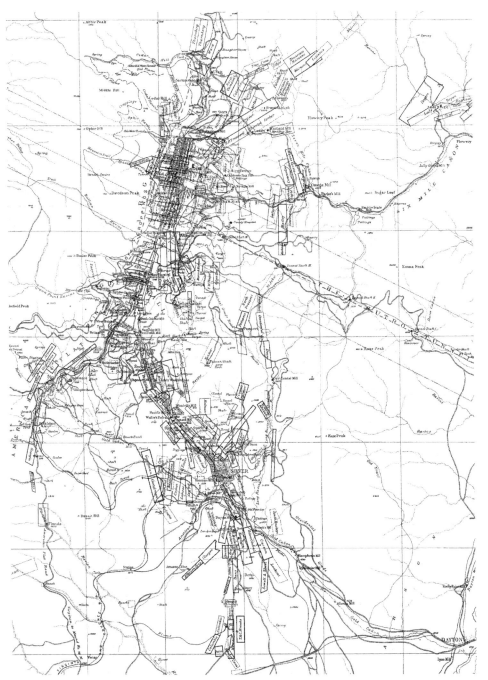

Outline Map of Washoe District Nev, Showing Comstock Lode etc. (detail), 1877, lithograph, George M. Wheeler 1876-1877 Expeditions, Corps of Engineers, U.S. Geological Surveys. Collection of Mark Diederichsen.

namely 108,000, and it is found that if the ore averages $100 per ton, each share of stock will receive in net dividends $1,046 and at $200 per ton will receive $2,322 in dividends. The stock is selling at about $400 per share, and a dividend of $10 per share $1,080,000 in all is paid regularly every month.

Whatever amount of wealth there may be in the Consolidated Virginia and California mines it is evident that their owners are quite confident that they will continue to yield as at present for many years to come, otherwise they would not expend money as lavishly as they are doing in preparations for their long continued and more extensive working. They are sinking a new and very large shaft 1,000 feet east of the present main shaft of the Consolidated Virginia, the machinery to be set up at which will cost $200,000. Through a drift run from this shaft ore will be extracted from both the California and the Consolidated Virginia mines. The two companies are equally interested in the shaft. The new mill being erected by the California Company will cost $400,000. The mill containing the stamps will be near the mine, and the crushed ore as it runs from the batteries will be conveyed in a flume to the pan-mill, nearly half a mile below on Six Mile Cañon.

Besides these heavy expenditures the two companies have bought 12,000 acres of timber-land high in the Sierras, to which has been constructed a flume through which to float wood, lumber, and timber, and the cost of this flume (twenty-one miles in length) was $250,000. These grand and expensive preparations show that the companies in question are but getting ready to mine.

Notwithstanding that this Comstock bonanza is the largest and richest deposit of silver in the world, none of the scientific men of America have yet taken the trouble to visit and examine it. It has been visited by many mining men from Europe, however. The majority of the European visitors are Englishmen, though many Germans and Frenchman, and a few Russians, have come to see and inspect this wonder of the modern mining world. All these foreigners are not only astounded at the great size and richness of the vein, but are also forced to admit that the mining and milling machinery of Nevada is far superior to anything of the kind to be found in Europe.

The northern extremity of the bonanza penetrates the Ophir ground where, however, it as yet appears to be somewhat broken and is found to lie in huge detached masses, between the 1300 and the 1600-foot levels. Much of the ore found is exceedingly rich, carrying a large percentage of gold. Stopes have been opened in several places in the Ophir, and ore is being extracted at the rate of three hundred tons per day. Here, too, are being made very extensive preparations for future mining operations. Hoisting-machinery for the incline is being erected that will be capable of sinking to the depth of 4,000 feet—well on toward a mile. Machinery for the pumping from the same great depth is also being erected. Their present greatest depth is 1700 feet, at which point they are drifting for the vein. Their present shaft is on a line, north and south, with the Consolidated Virginia, and Gould & Curry shafts, and is about one thousand feet east of the old shaft, and the point where silver was first discovered in 1859 by Pat McLaughlin and Peter O'Riley.

It is a circumstance worthy of note that fourteen years after the discovery of silver, the big bonanza, the mammoth deposit of the lode, should be found near where the first silver ore was turned up to the light of day. About one thousand feet eastward from the spot where O'Riley and McLaughlin first saw and wondered at the strange "blue stuff" in the bottom of their rocker we now have the bonanza, a second wonder. Still to the eastward one of these days a third will be found. Out of the first bonanza, into the top of which O'Riley and McLaughlin luckily struck their picks, was taken about $20,000,000 before the deposit was exhausted; out of the Consolidated Virginia mine alone has already been taken $15,500,000 and as yet they have hardly begun working in real earnest, What they have worked out in the bonanza is as one room to a whole block of buildings. In regard to what is still below, they only know that at the greatest depth yet attained they still have the same rich ore that is found on the 1500-foot level.

By referring to the map of the 1500-foot level it will be seen that the Consolidated Virginia Company still have a great amount of unexplored ground lying to the southward of where they have drifted and opened stopes in the great ore-body. What is in the ground remains to be seen, but undoubtedly it contains a vast amount of rich ore. As is to be seen, the California Company have to the eastward a vast unexplored region into which no less than five cross-cuts, one hundred feet apart, are being extended. All of these are in ore of the richest character, and the width of the bonanza at that point is likely to prove as great as at cross-cut No. 2, in the Consolidated Virginia, namely eighteen or twenty rods. To cut off and estimate "slices" through the whole length of the California ground would count up more hundreds of millions of dollars than I dare name. When the new mill of the California Company shall have gone into operation, silver will be produced so rapidly, and in such amount as to astonish the world, and may perhaps reduce the market value of the metal. When they begin the work of extracting ore they will be able to take out all that they can reduce in their own mill and as many other mills as they can secure, whether the amount required be five hundred or one thousand tons per day.

In the Mexican and Union Consolidated mines, lying just north of the Ophir, the work of prospecting has but recently been commenced, yet very promising assays are obtained. The Sierra Nevada mine, which lies next to the Union Consolidated, on the north, has yielded a large amount in gold from surface earth, and from decomposed rock and earth extracted a short distance below the surface, but as yet nothing that could be called a bonanza has been found. In the early days, about 1862, a great deal of gold was extracted from the surface earth by washing with the hydraulic apparatus, as the placer-mines of California are worked. As at Gold Hill, and at the head of Six Mile Cañon were found great bonanzas where were at first found gold-diggings on the surface; so the Sierra Nevada Company may yet expect to find a bonanza in some part of the large mountain on which their mine is located. To the eastward of the mines in which is situated the big bonanza a score of new claims have been located, and on many of these, machinery has been set up, and large shafts are being rapidly sunk. A new bonanza is liable to be found in this direction, as it is a part of the silver belt that has been but little explored.

The excitement in regard to the grand development in the Consolidated Virginia and California mines had the effect of sending up the price of stocks along the whole line of the Comstock. Mines that could show no manner of improvements in their prospects went up with the rest, under the pressure of the excitement. The aggregate value of mines in Virginia and Gold Hill districts, whose stocks are called in the San Francisco Stock Board, was about $93,000,000 November 22, 1874. On the same day of the following month their market value was as follows:

ANDES	$250,000
ARIZONA & UTAH	18,000
ALPHA	159,000
AMERICAN FLAT	240,000
BALTIMORE CONSOLIDATED	450,000
BACON	240,000
BELCHER	5,720,000
BEST & BELCHER	3,528,000
BULLION	1,700,000
CALEDONIA	520,000
CALIFORNIA	54,000,000
CHOLLAR	2,464,000
CONFIDENCE	1,123,200
CONSOLIDATED VIRGINIA	54,000,000
CONSOLIDATED GOLD HILL QUARTZ	140,000
CROWN POINT	5,200,000
CHALLENGE	600,000
CROWN POINT RAVINE	100,000
DARDANELLES	670,000
ECLIPSE	250,000
EMPIRE MILL	800,000
EXCHEQUER	900,000
GLOBE	25,000
GOULD & CURRY	2,880,000
HALE & NORCROSS	1,024,000
IMPERIAL	1,900,000

JULIA	210,000
JUSTICE	1,470,000
KENTUCK	660.000
KNICKERBOCKER	120,000
KOSSUTH	216,000
LADY WASHINGTON	7 5,000
LEO	40,000
MEXICAN	3,456,000
NEW YORK CONSOLIDATED	144,000
OPHIR	18,900,000
OVERMAN	2,944,000
ROCK ISLAND	125,000
SAVAGE	2,000,000
SEGREGATED BELCHER	960,000
SILVER HILL	540,000
SIERRA NEVADA	340,000
SUCCOR	114,000
TRENCH	50,000
UNION CONSOLIDATED	1,400,000
UTAH	160,000
WHITMAN	150,000
WOODVILLE	252,000
YELLOW-JACKET	1,920,000
TOTAL	$175,147,200

By the above it will be seen that the appreciation in the value of forty-nine mines was over $82,000,000 in thirty days. Besides the mines given in the above list there were a score more that have a market value, all of which were more or less affected by the excitement, and were bought by persons who not having money to purchase bonanza stocks were yet determined to get into mines of some kind.

The body of ore in the California and Consolidated Virginia mines, known as the "Big Bonanza" is by no means the only bonanza found on the Comstock that was worth having. From the first Ophir bonanza was extracted, all told, about $20,000,000; from the Savage, $15,750,000; Hale & Norcross, $8,000,000; Chollar-Potosi, $16,000,000; Gould & Curry, $15,550,000; Yellow-Jacket, $15,000,000; Crown Point, $20,000,000; Belcher, $25,000,000; Overman, $3,000,000; Imperial, $2,500,000, and many other mines sums running into millions, or well up in the hundreds of thousands. The Belcher and Crown Point mines are still yielding about 500 tons of ore each per day. The Belcher mine has paid its stockholders dividends to the amount of $14,135,000; the stockholders of the Crown Point have received $11,588,000; the Consolidated Virginia has paid $9,720, 000; Chollar-Potosi, $3,080,000; Gould & Curry, $3,826,800; Hale & Norcross, $1,598,000; Savage, $4,440,000; Yellow-Jacket, $2,184,000; and many others sums ranging from fifty thousand to one million dollars.

There is, of course, a vast deal of money paid out in the shape of assessments levied for the purpose of opening new mines, and sometimes on mines already opened, when they get into a "bad streak"—are in "borrasca"—but, taking all kinds of mines together, the dividends have far exceeded the assessments. From first to last, on all the mines the stock of which is bought and sold in the San Francisco Stock Board, there have been levied assessments amounting to $54,258,500; showing a balance of $28,256,708 in favor of the mines; there is also the present market value of the mines to be taken into consideration, which is a grand item.

The mines of the Comstock give life to the whole Pacific Coast, and are the main-spring, so to speak, of all kinds of trades and every kind of business. They furnish to the California mechanic that employment which gives him his bread. The army of workmen of all kinds, who were employed in the building of the famous Palace Hotel, of San Francisco, the largest and most costly structure of the kind in the world, were all paid with money taken out of the mines of the Comstock. Washoe money also reared the Nevada Block, and scores more of the finest and most costly buildings in San Francisco—buildings which are the pride of the city.

All the foundries and machine-shops of San Francisco and other large towns on the Pacific Coast are running day and night to fill orders from Nevada for engines, boilers, pumps, and all manner of mining machinery; but for the Washoe silver-mines nearly all the workmen employed in these foundries and machine-shops would be obliged to migrate to some other land. The ranchmen and fruit-growers of California would find times very dull with them but for Nevada, as in the towns of the silver-mines, they always find a market for all their products at high prices in ready coin. Without the "big bonanza," and the many other silver-mines of all classes in Nevada, times would be very different from what they now are in San Francisco, and, indeed, throughout California and over the whole Pacific Coast.

The influence of the Washoe silver-mines does not stop on the Pacific Coast, but extends throughout the United States and is also felt in Europe. Not only are manufacturing establishments in California running to fill orders for machinery for the mines of Nevada, but many establishments in the Atlantic States and a few in European countries are also at work on certain kinds of machinery required in the silver-mines; as steel-wire cables, air compressor power-drills, and the like. Not alone to the deposit of ore in one or two mines, but to the whole Comstock lode should be given the name of the "Big Bonanza."

CHAPTER LXVI

Concerning Ventilation

Too Hot for Comfort—Blowers—Down Deep—The Sutro Tunnel

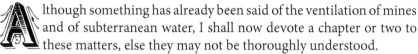

lthough something has already been said of the ventilation of mines and of subterranean water, I shall now devote a chapter or two to these matters, else they may not be thoroughly understood.

The proper ventilation of a mine is a matter of the first importance. Without ventilation no mine can be worked. Without ventilation the whole mine, even to the mouth of the shaft, would be filled with stagnant and foul air, in which men could not live for half a minute. No mine can be worked unless air from the surface of the earth is introduced into it. It is even impossible to sink a straight shaft to the depth of one hundred and fifty or two hundred feet—all the circumstances being the most favorable possible—without carrying fresh air down to the men working in its bottom. When mining was first begun on the Comstock, wind-sails were used to carry air down into the shafts. This is a contrivance of cotton-cloth, and is a cross between a sail and a bag. The mouth of the baggy sail is turned to the wind, and when it fills, air is forced down a tube that leads from its lower end. Sometimes air was forced into a shaft by means of a common blacksmith's bellows—slow and hard work. When water and a proper amount of fall can be obtained, a water-blast is sometimes used. In this the water falling through a tube carries down with it and forces into the shaft or mine a certain amount of air.

At the present time, however, the only manner in which air is forced into mines is by means of rotary blowers or fans—precisely the same as those used at the foundries for furnishing a blast to the cupolas in which iron is melted. At all of the mines along the Comstock these blowers are seen in operation. The best, cheapest, and most thorough means of ventilation is by making connection with the shaft of an adjoining mine. The moment such connection is made, the air from the surface goes down one shaft and comes up the other. In passing to the shaft through which it again rises to the surface, the air, of course, takes the most direct route, yet a great volume of pure air is introduced into the two mines. By means of doors fitted to the connecting drifts between the two mines, the air thus introduced may be distributed pretty evenly through the principal levels, as it can be made to circulate at a considerable distance from what would be its direct and natural route.

In all mines, however, there are always drifts, cross-cuts, winzes, and upraises in remote places to which it is impossible to convey the air circulating in the body of the mine. To provide a supply of air at these points the blowers are used. They send a column of air down into the mine through a large iron pipe, and on the several levels are smaller pipes which convey it to where it is required. In many of the mines there are small blowers on the lower-levels that are run by engines driven by compressed air. These are very useful in furnishing a supply of air in out-of-the-way places.

It is not only necessary to furnish pure air for the miners to breathe, but fresh air is required in great volume to cool off the rock and keep down the heat in the drifts and crosscuts of the lower-levels. As the shafts and inclines increase in depth there is a constant and corresponding increase of heat in the rocks into which the works are advanced. At the depth of from 1,500 to 2,000 feet the rock is so hot that it is painful to the naked hand. In many places, from crevices in the rock, or from holes drilled into it, streams of boiling water gush out. In these places the thermometer often shows a temperature of from one hundred and twenty to one hundred and thirty degrees. It is as hot as in the hottest Turkish bath. In these places men could not live but for the supply of cool air that is pumped into the drift or other place in which they are at work; even then the temperature often remains as high as one hundred and ten degrees. The rock in a newly opened level retains its heat for months, however much air may be brought into the mine. Nearly all the leading mines on the Comstock are down to where the rock is exceedingly hot. The Crown Point and Belcher Companies are down 1,700 feet; Yellow-Jacket, 1,740; Bullion, 1,700; Imperial-Empire, 2,100; Gould & Curry, Best & Belcher, Consolidated Virginia, and Ophir, each 1,700; while the Savage Company are down nearly 2,300, and the Hale & Norcross, about 2,200. In the two mines last named they find it fearfully hot. As the Savage Company have started up machinery capable of sinking to the depth of 4,000 feet, they will presently be in danger of dropping into the great central fires of the earth.

As depth is attained it is found necessary to increase the size and capacity of the blowers used and the main pipes through which the air is forced into the mines have now been increased to about two feet in diameter, whereas the diameter of those first used was only about six inches. With a small pipe the air backs up on the blower and there is a waste of power. The pipe should be so large that there is no longer any perceptible back-pressure—so large that all the air blown into it finds an abundance of room in which to advance without encountering the resistance of its own elasticity. The pipes should be enlarged until the air goes through without any rebounding.

It is a question in many minds whether the miners of Nevada have gone the right way about the ventilation of their mines; whether instead of forcing air into the lower-levels they should not pump the foul and heated air out, when pure air would rush down and fill the vacuum thus created. In the mines of Germany they practice this plan of pumping out the foul air. In Nevada, however, it is not likely that it would answer so good a purpose as the plan of pumping in fresh air. By blowing in air as is now practiced there is always more or less good air at the face of a drift about the end of the pipe, but by the pumping-out plan the air surrounding the end of the pipe would be sucked into it, and that which would reach the men would be such as flowed a long distance in contact with the heated rock forming the walls of the cross-cut or drift. American miners work so fast that the rock does not have much time in which to cool behind them. Therefore the better plan for them seems to be the reverse of that practiced in the Old World.

It remains to be seen what effect the Sutro Tunnel will have in creating a circulation of air in the lower-levels of the mines when it shall have been completed. This tunnel, about which so much has been said in Congress and elsewhere, starts at the edge of the valley of the Carson River, in a south-easterly direction from Virgina City, and is intended to tap the Comstock lode at the depth of 200 feet. Its total length will be 20,145 feet. Work was commenced on it in October, 1859, and it has now been extended a distance of between nine and ten thousand feet. About 1,100 feet of the tunnel, from the mouth in, has been made of full size, twelve by sixteen feet; the remainder, what is called the header, is six by seven feet in size.

There are along the line of the tunnel, which runs under several mountains of considerable size, four shafts. These were designed to be sunk down to the level of the tunnel, when work on the tunnel might be prosecuted in two directions from the bottom. Shaft No. 1 is located at a distance of 4,915 feet from the mouth of the tunnel; shaft No. 2, 9,065 feet from the mouth of the tunnel; No. 3, 13,545 feet from the mouth of the tunnel; and shaft No. 4, 17,695 feet from the same point, and 2,450 feet from the point where the tunnel will intersect the Comstock lode. Shafts Nos. 1 and 2 are down to the level of the tunnel and work has been done through them. Shaft No. 1 is 523 feet, and shaft No. 2, 1,041 feet in depth. Shafts Nos. 3 and 4 are not yet down to the level of the tunnel, the "header" of which is progressing between shafts Nos. 2 and 3. When the tunnel shall have been completed, there will be a connection between the Comstock lode and shaft No. 4 through which there will be a circulation of air. This shaft (No. 4) will be 1,485 feet in depth, and when the connection is made the air will either pass down it, along the tunnel a distance of 2,450 feet and out through the mines at the point of intersection, or will pass down through the mines and out through the shaft. Which way the draught will be, no man can say, as the course of currents of air underground is governed by laws not yet well understood. Whichever way the draught may be, however, there will be a great improvement in the circulation of the air in the lower-levels of the adjacent mines, to the depth of 2,000 feet.

However diligently work may be prosecuted on the Sutro Tunnel, it must be some years yet before it can be completed to the point of intersection with the Comstock lode. Meantime there is being sunk at the distance of about 2,000 feet east of the lode, and about 450 or 500 feet west of shaft No. 4 of the Sutro Tunnel, a shaft which will be the largest and most perfect in every respect ever sunk in that country. This shaft is being sunk by a combination of three leading mining companies—the Chollar-Potosi, Savage, and Hale & Norcross. It will be ten by thirty feet in size, divided into four compartments by stout plank partitions, and the machinery placed over it will be of a capacity to sink it to the depth of one mile.

Rapid progress is being made in the sinking of this great shaft. At proper intervals drifts will be run from it to the Comstock lode. The first drift will probably be run at the depth of 2,000 feet, and it will reach the lode long before the completion of the Sutro Tunnel, and as regards ventilation, will

Plate I.

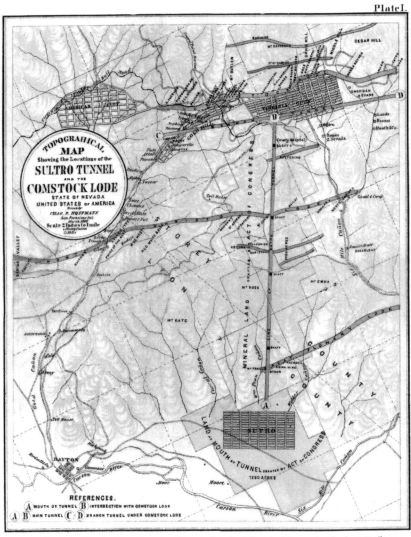

Topographical Map Showing Sutro Tunnel and Comstock Lode, 1866, color lithograph, Charles F. Hoffmann. Collection of Mark Diederichsen. North is to the right on this map.

do all that could be expected of the tunnel. As two or three of the leading mines are already working at a depth of nearly 2,500 feet, the big shaft must be looked to for ventilation, everywhere below the depth of 2,000 feet; therefore below this depth drifts will doubtless be run between the lode and the shaft at frequent intervals.

Owing to the lead dipping to the east at an angle of from thirty to fifty degrees, the distance necessary to be run to connect the lode and shaft will constantly decrease until at a certain depth the shaft itself will cut the lead, after which time the drift to reach and ventilate the vein must be run to the eastward. A branch-track connects this shaft with the main Virginia and Truckee Railroad.

Inside the Sutro Tunnel, 1862, collodion/albumen, attributed to Charles L. Weed (Lawrence & Houseworth). Library of Congress Prints and Photographs Division.

CHAPTER LXVII

BELOW THE WATER-DEPOSITS
Deeper than a Well—Bottom Dropped Out—Creeping Propensities— A Skull Discovered—An Unlucky Slip

In countries where no mining is done it is the prevalent opinion that at a certain depth the earth is full of water, and that the deeper we go the more water will abound. This is a mistaken notion. After delving beyond certain bounds, water ceases to be generally disseminated in the earth. This is after we have gone below the "scalp" or surface-water of the country. Until we have passed through this scalp, water is found almost everywhere. This being the case, it is quite natural that persons residing in countries where wells sunk in search of a supply of water are the deepest works of the kind undertaken, should imagine overwhelming floods of water to exist everywhere far down in the bowels of the earth.

In Nevada—and the rule probably holds good in every country— after passing the more open and softer matter—drift and rock—there is reached the solid rocky mass forming what might be termed the "skull" of the earth—the hard shell lying between the comparatively spongy exterior strata, and the molten interior mass. This intermediate shell of hard rock is where the miners along the Comstock are now delving in all the deeper mines. Here we find that solid rock takes the place of water in most situations—solid rock is the rule. When the rock is not solid and perfectly homogeneous, there water finds its way and forms subterranean reservoirs of all sizes and shapes, which, in mining parlance, are called "pockets."

These pockets may be of almost any shape, but are generally in the form of a crevice. As a rule, the crevices are not open spaces like caverns, but are filled with some permeable material into which the water may find its way and settle, as in the ground composing the "scalp" above.

The water at the depth of from 1,000 to 2,000 feet lies in detached bodies. In the country-rock (the rock lying on each side of a vein and forming the general rock of the country) there are fewer of these pockets of water than within the bounds of a vein, as the solidity and homogenous character of the outside rock leaves no space in which water may be contained. The Comstock lode occupying an immense fissure, extending into the intermediate crust of the earth to an indeterminate depth, there are naturally many openings in it, through which water may descend; besides, the material of which the vein is composed is in general much softer, and therefore more pervious than the great mass of rock outside of the vein. The pockets of water are confined within walls of clay or hard, impervious rock. Thus drifts may be run on all sides of, and even under, these subterranean reservoirs, and no water is seen until the confining walls are cut. When a body of clay is encountered and there is reason to suspect that a body of water is being approached, a long drill is used with which to feel the way in advance of the drift, and let the water out, if any there be, in a controllable stream. Were the miners to push ahead with a drift of full size, the pressure of water would presently burst in the whole face of their opening, tear down the timbers, cause extensive caving of the ground, and perhaps flood everything, and drown the men before they could escape.

When once the works of a mine have been carried down into the solid shell of the earth, the work of draining any body of water that may be encountered is a mere question of time. If the underground cistern is small it is soon pumped out; if large it takes a proportionally longer time, the same pump being used in each case; but, sooner or later, it must be exhausted. If water were not thus found in detached bodies (instead of being universally diffused) in that zone of the earth under consideration, there could be mining under seas, lakes, and rivers, as is now successfully practiced in many countries.

In illustration of the manner in which miners often drift under and around bodies of water, I may give an incident of the early days of Washoe, when drifts and tunnels had not yet drained off the surface-water, and wells were yet a possibility in Virginia City.

A lady resident of the town one day went to a well in her door-yard to draw some water. Being in haste, she let the bucket go down from the windlass "by the run," and the instant it struck the water out dropped the whole bottom of the well. Every drop of water instantly disappeared and nought was seen where it had been, but a black, yawning chasm in which hung and dangled the bucket. Amazed almost beyond the power of speech, the lady for a time stood and gazed into the bottomless well, then rushed to the house. She had considered the matter and comprehended it.

"What did I tell you?" cried she, addressing her rather easygoing husband. "I knew that the men who dug that well were taking no pains with their work!"

"What is the matter now?" said the husband.

"Matter?—matter enough! The bottom has dropped out of the well!"

"Bottom dropped out of the well!" exclaimed the husband, beginning to become interested.

"Yes: the bottom has dropped out of the well, and I am not at all surprised—I am not one bit astonished! I knew when I saw the men putting the bottom in that well that it would never be of any account!"

The cause of the accident was simple enough. The well had been dug in the line of a tunnel advancing from a distant point below. The miners, all unconscious of the presence of the well, had drifted under it, and at no great distance below its bottom. Being without adequate support the bottom must soon have fallen out, of its own accord, but the sudden jar of the bucket on the surface of the water undoubtedly precipitated the event. A peculiar kind of clay is found in many places on the Comstock lode which is not a little curious on account of its creeping propensities. A stratum of this clay will be seen to crawl out into tunnels and other openings in a manner much resembling the action of the toy known as Pharaoh's serpents. You are unable to see where it is coming from or what moves it, yet it is constantly crawling out into all the openings that reach it.

In places where drifts have been run into this clay it is necessary to keep one or two men constantly at work at cutting it away in order to keep the drifts open and passable. This is not owing to the slaking and swelling of the exposed surface, as in that case after a few removals of the surplus material a hole would be left, and there would be no more trouble. The whole body of the clay appears to be creeping. It has the almost imperceptible motion of the glacier, irresistibly advancing, crushing everything in the shape of timbers that may be placed before it. All that can then be done is to set men to work at cutting it off as fast as it comes out. The cause of this creeping is probably to be found in the pressure of the superincumbent or surrounding strata of rock. Its motion is not unlike that seen in the straightening out of a piece of pith that has been compressed. There is a limit to this creeping power of the clay, but it is not reached till many feet have crept out into the drift, tunnel, shaft, or chamber, and have been cut off and removed. Its action is so mysterious that some of the miners are ready to explain it by saying that the clay comes out and fills up the drifts because "Nature abhors a vacuum."

If left to its course the clay would very soon close up the drift, as completely as if none had ever been made. Thousands of feet of drifts and tunnels in the mines are closed in this way.

In the Caledonia mine, American Flat, much trouble was experienced with this creeping clay. On one occasion a streak of it two or three feet in width continued to rise from the floor of a tunnel until over thirty feet had thus come up and been cut off. It is bad anywhere, but is most mischievous in the main shaft. For this reason mining men always seek a spot in which to put down such shafts, where they are likely to pass through solid "country-rock" to a great depth below surface. The sad experience of early days taught them this lesson. The clay is generally found within the wall of the vein. It abounds in the mines south of Gold Hill, about American Flat. The ordinary clay found next to the foot, and hanging walls in all mines is liable to swell—on account of the lime it contains—when exposed to atmospheric action, but after the pressure on the timbers has been eased by cutting away behind them a few times, there is no more trouble.

The power of this swelling, slacking clay is immense. It crushes in, and splinters all the timbers that can be placed before it: it somewhat resembles the power exerted in the expansion and contraction of large masses of iron, as seen in iron bridges and similar structures. The following curious Comstock "find" may be of interest to some readers.

In working out the first or upper bonanza of the Ophir mine, there was brought to light a human skull of a very ancient and curious type. The skull was dug out where a drift was being run in the ore-body at a depth of about three hundred feet below the surface. It was brought out, and dumped with a carload of ore, not being observed by the miners. United States District Judge A. W. Baldwin, since killed by a railroad accident in California, happened to be present when the car-load of ore was dumped. Seeing an object of peculiar shape roll toward his feet among the ore dumped from the car, the Judge picked it up, and found it to be a human skull of a peculiar form and thickly crusted over with sulphuret of silver. He carried it into town and presented it to Wm. Shepard, of the firm of Tinker & Shepard, who placed it in a cabinet of curiosities, where it still remains.

The skull attracted no attention outside of Virginia City until 1874, when, mention being made of it in the newspapers, the Academy of Sciences, of San Francisco, sent for it for the purpose of making a critical examination of it. While it was in San Francisco a plaster cast was made of it, and at a meeting of the Academy of Sciences, Dr. Blake exhibited the cast and spoke of it as follows: "There is in this skull a peculiarity that is seen in some of the ancient Peruvian skulls, namely, on interparietal bone. The general *contour* of the skull is of a very low type; the anterior portion is very slightly developed and receding; the hinder portion is largely developed. It bears a similarity to the skull of the carnivorous apes, the cavity for the lower jaw-bone being very deep and not allowing of any grinding motion of the jaws. The skull when found was covered with a metallic layer. It is of a different type from any that have been found, and belonged to a carnivorous man, who could walk easier on all fours than on two feet." Several ancient Peruvian skulls were then produced in order to show the interparietal bone.

Professor Whitney was very anxious to be allowed to send the skull to the Atlantic States and Europe, but the owners would not part with it for that purpose. The plaster cast taken was sent to Dr. J. Wyman, of Cambridge. It would seem that the conclusion arrived at in San Francisco was that the skull was that of a man belonging to a pre-historic race. He probably was adorned with a tail. At the time the great fissure was formed in which the Comstock lode was deposited, or perhaps at the time the fissure was being filled with its rich ores, this pre-historic creature was probably fooling about the edge of the chasm, looking down into it to see what discoveries he could make, when the earth crumbled beneath his weight, and he rolled down and was incorporated in the heart of the vein. His sad fate must have proved a salutary warning to all others of his tribe, as his skull is the only thing in the way of ancient human remains that has ever been found in any mine on the lode.

CHAPTER LXVIII

SOME INTERESTING CREATURES

Carson City—Lizards and Scorpions—A Pleasing Insect—
A Wicked Way of Laying Eggs—Another Agreeable Insect

There are in operation, in all, in the vicinity of the Comstock, mills, the aggregate of whose stamps is over one thousand.

The Consolidated Virginia Company give employment to the following mills: Consolidated mill, sixty stamps and crushing capacity of 230 tons per day; Sacramento mill, 50 tons; Mariposa, 12 stamps, 40 tons; Hoosier State, 18 stamps, 50 tons; Devil's Gate, 10 stamps, 35 tons; Kelsey, 15 stamps, 45 tons; Bacon, 20 stamps, 50 tons; Occidental, 20 stamps, 50 tons; total, 195 stamps, 600 tons per day. The pay-roll of the men employed in these mills amounts to $35,000 per month.

At Silver City, about five miles below Virginia City, on Gold Cañon, are a considerable number of fine mills (some of those mentioned above among the number) in all of which steam is the motive power. A branch of the Virginia and Truckee Railroad runs to Silver City and supplies these mills with ore, wood, and all other articles required. Near the town are several mines—the Silver Hill, Dayton, Kossuth, Daney, and Buckeye—on which are in operation first-class hoisting-works, and the southern continuation of the Comstock is supposed to pass through the ground on which the village stands. It is already a lively camp, boasts a tri-weekly newspaper—the *Lyon County Times*—and should the hopes of the mining-companies now at work in that vicinity be realized, will soon be one of the leading mining-towns of the State.

On the Carson River are a large number of first-class reduction-works that are driven by water-power. The Eureka mill, of the Union Mill and Mining Company, of which company Mr. Sharon is a principal stockholder, is one of the finest mills on the river. It contains sixty stamps (the same number as the Consolidated Virginia mill) and is provided with a proportionate amount of amalgamating-machinery. It is run on ore from the Belcher mine. It is connected with the Virginia and Truckee Railroad by a tramway over two miles in length. The Brunswick mill, also on the river, contains fifty-six stamps and works Crown Point ore. The Merrimac, Santiago, Morgan, and Mexican mills are all on the Carson River and receive their supplies of ore over the Virginia and Truckee Railroad. Some of these mills are very picturesquely situated, being surrounded by high, rocky hills and having near them, on the bars of the river, handsome groves of willow and Cottonwood trees.

Carson City contains no mills, but the interests of her business men are identified with those of the mining towns above. The town, which contains about 8,000 inhabitants, is situated in Eagle Valley, at the base of the Sierra Nevada Mountains, and contains many fine buildings, both public and private. Carson City is the capital of the State. The capitol building and the United States' Mint are imposing structures, built of a handsome grey sandstone obtained at the State Prison quarry, about one mile east of the town. The Virginia and Truckee Railroad Company have large machine-shops and other large and substantial buildings at Carson.

At Carson trees are grown, and about the town are to be seen some very handsome private grounds. The plaza surrounding the State House, some ten acres in extent, is inclosed by a handsome wrought-iron fence, the successful bidder for the construction of which was an enterprising New England schoolmarm.

Although Carson is an oasis where something in the shape of verdure refreshes the eye, yet to the eastward, northward, and in all directions but westward—where the Sierras rise— all the landscape is made up of brown and sterile hills and mountains capped with piles of grey granite. These hills are not only barren and dreary in aspect, but are, in fact, as desolate as they appear. In traveling among the rocky hills and desert valleys there is apparent an absence of animal life that causes one to feel very lonely. Out in the great wilds all is silence. Not the note of a bird is heard—not a bird is seen. Although the wind may be blowing a gale, nothing is stirred by it, for there is nothing to stir. It seems strange to feel the force of the wind, yet hear no sound from it nor see anything moved by it. In these wild regions we find basking upon the rocks or gamboling over the barren ground great numbers of lizards. They are seen in great variety, and some of them are very handsome, being striped in red, yellow, black, white, brown, and many other colors. Some kinds are over a foot in length. All are very active, and it is a difficult matter to catch them. Some of the larger kinds have long and sharp teeth and know how to use them. I have never heard of anyone being bitten by one of them, but the Mexicans say that the bite of one variety, which has a black ring round its neck, is fatal.

On one occasion I assisted a gentlemen in catching a dozen or more of all kinds, the object being to preserve them in alcohol. They were placed in a sack as caught. On getting home with them, after carrying them about two miles, it was found that they had torn each other to ribbons.

A curious little reptile is found everywhere throughout the country, which is called a horned toad. It grows to be four or five inches in length and looks like a cross between a lizard and a terrapin. What are called its horns are nothing more than several diamond-shaped scales that grow on its head, and which it has the power to erect or depress. It is of a buff color, sprinkled with spots of dull red. Like the chameleon, it appears to live on air. Specimens have been kept for months in glass jars and have never been seen to eat, though flies and other insects in abundance were furnished them. Persons in Nevada sometimes send these pets to friends in the Atlantic States through the mails. They generally go through all right. Scorpions abound among the loose rock on the sides of the hills. They have a sting in the end of the tail with which they are very handy. Their sting is very painful, but not fatal. The antidote is ammonia, taken internally, and rubbed upon the wound. These unpleasant creatures are from three to five inches in length, and present much the appearance of a shrimp or a craw-fish. When the prospector is camped in the hills the scorpion is fond of crawling down his neck as he lies sleeping on the ground. When objection is made to this familiarity the scorpion uses his sting.

A few centipedes are found in the country, but they are not very large or venomous, and are not much boasted of. In the spring of 1875, a lady residing in Silver City awoke one night to find something crawling about in her bed, and getting a light discovered it to be a centipede about eight inches in length. She was stung in two or three places by the insect, but eventually recovered. In countries further south the centipede is more dreaded than the rattlesnake.

Tarantulas are abundant in Nevada, but persons are seldom bitten by them. They are sometimes so large that they stand three inches high when walking, and their legs and bodies covered with hair as long as that of a mouse. Their fangs are about the length of those of a rattlesnake, and the little, found mouth from which they project is blood-red. When the end of an iron ramrod is presented to them their fangs may be heard to grate upon it. They make a nest in the ground about four inches in diameter, which is lined by a fabric, spun by the creature itself, which is as fine and glossy as white satin. A lid, made of small bits of rock and soil glued together, covers the entrance to the nest. The under side of the lid is also lined with the satin-like substance, and is hung on a hinge of the same. Although the tarantula travels slowly, yet when it has reached its nest it darts within it and closes the lid so quickly that the eye can hardly follow its motions. When the lid of the nest has been closed it is a difficult matter to distinguish it, as its upper side presents precisely the same appearance as the pebbles and earth surrounding it. Once it is within its nest the tarantula is able to hold the lid down and to resist any small force used for the purpose of raising it. When the lid is raised the creature shrinks back in its nest and there sits with its malignant little eyes shining like two beads of jet.

Tarantula, Carson River Pet, 1876, collodion/albumen, Carleton E. Watkins. California State Library.

By using great care the nest of the tarantula may be extracted from the ground, when it is found to be a ball about four inches in diameter composed of agglutinated pebbles, bits of clay, and other components of the soil in which it is built. In this shape they are sometimes placed in cabinets with the tarantula imprisoned within, a thread being tied over the lid of the nest. A tarantula, however, is not a very desirable pet. The tarantula has an enemy in a large wasp, of which he stands in mortal fear. When the tarantula goes out for a quiet stroll this wasp frequently finds him, and if he is more than a few feet away from his nest he never reaches it.

As vultures appear to drop out of the sky when an animal has fallen dead in the desert, so this wasp, the deadly enemy of the tarantula, comes upon the scene. Straight as an arrow from the bow, and as swift as light, he comes from the upper air and pierces the tarantula through the body. The tarantula turns upon his back and in mortal terror claws the air, but the wasp has disappeared—can nowhere be seen. After watching for a time, with his legs in the air, the tarantula gets upon his feet and travels at his best pace for his nest. Almost instantly there is a whiz, and the wasp has given him another thrust—perhaps two stabs, as he is quick as lightning.

Although I have called the enemy of the tarantula a wasp, it is not a wasp, though looking much like one. The lance which it thrusts into the tarantula is not a sting, but an ovapositor, and at each stab an egg is deposited in the body of the tarantula. All this appears to be well understood by the tarantula himself and from the time the first egg has been planted in his back he seems to feel that his days are numbered; as the egg will soon hatch a grub—a worm—that will devour his vitals. At each encounter the tarantula throws himself upon his back and tries to fend off or to grasp his antagonist with his claws, but the wasp patiently waits somewhere high in the air, till he gets upon his feet, then darts down and pierces him with his lance. The tarantula soon grows weak, and then the wasp thrusts into his body half a dozen eggs at each visit. Soon the tarantula is unable to move and after a few stabs is quite dead. The wasp then digs a hole in the ground two or three inches in depth, crams the dead tarantula down to the bottom of it, and then closes it up. When the eggs of the wasp hatch, the young grubs find their food at hand in the body of the dead tarantula.

Another agreeable insect found in the hills of Nevada is an ant that is armed with a sting. It is black in color, and has a few scattering orange-colored hairs on its back. It is seldom seen, and appears to lead even a more solitary and secluded life than does the tarantula.

CHAPTER LXIX

MILLIONAIRE PROPRIETORS

Mr. John Mackay—The Hon. William Sharon—
How his Fortune was Made—Mr. James C. Fair—
Mr. Samuel S. Curtis—The Hon. J. P. Jones—A Big Business

A chapter giving a few words in regard to persons prominently connected with the big bonanza and the Comstock lode may be of interest to some readers. I cannot undertake to give more than the outlines in each instance. The biography of almost any man who has been ten years on the Pacific Coast would make a large volume, were all of his experiences written up

John Mackay Esq., the millionaire miner of the "big bonanza," was born in the city of Dublin, Ireland, and served his time as a ship-carpenter. He came to California soon after the discovery of gold, and mined at and near Downieville, Sierra county, for many years. In the placer-mines he had his "ups and downs" the same as other miners, and often did a vast amount of hard work for a small amount of gold. Mr. Mackay came to the silver-mines of Washoe in the early days, and for a time after his arrival worked for wages at the Mexican and other mines—swinging a pick and shovel as an ordinary miner. It was not long, however, before he began to get ahead financially, and, it is said, made his first "raise" in the Kentuck mine, Gold Hill. He finally obtained a large interest in the Hale & Norcross mine, Virginia City. Here he took Mr. Fair in as a partner and the two men secured control of the mine, rescinded an assessment that had been levied, and began paying dividends. The Hale & Norcross being "in bonanza," the partners soon had money with which to secure other mines. Finally, in company with Messrs Flood & O'Brien, of San Francisco, they purchased the Consolidated Virginia ground, getting it for about $80,000, and eventually acquired a controlling interest in the California mine.

John W. Mackay, c. 1890, dry plate/albumen, Louis Thors. University of California, Berkeley, Bancroft Library.

Although Mr. Mackay is now worth fifty or sixty million dollars, yet, like Mr. Fair, he spends much of his time, when at Virginia City, in the lower levels. Almost every morning at six o'clock he descends into one or another of his mines, and often remains underground for several hours, passing through all the levels where work is being done, when there is anything that requires his attention. In passing through a level he sees all that is going on at a glance. Mr. Mackay is one of the most modest and unassuming of men, yet he is a shrewd observer of character, and of all that is going on in the world about him. Generally he has but little to say, but that little is to the point—goes directly to the bull's-eye. He is not often misunderstood. He most thoroughly understands mining in all its branches, as there is nothing required to be done in a mine that he has not done with his own hands. No man is more ready to adopt improvements than Mr. Mackay. He is ever ready to spend money for labor-saving machinery. Those of his men who imagine they have discovered a new plan of doing any kind of work whereby a saving in time or muscle can be effected, always find an attentive listener in Mr. Mackay, and all the encouragement they require. He frequently stimulates their inventive faculties by telling them of certain things for which he desires some new mode of working to be thought out, or some new machine to be constructed.

Although one of the most kind-hearted and generous of men—as the hundreds he has befriended can testify—I may here state, for the benefit of a certain class of persons, that he pays no attention to the bushels of silly begging-letters which he receives from all parts of the United States and even from the remotest corners of Europe—all are tumbled into his wastebasket.

Notwithstanding that Mr. Fair is the superintendent of the mine owned by the Arm, Mr. Mackay also does duty as superintendent, and the pair generally hold a grand council on all matters of moment. When this council is in session in the private office at the works, the miners in passing back and forth hold up their fingers to one another as a sign that no noise is to be made that will interfere with the deliberations that are in progress near at hand. No man in Nevada more thoroughly understands the Comstock lode than Mr. Mackay. He has made it his study for years. No change of rock can occur but that he knows what it portends. He appears to know almost every clay-seam, and streak of quartz, and porphyry that runs through the vein. By looking at a sample of ore he can tell the amount of silver it contains almost as well as if he had seen it assayed. He is particularly at home in the northern part of the Comstock, where he has had most acquaintance with the mines, and may be said, to have that part of the lode by heart. As regards mining knowledge, Mr. Mackay is the "boss" of the big bonanza.

William Sharon, c. 1875, collodion/albumen, Mathew Brady. Library of Congress Prints and Photographs Division.

The Hon. William Sharon, who for many years figured so prominently in the mining and milling interests of the Comstock lode as to earn for himself the title of the "King of the Comstock," was born in Jefferson county, Ohio, in 1821. His family were Quakers and his ancestors were among those who settled at Philadelphia with William Penn. When a boy of seventeen Mr. Sharon thought that the life of a boatman would suit him. He purchased an interest in a flatboat, and started down the Ohio River, bound for New Orleans, but "landed his boat" when he reached Louisville. At this point the boat struck a rock in crossing the falls, and was left a total wreck. Mr. Sharon then returned to his native town disgusted with a "seafaring" life, and went to college a few years, then studied law and practiced for a time in St. Louis, Missouri.

Giving up the practice of law on account of bad health, he figured as a merchant, at Carrollton, Illinois, until the discovery of gold in California. He was among those who crossed the Plains in 1849, and in August of that year reached Sacramento, where he purchased a stock of goods and opened a store. The floods of the winter of 1849-50 swept his stock into the Pacific Ocean, leaving him about as he was left when he struck the falls at Louisville, on the Ohio River.

After his store had been carried away by the flood he went down to San Francisco and opened a real-estate office. He continued in this business until 1864, and had accumulated a fortune of $150,000, when he began speculating in mining-stock. In this he again struck the Louisville Falls and again "landed his boat," a total wreck. Being once more foot-loose and ready for anything that might offer in the way of business, he was sent over the Sierras to Virginia City, Nevada, by the Bank of California to look after certain of the affairs of that institution which required attention. After reaching Virginia City he soon arranged all the affairs of the Bank of California, and while looking about and probing into matters in so doing, was shrewd enough to see that he had at last reached the place where all the money on the Pacific Coast was coming from. He at once urged upon the officers of the Bank of California the necessity of opening a branch at Virginia City, which was done and Mr. Sharon was placed at the head of the new institution, with unlimited powers. He remained in Virginia City a number of years as the head of the branch bank in that place, and finally resigned in order to look after affairs of his own, leaving in his place an excellent and capable man in the person of Mr. A. J. Ralston.

Mr. Sharon is the father of the Virginia and Truckee Railroad, undoubtedly the crookedest railroad in the world, and a wonderful road in many other respects. In building this road Mr. Sharon secured a subsidy of $500,000 from the people of Washoe in aid of the project, constructed as much of the road as the sum would build, then mortgaged the whole road for the amount of money required for its completion. In this way he built the road without putting his hand into his own pocket for a cent, and he still owns half the road—worth $2,500,000 and bringing him in as Mr. Adolph Sutro says, $12,000 per day. On this trip he got his boat over the falls in good shape. The road, however, has been of great benefit to the country, and Mr. Sharon was a good man for the country while he was at the head of the Virginia branch of the Bank of California, as he had the nerve to advance money for the development of mines and the building of mills at the time when no outside banking-house would have ventured a cent. He saw that, though some of the mining companies were in "borrasca" there was every likelihood of their being in "bonanza" soon again, provided they were furnished with a sum sufficient to make proper explorations.

Mr. Sharon is the principal owner of the Palace Hotel, San Francisco, the largest and most costly hotel in the world, and of a vast deal of other property in the city named, and in various places in California and Nevada. In all he is probably worth seventy or eighty million dollars. In 1874, he was elected United States' Senator from Nevada, for six years, to take the place of Mr. Stewart. Mr. Sharon has a very clear head, a thorough understanding of financial questions, is a shrewd business man, and a man of large capabilities in all the walks of life.

James G. Fair Esq., one of the principal owners and the superintendent of the Consolidated Virginia and California mines, was born in the north of Ireland. He came to the United States in his youth and settled in Illinois. Upon the discovery of gold in California he determined to try his "luck" as a miner. He left Illinois, in 1849, and reached California, in August, 1850, when he went to Long's Bar, Feather River, called by the Mexicans *el Rio de los Plumas*— the river of feathers.

On Feather River, Mr. Fair learned the art of mining for gold in the bars and river channels, among boulders so large that to look at them made one sick at heart. In 1860 he gave up mining for gold, and made his way across the Sierras to Virginia City, where he

James G. Fair, c. 1881, collodion/albumen, Mathew Brady. Library of Congress Prints and Photographs Division.

has ever since made his home, and where he has constantly been engaged in mining and other enterprises. In 1857 he became the partner of John Mackay in the Hale & Norcross mine, when both he and Mr. Mackay made a "snug bit" of money.

Since becoming partners, Messrs Mackay & Fair, and their associates, Messrs Flood & O'Brien, of San Francisco, who are interested with them in many speculations, have acquired controlling interests in the Gould & Curry, Best & Belcher, Consolidated Virginia, California, Utah, and Occidental mines; also, of the Virginia City and Gold Hill Water-Works, of a large number of quartz-mills, of the Pacific Wood, Lumber, & Fluming Company, in the Sierra Nevada Mountains, and are concerned in various enterprises in California. Messrs Mackay & Fair also have mines in Idaho, Montana, and Utah—have even reached down into Georgia and taken hold of some of the gold-mines in that region, sending old and reliable Comstock mining superintendents to examine and test the mines. They have probably also viewed the New Hampshire silver-mines through their agents, and weighed and estimated Silver Isle, Lake Superior.

At the time of the Arizona diamond excitement, and swindle, Mr. Fair had a man there and all over the ground as soon as the first whisper in regard to the finding of precious stones in that region had gone abroad. While nobody in Virginia City knew that he was taking the slightest interest in the diamond excitement, or that he had even heard of it, Mr. Fair had "prospected" the whole thing and found out all about it. Still he said nothing, and probably not five men on the Comstock range today know that Mr. Fair was close upon the heels of the men who put up the great Arizona diamond swindle and prospected their "salted" ground about as soon as the "salt" was sown. He now has in his house at Virginia City a whole drawer-full of stones of all kinds that were brought to him by the agent he sent down into the diamond-fields.

Samuel T. Curtis, c. 1876, illustration from the first edition of *The Big Bonanza*, after a photograph.

Mr. Fair is a man who never talks when he is acting, and no one knows exactly what "Uncle Jimmy," as the "boys" call him, is up to. You see the hole by which he goes into the ground, but when once he is down out of sight you never know in what direction he is drifting. Mr. Fair is worth thirty or forty million dollars, yet he spends as much time in miner's garb, down in the seething lower levels, and "poking, about" in all manner of old abandoned drifts, and tunnels, as though he were working for four dollars per day, and had a very hard and exacting "boss." He is a shrewd and enterprising business man, and thoroughly understands mines and mining. In his mills he is as much at home as in the mines, and perfectly understands the reduction of silver ores, and all the operations connected therewith. He is quite unassuming, and always has a cheerful word for the "boys" of the lower levels when passing through his mines. Like Mr. Mackay he is ever ready to give all kinds of machinery a trial and to adopt it if it is found useful.

Captain Samuel T. Curtis, superintendent of the Ophir mine, is a miner of great experience both in the silver-mines of Nevada and the gold-mines of California. He was born in the south of Ireland, but came to the United States when quite young, settling in Western Virginia, where he lived many years. From Virginia he went to Cincinnati, Ohio, where he resided until the discovery of gold in California.

In common with thousands of others of an adventurous disposition, he caught the gold-fever, and in April 1849 started across the Plains. After many hardships and adventures of all kinds, he landed at Lassen's Ranche, in the northern part of California, in November of the year named. His party started across the Plains with saw-mills, and an immense train of wagons loaded with all manner of machinery and stores, but abandoned everything, and were glad to reach California alive. Mr. Curtis at once made his way to Feather River, where he mined until 1858 when he went to Nevada county and engaged in mining in that place. In 1859 he was elected to the California Legislature, and when he went to Sacramento to take his seat was the first time that he had been out of the mountains for ten years—he had seen no towns larger than the mining camps of the Sierras.

John P. Jones. Published in *Autobiographies and Portraits of the President, Cabinet, Supreme court, and Fifty-fifth Congress, Volume 1,* by Walter Neale, The Neale company, 1899.

At the time of the Indian trouble in Washoe, in 1860, Mr. Curtis raised a company of volunteers in Sacramento, and, as captain of the company so raised, brought over the Sierra Nevada Mountains a timely supply of arms and ammunition. Being obliged to provision his company for some time after arriving in Nevada, the part he took in the "war" cost him over $3000. It was no better as a speculation than bringing saw-mills across the Plains. During his residence in Washoe, Captain Curtis has had the superintendence, of the St. Louis, Empire Mill Mining Company, Union Consolidated, Sierra Nevada, Mexican, Savage and several other mines, and now is in charge of the Ophir. As a mining superintendent he has always been very fortunate, and, from his many years of experience in various mines along the Comstock, he knows almost every foot of the vein. He has given much attention to the stratification of the vein, and to the crystallization and other characteristics of the rocks found within its walls. So fortunate has he been in hitting upon bonanzas that when he has taken charge of a mine the men say: "If there is anything in the claim the Captain will find it!" When in charge of a mine he is indefatigable. He is about as much underground, and about as much at home there as upon the surface.

The Hon. J. P. Jones, United States Senator from Nevada, is a man who had much mining experience in California, previous to his crossing the Sierras and taking up his residence on the Comstock lode. He has long had control of the Crown Point mine, at Gold Hill, and from its several bonanzas has extracted many millions of dollars. He thoroughly understands the business of silver-mining and is an excellent judge of the ores of the Comstock. He is not only well acquainted with that portion of the great lode which passes through Gold Hill, but also with the mines on all parts of the vein, He owns a controlling interest in the Savage mine, in Virginia City, and still retains the Crown Point mine which is yielding as largely as ever, though the ore extracted is less rich than that which was being extracted some years since.

The mills of the Nevada Mill Company, nine in number, and containing 222 stamps, are owned by Mr. Jones and Hon. Win. Sharon and are capable of crushing 650 tons of ore per day. The Rhode Island mill, 24 stamps, belongs to the Crown Point Company. Besides his many interests along the Comstock range, Mr. Jones has a large number of mines and much mining property at Panamint, has town-sites down on the coast of California, and is engaged in enterprises of various kinds in all parts of the Union. "No pent-up Utica contracts his powers," he has a genius for mining and for surface business of all kinds, and when he rises in his place in the United States Senate can make a good talk—is about as much at home as though among the men on the lower levels of one of his mines, giving directions for the opening of a new stope. Mr. Jones counts his dollars by millions. It is said that he has about five times as many millions as he has fingers and toes.

CHAPTER LXX

FUN AND FROLIC

*A Secret Expedition—Bitten by a Snake—All a Mistake—
Camping Out—Manufacture of Slapjacks—"It never came Down"*

As it may be of interest to persons who have never been in the mining-regions of the Pacific Coast, I shall give an account of a prospecting trip which I took in Washoe, in 1860, just after the Indian troubles. Although no grand discovery was made, a sketch of the trip will serve to show the manner in which such expeditions were at one time conducted.

I was at that time camped at Silver City. One day a miner came to my cabin in a great state of excitement and said he had just learned that some men had struck placer-diggings of extraordinary richness on El Dorado Cañon, a large cation to the southward of the Carson River. He said: "They are getting gold as large as peas, and are making from $10 to $20 per man with rockers." A dozen or more in the camp were let into the secret, and we soon had several mules packed with "grub"—flour, beans, bacon, tea, and sugar—and were ready for a start. We wished to reach the new gold-region in time to get good claims and in advance of the rush of prospectors that was likely to occur as soon as news of the new strike should leak out. Not a soul in the camp knew where we were going, and as we marched down Gold Cañon, the miners pushed aside the blankets which were hung up as doors to their cabins and gazed in wonder upon our caravan. Each countenance said more plainly than words could have expressed it: "A big strike has been made somewhere. Those fellows know where it is and are going to it. I must find out about it and be off after them!" With a great clatter of pots, kettles, gold-pans, and frying-pans, our mules trotted into Chinatown (now Dayton). In this camp our "grand entry" created something of a sensation, and curiosity was seen in every face. Even the unimpressible Chinamen gazed upon us in almond-eyed astonishment. We were nearly all on foot and carried picks and shovels upon our shoulders, and long knives and six-shooters slung to our belts.

All who saw us were dying to ask us what was up; but, evidently feeling that it was a secret expedition, no man ventured to question us. Already we were rich, in imagination, and all felt as jolly as so many millionaires setting off on a pleasure excursion. Indeed, miners generally make these trips a sort of pleasure excursion and give about as much time to deviltry, and to curiously wandering about and viewing the wonders of the wilds, as they do to the real business of the journey.

Passing through Chinatown, we were soon at the Carson River, where we found trouble that we had not thought of. The river was high and swift; nearly all of our party were on foot; the mules were heavily packed, and there was but one horse without a load. This horse, however, was a large and powerful animal. Tom Lovel, his owner, finally rode across the stream and found that the water just reached to the horse's back. The pack-mules were driven across the stream after Tom by means of clubs and stones thrown after them. All got safely over but one puny and unlucky beast that was carried down the stream. The little rascal never attempted to swim until he had been swept some distance down the river, when he turned his head against the current and paddled away like a good fellow, for about ten minutes, without gaining or losing an inch, then with a mournful, despairing groan he gave up and floated ashore on the same side from which he started. Tom then came back on his horse, and throwing a lasso about the neck of the dripping little beast, towed him to the other shore, despite his moanings, and sundry other expostulatory demonstrations. Next we footmen were, one at a time, mounted behind Tom and borne across the stream, all but myself landing in shape. I was the last to cross, and, on mounting the opposite shore, Tom, having overmuch confidence in the strength and activity of this horse, insisted upon trying to ascend a perpendicular bank. The consequence was that we both slid back upon the horse's rump, causing his hind feet to sink into the mud until he assumed a perpendicular position.

The next thing I saw was that horse's head coming straight into my face. There was then a dull splash and a surging sound, and I was at the bottom of the Carson River, with Tom and horse a-top of me. I did some lively work for a time, and finally came to the surface with my mouth full of black mud. Tom got out in some way before I came to the surface. While I was pouring the water out of my boots, wringing out my shirt, and firing off and reloading my revolver, the majority of our party moved on, Tom allowing a friend to ride his horse. Only Tom, myself, and a Missourian known as "Pike" (the man who found the "stuff compasses are made of") remained behind; and when we finally started the others were nearly a mile away. We had not travelled half a mile before we came to a bayou or slough, half as large as the river itself and of which it was a sort of a cut-off. Here we halted. The "boys" had gone on with the animals, and, seeing that there was no other way—and being about as wet as water could make me—I plunged in and waded across, the water coming almost to my armpits. Tom hesitated and hallooed to try to make those in advance come back with his horse, but they were beyond hearing. Finally he offered Pike half a dollar to carry him across the slough on his back, which offer Pike gladly accepted. When Tom mounted Pike's back he settled him down in the mud nearly to his knees, and when he got out into the stream, Pike floundered about alarmingly.

Tom drew up his legs and wrapped them about Pike's hips, hugging to him as closely as a young Indian.

All on a sudden Pike began to shout: "Snake! Snake! For God's sake, Tom, get off my back, a snake is biting me all to pieces!"

"What in thunder do you mean?" cried Tom. "Don't you try foolin' with me about a snake!" "Snake! Snake!" cried Pike, striving to run, but Tom clung to him like the Old Man of the Sea, thinking that he was putting up a job to throw him into the water.

"Stop your foolin' or I'll hit you!" said Tom.

But Pike still plunged furiously, and then began calling upon Tom to put down his legs. "Put down your legs, confound you! Don't you see that you are killing me—that you are cutting me all to pieces with—" But Pike was not allowed to finish the sentence, as Tom, who was by this time blind with rage, drew back his fist as well as he was able and struck Pike in the mouth.

The unexpected blow caused Pike to throw his head back so far that both went over backwards and disappeared under the water. They came up about four feet apart, and as soon as Tom got his hair out of his eyes he made for Pike. The latter was on his guard and stepped aside, at the same time grasping Tom and giving him such a plunge as must have sent him to the depth of a foot into the mud at the bottom of the stream. Pike then broke for the shore with such furious strides as to nearly lift the waters from their bed. By the time Tom had reached shore Pike was at a safe distance, yet when Tom began snapping his revolver at him he danced about at a lively rate.

"Hold on! hold on!" cried Pike, "stay where you are! Don't shoot till I tell you about it! Blast it, don't you know that down in the water thar you was jist cuttin' me all to pieces with them infernal spurs of yours!"

Tom glanced down at his heels and saw it all. There were his huge Spanish spurs, sharp as needles, and there he had been digging into poor Pike's flesh while riding him through the water, causing him to think he was being bitten on all sides by water-snakes.

"Haw! haw!" laughed Tom. "Why Pike, you fool, why didn't you tell me that I was hurtin' you with my spurs?"

"I didn't know what it was myself, at fust; then when I did find out you wouldn't give me time to say it."

After these explanations Tom and Pike shook hands and called it even. Peace being restored, we set forward along the trail on which our companions had preceded us, but did not overtake them until we had reached the mouth of El Dorado Cañon, the gulch on which we expected to find the diggings. Up this cañon we travelled a considerable distance, when we found our friends had halted for dinner. Most of the way we had found the cañon but a few rods in width and walled in by almost perpendicular piles of granite and slate, but where our party had halted there was a beautiful little valley, several springs, and two or three small groves of willows and cottonwoods.

It does not take long for a party of prospectors to prepare a meal. The mules are first unpacked and turned out to graze; wood is then collected and a fire built, and by the time this is blazing several cooks are getting ready for business. Self-rising flour is placed in the same pans that are used in prospecting for gold; water is then added, and the whole is then stirred up with a spoon until of the proper consistency for pancakes. Soon two or three men, each with a frying-pan, are at work baking slapjacks, while as many more are frying the savory bacon; tea is being made in a coffee-pot, and soon all is ready. Each man then hunts up his tin plate, puts a handful of earth upon it and scours away all traces of the last meal, when he is ready for his allowance of bacon and slapjacks. Tin cups are used for the tea. These meals in the wilds of the mountains are eaten with a relish by the hardy prospector. There are generally a few raw onions to go with the bacon, and when a camp is made at night beans are cooked.

Of nights, too, when there is more time for cooking than during the noon halt, bread is baked. In making bread the miner mixes it in his prospecting-pan, as for slapjacks, and when it has been properly kneaded, takes it between his huge paws, and hammers it out in the shape of a large flat cake. This cake he places in his frying-pan and then stands it in front of his fire to bake, turning it over when one side is done.

Sometimes a regular loaf is made. When a loaf is decided upon, a large hole is dug in the ground, and a fire made in it. By the time the fire has burnt down and there is nothing left but a bed of coals, the loaf is manufactured. The coals are raked out of the pit, and the loaf is placed in a gold-pan and set in its bottom. Another gold-pan is turned over that containing the loaf, when the whole is covered with live coals, hot ashes and earth. In this way is made a loaf that is as sweet as any that ever came out of the oven of the baker. Beans— after they have been boiled until soft—are often baked in the same way, the camp-kettle containing them being buried in a pit in which a fire has been made.

In making slapjacks a miner considers himself a greenhorn if he is not able to turn them without doing it with a knife, after the fashion of a woman. He shuffles the cake about in the pan till it is loosened, then deftly tosses it into the air, catching it, batter side down, as it descends. This way of turning slapjacks is a trick, however, that some men find it impossible to learn. I once had a partner whose one dream of life it was to be able to turn a slapjack in this way. If he could but flip a flapjack into the air and catch it all right, he thought he would be perfectly happy, whether the diggings paid or not. One day, while in the cabin cooking slapjacks, he announced that he would turn one in the air or die. He was a man who weighed about one hundred and eighty pounds and had somehow got it into his head that in order to successfully perform the feat a great outlay of Strength was required.

Taking hold of the handle of the frying-pan with both hands and getting out into the middle of the floor, where he could have plenty of room, he hustled the cake about in the pan until he found it was loose on all sides. He then squatted nearly to the floor, and, giving a mighty heave, sent the pancake flying upward. This done, he stood, frying-pan in hand, waiting for the cake to come down, in order that he might catch it. But that pancake never came down, it struck batter side against the ceiling, and there it stuck as fast as the wafer on a love-letter.

I have heard of men who were able to throw a slap-jack up through the chimney, then run outside of the house and catch it before it struck the ground, but I have never had the good fortune to see the feat performed.

CHAPTER LXXI

THE BRIGHT SIDE OF PROSPECTING

*Off for the Land of Gold—Something in his Boot—Afraid of Tom—
Tom's Intentions—Pike Outwitted—Left Behind*

In the place where we had encamped for dinner there was on one side of the ravine, and at the height of about fifty feet above its bed, a long bench of rocks on which were piled, tier upon tier, rocks that bore a striking resemblance to sacks of grain. Always having the "evil one" in their winds when not in the wilderness, the boys called this place the "Devil's Levee." Another place, on the opposite side of the cañon, where a dozen or more huge, egg-shaped boulders, set on end, stood nodding this way and that, they christened the "Granite Polka.

Continuing our journey up the cañon, we presently arrived at the place where the miners were at work who were reported to be making from $10 to $20 per day. They seemed much surprised to see our party and told us that they were making nothing. None of us believed this, and, without waiting to unpack their animals, two or three of our men rushed off up the ravine to secure claims. I asked to see the kind of gold they were getting, and was shown a pan in which were five or six specks about one fourth as large as the head of a pin. The man who had told me in Silver City, about the big strike, and who had induced me to join the expedition, said the men were fooling us; he was sure they had rich diggings. Taking the pan, this man got down into the hole that had been dug by the miners, and got a pan-full of the best-looking gravel he could find. Winking for me to follow, he started down the stream to a small pool. When we were out of hearing he said he thought the men were trying to "play us." "They don't want it known that there is anything here," said he, "until their friends are all on hand to gobble up the ground. You can bet high that I'll get a good prospect out of this pan of dirt. It looks like the right stuff."

Meanwhile he was washing it down, stopping once in a while as he neared the bottom to flit the water over it in the expectation of seeing a "chispa" or a "nugget." The less sand there was in the pan the longer grew his face. At last all was panned out, even to the last grain of "black sand," and nought remained but the few little specks of gold ("colors") originally in the pan.

"Skunked, by the holy spoons," cried he. I then washed out the pan and filled it with earth out of a crevice—the best I could find—panned it down, and had three small colors.

We then went back to the camp of the miners who had dug the prospect-hole and asked how the story got started that they had found gold of the size of peas and were making from $10 to $20 per day. They knew nothing about it, but one of them finally recollected that when he went to Silver City for a rocker he had said to some one that from the number and shape of the "colors" they were finding on the surface he did not doubt they would find them as big as peas when they reached the bed-rock. Some one then remarked—"If you do you'll be able to make from $10 to $20 per day,"—from this grew the story of the rich strike in El Dorado Cañon. We all felt rather "cheap" when we heard this explanation, the perfect truthfulness of which we could not doubt. I have known many grand mining excitements that had even less foundation. Even this little "sport" did not end with our visit to the cañon.

After we had been at home a week, and when we supposed it was well understood that the diggings were too poor to pay, parties were still rushing thither. Presently the story crossed the Sierras, and the California papers said that, "in the El Dorado Cañon diggings, Nevada, miners are making from $20 to $40 per day with rockers; and the gold is of fine quality, being worth $17 per ounce." Though our ardor was a good deal cooled by what we had learned in regard to the diggings, we were not altogether discouraged. The boys got their picks, pans and shovels, and dividing into small parties, struck out in various directions, up and down the cañon, and among the small ravines putting in from the hills; agreeing that wherever the best prospects were found, claims should be staked out for all. At night all hands returned, and nothing had been found that would pay—a few small colors was all that could be found, and they could be obtained almost everywhere. It was something like the present Black Hills mines. Lighting our campfire we baked our slap-jacks, fried our bacon, and made a glorious meal, after which pipes were lighted, and many stories told of the good old days of "49," when the pockets of every honest miner overflowed with gold. When each man had spun his yarn it was time to think of sleep, and every man rolled himself in his blankets and stretched himself in the best and softest spot he could find, looking up at the stars in the ceiling of his bedroom until he fell asleep. At daylight we were astir, Pike was among the first up. Tom did not "unroll" till breakfast was almost ready. He then crawled out and proceeded to pull on his boots, taking a seat on a pack-saddle.

About this time I observed that Pike was closely watching Tom's movements. Tom had got one boot on and his toes started in the other, when he stopped and yawned lazily. Rousing himself, he then drew his boot on with a "chuck." His foot had hardly struck bottom before he gave a yell and turned deadly pale. Grasping his foot he tried to pull his boot off, but lost balance and rolled to the ground.

"Pull off my boot, quick, somebody! There is a scorpion in it!" cried Tom.

Pike managed to be the first to reach Tom, and catching him by the ankle began tugging desperately, dragging Tom here and there, with nothing but the top of his head touching the ground.

"Your foot is swelled, Tom, and this boot can't be got off!" said Pike.

"Yes it can," cried Tom. "Pull, confound you, pull! He is stingin' me all the time. Pull, Pike—confound you, pull! He's stingin' me to death!"

Pike gave several desperate plunges, lifting Tom clear of the ground each time; then stopped.

"I tell yer, Tom," said he, "it ain't no use; it'll never come off, your foot is swelled so bad."

"Cut it off then!" roared Tom, "cut it off, I can't die this way!"

Pike drew his bowie-knife and had ripped the leg of Tom's boot half way down when, thinking the joke had been carried far enough—for I was satisfied Pike had been playing a trick of some kind—I pushed Pike aside, and pulled the boot off at once. When the boot was off, behold! sticking to the bottom of Tom's stocking, a small prickly pear.

On seeing the prickly pear, where there should have been a scorpion, all hands laughed, and all were pretty well satisfied that the trick was Pike's, as a good deal of sport had been made of him in regard to his having been snake-bitten. To the surprise of all Tom neither raved nor swore—said not a word, in fact—but set quietly to work at extracting the spines which had penetrated his foot in fifty places. He then examined his boot, which was cut down almost to the heel, drew it on and took his seat in silence at the camp breakfast. This conduct on Tom's part gave Pike great uneasiness, as all could see. At last he said:

"Who in thunder do you suppose put that air cussed par in your boot, Tom?"

"I suppose you know as much about it as anyone here," said Tom.

"Me! good Lord I don't purtend to know. I can't account for it nohow, without one of them mountain rats might of done it."

"Yes," said Tom, dryly, "mountain rats are mighty fond of runnin' about with prickly pears in their mouths, so we'll say no more about it."

Pike felt very uneasy about the matter. He didn't like the way Tom was acting. After breakfast, when we were alone, he asked me if I didn't think Tom would watch his opportunity and shoot him. When all had breakfasted it was concluded to scout out and prospect at a greater distance from camp than we had yet done. While some of us prospected the ravines others were to take the animals and go out into the hills to look for quartz ledges. Pike wished to go with the quartz-hunters, but had no animal to ride. To the surprise of all, and almost to the terror of Pike, Tom offered him his horse. Pike stammered his acceptance and turned away, looking very quiet. In passing off it fell out that Tom and myself were to prospect certain ravines. We dug a number of holes down to the bed-rock and washed and washed out many pans of earth, but a few small colors was all the gold we could find. During the day Tom said:

"Do you know that was a villainous trick that Pike played me? To pretend, too, that he couldn't get my boot off, when all the time he had hold about my ankle. Then to go and cut my boot!"

"But you told him to do that."

"Yes, I know I did, for between you and me, I was awful scared. I thought I was gone in sure. I'd have bet my life on there being a scorpion in my boot."

"Do you know that Pike thinks you intend to kill him?" said I.

"No. Is he such a fool as that?"

"You know men are killed in this country for more trifling things."

"I don't want to kill any man, but I do want to play even on Pike. It was mean on him to put that thing into my boot after we had shook hands down at the river."

After a time Tom said: "Pike is a great coward and I'll watch my chance and scare the life out of him before this trip is over."

"So be it," said I.

As we could find no gold we turned our attention to prospecting for the beauties of nature. In one place, standing high and dry at some distance from the cañon, we found a very handsome natural bridge or arch. It was about eighty feet high, with a span or opening thirty feet in width by fifty feet in height, and beautifully set off with turrets and spires which rose from the top of the arch. Near this natural arch we found a cave, but it proved to be of no great depth. From the remains of fires in it, it appeared to have been used by the Indians as a place of shelter.

After wandering about in the hills for some hours we started for camp, and as we neared it saw a great bustle there among the men. They had brought in all of the animals and were busily engaged in packing up. As soon as they saw us approaching they called to us to make haste. Pike came running towards us, and laying his hand alongside of his mouth, sang out in a hoarse whisper: "Injuns!"

"Injuns?" said we.

"Yes," said Pike, "Injuns! Hills full of 'em! Hurry up, we're goin' to light out o' here!"

The long and short of the story was that Pike and his partner had crossed the mountain into what was called Sullivan district, when they found all the miners packing up and leaving for Carson City, on account of Indians having been seen watching them from the rocks. One of our boys who was lying in the shade of a bushy cedar, with his boots off, cooling his feet, had also seen Indians and had rushed into camp. His story was that, as he was lying under the tree, eleven Indians, all in war-paint, and each armed with a minie musket and revolver, passed along a trail about five rods away. They were in single file and were going eastward at a dog-trot. Thus were the Indians running one way and the whites another—the opposite direction.

On reaching camp we tried to prevent this stampede, telling the men that the Indians seen were merely a scouting party, and were probably then many miles away in the direction of Pyramid Lake, but several said they would bet any money that the redskins were even then watching us from the tops of some of the surrounding rocky hills. They could see rocks on the hills that looked like the heads of Indians, and by watching these some said they could see them move.

The miners whom we found on the cañon had pulled up stakes and left on the first alarm. After much talk, a majority of our party declared in favor of remaining on the cañon another day, but the minority owned the mules, and swore they were going to leave at once. They said they did not imagine the Indians would attack us, but they were tired of prospecting and were going down to Carson River to *fish*. Pike was very anxious to try his luck at fishing, and was ready to start at once for Chinatown to buy hooks and lines, if anyone would furnish him a horse.

After much talk, Tom came to me, and said: "Let us go down the cañon a few miles with these fellows, and then make them camp, where we can have a night-attack by the Indians, and scare Pike out of his wits." This was agreed to, and off we all started. About sundown we reached an open, grassy spot calling a halt proposed to camp there. The minority would not hear of such a thing. Pike was the most determined of any, and was bound to go to the river. The joke of the night-attack had been whispered among our men, and they determined to keep Pike with us. One of them took him aside and told him that we had reason to believe that the Indians were lower down the cañon; that, in fact, they were lying in wait for us in the rocky hills about its mouth, and that all who went down that night would be killed.

"Good Lord!" cried Pike, "you don't say so. Well, if that's the case I'll be dogoned if you ketch me goin' down thataway!" But Pike presently had a doubt about this plan. Said he: "If we stop here won't the cussed Injuns get tired of waitin' and come up here after us?"

"Well," said our man, "but you see we'll let these fellows go that want to go so bad, and when the Injuns git them they'll think they've got us all and so will be satisfied. However, it is almost too bad to let them go down there and be killed. I guess I'll go and tell them where the Injuns are."

"No, no!" cried Pike, "what are you about. If you tell them and stop them from goin' down, thar won't be no place safe! Don't talk so loud or they may take the hint and not go."

"Come, Pike," called the fellows who were so anxious to go fishing, "if you intend to go with us, hurry up, or we'll leave you!"

"Leave me and be dogoned to you!" cried Pike. "I've got a pistol now (a lie) and I'm goin' to stay here and have some fun a fightin' Injuns 'fore mornin'. Go along with you. I'm all right now!"

Pike's friends were evidently amazed at this sudden exhibition of courage on his part. They whispered together for a time; then one of them said: "Gentlemen you may think that you are exhibiting bravery; but, gentlemen, it is not bravery, it is madness." This earnest speech was greeted with a laugh from our side of the house, and the "fishermen" turned the mules into the trail and were soon out of sight.

CHAPTER LXXII

THE COMICAL STORY OF PIKE

Tom Sings—The Joke Successful—Pike Vanishes—A Pretty Big Story— Doubtful Dreams—Self-deceived—Our Journey's End

As soon as we were left to ourselves we built a roaring fire, in spite of all Pike's remonstrances. "It's jist as good a thing as the Injuns want," said he. "It's jist showin' 'em whar we are. We'll all lose our skelps afore mornin.'"

When we began to think of supper, we found that we had played a little joke on ourselves, in our hurry to get the other fellows away in order to make sure of Pike. We had nothing in the shape of provision except a few pounds of rice, which happened to be on Tom's horse. We put some of this into a gold-pan and boiled it, but it was rather poor eating without either butter or salt. As we were sitting about the pan scooping up this rice with knives and wooden paddles, Pike said: "I allers knowed I didn't like rice as well as I thought I did, and now I'm sure of it." But we had plenty of tobacco and what we lacked in "grub" we made up in smoke. As soon as it grew dark Pike became very restless.

"What was that?" he would say. "Did you hear the rocks rattle upon the hillside?" and he would peer out into the darkness.

Tom now began to sing as loud as he could roar:

"My name it is Joe Bowers, I've got a brother Ike, I come from old Missouri, yes, all the way from Pike."

"Stop singin' so loud, Tom," cried Pike in alarm. "Don't!" But Tom roared the louder—

"I'll tell you why I left thar, and how I came to roam, And leave my poor old mammy, so far away from home."

"Let go of me, Hank, there's five hundred of 'em comin'!"

"I'll never let go of you," said Hank. "Carry me off!"

Pike then lifted Hank who was groaning at a terrible rate, and carrying him about two rods, pitched him, neck and heels, into a clump of thorny bushes. This done, Pike rushed down the cañon at the speed of an antelope. Tom rolled on the ground and laughed until he almost smothered himself. "I'm even with Pike on the prickly-pear business!" cried he, as soon as he was able to speak, "he shall never hear the last of this Injun fight!"

For my part, now that the fun was all over, I began to feel quite miserable over the whole affair. I feared that in his great fright Pike might dash his brains out against a tree or break his neck among the rocks. I firmly resolved never to take part in another affair of the kind, calling to mind several sham fights and other deviltry in California that had been attended by fatal results to the victims.

In the morning we were ready for a start at sunrise. The first thing I saw was Pike's hat, lying near the place where he had spread his blankets the night before. The sight gave me quite a shock, as it seemed to be the hat of a dead man. I soon found that the others were beginning to feel much as I did about the matter, for, as Pike's blankets were being rolled up to be packed on Tom's horse, one of the boys said: "I hope nothing has happened to Pike." Another said: "O, he's all right!" but at the same time it was easy to see that the speaker feared that he was not "all right."

As we passed down the cañon, I could not help thinking that we should presently find Pike lying wounded or already dead in some rocky pit or pile of boulders near the trail, and most of our party looked quite solemn. The man who carried Pike's hat looked as though he were in a funeral procession, carrying a portion of the corpse. At length we were through the cañon, and having reached the level plain without finding Pike's remains, we all felt quite jolly again and immediately set to work and planned another surprise for him, when we should find him. Instead of fording the river, as we had done in going out, we went some two miles further down and crossed at a ferry. We inquired of the colored man in charge if anyone had crossed during the night. He assured us that no one had crossed, as he found the boat tied up on the west bank, as he had left it the evening before.

We now knew that Pike must have crossed at the ford and again began to feel uneasy, fearing that reaching the river in a state of exhaustion, he had plunged in and had been swept under by the current. One of two things was certain: he was either safe across, or was drowned, as the Mississippi itself would not have stayed his flight. On turning into the main street of Chinatown we came suddenly upon a group of men with minie muskets in their hands and in their midst stood Pike, with a handkerchief tied about his head. He had a musket in his hand and was the centre of attraction. We could see that he was telling those about him of the dreadful affair of the previous night. All those surrounding him were listening so intently that we approached without being observed. Pike was just saying: "Yes; Hank may be alive. I carried him about two miles on my back, with the red cusses yellin' at my heels, then laid him down and kivered him up with brush. But all the rest—" Here Pike turned and saw our party. His jaw dropped, and his eyes almost started from their sockets.

"Well, what of the rest?" said one of his auditors.

"Why, my God! they are all here!" said Pike. "There they all stand!"

The crowd now turned to us, and began to ask: "Who was killed?" "Were there many Indians?" and many other like questions. Not a word of this, however, could we be made to understand. We had seen no Indians; we had never dreamed of any danger from Indians. The whole crowd at once turned to Pike for an explanation. Some of the men hinted that unless he gave a pretty satisfactory explanation of his strange stories he would get into trouble. Pike was thunderstruck and gazed at us with a look of utter helplessness. At last he stammered: "Tom, wasn't you killed?"

"If I was killed I wouldn't be here, would I?"

"I thought I saw you fall," and Pike's face wore the most puzzled look imaginable. His fingers sought the yellowish tuft of hair on his chin and gazing at one and another of us he sighed: "I don't understand it all."

"We none of us understand it," said one of the crowd, sneeringly.

"All here—all here!" said Pike, his countenance wearing the look of an insane person.

"Pike," said I, "you must have dreamt all this about Indians."

Pike's face brightened for a moment, but soon resumed its old look of despair. "No, no," said he, "no dream. I saw them all killed."

"But, Pike, look at us; we are all here—all alive and well!"

Pike looked vacantly about him at the boys, and said: "Yes, I know, but I don't understand it at all."

"Well," said I, "all there is about it is that you were dreaming and suddenly rose up shouting 'Injuns! Injuns!' and before we could stop you, you ran away down the cañon."

"Yes," said Pike, "it must have been a dream. You are all here—it must have been a dream. But it don't seem that way at all."

"Don't seem what way?"

"Why, the way you tell it."

"Well, how does it seem. Let us hear you tell it. Let us have your dream."

"Give us the dream! Let's have yer dream!" cried the crowd.

"Well, you see I was a layin' thar in my blankets—But I'll be dogoned ef I believe I did dream it!" cried Pike. "I can almost hear the guns crack now!"

"Of course you dreamt it. Ain't we all here?"

"Yes; I know. But how did I act—what did I do?"

"Why, I've just told you all you did. You know that after you went to bed you was bouncing up on your knees every five minutes, and at last you bounced up and took to your heels."

"Yes; I know I was a little uneasy like. I kept a-hearin' somethin' rattle up on that hill, so I kinder kept on my guard like."

"Well, let us have the dream," all again cried.

"Well," began Pike, "at first I was a-dreamin' along kinder nice and easy like, when all at once I heard the rocks clatter—I mean I thonght I heard 'em clatter. Then bang, bang! pop, pop! went the guns, and O! sich yells— sich yells! I thought my hair riz straight on end, and I seed niore'n five hundred Injuns, all a-hoppin' down the hill like turkeys. All this time I thought that you fellers was a blazin' away at about two hundred of 'em that was all round you, and about five hundred on the hill. Then I thought I grabbed up a pick and went right inter the thick of the cusses and fit and fit till I'd wore out the pick, and then fit a long time with the handle. By this time I thought you fellers was all killed and I thought I'd git up and dust. But jist then I thought that Hank got holt round my legs and said he was wounded, and wouldn't let go of me, thout I'd carry him off. I thought I tuck him on my back and carried him 'bout four miles, and hid him in some brush. Then I thought I run on and waded across the river—"

"No, no! you didn't dream that! You did actually wade across the river."

"Well, then what part of it did I dream? Can anybody tell me that?" and poor Pike looked more puzzled than ever.

"You must have waded the river, you know, or you would not be here."

"Well, yes; I s'pose I did, but that don't seem a bit plainer, nor hardly half as plain as the shootin' and yellin' part. That was the dogonest plainest dream I ever did hev!"

"Yet, as we are all here, alive and well; it must have been a dream?"

"Oh, yes, it was a dream, sartain and sure, but what gits me was its bein' so astonishin' plain—jist the same as bein' wide awake!"

Pike continued to tell his dream for some years, constantly adding new matter, till at last it was a wonderful yarn. He enlarged greatly on the part he took in the fight, and after wearing out the pick on the skulls of the Indians, wound up by thrusting the handle down the throat of a brave, as his last act before beating a retreat. Tom more than once told him the truth about the whole affair, bringing in half a dozen of the "boys" to corroborate what he said, but not a word of it would Pike believe.

"Do you think," he would say, "that I was fool enough to believe that sich things actually happened? No, it was all a dream from fust to last, and the biggest and plainest dream I ever had!"

The account I have given of our prospecting trip is a fair sample of all such expeditions—though this trip "panned out" rather more than the usual amount of deviltry. Parties of men frequently travel two or three hundred miles to prospect a certain region, and when they reach it, merely scratch about on the surface for a day or two and if nothing is then found they curse the place and strike out for some other section, when the same surface scratching is repeated. With prospectors the "big thing" is always just ahead, never in the place where they are. Of course good miners are frequently found, but in nine cases out of ten a prospecting trip results about as did the little scout given above.

When we were prospecting there were things worth looking after, but we did not pay any attention to them. We saw in the cañon abundant indications of coal, but we were looking for gold alone. The coal, the croppings of which we saw, is now being extracted by a company and their mine is one of great value. Near where we camped while prospecting in the cañon now stand the steam-hoisting works of the coal company. It may look as though we did very little work for a prospecting party, but I have known a party of men to travel three hundred miles without having washed a pan of dirt; half the time they did not even dismount from their horses when looking at mining ground. Large parties do less work than small ones, as they can never agree in regard to where they are to set in or what is to be done. If one or two men wish to stop and prospect, the others are pretty sure to say: "Confound the place! there is nothing there. I know by the looks of the ground that it is of no account," and so the whole party moves on, and a *good* place in which to set to work is never found.

A majority of those who go on prospecting expeditions do not want to find a place where there is going to be much hard work to be done. They prefer rambling through the country and viewing new and curious sights to sinking shafts and running tunnels. If they can't find gold or silver in rock that shows itself on the surface, they continue to travel. The novelty of delving in the earth for the precious metals has long since passed away in the case of the old miner or prospector. New-comers—known as "pilgrims" or "greenhorns"—are much more likely to do real work when on a prospecting trip than any of the old miners. In the case of the pilgrim there is a fascination in the bare fact that he is digging for silver or gold which drives him on and lends strength to his muscle.

THE GREAT FIRE

OCTOBER, 1875

Many large fires have at various times swept through Virginia City, but the greatest and most destructive that ever occurred in the town was that of October 26, 1875. At 6 o'clock on the morning of that day a fire started in a little wooden lodging-house on A street, in the western part of the town, which in a few hours destroyed all the buildings standing on an area of ground half a mile square, in the heart of the city. Most of the public buildings and the hoisting-works, and many other buildings of the bonanza mines, were burned. In all, property to the value of over $10,000,000 was swept away. About two thousand buildings were reduced to ruins, and hundreds of persons left homeless and destitute.

The fire started at an hour when few persons were abroad. Only the butchers, bakers, marketmen, and other early risers were astir. The "owls" of the city, birds of prey that haunt the place all night, had disappeared with the grey of dawn and were in their first deep sleep; the time was an hour too early for the change of shifts in the mines, therefore at no other time, day or night, could the streets have been found more completely deserted.

When the first fire-bells rang few persons heeded, even though they heard them. Soon, however, the mournful and long-drawn wail of one steam-whistle after another, in quick succession, was heard to join in sounding the alarm till the fierce clangor of the bells was almost drowned. The bells, loudly as they rang, only said: "There is a fire," but in the fierce, wild shriek of the whistles there was that which thrilled all, and which said as though with a human voice: "There is a fire, and a great and most dangerous one!" In the sounding of the whistles it was to be noted that there was no hesitation or timidity anywhere shown; each engineer pulled open the valve of his whistle to its full extent, at the first grasp of his hand.

The fire started in the midst of scores of wooden buildings, and seemed to dart above all the surrounding roofs at the first bound. In addition to their being constructed of wood, nearly the whole of the buildings in the neighborhood were lined with cotton cloth, on which was pasted paper, as on a plastered wall. The partitions dividing the room, and the ceilings of all the rooms, were also constructed of muslin and wall-paper. Hardly a drop of rain had fallen during the preceding summer months, and the whole town was as inflammable as scorched flax.

Almost instantly the column of fire that was at first seen to arise began to assume the form of a pyramid. The base of this pyramid rapidly extended into the sides of houses in all directions—the glass falling in showers from the windows to give ingress to the flames—and structure after structure burst out in sheets of fire more rapidly than could be counted or noted down. Shouts of men and women rang through the halls of all the large hotels and lodging-houses in the neighborhood, and loud rappings, to arouse the sleepers, were heard at the doors of rooms. Nearer the scene of the fire, persons of all ages, both sexes, and every condition were fleeing for their lives in all stages of dress and all manner of undress. Many of those nearest the building in which the fire broke out had only time to leap from their beds and rush into the streets, as their houses were wrapped in fire before they were aware of their danger.

At the time the fire burst forth a fierce gale was blowing from the west. This carried great sheets of wall-paper, blazing shingles, and a great shower of fiery missiles of all kinds high into the air and far to the eastward, kindling fresh fires in advance of the main roaring mass of flame. The main body of the fire streamed before the gale as fierce as the flame from a blowpipe. It stopped for nothing. It was seen resting against the side of a stone or brick building for a minute, then black smoke began to roll up through the roof, and a moment after the smoke became flame—flame that joined the main stream and darted on and through all that stood in its way.

Many of the buildings destroyed were such as had always been thought fire-proof; but they fell before the fire as quickly as though they had been the commonest of wooden structures. There was apparently much fire in the midst of the streets as within the buildings; indeed the whole air seemed on fire. Water thrown into the midst of the flames produced no effect unless, as many thought, it added to their fury and fierceness. Although the firemen were at work with both hard-engines and steamers, while yet but few buildings were involved, the water they threw upon the burning buildings might as well have been as much oil, for any effect it had in checking the flames. The firemen were driven back from every point where they attempted to make a stand, and it soon became evident that no efforts of theirs could check the progress of the fire. It was such a fire as that which swept Chicago and Boston—a fire as fierce and uncontrollable as though belched up from the bottomless pits of the lower regions.

When it was seen that the fire was wholly beyond control, that it must take its own course and burn its way out through the city, the wildest confusion ensued. It was as when a beaten army begins its retreat. All took what they could conveniently carry in their hands, those things they most prized, and fell back out of the track of the fire. Men, women, and children thus leaving their homes, and house after house being thus deserted, a great human wave was pushed back on all sides toward the suburbs of the city. Hundreds moved their goods again and again, each time losing something, until at last they found themselves driven far up on the open face of the mountain, empty, handed, panting for breath, and parched with thirst. While the whole face of the mountain seemed a sea of fire, with great billows tossing to and fro, the sounds that reached the ear were as fearful as the scene spread before the eye. From the armories of the various military companies, from the gunsmith shops and from many of the variety-stores, there came a constant roar of exploding cartridges, guns, pistols, fire-crackers, bombs, rockets, and all manner of fireworks, sounding like the steady

C Street, Looking South from the International Hotel, 1862, collodion/albumen, attributed to Charles L. Weed (Lawrence & Houseworth). Library of Congress Prints and Photographs Division. All of these buildings were destroyed in the Great Fire.

discharge of small arms in a great battle. Amid and above all this din were heard the frequent and startling discharges of giant-powder, gunpowder, and Hercules powder, as building after building was blown up in various parts of the town.

As the fire began to approach the great mining-works these heavy reports became more frequent and terrific. The miners carried into buildings, not a few cartridges only of the powerful explosives they were using, but whole boxes of them, and when there were fired they seemed to shake Mount Davidson from base to peak. By the blowing up of buildings, and by almost superhuman exertions at carrying water and wetting the roofs and sides of houses, the progress of the fire was stayed at a few important points, and a great amount of valuable property saved that would otherwise have been destroyed; yet, in the main, the flames held their course through the heart of the town.

Southeast View from the International Hotel, 1862, collodion/albumen, attributed to Charles L. Weed (Lawrence & Houseworth). Library of Congress Prints and Photographs Division. All of these buildings were destroyed in the Great Fire.

Thus in a few short hours was swept away the best part of what at dawn had been a fair city—a city filled with elegant and comfortable homes, handsome and costly public buildings, large stores, packed with all manner of valuable goods, and mills and mining-works the most complete of the kind in the whole world. All these were licked from the face of the mountain, and but a wilderness of toppling walls and smoking ruins showed where they had been.

This great fire was started in a low lodging-house kept by a woman known as "Crazy Kate"—Kate Shea—by the breaking of a coal-oil lamp in a drunken row, as is asserted by those who occupied the adjoining houses.

In its march to the eastward down the slope of the mountain, the Court-house was the first large public building that was destroyed; the building and rooms of the Washoe Club, filled with elegant furniture and costly paintings, was the next to fall. Devouring at a gulp a score of smaller build-ings, the International Hotel, the principal hotel of the city and a huge brick structure, filled with stores, saloons, and other places of business on its first floors, was soon reached by the flames and became a volcano of fire. About the same time, further to the southward, the Bank of California, the *Enterprise* (newspaper) build-ing, and many large brick and stone structures, from three to five stories in height, were vomiting fire from every window and door from roof to basement. Soon Pipers Opera House, a huge frame building, like some great fire-ship was spreading terror through the neighborhood; while to

International Hotel, 1862, collodion/albumen, attributed to Charles L. Weed (Lawrence & Houseworth). Library of Congress Prints and Photographs Division. This building was destroyed in the fire.

the right the southward the Methodist, Catholic, and Episcopal Churches were towering pillars of fire, with seas of fire below and about them. To the left and northward the freight and passenger depots of the Virginia and Truckee Railroad Company, with many smaller buildings, were pour-ing great streams of fire to the eastward into the hoisting-works of the Consolidated Virginia Mining Company, which in turn, with over a mil-lion feet of lumber, sent a broad river of flame into and over the big mill of the company—a mill the most costly and complete then in operation in any part of the world. Not only this mill, but also the California stamp mill, near at hand, was here swept away. The buildings of the new "C & C" (California and Consolidated Virginia) shaft were saved through the most strenuous exertions of many miners, and after blowing up many houses.

To the northward at this time, the City Hall and scores of large and costly private residences were wallowing in a lake of flames, which lake overflow-ing on the east, inundated the several buildings constituting the works of the Ophir Mining Company, sweeping them from the face of the earth. Building after building was hurled hundreds of feet into the air to prevent the fire reaching these works, but nothing stayed its advance. Shattered buildings seemed to burst into flames in mid-air and their wrecks served but as trains laid to lead the fire more surely to the doomed works.

At times great whirlwinds came down the side of the mountain and waltzed about in the midst of the burning buildings, carrying spiral columns of flame and fiery missiles thousands of feet into the air. The tops of some of these pillars of fire were seen by persons fifteen or twenty miles away. An Indian who was on the opposite side of Mount Davidson, and on the west side of Washoe Valley, at the foot of the Sierra Nevada Mountains, fifteen miles distant, observed one of these whirlwinds of fire, which he said "looked like an augur," and started for the city to see what had befallen it. Jonah-like he wanted to see whatever trouble there might be in store for the place. He reached the top of Mount Davidson in time to see the churches all aflame. A grand view of the burning town he must have had from the top of the mountain!

At first, while but a few houses were on fire, there was heard some wailing among the half-dressed women and children, but as block after block became involved, the ruin being wrought was on a scale so grand that the excitement and terror of the scene forbade all thought of anything so small that tears could prove a solace for its loss.

When all was over, the people for a time seemed stupefied, or rather drunk, with the excitement of the day, and it was almost night before many of them remembered that they were without homes. All the houses left standing were soon filled; many young men, who could do so, went by rail to neighboring towns, while, for one or two nights, persons camped out on the sides of the hills—the school-houses and other public buildings remaining being filled to overflowing. The next morning after the fire, relief came pouring in from all quarters, for over two thousand buildings were destroyed, and hundreds of people were left homeless and destitute. Carson City sent two or three car-loads of provisions, ready cooked, early the next morning after the fire, to supply the immediate wants of the sufferers, and San Francisco and other towns and cities of California, at once telegraphed money and started clothing, blankets, bedding, and provisions over the Sierras, by express. A Relief Committee was organized in the city, and similar committees in San Francisco and other towns and cities of the Pacific Coast, and soon all the sufferers were made as comfortable as shelter, food, and clothing could make them. All the towns of Nevada and California contributed as generously as though their own people had been in distress, and San Francisco was untiring in her efforts for the relief of the sufferers as though the people of Virginia were her own sons and daughters. But two persons are known to have perished in the flames, though there were scores of narrow escapes. After the fire two or three men were killed by falling walls.

The insurance on the property amounted to $2,500,000, and this, with what many had left in money, stocks, and other kinds of property, joined with stout hearts and unlimited faith in the inexhaustible wealth of the mines, gave all courage to set to work at re-establishing themselves.

To rebuild the town was the one thought of all. The next morning after the fire the work of cooling down and clearing away the ruins of buildings was in progress in hundreds of places; lumber was coming in by rail and was being hauled up on the still smoking ground. From that time forward the work went on almost day and night, and in all kinds of weather. A week after the fire a tornado blew down and demolished a great number of the newly erected and partially completed wooden buildings, but the moment the storm ceased the wrecks were cleared away and building was again resumed. The mining companies whose works were destroyed showed undaunted spirit and indomitable energy. The Consolidated Virginia Mining Company's hoisting-works and mill, and the California. Mining Company's stamp mill, were a loss of over a million dollars at one fell swoop.

Eagle Engine Company No. 3, Virginia City, 1863 collodion/albumen. Comstock Firemen's Museum

The Consolidated Virginia hoisting work's assay-office, 1,250,000 feet of lumber and timbers, 800 cords of wood and the stock of mining supplies on hand was a loss of $800,000.

The loss by the burning of the Consolidated Virginia mill was $431,000; battery mill of the California Company, $80,000; hoisting-works and building of the Ophir Company $150,000; a total loss to the bonanza mines of $1,461,000. Large as were the losses of the several mining companies they had hundreds of men at work the day after the fire at clearing away the still burning ruins preparatory to immediate rebuilding. There was not a moment's hesitation.

In November the Consolidated Virginia Company declared their usual dividend (No. 19), of $10 per share on their capital stock, aggregating $1,080,000; and again in December a dividend (No. 20), amounting to the same great sum was declared. Thus did this Croesus of mining companies pay out to stockholders the princely sum of $2,160,000 during the time they were engaged in the costly business of rebuilding their works and filling them with expensive machinery. That they could do this must seem incredible to persons unacquainted with the almost inexhaustible deposits of rich ore in the bonanza mines.

The withholding of one of these dividends would have furnished more than enough money to have rebuilt both hoisting-works and mill, but having millions in sight in the lower levels of the mine which could be rapidly taken out when once the works were again running, the company gave the stockholders their regular dividends, just as though nothing had happened. The California Company had both their stamp-mill and their pan-mill almost completed and in a short time, but for the fire, would have been extracting ore. Their pan-mill (an improvement on the big mill of the Consolidated Virginia Company), one of the finest in existence, was saved, being nearly half a mile to the eastward of the mine and the scene of the fire. The shafts of the Ophir and Consolidated Virginia mines were blocked up and filled in with earth about their mouths when it was seen that the buildings covering them were doomed to destruction, yet the fire worked its way some distance down the latter and was with difficulty extinguished. Had the fire reached the immense masses of timbers in the underground works it would perhaps have gone through the whole of the mines on the northern part of the Comstock range, when the loss would have been many times greater than that of all that was destroyed on the surface, counting in all that was swept away in the town as well as on and about the mines.

In San Francisco the wildest excitement prevailed on California Steeet and, indeed, in all parts of the city as soon as it become generally known that a great fire was raging in Virginia City, and that the mining-works were in danger. Those who first received news of the fire did not make it public, but began selling their stocks on the street. Ophir, which closed at $52.75 on Monday evening, October 25, was offered, Tuesday morning, October 26, at $50, and considerable amounts of the stock were sold at this figure. As the news spread all stocks fell, and before the panic ended Ophir sold as low as $36 per share, but before night rallied to $41. Thousands upon thousands of shares of stocks were sold on California Steeet (the grand rallying place for dealers in stocks) before the Stock-Boards opened, the street being a surging mass of pale-faced and excited humanity. In the San Francisco Board, when the calling of the list of stocks began the place instantly became a perfect bedlam.

In the evening, when the full extent of the damage done by the fire had reached San Francisco, the people became quiet and began to gain courage. They reasoned that although the surface-works of the leading companies had been destroyed the mines were still there and as rich as the day before the fire; that the resumption of the extraction of ore was only a matter of time and all would be going on as usual in from forty to sixty days. Finally all retired for the night, greatly reassured, and the terrible panic was over. The people of San Francisco were correct in their estimate of the energy of the men who were at the head of the affairs of the mining companies— Col. James G. Fair and John Mackay, of the Consolidated Virginia and California, and Capt. S. T. Curtis, of the Ophir. In less than thirty days new buildings stood in the place of those that had been burned, both at the Consolidated Virginia and Ophir mines; and on Thanksgiving Day, just thirty days after the fire, the hoisting engine of the latter was started up amid the rejoicings of some hundreds of persons who had collected at the works, and (merely to be able to say that it was done) a few car-loads of ore were hoisted from the 1,300 foot level, though the business of regularly hoisting ore was not resumed until after the starting of the large pump and the proper draining of the mine, some time afterwards.

Before the expiration of the sixty days allowed (by close calculators at the time of the fire) for the rebuilding of the Consolidated Virginia hoisting-works, they were not only put up in better style in all respects than before the fire, but they were again taking out ore at the rate of over $1,500,000 per month. The Ophir Company were also soon after hoisting ore as before the fire, and ere long the work of extracting the vast stores of immensely rich ore (hitherto untouched) standing in great squares in the mine of the California Company was begun, giving full employment to the splendid mill of that company and, with the yield from the Consolidated Virginia, adding $3,000,000 per month to the hard-money wealth of the world.

In order to guard against a recurrence of such a calamity as that described in this chapter, the people of Virginia City at once set about the construction of a series of large reservoirs upon the side of the mountain above their town which, with a proper system of mains and hydrants, should afford them better protection against fire than they had ever before enjoyed. In sixty days after the fire the principal streets running through the burnt districts were again lined with business houses, the majority of which were of a better class than those destroyed, and dwellings once more covered what a few weeks before a good deal resembled the bottomless pit. The gap left in the city by the fire was again filled, and was not readily distinguished by strangers, except by its striking resemblance to a new patch placed on a pair of old pantaloons.

But for the Virginia and Truckee Railroad all this work could not have been done in a year. Indeed it would have taken the whole winter, with all the teams that could be pressed into the service, to have hauled from the mills in the mountains sufficient lumber to rebuild the mining-works alone. Nearly all of those whose homes were destroyed would have been obliged to seek shelter in California, and it would have been a difficult matter to bring in enough provisions and other supplies to comfortably keep such as remained in those parts of the city left intact.

The Railroad Company not only poured into the city an unbroken stream of lumber, timbers, and supplies of all kinds for the use of the mining companies and citizens, but at the same time did a vast amount of work for themselves. Their depot buildings, trestle-work, bridges, switches, the timbers of a tunnel, track, and, in short, all of their improvements in the city were destroyed. All these were replaced and at the same time all the other work done. Trains ran day and night—as many as forty-five trains passing over this road some days—and thus was the great work of rebuilding so speedily accomplished that a new town seemed to spring up out of the ground.

APPENDIX

Mexican Mining Terms

Acciones—Shares in a mine.

Ademada—Timbered.

Abonar—To pay a debt by installments.

Afaderas—All kinds of wood used in a mine for any purpose.

Afccati—A small line.

Agua—Water.

Ahogar—To gouge out a mine by working narrow and only in rich places.

Aire—Air.

Atinero—A miner.

Azogue—Quicksilver.

Bartolina—A chamber cut out in a mine in which to keep tools and stores.

Barranca—A precipice.

Barretero—A miner.

Barrena—A drill.

Batea—A wooden bowl used in washing auriferous earth.

Bonanza—A large and rich body of ore—prosperity.

Borrasca—Barren rock—bad luck—adversity,

Buena saca—Doing well.

Cairesle—A hair rope—a line.

Calabrote—A large rope.

Canada—A deep ravine, gulch.

Cavallo—A "horse"—a block of barren rock in the midst of a body of ore.

Cavassos—Borings drillings.

Cavasal—A cross-piece—timber.

Charqueo interior—To lead water to a drain.

Chorrerra—A cave—the caving in of a mine.

Cinta—A streak of ore.

Contra Mina—An underground connection.

Contro-pozo—An "upraise" to meet a winze,

Cuarzo—Quartz.

Cascajo—Gravel.

De Cielo—The roof—working overhead.

De Pied or a *Pique*—Beneath the floor—sinking, or working down.

Derotada—Gutted, spoiled and abandoned.

Destajo—A contract.

Dispacho or *Dispensa*—An ore-house.

Echanlero—A platform for weighing, sorting, or packing ore on. A Patio of a mine.

El Alto—The hanging wall.

El Abajo—The foot wall.

El Cordon—A ridge or spur of a mountain.

El Creston—A crest or outcropping.

El Crucero—A cross-cut.

El Fronton—An ore breast.

El Manto—(mantada)—A flat deposit.

El Patio—The level space at the mouth of a mine or tunnel.

El Rumbo—The course.

El Socabon—An adit.

El Tajo abierto—An open cut.

El Tiro general—The main shaft

En Borra (Emborrescade, Borrasea)— Not in pay ore— "petered out"— applied to the barrenness of veins, not to dead work, as a tunnel run to reach a vein.

En Frutos—In ore.

Escabar—To strip a claim on the surface merely

Fueros—Special privileges.

Fundi do—Filled with water.

Grantio—Granite.

Guardas de Labor—Roof and walls of a mine in general.

Hilos—Threads of ore.

Hundido—A settling or sinking.

La Bocca-vieja—The mouth—the old mouth.

La Cata—A small pit—a "coyote hole."

La Demasia or *Hueco*—The unclaimed ground between two claims.

La Guia—A guide, or the float rock.

La Lumbrera—The air shaft.

La Obra—The tunnel—the work.

La Patia—A narrow footpath in a mine.

La Quebrada—A ravine.

La Recuesta—The dip.

La Tabla—A stope.

La Tronada—The rocks thrown down by a blast

Las Afedias—The boundary lines of a claim as marked by Las Escatas, stakes, or Estaeada, staked off.

Las Cañones—The drifts.

Las Guardas Rayas—Monuments of wood or stone.

Las Desagues—The drains of a mine.

Las Escaleras—The notched stepping poles or ladders in a mine.

Las Respaldas—The walls of a mine.

Las Sierras—Mountains or mountain ranges.

Latones—Small poles

Los Caminos—The travelled roads in a mine of any kind.

Los Pilares—The pillars of a mine—place of timbers—to "dispilar" a mine is to dig down the pillars.

Los Planes—The deepest workings or bottom of a mine.

Lot Llavis—Beams, timbers.

Nivel—A level.

Obsa muerta—Dead work.

Oreones—Forked poles.

Oro— Gold.

Oro en fasta, brulo or *virgin*—Gold bullion.

Oro en polvo—Gold dust.

Pala—A shovel.

Paradera—Sluice-gates.

Pedregal—a stony place

Pico—A pick.

Pied direcho—A stud.

Pileta—A sump or tank.

Pizarra—Slate rock.

Plata—Silver.

Plata virgen or brulo—A rude mass of silver—native silver.

Pohora—Powder.

Presa—A dam.

Puertas—When a vein pinches—"cap rock."

Reata—A rope for tying mules or horses.

Risco—A steep rock.

Roca—A rock

Suffocante—Hot, bad air.

Terrero—A pile of waste rock.

Un Mineral—A mining district

Una Vita—A lode or ledge—a true fissure vein.

Una Vena—A vein—a narrow seam or streak.

Una Veta tapada—A "blind" ledge or lode—a' lode that is covered with soil.

INDEX

Bold page numbers indicate illustrations.

Index

Made in the USA
Middletown, DE
26 December 2014